The Cleveland Rams

The Cleveland Rams

*The NFL Champs Who Left
Too Soon, 1936–1945*

James C. Sulecki

McFarland & Company, Inc., Publishers
Jefferson, North Carolina

LIBRARY OF CONGRESS CATALOGUING-IN-PUBLICATION DATA

Names: Sulecki, James C., 1961– author.
Title: The Cleveland Rams : the NFL champs who left too soon, 1936–1945 / James C. Sulecki.
Description: Jefferson, North Carolina : McFarland & Company, Inc., Publishers, 2016 | Includes bibliographical references and index.
Identifiers: LCCN 2016040923 | ISBN 9780786499434 (softcover : acid free paper) ∞
Subjects: LCSH: Cleveland Rams (Football team)—History. | Cleveland (Ohio)—History—20th century.
Classification: LCC GV956.C63 S85 2016 | DDC 796.332/640977132—dc23
LC record available at https://lccn.loc.gov/2016040923

BRITISH LIBRARY CATALOGUING DATA ARE AVAILABLE

ISBN (print) 978-0-7864-9943-4
ISBN (ebook) 978-1-4766-2645-1

© 2016 James C. Sulecki. All rights reserved

No part of this book may be reproduced or transmitted in any form or by any means, electronic or mechanical, including photocopying or recording, or by any information storage and retrieval system, without permission in writing from the publisher.

Front cover: Cleveland Rams tailback Parker Hall carries the ball in a 1939 game at Municipal Stadium (Cleveland State University Library)

Printed in the United States of America

McFarland & Company, Inc., Publishers
  Box 611, Jefferson, North Carolina 28640
  www.mcfarlandpub.com

For Dad, who gave me a love of football;
Mom, who gave me a love of Cleveland;
and Louise, who gave me everything.

Table of Contents

Preface — 1
Introduction: "A Champion scram team" — 6

Part I: Start-Up

1. "We became the Rams" — 15
2. Razzle-Dazzled and Bedraggled — 26
3. This Time Pro Football Was Going to Work in Cleveland — 39
4. Rams to the Slaughter — 51

Part II: Upstarts

5. Race-Wrecking Rams — 60
6. The Rams' Lewis and Clark Expedition — 76
7. "The public be pleased" — 89
8. The War Year, the Lost Year — 106

Part III: On the Up and Up

9. Twenty Months to a Title — 117
10. The Hero's Journey to Cleveland — 131
11. A New Power Rises in the West — 142
12. "An even zero": The Title Game — 162

Part IV: Up and Gone

13. "The public be damned" — 177
14. "The Cleveland Rams ceased to exist" — 196

Appendix: What Became of Selected Individuals — 217
Chapter Notes — 225
Bibliography — 245
Index — 268

Preface

"You tell somebody you played for the Cleveland Rams, their face will drop. They don't have any idea who the Cleveland Rams were."—Johnny Wilson, Cleveland Rams, 1939–42[1]

The idea for this book, the only in existence that I know of devoted solely to the National Football League's Cleveland Rams, was seeded, though it would take many years to germinate, in 1995. This was when the former Los Angeles Rams just had moved from Anaheim to St. Louis, and I—insecure about Cleveland Browns owner Art Modell's cryptic pronouncements about his team's future in my hometown, and with my work as a business journalist taking me several times that year to Missouri—seized the opportunity to ask numerous St. Louisans I happened across whether they knew where their new football team had originated. *Sure*, each said with solemn self-certainty, *in Los Angeles.* In vain I corrected them and suggested that if they were going to have an NFL team again in their city they might as well know its history. And that history assuredly is noteworthy: The 1945 Rams are the only NFL championship team to play the following season, fully intact, in a different city; the Rams now are the only NFL franchise to win titles in three different cities.

This book concluded in January 2016 when Rams owner E. Stanley Kroenke, after months of speculation in the media while I set about researching and writing what you're about to read, finally received permission from his fellow NFL owners to move his team back to Los Angeles. Just a few weeks later my wife and I took a cross-country flight to California to meet with the sons of a few men who had been major participants in the team's initial move from Cleveland to L.A. In so doing I had a keen awareness—as we followed first the southern shore of Lake Erie, then hurtled past the flat corn and soybean and wheat plains, then over the Rockies and then the Sierras, and finally over the coastal mountains and into the L.A.

basin—that we were retracing the franchise's cross-continent exodus exactly 70 years earlier as it left behind a black-and-white Midwestern winter landscape to be reanimated in the West. It was a dash to the West Coast that abruptly ended Cleveland's complicated relationship with the team, but it also widened, once and for all, NFL football to every person and region in the United States.

Sometimes history doesn't wobble but instead spins to a perfect symmetry. On January 12, 1946, owner Daniel F. Reeves (no relation to the Dan Reeves who coached the Denver Broncos) received permission to move the Rams from Cleveland to Los Angeles. On January 12, 2016—70 years later to the very day—Kroenke was given allowance to move the Rams from St. Louis back to Los Angeles.

And somewhere between it all, in my personal realm, was my own troubled relationship with the team that rose in the Rams' wake, the Browns—my birthright, as a fourth-generation Clevelander, of orange and seal brown, of teams that have been mostly mediocre in my lifetime, their greatest successes in the 1940s and 1950s burned out before I was born like a distant Big Bang detectable only through a telescope. I don't believe I was fully aware until my teens of the Cleveland origins of the Rams—glorious on 1970s color TV in uniforms of yellow like the California sunshine and blue like the Pacific, and playing under the arches of the L.A. Memorial Coliseum with its backdrop of palm trees swaying in the afternoon.

And then I learned more: The Rams' colors had started in Cleveland. The iconic ram's-horn logo had started in Cleveland, in smokestack and snow-slushy Cleveland. It was here that quarterback Bob Waterfield and his movie star wife Jane Russell—she, later, of *Gentlemen Prefer Blondes* with Marilyn Monroe—had lived briefly, in a one-room apartment on Euclid Avenue, won a championship, and … moved. When the Rams departed for L.A. in early 1946 a door was opened for the Browns, and that opened a door for Modell eventually to buy the team, and much later that opened another door for … Modell to transfer the Browns to Baltimore. It was a chain of events whose impact, looked at in hindsight from a city that just sat out its 50th consecutive Super Bowl, still rattles defiantly proud Cleveland football fans nearly three-quarters of a century later.

I also learned my father and my grandfather were in attendance at the game in 1945 in which the Rams won the NFL Championship, only to announce a scant 27 days later that the team was leaving town. My father was but ten then and recalled little about that afternoon in Cleveland Stadium other than the extreme cold; the snow; the brown field; the insulating straw on the field and in the stands, the latter set afire by ne'er-do-wells;

and Sammy Baugh's controversial safety that spelled the difference in the game. Nine months later the Browns' debut on a late-summer evening on that same field, by then vibrant green, would be like a Technicolor revelation for my father, and he—like many other Clevelanders—would fall for the Browns and forget the Rams almost instantly.

I realized as well, as I conducted interviews in 2014, 2015, and into early 2016, that Walker Gillette, Dan Reeves, Jr., Buck Waterfield, and Bob Gries—all of whom made contributions to this book—are linked, as am I, by our fathers having somehow participated in that arctic day in Cleveland Stadium. Sports has a unique knack for threading commonality across generations and geography, and family is what binds this book as much as anything.

I've written this book, finally, to set the record straight—to dispel a myth in some corners about near-universal apathy for the Rams franchise in the city of its origin. Many earnest attempts in fact were made to establish the Rams in Cleveland. John Dietrich, the *Cleveland Plain Dealer*'s sports writer who covered the team through its entire decade there, believed that the Rams playing in Cleveland Stadium "could have been a gold mine."[2] Instead Reeves bought the team and quietly offered the city an untenable proposition: lose and the team stays, win and it leaves. And so the Rams won and left, becoming a perpetual flight risk compared to most other modern professional sports franchises, as the account of where and how they started became lost amid the team's shuffling from Cleveland to Los Angeles to Irvine to St. Louis and back again to Los Angeles. Even Clevelanders, who presumably might be more acutely interested than sports fans in other parts of the country in laying claim to any stray championship, seem not to know very much about the Rams' beginnings or fleeting success here. Maybe this will change.

They say history is written by the winners, but the truer account often is about the losers. As such, the Rams' experience should be familiar to any sports fan. It's about missed chances. Meddling and prevaricating owners. Well-intentioned coaches who fall short on game day. Personalities off the field. Stumbling in failure and reemerging in triumph. Self-serving sports organizations. The intrusion of business into sports; the intrusion of *sports* into *business*. Local civic pride relying paradoxically on out-of-town personnel as guns-for-hire. The age-old argument over who really has purchase on a sports franchise: the geographic area that hosts it, or the business entity that owns it.

But as much as anything this account is about sports as presented to us through the prism of the media, to which we've all grown fully accustomed. The maturation of sports writing and sports commentary seems to have accelerated particularly in the late 1930s and 1940s, in which nearly this entire experience takes place. Writers took the Rams seriously; they devoted a fair amount of space to coverage of them. So newspapers, not surprisingly for the era, are a leitmotif of this book. The co-founder of the Rams franchise initially had aspirations as a newspaper artist. Newspapermen helped to choose the name "Rams" because it fit well into headlines. An enterprising newspaper reporter very nearly blew the team's cover story about its impending move to L.A.; and when the departure indeed happened, the news thereof was stifled by a pressmen's strike at all three newspapers then in Cleveland.

Nearly four decades ago, on the eve of the Los Angeles Rams' appearance in the Super Bowl following the 1979 season, it was another sports writer—Hal Lebovitz—who wrote an article in the *Plain Dealer* titled "Remember the Cleveland Rams?" It seems appreciably few did based on the need for the article. But in it, Lebovitz—dean of Cleveland sports writing and an *eminence grise* on the *PD* copy desk by the time I met him one 1970s evening as a teenaged would-be journalist—reports that a colleague had not known of the team's origins and had told him, "I'd like to read about the team, how it came to be, how it did, why it was transferred to Los Angeles. I'll bet everyone in town would."[3] Lebovitz never did write a book on the Cleveland Rams, so I did.

His extensive newspaper piece of course serves as this book's essential scaffolding, but there's so much more to what went on, and for this I am indebted to the long-ago reporters who created those first drafts of history—especially Dietrich and Gordon Cobbledick of the *Plain Dealer,* and the legendary Franklin Lewis of the *Cleveland Press*. Solid reporters all, they clearly pulled for the success of the Rams and for pro football in general in Cleveland—hardly a sure thing at the time—while also remaining journalistically objective.

Also immeasurably valuable in my research were the archives of the *New York Times*, the *Chicago Tribune*, and the *Los Angeles Times*. Newspaper accounts, though hardly flawless, contain no small element of truth because they were written while events still were fresh and were cross-checked by competition in what then were multiple-newspaper cities like Cleveland. Sometimes reports were at variance, and when this was the case I did my measured best to provide the closest representation of the truth I could divine.

Yet newspapers articles alone would be flat without the personal recollections and access to personal mementoes so generously granted by the families of former Rams who welcomed me into their homes. For this I thank Walker Gillette and Marguerite Gillette; Bob Gries and Donald Gries; Dan Reeves, Meghan Reeves, and Rick Reeves; and Buck Waterfield and Etta Waterfield. Buck Waterfield's, Walker Gillette's, and Donald Gries's collections especially contribute to much of the imagery you see in this book.

My father Jerry Sulecki provided recollections of the Rams' championship game and of that era in general, counsel on the overall direction of the book, research for the "What Became of the Cleveland Rams" postscript, and insight into pro football he gained while officiating Browns practices in the 1980s and 1990s.

Family friend Bob Valerian, a retired attorney and a longtime Cleveland football fan, provided insights into the legal machinations that attended to the Rams' move. Maggie Puskas devoted her spare time to helping with a number of the images you see in these pages, and joined many of my colleagues at Meister Media Worldwide as a source of general support and advice as I molded this book's central thesis.

On-site research at the Pro Football Hall of Fame in Canton, Ohio, with the aid of Jon Kendle and my interview with Joe Horrigan there were very helpful, as was poring over the *Cleveland Press* archives at Cleveland State University with the help of Lynn Duchez Bycko. Online resources that were the very backbone of my daily research included Pro Football Reference, Pro Football Archives, and the website of the Professional Football Researchers Association, of which I am a member.

I also consulted many books on pro football, many of which touch only briefly on the Cleveland Rams and/or focus largely on the Rams' post–Cleveland existence; instead I have isolated the events here almost exclusively to the years 1936 to 1946, with some additional detail on the team's subsequent move to L.A. I found one book in particular to be especially valuable and praiseworthy as background. Craig R. Coenen's *From Sandlots to the Super Bowl* is a scholarly treatment of pro football from 1920 to 1967 and is not to be missed by anyone hoping to understand or write about the origins of the NFL.

My children Erika Sulecki and Nathan Sulecki were very patient and I think even occasionally interested as I regaled them with anecdotes from the era of their great-grandparents. But more than anyone, my wife Louise Sulecki was—is—my best friend, my preeminent sounding board, my tireless traveling partner, always enthused and encouraging about this project, and always with a deep reservoir of patience as I sequestered myself away for endless hours to work on this book. Without her it would have been absolutely impossible, and I thank her most of all.

Introduction
"A Champion scram team"

On December 16, 1945, Bob Waterfield, the kid quarterback from southern California, nearly lost sensation in his extremities from the Cleveland cold. But he well could feel the pressure of the city's championship hopes as he played for the first time ever—a rookie National Football League quarterback—on the ice- and snow-torn tundra of the field at Cleveland Municipal Stadium. Red, white, and blue bunting snapped against the steely face of the stadium's upper deck in a sideways-racing Lake Erie wind. More than half the seats in the expansive ballpark lay empty, and spectators huddled as close as they could to the field for warmth and a better view. Football sounds were hushed and muffled by frozen lake air and the layers of clothing that lined players' uniforms.

From the corner of his eye Waterfield could see fans beginning to swarm the sideline, having slipped the stadium grandstand, having climbed over snow piles and straw bales that lined the stadium's rim, having penguin-walked across the slippery surface. They wore parkas, earmuffs, flying suits, ski troop uniforms—blankets, even—and more than a few surreptitiously carried flasks in their coat pockets. Some raced across the field to be near the Cleveland Rams' bench when the final gun was fired.

This was not the pro football city of popular perception. Cleveland, nurturing yet another NFL franchise after a dozen-some years of teams variously called the Tigers, the Indians, and the Bulldogs, was "never one of the stronger towns in the circuit."[1] Instead the city had its Major League Baseball, its Indians, its Bob Feller; its boxing, its horseracing, its minor-league hockey, its high-school and college football. The seven previous editions of Rams teams before Waterfield had come to town had posted seven consecutive non-winning seasons—one with a record of 1–10, another 2–9—and Clevelanders clearly "found no reason to support bad pro football franchises when they had other more appealing options for their entertainment dollar."[2]

Rams attendance routinely scraped the bottom or near-bottom of the league. The owner lost money. Rumors that the team might move—to Boston, to Cincinnati, to Baltimore, to Los Angeles—had hounded the Rams for years. Newspaper writers charged the NFL with giving Cleveland a raw deal, sending the Rams on the road for most of their games and diverting marquee opponents away from the city on the spare three, four, or five autumn Sundays the team usually was home during its 10- or 11-game seasons. And really, at their core the Cleveland Rams were little more than road kill for the Chicago Bears, New York Giants, Green Bay Packers, and Washington Redskins—the well-funded and well-supported big four that lorded over the NFL and had locked up 23 of the 24 spots in the young league's first dozen championship playoff games.[3]

But in 1945, things suddenly were different. With Waterfield an unexpected sensation and a surrounding cast assembled and gelling after years of World War II military absences and careful draft selections and signings, the Rams marched to a 9–1 regular season record and into the championship game. And now, on the massive bleacher scoreboard clock at Cleveland Stadium, mere seconds remained—all that stood between the Rams and football immortality. Waterfield began his cadence and looked over the line at the Rams' opponent: Washington in its familiar burgundy and gold, exuding confidence, steam, and breath. The Redskins were playing in their sixth NFL title game in ten years, but there now was no chance of them winning today. Rams center and team captain Mike "Mo" Scarry snapped the ball, Waterfield dove into the line, and it was over: The Rams had defeated the Redskins 15–14. The Cleveland Rams were National Football League champions.

The world looked quite different for them now.

In the fading early-winter afternoon of the nearly zero-degree day, Clevelanders flooded the frozen field. They surrounded the Rams. They hoisted Waterfield and carried him off the field. They asked him to sign autographs until the Californian suggested they might all freeze to death if they did not find warmth and shelter soon.

With Waterfield a magician in reading and eluding defenses, with end Jim Benton fearless in his horizontal airborne stretches for passes, with the so-called G-men backfield of Don Greenwood and Fred Gehrke and Jim Gillette blending into a potent combination of power and speed, and with star linemen Riley "Rattlesnake" Matheson and Milan "Mike" Lazetich blasting holes and fending off pass rushers, the Rams were "sport's first spectacular postwar team," *Sporting News* reported.[4] In victory the Rams had set new NFL championship-game records for gross gate, net gate, and radio

The 1945 NFL Champion Cleveland Rams. Key personnel included: (bottom row) Don Greenwood (66) and Fred Gehrke (18); (second row) Eberle "Elbie" Schultz (40), Steve Pritko (30), Jim Benton (49), Riley Matheson (11), head coach Adam Walsh (in jacket), and Jim Gillette (24); (third row) Mike "Mo" Scarry (39, far left, next to assistant coach George Trafton), Gil Bouley (42), Bob Waterfield (7), Milan "Mike" Lazetich (27), and general manager Charles "Chile" Walsh (in overcoat); (back row) assistant coach Bob Snyder (far left) *(Walker Gillette Collection)*.

broadcast rights.[5] Waterfield was a media darling—a one-time Hollywood extra who was married to the sex symbol of the era, Jane Russell. Matheson was a rancher in the offseason, folksy and colorful—a reporter's dream. Gillette was Virginia-gentleman handsome. Head coach Adam Walsh was a California-bred scholar, bespectacled and articulate, while his brother Charles "Chile" Walsh, the team's general manager, was among the league's premier evaluators of talent. Owner Daniel F. Reeves, a sharp New Yorker, possessed a seemingly endless fortune from the sale of his family's grocery business and an equally endless willingness to spend his money in pursuit of a winning team.

The Cleveland Rams were "ushering in a new and dynamic era for the National Football League," *Sporting News* said—but also especially "a bright one for their own town."[6] World War II was over; servicemen were streaming home; manufacturing was booming. Cleveland was the sixth-largest city in the nation, one place behind rapidly growing Los Angeles. And now: a football championship, Cleveland's first since the Bulldogs of 1924, and with it a hint of even more to come, as Chile Walsh's recent draft selections of two talented ends named Tom Fears and Elroy "Crazylegs" Hirsch looked especially promising. Perhaps rumors of the team's departure might finally abate.

"At long last, Cleveland is sold on professional football. More accurately, perhaps, sold on the Cleveland Rams," sports reporter Jack Clowser had written in the *Cleveland Press* that autumn.[7] It was going to be a happy Christmas in Cleveland. It felt like it was the beginning of the Cleveland Rams.

But it really was the end.

* * *

A few weeks after New Year's Day 1946, NFL owners gathered in New York City for their annual postseason meeting. Only a month had passed since the arctic game in Cleveland that crowned the Rams as champions. The proceedings began "so tamely" that reporters complained of a lack of news to the NFL's public-relations flack George Strickler, who reassured them: "Don't worry, boys. Before we're finished I personally will guarantee to produce at least one atom bomb explosion."[8]

A detonation occurred on the afternoon of Saturday, January 12, 1946. Reeves, the young owner of the Cleveland franchise since 1941, requested permission to transfer his champion Rams to Los Angeles—*terra incognita* for the NFL. Four of the owners, among the league's most powerful, objected strenuously. The cost and time it would take to dispatch entire football squads to play the Rams on the West Coast—2,000-plus miles and a 45-hour rail journey from Chicago and Green Bay, then the league's westernmost outposts—was untenable, comparable to establishing a 21st-century NFL team in Asia.

Reeves persisted. Attendance in Cleveland was lackluster. His Rams had posted a financial loss of $40,000 in 1945[9]—and this in a championship season. In L.A. he happily would pay $5,000 over the league's guarantee to each visiting franchise to compensate for travel expenses to the West. This was how much he believed "Los Angeles has the greatest football future of any city in America,"[10] a notion he developed a decade earlier while still in college when he saw a University of Southern California game at the grand Los Angeles Memorial Coliseum. "It is not that I love Cleveland less," he said, invoking Shakespeare's *Julius Caesar* amid a drama he himself had loosed, "but that I love Los Angeles more."[11]

Reeves, age 33, was a "slender, discriminating cosmopolite"[12] who routinely traveled to Cleveland for game days only, then hopped on the next available train back to Manhattan. He had no known interest in the blue-collar American heartland that a quarter-century earlier had midwifed the NFL in the smaller industrial Ohio cities of Canton, Akron, and Dayton. Instead his earliest exposure was to the big-city, Eastern-seaboard variety of pro football, joining tens of thousands as a teenager in Manhattan to watch the football Giants at the Polo Grounds.

By the time Reeves had left Georgetown University he was inspired by his brother's minority ownership of the NFL's Boston/Washington Redskins, then bolstered by his own share of the family fortune to buy a pro football franchise of his own—*any* pro football franchise. Had he gained control of the Philadelphia Eagles or the Pittsburgh Steelers as he had failed to do[13] he very possibly would have moved either of those teams and altered pro football history. But the Rams were the only NFL franchise available in 1941, presented to the market by a founding syndicate of wealthy Cleveland sportsmen and businessmen who were worried about the coming war and its potential effect on their cash flow; by their own later admission they had made each game "a weekly social event"[14] as they meddled in on-the-field football decisions.

Now Reeves had a championship organization as leverage, and notwithstanding his statement five years earlier that "there was no reason why big-league football couldn't be put over in a big way"[15] in Cleveland—a prediction that would come true with the Browns—he nevertheless was determined to fulfill his ambition to move to L.A. He threatened to pull the Rams from the NFL if the owners did not accede to his demand.

The other moguls assembled for a special session. Those in opposition to Reeves did not have a strong hand, as the league was about to battle the new All-America Football Conference for public attention and postwar dollars. Dan Topping, owner of the NFL's Brooklyn franchise, just had announced he was leaving the league to found a New York team in the AAFC. A second defection, by Reeves, would embarrass the NFL even more. The AAFC also was setting up franchises in Los Angeles and San Francisco, while the new Browns were about to share the Cleveland market with the Rams and take up residence in its huge stadium, leaving Reeves' team in the city's much smaller and less-remunerative League Park. Moving the Rams to Los Angeles, Reeves argued, would drive a preemptive stake into rich California soil and into the heart of the AAFC.

A vote was taken.

The following morning, January 13, 1946, the thick Sunday edition of the

The arctic-like 1945 NFL Championship Game was the Cleveland Rams' first and only contest in Cleveland Municipal Stadium that year—and the franchise's very last as the home team in Cleveland. Precisely 50 years and one day later the original Browns played their final game in the same stadium, and the historic structure, host to six NFL title games in its history, was razed shortly thereafter *(Christopher Noice)*.

New York Times thudded on street corners, newsstand piles, and doorsteps with a top-of-the-sports-page headline reading: "Cleveland Rams Transfer Eleven to Los Angeles."[16] Reeves had won his case; and further he revealed to writers that he "had applied for a transfer of his club to Los Angeles at every NFL annual meeting beginning with 1943."[17] Indeed he had wanted a team in L.A. since 1937, four years before he even had bought the Rams, and now he would "move as quickly as I can find a place and offices in California and as soon as I can close up the Cleveland setup."[18] It was a perfect end run: If Reeves could not get what he wanted for his team in Cleveland, he would maneuver around this obstacle and make his way to L.A.

And so it was that the Rams ended their decade-long opening run in the city of their founding. Cleveland, a charter NFL city in 1920, was gob smacked by both the team and the league, abandoned "without warning and without explanation or apology"[19] by its short-lived champions, and just as they had turned a competitive corner. A testimonial dinner hosted by more than 800 state and civic leaders, businessmen, and fans to celebrate the Rams' newfound success fortunately had been scheduled four days *before* the championship game. Within months of Reeves' announcement the Rams officially took up residence in the 103,000-capacity Coliseum and issued its *1946 Guide for Press and Radio* with cover lines that iced the hearts of Cleveland fans back east:

> L.A. Rams Football Club:
> 1945 World Champions[20]

Twenty-seven days. That was all that separated the Rams from a championship and an announcement that they were leaving. It was a significant gesture of financial self-interest even for the striving NFL, and it would not be replicated for at least 70 years afterward. Even well into the 21st century the Cleveland Rams would remain the Champs Who Left Town: the only championship franchise in nearly 100 years of league history to be based the following season, fully intact, in a different city.[21]

Clevelanders much later would vilify Art Modell for transferring the Browns to Baltimore, but Modell's financial problems—if often self-inflicted—were "legitimate," Joe Horrigan of the Pro Football Hall of Fame said. Reeves, by contrast, "fabricated his concerns for opportunity. Modell was moving to survive; Reeves was moving to accelerate his wealth."[22] Though the other NFL owners initially resisted the Rams' move, in time they would reward Reeves with a spot in the Pro Football Hall of Fame and a "Pioneer Award"[23] in his name. The Rams' daring dash for California, after all, had opened the Western frontier and uncounted riches for all of professional sports.

Cleveland, for its part, was the worse for wear, at least immediately. "My heart[']s bowed down," James E. Doyle, the *Cleveland Plain Dealer*'s sports laureate, wrote on February 6, 1946, when he finally was able to bleed public sentiment after a month-long, citywide newspaper strike had ended. "Our champion Ram team/has jumped the town—/A champion scram team!"[24]

* * *

Then largely forgotten, in the instant success and subsequent gathering failure of the new Browns that settled in after Reeves' franchise had left, was the role that the Cleveland Rams had played at a pivotal moment in NFL history.

Waterfield was a triple running, passing, and kicking threat whose all-around athleticism would look much at home on 21st-century flat-screen TVs. Benton set a single-game record for pass reception yards that stood until the 1980s and, decades after that, continued to rank among the very best of all time.[25] With the 1935 Detroit Lions the Rams broke through the hegemony of the NFL's early powers and foreshadowed the parity and any-given-Sunday advantage that would define and enrich the league decades later and make it America's number-one-sport. The Rams' overall winning percentage in Cleveland was better than many imagine or remember—a considerably better run cumulatively across their eight seasons than more established franchises the Steelers, the Eagles, and the Cardinals.[26] This gave the team's home city a preview of modern competitive NFL football that the Browns of the 1950s and 1960s finally would deliver.

The Rams' move from Cleveland to L.A. has been called "the most audacious and important relocation in sports history,"[27] simultaneously setting in motion the reintegration of pro football and the migration of sports franchises to the West Coast. The stories of Jackie Robinson breaking the Major League Baseball color barrier and of the Giants and the Dodgers abandoning New York for California are intertwined with that of the Rams. Innovation and influence, indeed, were common among those who passed through the Cleveland Rams organization. Sid Gillman drew on his one season as an end for the team in 1936 to launch a Hall of Fame career as "father of the modern passing game,"[28] taking his place among the ten most influential head coaches of all time and nurturing a coaching tree that took a dozen of his one-time assistants to head-coaching jobs of their own.[29] Rams general manager Chile Walsh selected three future Hall of Famers in two NFL drafts while in Cleveland and foresaw a day when the league would play midweek games in indoor stadiums. Ex-Rams Greenwood, Scarry, Chet Adams, Tommy Colella, Gaylon Smith, and coach Bill "Red" Conkright all were key contributors on the legendary 1946 edition of the Browns, whose founding owner Robert H. Gries also had been a charter investor in the Rams. End Howard "Red" Hickey later was credited with forming the spread-formation shotgun offense. Waterfield, Reeves, and Rams head coach Earl "Dutch" Clark were inducted into the Pro Football Hall of Fame, with Waterfield's iconic "7" inspiring Denver Broncos quarterback John Elway.

Off the field, Gehrke, with encouragement from Rams ex-player and coach Bob Snyder, crafted the team's groundbreaking horned helmet design that transformed football uniforms at all levels of the game. And the Rams, only five seasons removed from Cleveland, were among the first NFL teams to televise their games and were the darlings of Hollywood movie and television producers seeking real-life players for their productions.

All these superlatives occurred in or had some historical roots in Cleveland. And yet, just three decades after the Rams had won their championship there, letters began to appear in newspapers that probed the franchise's actual existence, as if its history were a runic artifact, knowable only by historians or unclaimed by the uncaring. "When I was a kid growing up in Cleveland," one letter in 1976 began, "I would have sworn that the Cleveland football team was the Cleveland Rams. My friends in Kentucky tell me I am crazy."[30] An obituary for former Rams player Dante Magnani in the *New York Times* declared that the franchise had "folded" in 1943.[31] In other instances the team's identity was attributed to that that of the Browns,[32] as if the Rams' history had been subsumed into that of their successors in Cleveland.

How had it come to this? The Rams were founded with high hopes by a football man steeped in a tradition of football excellence at The Ohio State University and by Cleveland investors who thought they had established an enduring civic treasure. The Rams were going to be a crowning achievement after numerous failed attempts at establishing pro football in Cleveland. They were going to be in Cleveland forever. Instead they very nearly went of business, twice—first when they dropped out of the league for one year in Cleveland because of World War II, then as they hemorrhaged money in Los Angeles in the late 1940s.

After transferring to St. Louis in 1995 the Rams had become the league's most preeminent wandering team in the modern era, picking up titles in three different cities—the only NFL franchise to do so[33]—and persisting 80-plus years after their start in Cleveland in perpetual pursuit of their one true home. Among the pioneers of modern teams in what would become an unhappily familiar pattern for sports fans, the Rams searched for a better and better stadium and more and more revenue until finally in 2016 they returned to Los Angeles, the city that had embraced them the longest and the most.

It was a meandering, itinerant path. It was an encapsulation of the NFL's struggle in its early years to gain a significant foothold in the American consciousness and reach its stratospheric success. It was a future that Damon "Buzz" Wetzel, a native of rural southern Ohio, never in his wildest dreams could have imagined for the one major achievement he was to have in his life: the founding of the NFL's storied, wandering, charismatic franchise, the Rams.

Part I: Start-Up

Chapter 1

"We became the Rams"

Damon "Buzz" Wetzel, a gadabout with an amiable smile, an artist's eye, and the hardness of a hoodlum while on the gridiron, pushed his way into establishing what would become a billion-dollar National Football League franchise. Though generally a solid player, he had multiple mishaps and injuries and quickly decided he would jump instead into the fray of coaching and general management, which was more financially remunerative and offered far more personal influence. Given more luck he might have ended up a celebrated player-turned-owner like the Chicago Bears' George Halas—with multiple championships and a drive in his name paved right to the front door of the Pro Football Hall of Fame in Canton, Ohio. But for Wetzel, as with so much else about the scrappy early years of the Rams football franchise that he and assorted Cleveland money men founded, things just did not turn out this way; instead he was to travel a road into obscurity that was very unlike Halas's.

Wetzel seemed destined to lead a successful professional sports franchise. He was born in 1910 in Roseville, Ohio, in the Appalachian foothills that were then in the birth-throes of professional football. Damon's father Henry, also nicknamed Buzz, was a baseball man who spent his son's childhood ascending through the ranks of manager and owner in the minor leagues and as a talent scout for Major League Baseball's Indians before he eventually moved his family to Cleveland. By 1938, with five minor-league championships in 15 seasons,[1] the elder Wetzel possessed what *Cleveland Plain Dealer* sports editor Gordon Cobbledick called "perhaps the most remarkable managerial and executive record in the modern history of the game"[2] to that point. But for all his achievements, Wetzel's chief regret that was his athletic son Damon did not follow him into baseball.

Young Wetzel instead took his beefy five-foot-10 and 190-pound frame, his "nimble feet" and "deceptive hip-shift,"[3] and his love of contact to the gridiron as a fullback for The Ohio State University, where he lettered for three seasons. (Even with his nimble feet he tripped during a sorority dance at the Columbus Country Club during his sophomore year and was hospitalized with head lacerations, making for front-page sports news back in Cleveland.) By his final collegiate season he and the Buckeyes were a raging success under new coach Francis Schmidt, who downplayed Ohio State's rivalry with Michigan by famously noting that the Wolverines "put their pants on one leg at a time, just like the rest of us."[4] Duly motivated, the Buckeyes dominated the Wolverines 34–0 in 1934, a year in which OSU ran up the score on opponents and finished 7–1. One game against Western Reserve University brought Wetzel to the historic playing field of Cleveland's League Park, future home of his own Cleveland Rams.

Wetzel was voted to the College All-Star team in a nationwide poll in 1935, right alongside Alabama's Don Hutson, eventual Hall of Fame end, and Gerald Ford, center for Michigan and future president of the United States. Yet Wetzel also was creative, an illustrator who was gaining notoriety as a "touchdown artist"[5] as well as "one of the hardest line smashers in the history of Ohio State university football."[6] His next practical progression after graduation might well have been moving back to Cleveland and settling in as an artist for a national newspaper syndicate, but Chicago's Halas pulled him fatefully into pro football.

The Bears then were the undisputed top dog of the NFL's Western Division and its representatives in the league's first two championship playoff games in 1933 and 1934. But the coming 1935 season looked foreboding. Legendary fullback Bronko Nagurski suffered chronic back injuries and would miss large chunks of the campaign. Halas knew of Wetzel's stardom at Ohio State and in fact had coached against him in a Bears exhibition with the College All-Stars. He figured Wetzel could fill in at fullback, but if Nagurski were indeed able to play, backfield coach Red Grange could plug Bronk right back into the lineup and slide Wetzel over to halfback (or onto the bench). Halas offered a contract to Wetzel, and he signed. If all went as scheduled he would return to Cleveland Stadium with the Bears when they played an exhibition game against the Cleveland College All-Stars. But he barely touched the ball during his short time with Chicago, carrying three times for no gain.[7] Nagurski did come back (or was hurried back) only two games into the regular season, and when the Bears departed Pittsburgh in late September after drubbing the Pirates 23–7 at Forbes Field, they left Wetzel behind.

Fortunately for Wetzel, Art Rooney—two years into a now-legendary

NFL ownership that initially was financed in part by successful bets on horseracing—again was willing to take a gamble, and he signed Wetzel. But even with lowly Pittsburgh, the back still frustratingly was a reserve. In his first game with the Pirates they were pasted 27–0 by the Green Bay Packers; in his second game they were flattened 17–6 by the Philadelphia Eagles. Then, "fist fights and a near riot flared" when the Pirates hosted the heavily favored Chicago Cardinals in a "rough, bitterly-contested affair," the *New York Times* reported.[8] Early in the fourth quarter the Pirates took the lead on a touchdown and extra point, though apparently not to the full satisfaction of Wetzel, who was caught punching Harry Nuuanu Field, a 230-pound Hawaiian-American tackle. Officials tossed Wetzel from the game. But the Pirates prevailed 17–13.

Trouble trailed Wetzel still. A few weeks before Thanksgiving 1935 the Pirates traveled to Ebbets Field to play the football Brooklyn Dodgers. A player on the Dodgers sustained a serious spine injury while Wetzel suffered a broken nose. The Pirates were on their way to a 4–8 record, and it likely was around this time that Wetzel began to entertain the possibility that a playing career in the NFL might not be for him. The money in pro football then was not in a per-game salary as a player, but as a coach or, even better, an owner—much like Wetzel's father, Henry, who by then had moved up to run a minor-league affiliate of baseball's Indians, the Zanesville Greys. Young Wetzel, 24, nurtured a plan to start up a pro football team in his hometown of Cleveland. All he needed was investment money, much as Halas had founded the Bears franchise with funding from the A.E. Staley Manufacturing Company.

But who would finance his team? And would pro football ever fly in Cleveland?

* * *

In 1935, pro football's shaky foundation in Cleveland was mottled with the memory of numerous failed franchises—this despite a gut feeling of then-league president Joe F. Carr, a native of neighboring Columbus, that Cleveland could be the perfect NFL location.[9] His hunch had merit. With and without a franchise, Cleveland often was at the NFL's crossroads or at least its periphery in the league's earliest years.

The National Football League was founded in 1920 in Canton, 60 miles south of Cleveland down the Cuyahoga River valley, just past Akron and the overland portage that links the Cuyahoga with the Tuscarawas River. Canton, along with nearby Massillon, was and still is rich football territory, hanging on the western edge of an arc extending through eastern Ohio and into west-

> **American Professional Football Association:
> Charter Franchises (1920)**
>
> | | |
> |---|---|
> | **Akron (OH) Pros** | **Dayton (OH) Triangles** |
> | Buffalo (NY) All-Americans | Decatur (IL) Staleys |
> | **Canton (OH) Bulldogs** | Detroit (MI) Heralds |
> | Chicago (Racine, IL) Cardinals | Hammond (IN) Pros |
> | Chicago (IL) Tigers | Muncie (IN) Flyers |
> | **Cleveland (OH) Tigers** | Rochester (NY) Jeffersons |
> | **Columbus (OH) Panhandles** | Rock Island (IL) Independents |
>
> *National Football League*

Cleveland joined four other Ohio cities as charter franchises in the American Professional Football Association in 1920. Two years later in a hotel in Cleveland, the organization changed its name to the National Football League.

ern Pennsylvania where local athletes once played independent (that is, noncollegiate) football in mostly small steel and blue-collar towns. Organizers of these games steered a wide berth around widely popular college contests and their siphoning effect on attendance by playing on Sunday afternoons rather than on Saturdays, but this schedule also ran them afoul of so-called blue laws restricting entertainment on Sundays in such large cities as Philadelphia and New York City. This had the effect of limiting early pro football to smaller Pennsylvania and Ohio towns where "blue-collar workers who slaved for six days a week ... didn't mind shelling out the fifty cents to a dollar admission to see a professional football game on their one day off."[10]

So it is no surprise that among the fourteen teams gathered inside Ralph Hay's legendary Hupmobile showroom in Canton in 1920 to form the American Professional Football Association (APFA), five were from Ohio.[11] These included charter franchise the Cleveland Tigers, a mostly forgettable squad that posted an inaugural record of 1–4–2; and the Akron Pros, the league's very first champions, led by Frederick Douglass "Fritz" Pollard, eventually to become the NFL's first African American coach. By 1922 the Tigers were a financial failure and were gone from the APFA, but the league hardly was gone from Cleveland. On June 18, 1922, the owners met in Cleveland's Hollenden Hotel and acted on Halas' recommendation to strike the word *professional* from the now–Columbus, Ohio–based organization's name—it was "superfluous," Halas said—and to use the word *league* instead of *association*, which in baseball connoted second-division teams. "And we were first class," the supremely confident Halas said. By the end of the meeting the "little group" formerly called the APFA was the National Football League.[12]

Los Angeles sportswriter Bob Oates observed lyrically that "Ohio was the anvil on which professional football was hammered,"[13] but attracting a paying public and making a financial go of the sport was something else entirely—a hopeful enterprise that usually ended with leaden familiarity. While franchises stayed soundly in places as diverse as Green Bay and New York, pro football teams in Cleveland and Ohio generally came and left nearly with the regularity of traveling vaudeville acts. Clevelanders were smitten with "more prestigious and meaningful sports"[14] like Major League Baseball, collegiate football, and boxing, and could be skeptical—even scornful, as was much of the American public—of pay-for-play football. In the popular view pro teams poached undergraduates and corrupted the fine morals of amateur collegiate players, turning the sport into "one for gamblers, drinkers and delinquent boys who refused to grow up."[15] Games frequently were boring, run-oriented, and low-scoring, and often ended in ties. There were hints of league affiliations with bookmakers and organized crime. A record 32 deaths and at least a dozen serious injuries were attributed directly to football in the 1931 season, frequently from the dangerous flying wedge play, and mostly among high-school and sandlot players. Insurance companies regarded pro football as so hazardous a sport that it was "classified with the most dangerous of professions."[16]

From 1921 to 1930, in a gambit for civic establishment and financial viability, the NFL ripped through 48 franchises in 38 different locations[17]—most of them small towns where pro football was a source of civic pride and boosterism and often was propped up financially by local business benefactors and fans. In big-city Cleveland the shuttering of the APFA franchise renamed the Indians, even with Jim Thorpe on the 1921 roster, opened the door in 1923 for another team called the Indians, but this next iteration finished a respectable 3–1–3 before it too folded. "This is too good a sport city to go without pro football," NFL president Carr protested in 1923, "and besides it's right in the heart of the region where pro football has its strongest hold on popular favor."[18] And so the Indians were followed by the 1924 Bulldogs—a merger of the legendary Canton franchise with the football Indians and Cleveland's first NFL championship team—but these Bulldogs also were financially moribund.

And the wheel of pro football kept turning. Some former Bulldogs players jumped to the Cleveland Panthers, a 1926 entry in the first of a series of NFL rival circuits to be called the American Football League. This version was founded by irrepressible football promoter C. C. ("Cash and Carry") Pyle, who was most famous for bringing college star Red Grange to the Bears and the NFL, but the Panthers fell quickly into financial receivership. Then came another NFL team called the Cleveland Bulldogs—a different franchise but with the same name as the 1924 champions. Quarterbacked by hometown hero Benny Friedman and playing their home schedule at Luna Park, an amusement attraction, the 1927 squad was billed officially as "Benny Friedman's Cleveland Bulldogs" and finished a respectable fourth in the league. But "the city wouldn't go for the pro game on a big scale,"[19] the *Plain Dealer* later concluded, and owner Sam Deutsch fell short of paying player wages, then averaging about $25 per week.

The team was sold to Detroit for one lone season before being shopped again, this time to Timothy Mara, a successful Manhattan bookmaker who never had seen professional football but whose young sons were enthusiastic about the sport. In 1925 Mara had figured a New York franchise in practically anything—shoeshine stands even—was worth the application fee, so he bought the rights to an NFL franchise. Four years later, in time for the 1929 season, eight former Bulldogs including Friedman were shipped to Manhattan to join the New York Giants, a budding dynasty that would enthrall young Daniel F. Reeves, future owner of the Cleveland Rams.

Big-time football thus ended in Cleveland for a decade save for a brief flash in 1931: one more experiment with another team named the Indians, this time sponsored by the NFL and managed by league employee Jerry Corcoran. Forming the Indians "was important because Cleveland was a big city, it was an industrial city, it had a large population base," said Joe Horrigan of the Pro Football Hall of Fame. For the NFL owners "it was [a city] that they really needed, and they didn't want to see failure."[20] Carr was encouraged by Cleveland's Depression-era investment in the newly opened Cleveland Municipal Stadium, capacity 78,000, and he predicted the Indians would be "packing the stadium within a couple of years"[21] right alongside their baseball namesakes. But the Indians defeated only the Brooklyn Dodgers and the Providence Steam Roller that season and were forced to move a home game against the Portsmouth Spartans to Cincinnati because of fan apathy at home. Many attendees to Indians' games came via distribution of free tickets—a common attendance-boosting practice of big-city NFL franchises. But Cleveland's three newspapers were indifferent, carrying "not a line regarding the team"[22] and its late-November week of road games—an 0-for-3 swing against Providence, Staten Island, and Chicago—that officially wrapped up this short-lived go at professional football. Cleveland was out of the NFL again.

By the mid–1930s the roll call of failure of pro football in Cleveland was extensive: Tigers, Bulldogs, Panthers, and Indians. There even was an entertaining semi-professional team called the Skeletons who wore full leather masks with luminescent paint and glow-in-the-dark bones on their jerseys. "When they ran out on the field there wasn't a lot of cheering because there was nobody there," Horrigan said.[23] The public, in Cleveland and nationally, still was years away from widespread interest in professional football. When the Associated Press conducted a poll of the best sports teams of 1933, sportswriters looked favorably on Major League baseball, college football, and pro hockey—and ranked pro football's sole nominee, the Chicago Bears, tied for dead last. Even three college rowing teams received more votes.[24]

Buzz Wetzel's ambition of establishing a successful pro football team did not seem at all promising. But he was persistent. At the very least he could line up former Ohio State teammates to help guarantee a winner on the field. Players like Sid Gillman, captain of the 1933 Ohio State Buckeyes and an All-American end who had turned down a contract offer from NFL's Boston Redskins to head into coaching—he might be coaxed into one more year of playing. And end Max Padlow—born in Russia, raised in Ohio, signed in 1936 to the Philadelphia Eagles. And Gomer Jones—one of the best centers in the college game, an All American, OSU captain in 1935, and team MVP his last two seasons. And Wetzel of course could join his old teammates as fullback if and when needed.

Getting a new team into the old boys' club of the NFL might prove to be a stretch. The established and insular league just had received—and promptly tabled—applications for franchises from Buffalo and Los Angeles,[25] and the owners were of no mind to add new members to their exclusive group. But a new rival circuit was starting up as a second version of the American Football League, and it was a players' league, with veteran players involved in managing their teams. If Wetzel could scrape together some financial support, he might really have something—a team of his own, like his father had.

Still—multiple attempts at professional football in Cleveland, and multiple failures. Who in their right mind would want to finance another one?

* * *

Homer H. Marshman, the so-called "real father of the Rams,"[26] may have looked like a blueblood with his piercing dark eyes and his sophisticated manner, but he started life very far from the wealthy Cleveland enclaves and Palm Beach getaways that later became his regular clime. In fact he grew up deep in Ohio football country.

Follow the Scioto River south from the flatlands of downtown Columbus where the early NFL once housed its headquarters and continue on through the paper-producing city of Chillicothe where, just south of town, Appalachian coal country abruptly opens up as fertile river bottomland with tree-covered hills that slope like an extended spine. Marshman was born in this area, in Jackson, Ohio, in 1898. Fifty miles southwest is Portsmouth—once home of the Spartans (later the Detroit Lions), birthplace of legendary sports executive Branch Rickey, and the last small city save for Green Bay, Wisconsin, to disappear from the NFL. Forty miles northeast is Athens, where Ohio University would offer an ambitious young man three years of rugged varsity football and a path out of small-town America. There, Marshman was granted his first law degree at age 22; then, at 25, he earned a second—this one from Harvard, where he befriended a future pro football colleague named Paul Thurlow. Then he lingered in Boston for awhile before returning to Ohio and joining a Cleveland law firm. His legal career blossomed in Ohio, his political aspirations less so. In 1930 he took out a petition to run as a Republican candidate for U.S. Senator and ultimately failed. In 1932 he lowered his ambitions to the Ohio Senate and that candidacy failed too. By 1934 he appeared to have reconciled himself to a successful life in law and business—partner in his own firm as "one of Cleveland's eminent attorneys"[27] and a regular eminence in executive positions and boards-of-directors across the region.

Marshman, age 38 in 1936, was a natural target for young Wetzel to approach when his own efforts to raise capital for his pro football team faltered. Marshman's old Harvard classmate was eager to intercede. Thurlow—a shipping magnate, secretary of the new AFL, and owner of the Boston Shamrocks franchise—teamed up to contact Marshman and request a meeting in Cleveland. "I never had seen a pro game and was something less than enthusiastic," Marshman recalled later.[28] Nevertheless he invited Thurlow and Wetzel to his house in the small village of Waite Hill and began contacting friends among the city's sportsmen and civic leaders to assemble his own fateful roster that would shape the course of professional football in Cleveland.

Wetzel no doubt felt some trepidation during his drive east from Cleveland to Marshman's house. Waite Hill, with a population of just a few hundred, exuded exclusivity and privilege. Sloping, leafy lanes curved around the picturesque Chagrin River as it winded toward Lake Erie. White clapboard houses and picket fencing imparted a feel of proper and prosperous New England. Many of Waite Hill's residents belonged to the exclusive Chagrin Valley Hunt and Kirtland Country clubs. To Wetzel, who undoubtedly was more familiar with Cleveland's smokestacks and steel mills and high rises 25 miles southwest of the village, the town may as well have been in a different state.

Gathered at Marshman's home were a half-dozen political and business powerbrokers at the city, regional, and national levels. Cleveland, haunted by the lingering Depression, still was at the height of its industrial might. That summer it would host the Republican National Convention which ultimately would bring Alf Landon to ringing defeat to incumbent Franklin D. Roosevelt. For many wealthy and influential men, ownership of sports teams was, variously, an act of civic altruism, a plaything, a distraction from the grind of business, and at worst a money pit. And here was solicitation for a sizable investment, in a sport that was not particularly popular or respectable like Major League Baseball, and for an upstart minor league at that.

Among the men in the room was Dan Hanna—or Daniel Rhodes Hanna, Jr., scion of a family business and political influence in Ohio. His grandfather U.S. Senator Marcus A. Hanna had engineered William McKinley's successful presidential campaigns in 1896 and 1900. His father Dan Hanna, Sr., publisher of the *Cleveland News,* two decades earlier had become so embroiled in a pitched readership battle with the *Cleveland Plain Dealer* that he enticed 25-year-old Arthur B. "Mickey" McBride to leave his hometown of Chicago and come to Cleveland to build the paper's audience as circulation manager.[29] McBride was extremely capable but had ambitions of his own, eventually tendering his resignation, acquiring real estate in Chicago and Florida and a taxicab company, growing spectacularly wealthy, and becoming a pro football owner in his own right—as founding owner of the Cleveland Browns. But that was a decade into the future. For now it was Hanna, nearly as much a real father of the Rams as was Marshman, who was in a position to resurrect pro football in Cleveland.

Wetzel, the son of a baseball man, wound into his pitch. The football team he was assembling would be stocked with All Americans. He himself had played in the big-league NFL; competing in the newly established and weaker AFL virtually assured success on the field, which could be the key to long-sought success for pro football in Cleveland. He would manage and coach the team; he might play as well. He would do whatever was needed to bring winning—and sustainable—professional football to Cleveland. Thurlow assured Marshman and the group that the new league was well financed. The established nine-franchise NFL had to be—*deserved* to be—challenged. It was insular, hesitant to admit new teams. Professional football was growing steadily in popularity among the American public; there was plenty of room for growth. Patience and initial investment were necessary, but in time the men's money would come back to them. Their investment would be well placed.

Marshman scanned the room and took a silent poll. Dan Hanna he knew well: A newspaperman like his father, Hanna probably would throw in his hat as an investor. Whether John A. Hadden, a fellow lawyer and until recently a member of the Ohio House of Representatives, would invest, Marshman may not have been entirely certain. But even if this small group of men was hesitant to put up funding, others could be persuaded. Ellis Ryan, for instance, was very much interested in sports; a dozen years later he would lead a syndicate to buy the Cleveland Indians from Bill Veeck. Marshman also was well acquainted with Steve O'Neill, prominent polo star and businessmen and also a future owner of the Indians. Robert H. Gries came from an old Jewish family in Cleveland dating to the 1830s and ran the prominent department store May Company. He had no athletic background but he was keenly interested in Cleveland's economic and civic well-being and was to take his family to every Rams home game—"a ritual he felt was important to show his family's civic pride," wrote his son Robert D. Gries,[30] who one day would be Art Modell's minority partner in the Browns.

And Marshman—what did he think? His competitive urge—ignited on the college gridiron, blunted by his short and unsuccessful turn in politics, so valuable in the courtroom and in business—was stirred. Owning a sports team could give him the high profile and local influence he originally had sought through public office. But his reputation in his adopted city of Cleveland could be on the line. He asked a few questions, raised a few objections. Wetzel responded eagerly, Thurlow forcefully, both trying mightily to persuade Marshman to invest in the franchise.

Marshman sized up the pair that had come out to Waite Hill. Thurlow, his old law school chum and would-be competitor on the field, already had an edge as secretary of the league. Of course it would be in Thurlow's own best interests to recruit another team; yet it also would be helpful for Marshman and the other Cleveland investors to know at least one of the other owners personally. And Wetzel, with his plump jowls and mischievous eyes, still looked like a college kid. He had been a star in college but he had the common sense to line up a backup career as a newspaper artist should his football dream fall through. And certainly, Marshman knew, his father was a success in baseball. The *Plain Dealer* just had run a photo of the "former scout for the Cleveland Indians, now president and general manager of their farm at Zanesville, O." alongside many of the successful major- and high minor-league players he had scouted—"his 'boys' who have made good."[31] Surely the father had passed on some of his sports instincts to the kid.

Owning a football team just might be fun, Marshman thought. He rose to his feet. Thurlow and Wetzel had themselves a deal. Cleveland was back on the pro football circuit.

* * *

Not long after this meeting in Waite Hill, Wetzel stood before Marshman and announced: "Now we've got to come up with a name."[32] The new franchise had opened up offices on Chester Avenue in downtown Cleveland,[33] and Marshman was beginning to fill the "neat and orderly" folder he kept in the "lower hand desk drawer in his office high in the Union Commerce building,"[34] Into this folder Marshman slipped the most important details pertaining to running a new football organization, and already the folder was beginning to swell. "We need a name," Wetzel said again. "For the team."

Lore has it that two sportswriters were present in the room. One almost certainly was the *Plain Dealer*'s John Dietrich, who would cover the Rams franchise's foibles and then fortunes beginning with the team's founding and continuing to its departure for Los Angeles ten years later. An Ohio State alum like Wetzel, and nearing age 40 like Marshman, Dietrich would serve as Virgil the chronicler to Marshman and Wetzel as the Rams descended into the inferno of pro football. Dietrich would chomp his cigar, peer "grumpily through his glasses,"[35] and leaven his game accounts and profiles of Rams management, coaches, and players with writerly cynicism, witty analysis, and bright exhortations to bring quality pro football at last to Cleveland. He would retire from sports writing in 1964, long after he had recommended to McBride a head-coaching candidate named Paul Brown,[36] and just before the Browns won their last NFL title in the 20th century to enter a long championship exile.

When Marshman suggested the new team should have a short name, Dietrich agreed and noted the frequency with which Indians was shortened to "Tribe" at the hands of sports editors. Yes, keep the name short, Dietrich and his colleague suggested, so that it could fit easily into a newspaper headline. Then Wetzel joined in. He was a fan of the powerful Fordham college team whose stout offensive line called the Seven Blocks of Granite included Vince Lombardi. Wetzel tossed out Fordham's nickname: the Rams.

There were nods all around. "I said to Buzz, 'We can't get one shorter than that,'" Marshman recalled. "We became the Rams."[37]

The *Cleveland* Rams.

A football franchise had been born.

Chapter 2

Razzle-Dazzled and Bedraggled

If one were to pinpoint the birth of the Rams—and with continuity in name and ownership from the American Football League to the National Football League there was just enough connective tissue to merit an argument that today's Rams began as an organization in the AFL[1]—the franchise officially debuted on October 11, 1936, against the Syracuse Braves. It was a Sunday afternoon of spicy leaf-fall, dwindling sunlight, and temperatures in the low 50s—a tease of warmth that lured about 5,000 curiosity-seekers to Cleveland's League Park to see what might transpire. A good many were fans of the Indians and American League baseball, then the dominant pro sport in town, and they came "possibly through force of habit,"[2] the *Cleveland Plain Dealer* speculated.

But the Rams' debut very nearly did not happen. Five weeks earlier Cleveland coach Damon "Buzz" Wetzel had announced his Rams were disbanding and his players were being released, the nascent team done in by a lack of financial backing. Among the six founding franchises—also New York, Rochester, Boston, and Pittsburgh—the Rochester group seemed unable to go forward and generated talk of forming a club in Brooklyn with money loaned from other teams. Wetzel did not think this would be a smart move given the spotty financial history of professional football, and he wanted out. "Another failure in Cleveland would ruin pro football here for 10 years," he said.[3] Betraying exasperation with the AFL, he hinted he would seek a spot for the Rams in the far more established NFL over the coming winter. But suddenly Rochester announced it would push forward, and it was a go for the AFL and the Rams. And for Wetzel too. He put aside his nascent career as a syndicated newspaper cartoonist so he could organize, coach, and manage this new hopeful enterprise. There now was no turning back.

AFL play commenced in late September 1936 with a ragged start not uncommon to game scheduling of the era. While the Rams were inactive for several weeks, the Braves hosted the Boston Shamrocks, took to the road to face the New York Yankees and the Pittsburgh Americans, and alighted in Cleveland on the second Sunday of October to oppose a Rams squad that had been practicing at a local golf club.[4] Wetzel was busy gathering the Ohio State stars whom Homer H. Marshman, Dan Hanna, Jr., and other investors—no fools—insisted be pressed into service as gate attractions to ensure a return on their investment.

When opening day arrived, Wetzel was anxious to see how his new team would fare. Physically the Rams players were not particularly large: More than half were under six feet tall,[5] including Sid Gillman, a five-feet-10 end who also was "a good share of the team's brains"[6] in helping Wetzel at coach. The heaviest player on the roster was Bill Sweeney, a six-feet-two tackle from Penn who weighed in at 260. At least 13 players were under 200 pounds, some well under. But with Gillman and six other college All-Americans the Rams were set to use a "highly diversified attack, centered around the Ohio State razzle-dazzle maneuvers"[7] of their former Buckeyes coach, Francis Schmidt. In an era that favored the run-centric single- and double-wing offense and use of tailbacks and halfbacks as well as the quarterback for forward passes, there would be plenty of throwing to complement laterals and gadget plays. Supplementing this Ohio State approach would be a combination of screen plays cribbed from the NFL's Chicago Bears, Green Bay Packers, and New York Giants into a style of offense which the players themselves came to dub, for want of a better description, as "Natpro."[8]

For their part the 0–3 Braves came to Cleveland with not much of an offense—nor with much in the way of uniforms either, as a portion of their gear had been stolen en route to Ohio as they journeyed along the shores of Lake Ontario and Lake Erie.[9] Missing a full complement of equipment hardly was cause for postponing a game in this bootstrapping era, however. Far from the sophisticated equipment of the late 20th and early 21st centuries, the get-up of players in the 1930s included helmets that were hard-leather shells with some fabric cushioning and no facemasks, shoulder pads made mostly of heavy leather, and mud cleats that had been developed just a few years earlier.[10] The Braves arrived with jerseys for their starting 11 players and not much more, so while the Rams took the field in vibrant red jerseys and matching red helmets along with pants, socks, and jersey numbers that very likely were gold/yellow,[11] the Braves possessed only two or three jerseys to be used by a dozen or so subs. They were reduced to "swapping shirts almost every time there was a substitution, so that as many as four or five men played under the same number."[12] This caused confusion in the crowd as to who was playing which position. As Marshman later observed, "kids' teams on any sandlot were better equipped."[13]

The Syracuse team's bedraggled appearance seems only to have added to an air of spectacle to this opening day, which was broadcast live on radio with commentary by veteran Indians announcer Jack Graney, first player-broadcaster in baseball history.[14] Not surprisingly, many of the spectators seem to have viewed the Rams' debut through the far more familiar lens of Major League Baseball, as did at least one reporter whose account in the next day's *Plain Dealer* would be headlined "Fans Just Can't Quit Baiting Umps."[15] Such partiality to baseball would not have surprised Wetzel, the son of a career baseball man. The Indians enjoyed a fair amount of success in League Park, including a World Series championship 16 autumns before the Rams' debut. Baseball then was king in Cleveland, and immortals including Cy Young, Shoeless Joe Jackson, Ty Cobb, Babe Ruth, and Lou Gehrig had roamed the city's field. Bob Feller had pitched his first game there just weeks before.

Though it was home to the baseball Cleveland Indians, League Park's rectangular shape was especially hospitable to football, with the gridiron set up between the third-base line on the north side and the home-run fence along Lexington Avenue on the south. The Rams played nearly half of their home games here in their time in the AFL and the NFL *(Strongsville, Ohio, Public Library/Wikimedia Commons).*

Still, League's Park odd configuration and seating capacity of 23,000 actually made it a surprisingly accommodating facility for football. The venue had hosted both NFL and college football teams, including Wetzel's own Ohio State Buckeyes, and the Rams would play nearly half of their home games within its cozy confines during their decade in Cleveland.[16] Located at a trolley stop at the corner of Lexington Avenue and East 66th Street, League Park was sewn into the middle of a neighborhood on the city's East Side, with automobile parking accommodated—for a small fee, of course—by local residents and their shallow front yards. Because two east-west avenues and two north-south streets defined the park's footprint, its configuration was fully rectangular and nearly perfect for football. One goal line was chalked along the first-base line while the other paralleled the park's left- and left-center-field bleachers, with the 15-yard line on the west end of the field drawn through the pitcher's mound. Box seats were especially close to the field and offered the ability for fans to shout to players, while bleachers that snaked around the third-base foul pole toward the scoreboard and flagpole in dead-center offered sublime views of the eastern end zone. Near the western end zone a 32-foot fence nearly as tall as the Green Monster at Fenway Park loomed behind the visiting football team's bench—on the same approximate patch of grass where any number of Indian right fielders pivoted to watch Ruth's home runs sail onto densely residential Lexington Avenue.

As Wetzel stood on the Rams' pre-game sideline, spectators shuffled through the concourse to take reserved seats that had some of the best vantage points in the house for $1.50[17]—equivalent to about three hours of a laborer's wage in one of Cleveland's many factories.[18] At game time a cold mid-afternoon breeze began to whisk in off Lake Erie, carrying a mixed scent of hot dogs, cigar smoke, raw turf and, if the wind moved in just such a direction, effluent from the steel mills in the nearby industrial Cuyahoga River flats. Streetcar bells clanged just beyond the home run fence along Lexington. The assembled murmured in charged anticipation of their new pro football team.

Cleveland Mayor Harold H. Burton tossed out the ceremonial first ball—a perfect spiral—to player Gomer Jones, as his fellow alumni from Cleveland South High School and Ohio State cheered wildly. A stocky five-feet-eight, 225-pound All-American from Ohio State, Jones was a smiling, round-faced center and the team's captain. Although that February the Chicago Cardinals had selected him in the second round of the NFL's inaugural player draft, he elected instead to join his old pal Wetzel in the AFL. It would be a fateful decision that would abort Jones's playing career before it barely got started, but on this opening day, as a gesture of thanks, it was Gomer Jones Day.

And it would be a good day for the Rams. Gillman, destined for the Pro Football Hall of Fame as a coach, scored the first touchdown in Rams history on a nine-yard pass from Lorain, Ohio, native Stan Pincura. Len Sadosky added to the tally on a lateral play as he filled in at fullback for coach Wetzel. Then Pincura, playing on both offense and defense as did virtually all players of the era, intercepted a Syracuse pass and returned it 46 yards for a touchdown. Very quickly the score was Rams 19, Braves 0. At halftime a drum-and-bugle corps performed, and the "home-town boys"[19] from Cleveland South High and Ohio State presented flowers to Jones, then baseball-besotted spectators continued to make wisecracks at the expense of the game. Kickoffs were accompanied by shouts of "Here's the windup!" Timeouts invoked exhortations to "Play ball!" A Rams touchdown run along the sideline roughly paralleling the third-base stripe invited regrets that the Indians might have done better than that summer's fifth-place finish had they only spent more time on that particular base path. "Razzle dazzle"[20] laterals quenched the crowd's quiet thirst for action, albeit to the "despair" of sports writers who tried to keep track of the ball as the Rams "did everything that is done on the basketball court but dribble the ball."[21] A good laugh was had during one of Syracuse's numerous "shirt-changing, time-out" periods when the field announcer took an opportunity to inform the assembled that the Rams' next opponents, the Shamrocks, were not only one of the best in the league but also among the "best equipped."[22]

Spectators seemed especially taken with the hard-as-nails play of halfback Harry "Horse" Mattos, son of Portuguese immigrants who emigrated first to Hawaii and then to Oakland. He had a permanent five-o'clock shadow, thick eyebrows, and heavy eyelids that made him look as if he were perpetually squinting at the sun. He was drafted by the NFL's Green Bay, found the Packers' contract offer too low, and signed instead with the Rams. At six-feet tall and a hair's-breadth under 200 pounds, he was 25 years old and a broad-shouldered specimen of a powerful back, taking shot after shot, unfazed.

The final score was Rams 26, Braves 0, prompting one excited writer to proclaim, "Give the Cleveland Rams a few seasons together and they'll take a place right alongside the best pro teams of the nation."[23] Wetzel seemed to be on his way to answering a tall order: making pro football relevant in Cleveland. Days after the game, Jones took Wetzel, Mattos, Pincura, and other Rams with him to the RKO Palace Theatre in downtown Cleve-

Rams franchise co-founder Damon "Buzz" Wetzel (10), with three other players from the American Football League team's 1936 inaugural season: Harry "Horse" Mattos (7), Mike Sebastian (4), and Bill Cooper (6) (*Family of Mike Sebastian/ Wikipedia*).

land to become special added attractions at a screening of a film in which he had made a cameo appearance. Then the *Plain Dealer*'s John Dietrich published a lengthy, glowing profile of Mattos. It was an early indication that the Rams would enjoy a higher profile than had their predecessors in pro football in Cleveland.

* * *

That the Rams were deemed newsworthy was especially notable given newspapers' previous apathy to pro football and with the bounty of local and national stories that reporters had to cover. Cleveland in the mid–1930s was the sixth largest city in America, and its signature skyscraper, the newly constructed Terminal Tower, cast a long shadow through the smoky haze of an industrial empire of steelmaking, "automotive production, lighting, electrical motors, and chemicals, paints and coatings."[24] Eight miles southwest of its Public Square the city had constructed the country's first municipally owned airfield, with the world's first radio-equipped air traffic control tower and the first airfield lighting system in the United States. The Great Depression may have laid Cleveland low, but the city still was running on the momentum of a half-century of "unrivaled industrial entrepreneurism"[25] and was churning through in-migrations of Eastern Europeans and Southern African Americans in search of steady low-skill work.

Cleveland also developed big-city problems as it teemed with industry and workers. In 1936 a string of mysterious killings and dismemberments that came to be called the Torso Murders was underway. The crimes ended abruptly and mysteriously two years later, unsolved, but they forever blighted the record of Cleveland safety director Eliot Ness, who had been hired to bring order to a city that was then a "large den of vice—bootlegging, prostitution, gambling [and] union-led extortion rackets, all protected by paid-off police."[26] Bustling, sooty, and corrupt, Cleveland that year hosted the Republican National Convention and the Great Lakes Exposition, a world-fair-like event on the city's lakefront, as it neared the close of a "bountiful era of cultural philanthropy"[27] that endowed such enduring world-class institutions as the Cleveland Orchestra and the Cleveland Museum of Art.

In and outside of Cleveland the seeds of a postwar era in which pro football would become America's favorite spectator sport were germinating. Birth control was legalized in 1936, enabling the women's movement and the liberalization of the fairer sex that would come to embrace pro football nearly as much as would men.[28] Amelia Earhart was preparing for an around-the-world flight that would presage common air travel. The Hoover Dam was completed, hastening the nation's shift to the West, while the Rural Electrification Act brought power to the nation's remotest areas.

Among African Americans, Jesse Owens won four gold medals at the 1936 Summer Olympics in Adolf Hitler's Berlin. Joe Louis would win the world heavyweight boxing championship the following year. In music Robert Johnson was making the first of his blues recordings that would become a blueprint for rock'n'roll, while Billie Holliday's slinky "Summertime" vied at the top of the music charts with Bing Crosby's "Pennies from Heaven." American society was changing—yet there was not a single African American then in the NFL. This was the result of a "gentleman's agreement"[29] among the league's owners, ostensibly to protect African American players from violence by racist white players, but also arising from a common belief that hiring black players in the midst of an economic depression might position them as competitors for what were perceived to be white men's jobs.[30] This policy one day would be reversed, with the Rams and Cleveland playing a vital role as pro football came under closer public scrutiny.

Still, nothing it seemed could thwart the inexorable rise of the popularity of pro football in America. In 1933 NFL president Carr audaciously had predicted that "in a few short years" the NFL would "outdraw baseball or any other sport, game for game."[31] To ensure his claim would come true, by the mid-1930s the NFL had overhauled its rules to create a "spectacular scoring game"[32] with wide-open play and frequent scoring. The Rams had begun play precisely at the dawn of an era in which a "changed and more marketable game" would "gain respect, exposure and acceptance from a national audience at a time when many spectator sports were stagnating or declining."[33] And in this era, in Cleveland as in many other cities, newspaper reporters would pay close attention and be ready to offer praise—or condemnation—for any representation of professional football.

For his part the *Plain Dealer*'s Dietrich was excited by the Rams' debut victory over Syracuse and delightedly had viewed the "extemporaneous lateral pass" as a way to "bewitch and befuddle the opposition."[34] But he quickly changed his mind after the Rams' second game, on October 18, 1936, as they fell to the Shamrocks and thudded to their first loss, 9–0. Suddenly Dietrich thought the Rams' vulnerability was "a rather bad case of lateralitis, or razzle-dazzleitis."[35]

The Rams rebounded with a 27–0 downing of the Yankees on October 25, 1936, in a contest that featured scoring passes to three receivers including Gillman, who was making the most of his one season as a pro player. Gillman, having turned down the NFL's Boston Redskins in 1935, considered the AFL a "rinky-dink startup"[36] but joined the Rams anyway because he wanted to help out Wetzel, his old Ohio State teammate. In truth he aspired to be a coach, and at age 25 he already was on the staff of Ohio's Denison College, where he began to explore use of game film to discern team and player strengths and weaknesses, devise plays, and learn the skills of a coach. Then on weekends he traveled 130 miles north to Cleveland to suit up for the Rams.

After five games the Rams were 2–1–2 and drawing 8,000 to 10,000 fans to home games at League Park. The situation looked guardedly positive, and Wetzel began to cut a prominent and dashing figure in town. He took up residence at 7609 Euclid Avenue, near a once-glorious area of Cleveland known as "Millionaire's Row."[37] When not in helmet and pads he sported a fashionable fedora, suit and tie, and knee-length coat, but prominence in the community did have its drawbacks for a young, sometimes-impetuous man. Wetzel made front-page news on his 26th birthday when he was involved in a fender-bender about 20 blocks from his house. Asked to produce a driver's license, he assured a police officer that he had left it at home. "O.K.," said the policeman as he called Wetzel's bluff, "I'll drive out with you to your house and we'll have a look."[38] He followed Wetzel to his driveway, whereupon the young coach finally came clean: Actually, he had intended to *apply* for a license. He was booked immediately at Central Police Station and released on personal bond.

Wetzel the novice sports executive soon was to discover that professional sports were no easy business. Marshman and the other Rams owners were interested in driving better attendance than 8,000 or 10,000 per game to League Park—something more in line with that of the Yankees and the mammoth 26,000[39] they had attracted for a game against Pittsburgh. Even in Boston, a city then considered no better a pro football town than Cleveland, the Shamrocks drew 13,500[40] for a contest against Syracuse. Wetzel's team was costing the owners money, beyond even the $53,000 in founding capital the dozen or so men initially had put up. Debt was accumulating by the week. Each Monday after a game, investor Robert H. Gries hosted the other owners for lunch at the May Company department store at which he was the operating manager. There they would add up, on a paper napkin, all of the week's expenses—payments for players, salaries for coaches, the laundry bill, etc. "I mean, it was *very* primitive," said Gries' son, Robert D. Gries, who later was a minority owner of the Cleveland Browns with Art Modell. The amounts were toted up, then divided, "and then everybody would reach in their pocket, and they'd take out the money, and that's how the team was paid in 1936."[41]

Robert H. Gries, founding investor in the 1936 AFL Rams, the 1937 NFL Rams, and the 1946 Cleveland Browns. Each week at the department store he managed, Gries hosted the other owners of the AFL Rams for lunch, during which they would tote up the team's expenses on a paper napkin and each pitch in cash to pay the team *(Donald Gries Collection)*.

Something clearly had to be done to keep the Rams' enterprise afloat. In early November the team reduced ticket prices, and Wetzel likely felt deflated. His 2–1–2 Rams were in third place behind Boston (6–1) and New York (4–2–2), his defense was the stingiest in the league in averaging only three points per game, and his razzle-dazzle offense was holding its own. But at least Marshman and the ownership group kept the marketing machine going. Advertisements for the team's game against the Brooklyn Tigers touted the Rams' signature razzle-dazzle attack and the throwing/receiving tandem of Mattos to Max Padlow. For their part the Tigers featured the prowess of Harry Newman, a star passer who had played on an undefeated team at Michigan with Gerald Ford, then led the New York Giants as a rookie to the NFL's first championship game in 1933 before he defected to the AFL. But the Rams were equal to the task. After building a 12–0 lead, then falling behind 14–12 late in the game, Cleveland moved into scoring position mostly on outstanding play by Gillman. Then they trotted out Declan O'Keefe for the game-winning field goal. The large O'Keefe was just "a hanger-on who had been sticking around for expense money—coffee and crullers,"[42] Dietrich informed readers. O'Keefe placed a rubber toe on his shoe, and with only a few seconds to play, dusk falling over the field, and more than 10,000 fans cheering and stomping their feet until the League Park grandstand shook, he lined up the ball and placed it neatly through the uprights for a 15–14 Rams win.

With Cleveland and Boston each carrying a .750 winning percentage and a claim on first place, a scheduled showdown between the two teams in Boston's Braves Field came into view. A report later would claim that the Rams and the Shamrocks played one of the wildest pro games Boston ever had seen, with "shuttle passes, shovel passes, flat passes, and now and then good old fashioned line bucking."[43] The teams exchanged leads until the Rams held a one-point advantage, then Cleveland halfback Mike Sebastian ran four successive reverse plays to pick up three first downs and, finally, a touchdown. The Rams had marched 75 yards on their final drive to push ahead for good 34–26 and move into sole possession of first place in the league.

Smarting from the home loss, Paul Thurlow, Marshman's old law-school pal, proposed that the teams append a third and final matchup to the end of the season schedule. This way, no matter what happened, the AFL would be able to say without hesitation which team had been the best—the Rams or the Shamrocks. Marshman readily agreed, because really there was no downside: The Rams would play a bonus game before its home crowd in Cleveland, generate additional revenue, and attract interest for a playoff-like contest. But unknown to Marshman, Thurlow had another surprise up his sleeve. When the time came for the Rams to collect their guaranteed $3,000 for traveling to Boston, Marshman asked Thurlow for a check rather than a stash of cash to take back on the train. Thurlow obliged, and Marshman returned home to discover that his check had bounced. Marshman swallowed hard and simply moved on in respect for his old law-school chum, but Monday's owner meeting at the May Company almost certainly was a bit tense.

The Rams, remarkably, were stiffed of their visitors' take again the following week, in Pittsburgh. Thirty minutes before their game with the Americans, Wetzel—alarmed by a near-total no-show at Forbes Field—approached opposing coach Dick Guy and demanded the Rams receive their $3,000 guarantee upfront. Guy refused. Wetzel left the clubhouse to take another look at the grandstand and, estimating there were fewer than 500 bodies, returned with a compromise: The Rams would play for 50 percent of all receipts after park expenses were deducted. Guy refused again. So Wetzel returned to the Rams' locker room and told his players to sit still. Once official game time had passed he instructed the entire squad to pack up their gear and get ready to take the train home. The game was canceled and the fans were given a refund. Then a he-said/he-said disagreement erupted. Wetzel acknowledged Guy had phoned him earlier in the week to suggest the game be moved to Cleveland, where a larger turnout than might be hoped for in Pittsburgh was almost certain. But Wetzel refused, believing the Rams were building a large following at home and hesitant to overexpose the team's presence.

Guy claimed a more nefarious motivation. "Cleveland did not want to play this game," he charged. "They are in first place and are determined to win the championship and they were afraid we would beat them."[44] Of course the Americans would have paid the Rams after the game, he reassured reporters. The Rams' response was to demand Pittsburgh's ouster from the league. Things had gotten ugly in the AFL, and for the Rams they were to end even uglier.

Cleveland lost its next two games while the Shamrocks won their last pair, and as the league's inaugural season limped to a close, Boston was in first place at 8–3 (.727)—percentage points ahead of Cleveland at 5–2–2 (.714). It looked as if the Shamrocks might walk off with the AFL's first title. But wonder of wonders, the Rams recalled that Thurlow and Marshman had agreed to a third, season-ending game in Cleveland—in essence, a playoff. A victory for either team would hand it the AFL championship. However, a funny thing happened along the way: bad Cleveland weather. Or more specifically, a mere *threat* of bad Cleveland weather on game day.

2. Razzle-Dazzled and Bedraggled

* * *

In a foreshadowing of the arctic weather that would accompany the epic 1945 NFL title game, snow descended for several days preceding November 29, 1936—the scheduled matchup between the Cleveland Rams and the Boston Shamrocks for what essentially would be the AFL championship game. More snow was in the forecast, and while the Shamrocks surely were no strangers to wintry weather in New England, they transmitted to Rams management their apprehension about possible game-day conditions at League Park. The Rams, fully aware they had everything to gain from the contest while Boston had everything to lose, would have none of it. They believed the Shamrocks' anxiety was a ruse. Just a week earlier, prior to a game against the Yankees in Cleveland, the Rams had lost several hundred valuable paying fans as debate broke out over whether to start a game in inclement weather. There would be no dithering this time. The championship contest was on, and Rams owners looked forward to a financial bonanza from an anticipated crowd of close to 15,000. A grounds crew cleared snow from the League Park field as newspapers carried ads and a sound truck threaded through Cleveland streets promoting the game.

But then a report came out of Boston that the Shamrocks had neglected to pay their players for several weeks, which certainly helped to explain Thurlow's bounced check. Many Shamrock players threatened to stay put in Boston rather than travel to Cleveland. The Boston owners, facing an insurrection, made a preemptive move by announcing—and making certain the Associated Press reported—that the game had been canceled on account of a forecast for heavy snow in Cleveland. The Shamrocks then laid claim to the AFL championship.

The Rams were beside themselves. Marshman flashed back to the meeting at his home in Waite Hill when Thurlow argued persuasively for him and other Cleveland civic leaders to invest in the new AFL. It was bad enough Thurlow's check was no good; now he and the Shamrocks had denied Marshman and the Rams a chance to lay claim to being the league's best team. The Rams should take the title by forfeit, the *Plain Dealer*'s James E. Doyle suggested, and the Shamrocks should "take a jump in the Atlantic Ocean."[45]

But Marshman and his partners would have the final word. They were through with unpaid guarantees, with empty grandstands and empty promises. Already they were paying out what Marshman had taken to calling "Irish dividends"—a rather impolitic way of saying "we lost money."[46] Just a few weeks earlier the Rams signaled they would continue in a "stronger and reorganized American League" the following year regardless of financial losses,[47] but as far as Marshman was concerned the AFL could forget all that now. "Count me out," he told his partner Hanna over lunch at the city's exclusive Union Club. "The American [Football] League is a failure."[48] If the Cleveland Rams were going to lose money, he said, they may as well do so on a bigger stage. Marshman would talk with NFL president Joe F. Carr about bringing the league back to Cleveland for the first time since 1931. Together they would get the Rams into the NFL.

Years later Marshman still thought about that $3,000 bounced check from Thurlow. "I've seen Paul since dozens of times," he said, "and he still promises to pay. Each time I tell him to forget it."[49] Marshman and the Rams had moved on.

It never did snow in Cleveland on November 29, 1936, in spite of the Shamrocks' misgivings about inclement weather. In fact, it rained. And Gillman was right: The AFL was a rinky-dink startup. The future of the Rams franchise clearly was in the big leagues. The NFL was coming back to Cleveland, and this time it was going to work.

CHAPTER 3

This Time Pro Football Was Going to Work in Cleveland

With their proposed exit from the American Football League, suddenly it was all business for the Cleveland Rams. Where before they had been a hastily thrown together organization making do with what they had and reacting to whatever weather, fate, and other teams in the AFL brought their way, now they were seizing their future as a legitimate business enterprise. It was as if the bungling of the AFL had brought into clear focus what the Rams adamantly did *not* want to be: a second-rate team. And with their quick success in the AFL—one cancelled game from a championship—came confidence they would need to succeed in the rougher circuit of the National Football League.

The Rams would be in the big time now, thanks in no small part to the support and encouragement of Joe F. Carr, who presided over the up-and-coming NFL from its first-ever offices on the 11th floor of the New Hayden Building in Columbus,[1] directly adjacent to the turret-shaped Ohio Statehouse. A former executive of charter NFL franchise the Columbus Panhandles, Carr maintained harmony among the powerful patriarchs of Halas, Mara, Rooney, Bidwill et al. He also was helping to pull the NFL towards increasing popularity and prestige. In 1937 General Mills placed a photo of the Chicago Bears' Bronko Nagurski on boxes of Wheaties cereal, a space typically reserved for baseball stars. That same year national sportswriters identified the growing popularity of pro football as the year's most striking development in sports.[2] Carr—bespectacled, dogged, and nearly evangelical in his pursuit of national prominence for the league he led at age 56—was resolved that during his tenure the NFL would sprout and sustain a new green shoot in the Sixth City of Cleveland just 140 miles from his office door. He understood, as a former sports journalist, the promotional value of establishing franchises in the nation's largest and most influential cities.

The timing was ideal for Rams founders Homer H. Marshman and Damon "Buzz" Wetzel. The Cincinnati Reds NFL franchise had failed in 1933, followed in 1934 by a hybrid Cincinnati Reds-St. Louis Gunners team—co-owned, coincidentally, by Charles "Chile" Walsh,[3] who later would become general manager of the Rams. The Reds-Gunners vacancy left nine NFL franchises in just seven markets—Boston, Chicago (Bears and Cardinals), Detroit, Green Bay, New York (Giants and Brooklyn Dodgers), Philadelphia, and Pittsburgh. It was a set-up that would continue into 1935 and 1936 until Carr convinced the owners to invite a new franchise into the Western Division. Carr would act as proxy for this franchise-to-be-named-later by drafting 10 rounds of graduating college players. As he prepared to make these selections, he visited Marshman[4] as he furthered his interest in seeing Cleveland back in the league.

On December 12, 1936, the evening before the Green Bay Packers defeated the Boston Redskins for the NFL title, the league's owners gathered along with hordes of Christmastime tourists at the Hotel Lincoln near New York City's Times Square. One hundred names of college seniors were written on a blackboard. The team with the worst record in the league in 1936, the Philadelphia Eagles, selected first, followed by the team with the second-worst record—the Dodgers—and so on until the Packers, the team with the best regular-season mark, made their selection. Only then would Carr draft for the incoming franchise—using the very last selection—with Carr emphasizing that there was only the *possibility* of adding a tenth team prior to the start of the season.

The very concept of a draft of college graduates still was relatively brand new for the NFL—started just a year earlier as a counterbalance to the every-man-for-himself approach to signing players that had tipped the league in favor of the powerful big four teams: the Bears, Packers, Giants, and Redskins. But its outcome in 1937 was familiar, and of less help to the Rams than they might have hoped. The best choice in the draft was made by the powerful Redskins, who competed with the AFL's Shamrocks in the Boston market and who were on the verge of moving down the Eastern seaboard to Washington, D.C. The Redskins selected "Slingin'" Sammy Baugh, a future Pro Football Hall of Fame passer who at six-feet-two and 182 pounds had "the arm of a god."[5] Baugh would lead Washington to the 1937 championship as a rookie and foster immediate and deep fan interest in the nation's capital; but had the Rams selected first instead of last, they might well have landed Baugh and begun their NFL existence with far greater initial success.

As it was, Carr did an adequate job with his selections. In the first round he picked up future All Pro and mainstay of the early Rams, Johnny Drake—a square-faced, wide-eyed fullback from Purdue who soon would gain notoriety for playing the game with reckless abandon. But like all the owners, Carr also left Clarence "Ace" Parker of Duke University on the board until the second round where he would be drafted by Brooklyn and begin his Hall of Fame career at quarterback.

Anxiously awaiting the conclusion of the draft was Marshman, there to make an initial presentation to the NFL owners on behalf of the Rams. Vying with Marshman for a spot in the NFL was an application from Buffalo along with two in-person hopefuls from Los Angeles who had traveled nearly 3,000 miles to New York City with hopes of entering the league. The ambitions of the latter were not unfounded. L.A. had a short-lived roving team called the Buccaneers in the league's formative years of the 1920s, during which Carr had predicted that one day their home city would be a credit to the league. But the NFL was not yet ready for a team in the distant West. Despite the California duo's offer to double the usual visitors' fee for their trouble in having to cross the Rockies—a compromise similar to that which Rams owner Daniel F. Reeves would make nearly a decade later—the L.A. application was shot down immediately by the Pennsylvania tandem of Eagles owner Bert Bell and Pittsburgh's Art Rooney. The reason: "great distance of travel,"[6] the identical protest Reeves would receive in early 1946. Buffalo and Cleveland, however, passed the initial screening, with league powers pointedly suggesting that strong capitalization would win the franchise when the decision-makers reconvened a few months later.

Marshman and Wetzel wasted little time preparing for that day: By the end of the year they had incorporated as Cleveland Rams Football Club, Inc., and on February 3, 1937, Marshman was confident enough to announce he had lined up a solid $55,000 in capital from 20 prominent Clevelanders[7] including several investors in the AFL Rams, among them department store executive Robert H. Gries, later to help found the Browns. Also in the mix was Albert C. "Al" Sutphin, who soon was to construct the Cleveland Arena, which would become home to the Cleveland Cavaliers when they debuted in the National Basketball Association in 1970. Joining the group, too, was Thomas E. Lipscomb, a local attorney who would play a pivotal role in Rams management and the drama that attended to the franchise's move to L.A.

There would be changes in day-to-day management as well. Marshman installed himself as president and secretary of the team, while Wetzel, at just 26, would conclude his short career as a player-coach to become general manager and fulfill his destiny as a sports executive. With Marshman, he would search for his successor as head coach.

On Friday, February 12, 1937—the official date of the Rams' initiation into the National Football League—the owners gathered at the ornate Sherman Hotel in Chicago, hometown of league powerbroker Halas. First order of business was selection of the league's tenth franchise. Marshman was ushered into a room where the NFL's executive committee was assembled and made his presentation, undoubtedly with more confidence than he had had in December given the investments he now had sewn up. News of strong financial support out of Cleveland was very agreeable to the owners, who now were accepting only well-funded applications from established major-league cities.

With Marshman's pitch complete, he was told to sit down and wait. A representative from Houston came in to make his proposition; the owners thanked him and asked him to leave, which Marshman thought was a bit strange and impolite given that he had been allowed to stay. Then a man from Los Angeles made his pitch, with the same result: He was told he could leave. "I couldn't understand it," Marshman recalled of the other hopefuls. "Their presentations were every bit as good as mine."[8]

Once the door had closed behind the representative from L.A., George Preston Marshall, a laundry business tycoon and owner of the team jocularly to be called the "Washing-Done"[9] Redskins, leaped to his feet and said, "I move we give it to Cleveland."[10] Population and geography, Marshman learned, worked strongly in Cleveland's favor. Houston still was something of a small town—then about the size of Toledo, Ohio. L.A. by contrast was more than a third larger than Cleveland but lacked a major-league baseball team—the NFL's requirement then for signaling big-league intent. The owners furthermore were quite content to keep their cozy league circumscribed to the familiar and compact East and Midwest regions of its origins. A vote was taken, and it was unanimous: Cleveland would receive the NFL's tenth franchise. Carr had promised as far back as 1923 that one day the city would "be given a real team that will be right up among the contenders."[11] Now he could return home to Columbus confident that this time pro football was going to work in Cleveland.

But first—business was business. Carr's family of owners wanted to know if Marshman had the money necessary for membership. If he wanted the franchise he had to pay them $10,000—immediately. "I had $7,000 in the bank," Marshman said. "This was depression time, you know."[12] He told them he had the money and wrote them a check on the spot. No Paul Thurlow, he rushed back to Cleveland, borrowed $5,000 from his friend Dan Hanna, withdrew another $5,000 from his savings, and ran to the bank on Monday morning to make sure his check would not bounce. *Then* it was official. For the first time since November 1931, when the football Indians had lost their last game before nearly 70,000 empty seats in brand-new Cleveland Stadium, the city was back in the NFL.

Now Marshman and Wetzel faced a countdown of only seven months to get an NFL-caliber team ready for play. The organization set up operations on the top floor of the imposing Guardian Building in downtown Cleveland, one block from the Union Club with its membership of the city's wealthy who would bankroll the team. Marshman's $10,000 check barely had cleared before a Rams logo appeared, likely for the first time ever. It was a detailed line drawing of a forward-facing ram's head with eyes narrowed in a pre-charge pose and tightly coiled horns—the prototype of what would become historic football iconography.

The new logo and the words "Cleveland Rams Football Club Incorporated: Member National Football League"[13] topped hand-typed letters that were tucked into lavishly designed envelopes, then sent with dispatch to 10 college seniors whom Carr had drafted on behalf of the team. "You are one of those men," read one such letter, signed by Marshman. "We should like to know first whether you are interested in playing professional football." The team offered assurances that it followed the same rules as other teams in the league regarding training, contracts, protection of players against injuries, "and matters of that sort." The letter promised "advancements … on the basis of merit," as if a place on the roster were a common entry-level position in business. A drafted player signing a contract with the Rams could be confident the organization was "interested in building a strong team," was in the midst of contracting other players recommended by college coaches, and now was "negotiating a few trades which will give us a nucleus of men experienced in professional football."

Payment would be arranged at a per-game rate—which, alas, would not be much, even for the era. First-round selection Drake would be paid $250 per contest, but only after he held out for more pay until practically the start of training camp. "You see, then the idea was to operate as cheaply as possible," Marshman explained later.[14] Drake's take was not bad, but his checks would be cut only 11 times that year—one for each of the Ram's regular-season games. Virtually all of the Rams would play for "meager wages and no job security."[15]

It might be a surprise to 21st-century football fans that college-educated

The Rams franchise sported a logo almost immediately upon its acceptance into the NFL in 1937. The rightward-facing ram's-head in profile, still in use in 2016, was evident as early as this financial document from January 1940 *(Donald Gries Collection)*.

men would risk injury at such modest pay to play in the early NFL. Many did not, including first-ever Heisman Trophy winner Jay Berwanger, who was selected with the top pick of the first NFL draft in 1936 but opted instead to become a foam-rubber salesman.[16] Many players did sign, however, mainly because they had been discharged into adulthood in the midst of the economic Depression. Even a modest professional football salary could help them pay off debts they had run up in college. In the 1930s NFL football still was not very distant from its founding as an "elitist collegiate sport,"[17] with an astonishing 85 percent of players holding college degrees.[18] Playing careers were short—an average of 3.4 years in the 1930s[19]—because of injuries, a perpetually refreshed supply of younger and therefore less expensive players, and better opportunities outside of football, especially in business. However, the game also could provide a springboard to coaching, which was the ultimate career aspiration of many players of the era.

Even still, the Rams were hard-pressed to find top-caliber players, mainly because the best talent of 1936 had been snapped up before Cleveland officially received its franchise. Marshman in fact still would be out scouting for talent just weeks before the regular season began. But the team would be a bit more fortunate in securing a well-known name as its first NFL head coach.

* * *

Hugo Bezdek came to the Rams trailing three colorful decades of coaching glory. In signing a three-year contract at a generous salary of $7,500 annually—several times more than his highest player would bring in that year—he instantly became the first person ever to have served as manager of a Major League Baseball team and head coach of an NFL team.[20] The idea for a three-year contract was his, for he felt that it would take that long to "make a respectable showing from a start at scratch"[21]—to build a team into a winner slowly, as he had done in the collegiate ranks. At age 53, with a shock of white hair, a wide Slavic face, and a hawkish nose, he "wag[ged] a square head on square shoulders, with just a nominal neck between."[22] Stockily built, he was at heart an academician, a pedagogical purist, and a creative thinker, perpetually dreaming of new ways to train and motivate his players, new rules to improve the game, new rationales for why sports—amateur sports, particularly—were the ideal way to build character in the young men of America.

He also was, it turned out, exactly the wrong type of coach for a young professional football team like the Cleveland Rams and its impatient investors.

Bezdek was born in 1884 in Prague, in the nation then called Bohemia, and was brought to the United States as a child to live in Cleveland where he once scaled the fence of League Park to watch Cy Young pitch for the Indians. His parents moved again, to Chicago, and he joined Amos Alonzo Stagg's original Monsters of the Midway football team at the University of Chicago. He became a fullback who "terrorized other Big Ten teams with his line-crushing power,"[23] and his squads suffered only four losses in four years and battled to a tie with archrival the University of Illinois.[24]

Along the way Bezdek became embroiled in a minor scandal when personnel at Illinois attempted to have him disqualified from college football for allegedly boxing professionally under the name of Young Hugo. Bezdek, it developed, only had been doing some friends a favor: whipping a local tough in a stockyards bout for no purse. But the truth of his amateur status came out only when the vanquished boxer—enriched $100 by Illinois for signing an affidavit stating that he once had fought Young Hugo—summoned newspapermen to a local tavern, lined them up at the bar, and said expansively: "What'll you have, mugs? Dis is on de University of Illinois."[25] The reporters happily drank up some of the proceeds from the ruffian's windfall, learned about the source of his newfound money, and ignored the bogus story about Bezdek entirely.

After graduation, with the American century still dawning, Bezdek headed west to become coach of the University of Oregon football team. Then he went south, where he coached a University of Arkansas team then called the Cardinals. In 1910 the carpet-bagging Bezdek was "impressed with the mean-tempered hogs that roamed the state" and helped himself to local lore by announcing to a joyous crowd that his Cardinal team, freshly victorious over archrival Louisiana State University, had "played like a band of wild Razorbacks."[26] The term was traceable to the nineteenth century but the nickname stuck, thanks to the coach, who departed after the 1912 season.

Bezdek bounced west again, taking first an Oregon squad and then a World War I military team to consecutive Rose Bowl victories, but Major League Baseball beckoned. The dispirited Pittsburgh Pirates, mired in last place in the National League in 1917, wanted Bezdek to take over the managerial reins from an apathetic Honus Wagner, who was then in the twilight of his career. Bezdek's appointment was "somewhat of a bombshell in baseball circles,"[27] but he had served as the Pirates' baseball scout on the West Coast for six years and was convinced his own ability to coach a football team was readily transferable to baseball. He ran his players through football-style workouts, explaining that his "system is merely the common-

3. This Time Pro Football Was Going to Work in Cleveland

Hugo Bezdek (back row, far left) in 1918, the first year he coached the Pennsylvania State University football team. His eventual ouster from Penn State in 1937 led him directly to the doorstep of the Cleveland Rams as its first NFL head coach. His time with the Rams was, unfortunately, an abject failure *(Pennsylvania State University/Wikimedia Commons).*

sense one of treating a player like a human being."[28] Bezdek instantly made good. His Pirates team jumped to fourth place and a record of 65–60 in 1918, then finished fourth again with a mark of 71–68 in 1919. "He was willing to listen to advice," said an "Eastern critic" in 1918, and "ready to discuss problems with experienced baseball men and to hear what they had to say."[29] Bezdek tutored Casey Stengel and Billy Southworth, both destined for their own highly successful managerial careers.

Then 34 years old and seemingly at the height of his powers, Bezdek nonetheless betrayed a budding dissatisfaction with big-league sports. "In the colleges the public uses a good deal of discretion in its attitude toward the football coach," he confided to a Pittsburgh reporter. "But in professional baseball the only thing that seems to count is games won."[30] Therefore Bezdek likely thought he had won his dream job in 1918 when he joined Pennsylvania State University as head football coach and, later, as director of its newly formed school of physical education and athletics. His success in the collegiate ranks resumed as the Nittany Lions compiled an overall record of 65–30–11 and two undefeated seasons. Bezdek even made a third visit to the Rose Bowl, though not without controversy. As three carloads of Penn State players remained stuck in a Los Angeles–area traffic jam, Bezdek withheld his team from taking the field until he had a full contingent. University of Southern California coach Elmer (Gloomy Gus) Henderson accused Bezdek of stalling as a way of taking the edge off his own Trojan players, to which Bezdek took umbrage and threatened violence if Henderson just would remove his eyeglasses. The two coaches nearly came to blows before a Tournament of Roses official stepped in and pulled the two apart. Henderson later admitted he had absolutely no intention of fighting Bezdek the would-be boxer.

Bezdek's clashes continued, though now on a more philosophical plane, as he increasingly challenged collegiate football's big money and single-minded emphasis on winning. In 1922 he strongly asserted "intercollegiate sports are maintained for one purpose only—to develop character in the men who take part."[31] It was a view he would hold for life. (Bezdek also urged a few semi-radical rules changes—for instance, that a team should receive four downs when inside the 10-yard line regardless of time left on the clock, and that the point-after-touchdown kick should be eliminated. Both suggestions went unheeded.) He turned down a doubling of his salary to manage the Philadelphia Phillies and instead stayed in the "wonderful service" of coaching at Penn State.[32] But by 1926 it was reported he was "alarmed" by the "monumental strides" of professional football and feared it would overshadow the purer college brand.[33] Now nearly a decade removed from managing the Pirates, he drew a parallel in observing that "professional baseball is a hum-drum existence for the players, who go through the same thing day in and day out with few of them getting anything out of it except the monetary reward."[34] He revealed that the key to his success in Pittsburgh had been not to emphasize money and victories but to "take inventory of the moral status of the players," remove the "bad eggs," and sign "players of honesty and integrity."

In 1927, afire with reformist zeal, Bezdek set in motion a process that would bring about his ouster from his position at Penn State and carry him to the threshold of the Rams: a radical policy of "de-emphasis"[35] that abolished football scholarships, recruited players from the general student body, and returned to the university a large building that had been constructed by and for the football program. In doing so he reduced what essentially was a semi-professional football system into one of "the purest amateurism."[36] After finishing 6–2–1 in 1927, the Nittany Lions dropped to 3–5–1 in 1928. They rebounded to 6–3 in 1929, but alumni had seen enough: After repeated efforts to coax Bezdek into resigning, they finally succeeded in early 1930, but kept him on as head of the athletic department.

Removal from the sidelines did not thwart Bezdek from his mission, however. In 1930 he went to co-members in the American Football Coaches Association and suggested that other schools do much the same as Penn State had done: to "frown on subsidization and recruiting of athletes," curtail scouting, require coaches to be faculty members paid no more than their peers, abolish spring practice, and "stress the educational value of football above all else." He was met with stony silence. A representative from Cornell wanted to know if this was a "one-man report" from the association's "stabilization" committee. Bezdek acknowledged it was. Another coach, from Wisconsin, moved that the report be "tabled."

"What's that?" Bezdek asked.

"That means," a representative of Georgia Tech interjected, "putting it in the lower drawer."[37]

Still, Bezdek persisted. In late 1931, now a professor at Penn State, he told a meeting of his fellow physical education directors that he sensed a growing change among student-athletes that was helping to bring "sanity back to a consideration of the game of football."[38] But the public was not buying it. Westbrook Pegler, a conservative columnist for the *Chicago Tribune*, characterized Bezdek as an "idealist" and a "bunchy proletarian."[39] Meanwhile mediocre records were piling up at Penn State: 2–8 in 1931, 2–5 in 1932, 3–3–1 in 1933, 4–4 in 1934, and 4–4 in 1935. The Nittany Lions opened the 1936 season with a dominating 35–0 win over tiny Muhlenberg, but the grand experiment was over: Bezdek, "storm center of alumni and student attacks over his athletic policies,"[40] was removed that day as director of Penn State's phys-ed school, given a one-year leave of absence, and told that at the end of that term he could return to a position outside of the athletic department or resign. He chose the latter and left.

In early 1937, out of work at age 52, Bezdek poked around for the next phase of his life. Reportedly he was a "gentleman farmer"[41] in Doylestown, Pennsylvania. Then in January 1937 it was reported that he was directing boxing at the agricultural school of what is now the University of California, Davis. Meanwhile, Marshman and Wetzel, on a search for their first coach, had their sights trained first on the Chicago Cardinals' Ernie Nevers, then on Dick Hanley, formerly of Northwestern, but they could not strike a deal with either. It was then that Bell, Eagles owner and later NFL commissioner, contacted Marshman and asked whether he had considered Bezdek. The old coach quickly signed and began wrapping up chores at his farm in Doylestown.

Bezdek was hailed as something of an approaching hero in Cleveland, accompanied by glowing accounts of his collegiate playing and coaching successes and his brief time in Major League Baseball. No real surprise was registered that he would assume the role of head coach in a pro sport he neither had played nor coached, and little if any mention was made of the controversies he had generated in the town of State College 250 miles to the east. Nor, it seems, was he held to question for the disparaging remarks he had made about big-time athletics. Rather, Bezdek, perhaps eager to hold onto his new job, told a *Cleveland Press* reporter blandly he had "been watching the pro game with interest for 10 years. Its growth, both in the matter of caliber of play and in public appeal, has been amazing."[42]

As events unfolded, Rams management would ride Bezdek to ensure "amazing" came quite quickly to Cleveland. In June, before the head coach even had made it to town to get the measure of his new team, Wetzel took the liberty of buying the contract of Bears star quarterback Carl Brumbaugh and installing him as assistant coach. It foreshadowed the back-seat coaching Rams management would do of Bezdek. Then in July Wetzel asked Bezdek to come to Cleveland, stash his bags in a local hotel, and join him at an Indians-Athletics baseball game. There the two ran up to the press box at Cleveland Stadium to meet and greet local newspapermen. To one sportswriter Bezdek already had noted that the NFL was "a tough league," that it would take "some time to determine the real possibilities" of his new team, and that he expected to have a winning record "certainly not later than next year."[43] To another he laughingly told a story about a local man who bet him the Rams would not win a single game that year.

This was not a laughing matter to Marshman, Wetzel, and the rest of Rams ownership, however. The investors expected a winner immediately and a crowd-pleasing one at that—a team that could make the turnstiles at Cleveland Stadium spin. Wetzel had established a pass-oriented, lateral-laden, razzle-dazzle offense, and this was to be the signature of the Rams. The team would be competitive in the NFL, not fodder for the big-four Bears, Packers, Giants, and Redskins.

Reality, unfortunately for the Rams, would prove to be much different.

Chapter 4

Rams to the Slaughter

A measure of the respect head coach Hugo Bezdek and his Cleveland Rams would command among their National Football League foes in their first season was foreshadowed on the first day of training camp—at a women's college some 30 miles east of downtown Cleveland. In a "cute secluded nook" behind the "ivy-clad halls"[1] of the Lake Erie College for Women in Painesville, Ohio, the Rams opened practice in August 1937 on a lawn usually reserved for ladies' field hockey. Swifty the Ram, the new team's mascot, grazed languidly on clover until newspapermen arrived, at which time the animal was dragged or carried around the field for photo opportunities with various players as cameramen propped up and stood upon field-hockey nets to gain higher perspectives for their shots. When night fell, very large, very tanned, and "very formidable-looking fellows"[2] folded themselves into tiny beds in the women's dormitory.

Surveying it all was youthful general manager Damon "Buzz" Wetzel who, with obvious nerves about having turned over his squad to an aged but nevertheless brand-new pro football coach, successfully had convinced Bezdek to open training camp a three full weeks before the rest of the league to make sure the team was organized. Bezdek, or "Bez" as he often was called, was twice the age of the new general manager and girded his ample frame with tank-top undershirts, full-length trousers, and street shoes when taking to the grass of the Lake Erie College practice field. On occasion he jumped in to demonstrate fundamentals and often understandably finished a "bad second"[3] to the players in drills. But on the whole he offered a sort of hands-off, avuncular presence.

Bezdek, having coached football only at the collegiate grade, and at the professional level having managed only the more individualistic sport of baseball, apparently discerned the opportunity for an experiment in self-governance among his young players. Many of the Rams' team rules were standard for the era: There would be gentlemanly conduct and proper attire at all times; only petty, low-stakes games of chance would be allowed; there was to be no smoking in uniform, in the locker room, or in conspicuous public places; room curfew was at 10:30 p.m. on nights before games and 11:30 p.m. on all other nights.

What was *not* typical of the Rams' rules system, however, was its means of governance: by committees composed of players—a central committee, for instance, and a conduct committee, an equipment committee, and a social committee, all of which would make and enforce rules and essentially run the team. "You see, Bez is a psychologist," explained tackle Ted Rosequist, a four-year NFL veteran who had been a teammate of Wetzel, Red Grange, and Bronko Nagurski on the Chicago Bears. "He figures we won't be so likely to break our own rules as his, so he lets us make 'em."[4] The central committee could recommend to Bezdek, for instance, that the linemen needed to spend more time practicing blocking. Bezdek of course always had veto power, but he carried his authority lightly, as the players were doing just fine in his estimation. He still believed in treating a player like a human being, as he had when managing baseball's Pittsburgh Pirates. He publicly wondered why more teams had not used such a system of self-governance.

Bezdek's laissez-faire style of coaching might well have worked with a veteran team; it even could have succeeded with a reasonable mass of Rams players returning from the near-championship American Football League squad. But as it was, "only in name are the Rams the team that competed in the American League, rival pro circuit, last year," reported John Dietrich in the *Cleveland Plain Dealer*.[5] The Homer H. Marshman/Wetzel management duo was the same, as were the team name, the civic identity the franchise carried, and many of the investors, but among players the sole holdovers were reported to be backs Harry "Horse" Mattos, Stan Pincura, and Bill Cooper.[6] They were augmented by NFL veterans including Bill O'Neill of the Lions; and Rosequist, Carl Brumbaugh, and Charles (Ookie) Miller of the Bears. Bob Snyder, formerly of the AFL's Pittsburgh Americans, also had signed with the team, as did collegiate stars Dick Zoll of Indiana and Johnny Drake of Purdue.

First-round pick Drake was a native Chicagoan who had hoped to play locally in the Windy City and held out for a higher salary with Cleveland until the day before training camp opened. Marshman and Wetzel finally acquiesced once they saw him put on a solid performance for the College All-Stars, breaking loose and nearly scoring a touchdown in a 6–0 defeat of the defending NFL champion Packers. Further previewing his toughness and wits was a searing experience he had lived through at Purdue—a locker room explosion a year earlier that killed one of his teammates and prompted Drake to dive into a nearby swimming pool to extinguish flames on his body. With a proper perspective on life well gained, he said he was joining the team with a positive attitude and planned to embrace the togetherness of the expansion Rams as something akin to college spirit.

Beyond Mattos, Pincura, and Cooper, the rest of the previous-year's roster had been released, scattered to other teams, never played again—or were banished by the league outright. In late August the NFL owners deliberated whether to punish Sid Gillman, Gomer Jones, and Max Padlow for having jumped to the Rams in the rival AFL—a grievous sin in the eyes of a league that was highly vigilant of outside rivals. Marshman, the successful attorney he was, traveled to a meeting in Chicago to argue on behalf of the trio. He noted that the Cleveland franchise had been admitted to the NFL in no small part because of the team's success brought about by the on-field prowess of Gillman, Jones, and Padlow. At minimum, he maintained, the three should be returned to their original NFL claimants—Gillman to the Redskins (where, tantalizingly, he might have been a pass target for rookie passing sensation Sammy Baugh), Padlow to the Eagles, and Jones to the Cardinals. But the other owners would have none of it. They handed five-year suspensions to all—essentially lifetime bans in an era when average playing careers were three or four years.

Jones could not figure it out. He thought he had received permission from the Chicago team to jump to the AFL and play in his hometown of Cleveland, and it never had occurred to him to secure a formal written release from the Cardinals. Thousands of Jones's many friends and admirers in Cleveland's Glenville neighborhood took up a petition to send to league president Joe F. Carr and the NFL's executive council, but it was to no avail: Jones was out of the league.

For his part, Gillman had been gone even before the ruling; he was destined for coaching glory and the Pro Football Hall of Fame. The other two came to sadder endings. Jones coached for many years at the University of Oklahoma, first on the line, then for just two seasons as head coach until he grew "tired of the criticism" and resigned in 1965 "for the good of the university."[7] He had compiled the worst record in school history to that time. Meanwhile, Padlow jumped to the AFL's soon-to-disband Cincinnati Bengals, then in 1938 received word his NFL ban had been commuted—Carr felt the running back was "up against it"[8] and had been punished enough. But like Jones, he never played pro football again. Both men died tragically, on the job, in 1971—Padlow in an auto crash while working as an inspector for the Ohio State Highway Department, Jones of a heart attack on a train platform en route to a college basketball tournament at New York City's Madison Square Garden. The two had been banished so close to the Rams' NFL debut that each was pictured in the Rams' 1937 team photos. Padlow mysteriously was the only player to be pictured not wearing a helmet.[9]

With the roster shakeup complete, Bezdek was asked to assess the roster he had been given. "Can't say exactly as yet, but I wouldn't say too good," he said. "Still, I never had a championship team that didn't look bad at the outset."[10] He soon was to discover how bad a team could be—far worse even than his Penn State teams became after he de-emphasized football there. The young Rams were about to be thrown to the Lions.

* * *

Many misapprehensions persist about the Rams' fleeting decade in Cleveland, not least of which is that the general community did not embrace the team. At least for the team's debut, nothing could have been further from the truth. The media, having witnessed three NFL franchise failures that reflected poorly on the city, was solicitous about the fledgling Ram operation's success. On opening day—September 10, 1937—the *Plain Dealer*'s Dietrich reported that "apparently every precaution has been taken to avoid another failure." The Rams were well backed financially, he noted; the team had trained for six full weeks at Lake Erie College rather than the customary three for other teams; and a successful collegiate coach in Bezdek was at the helm. Nevertheless the team needed to "prove to the public that they really have the foundation of a winning team,"[11] and that would be a tall order. Dietrich thought that if Bezdek could win half his games he would be a "miracle man."[12]

Pomp and circumstance accompanied the Rams' NFL debut on a warm, early autumn Friday evening in Cleveland. With skies threatening rain, a parade of military veteran musicians stepped off a little more than an hour before the game, covered 13 blocks heading west on Euclid Avenue, turned north on East Ninth Street toward the lakefront where the Great Lakes Exposition was in the final week of its two-year run, and concluded at Cleveland Stadium. There a Rams flag was hoisted up a pole in center field, and Cleveland Mayor Harold Burton, just as he had eleven months earlier at League Park, tossed out the ceremonial first pass. Though Rams management had expected 35,000 spectators, the Stadium actually hosted a crowd of 24,800, several thousand of whom were Detroiters who chartered

4. Rams to the Slaughter 55

A Rams pennant circa late 1930s. Though the franchise was well backed financially by local Cleveland businessmen, civic leaders, and sportsmen, the team struggled on the field and at the box office *(Donald Gries Collection)*.

a boat and crossed Lake Erie expressly for the game. Ticket prices were decidedly big-league—$2.20 at the premium end[13] versus $1.50 a year earlier in the AFL[14]—but the Rams had taken pains to ensure the best fan experience possible, sliding the gridiron closer to the southwest corner of the stadium to replicate some of League Park's coziness the previous season.

Unfortunately for Cleveland fans, the evening's opponent was far superior to the hapless Syracuse Braves in the Rams' AFL debut. The Detroit Lions had finished 8–4 and 7–3–2 and two previous seasons and claimed the 1935 league title in only the third championship game in NFL history.[15] They were led on the field and coached by the estimable Earl "Dutch" Clark, the highest scoring and highest paid player in the NFL to that time.[16] But the Rams were, by all appearances, undaunted. A loud ovation greeted them as they took the field in snappy new uniforms dominated by the key color of their one year in the AFL: satin pants, helmets, numerals, and sleeve panels of all red, accenting jerseys and socks now of black rather than gold. A live radio audience was tuned into WGAR and announcer Bob Kelley, who would follow the team to California and remain the Rams' broadcaster well into the 1960s.

The stadium's lights were lowered just before kickoff as each Cleveland player took the field to a single spotlight. "The finest set of floodlights in the country"[17] had been installed on the roof of Cleveland Stadium, but even with lighting back to full power and the game begun, the proceedings were dim in the early September night. The *Plain Dealer*'s Dietrich witnessed through drizzling rain the debut of an NFL franchise playing in the "murky depths of the stadium."[18] Despite Wetzel's dictate that the Rams' play must be fan-friendly, Bezdek quickly dispensed with the old razzle-dazzle and ground down instead into the run as the Lions pushed around the Rams' jumbo-sized linemen. Only four passes were attempted the entire evening—all by the Rams—as the two teams tied an all-time NFL record for fewest total pass attempts in a game.[19] One Detroit touchdown occurred on a wild snap that sailed past Rams tailback O'Neill and into Cleveland's end zone where the Lions pounced on the ball. Another came on a pick-six. At halftime the score was Detroit 21, Cleveland 0, and the mascot Swifty the Ram was brought onto the field for what at least one wag could not resist calling a suitably "sheepish"[20] appearance.

The Rams neared midfield early in the third quarter before yet another bad snap dropped them back to their own 30. The Lions took over on downs, and soon Detroit's Ernie Caddell was whisking 23 yards for a touchdown and a 28–0 score. The crowd began chanting for Harry "Horse" Mattos and erupted with a great roar when the former AFL star, now riding the bench in the NFL, was sent into the game early in the fourth quarter. But the contest was over. The Rams were routed by a demoralizing four touchdowns in their much-heralded NFL debut.

Management had no delusions; the Rams were a new team, attempting to hold their own against a championship-caliber franchise. But when Bezdek shook up the roster a bit in the second game against the bottom-dwelling Eagles, the Rams gave their new fans some hope. Snyder and Drake connected for the first-ever touchdown in the Rams' NFL history, then repeated the feat later in the game, while Joe Kebble made a somersaulting catch of a Mattos throw in the end zone as the Rams collected their first-ever NFL victory 21–3. Things seemed to be on the up and up, especially with the mediocre Brooklyn Dodgers and Chicago Cardinals dead ahead. At Ebbets Field Cleveland indeed had the Dodgers neutralized for most of the game and nurtured a 7–6 lead late into the fourth quarter via a four-yard touchdown run by Mattos—until the Dodgers staged a late drive and kicked a field goal to extract a 9–7 win. A similar collapse occurred the following weekend. The Rams were back in familiar environs before 10,400 fans at League Park and were battling the Cardinals to a scoreless tie until Mattos dropped a fumble that was scooped up by Chicago and returned for a touchdown. Cardinals 6, Rams 0.

Quickly Cleveland's record was 1–3, and the Rams—not yet at the halfway point of the season—already had accumulated more losses in the NFL than they had in their entire year in the AFL. Worse, Dietrich complained that the Rams offense in the Cardinals game—as in the opener against the Lions—"lacked the open play the crowd had been led to expect."[21] Bezdek seemed to be playing the game conservatively by developing the run in order to pass. If the jaded fans were not yet growing restless, Rams management certainly was.

When the Bears came to Cleveland in mid-October it was thought the Rams' only hope for a win would be the old razzle-dazzle—forward passes and laterals. Even that small chance was squashed. "Against the gigantic Bears," Dietrich reported, "the Clevelanders looked like little boys."[22] A mere 5,000 spectators showed up in a drizzling rain to watch Bronko Nagurski and the rest of Chicago play nearly the entire game on Cleveland's muddy half of the League Park field. The Rams did finally score—their first-ever points at home in the NFL—when they turned the ball over on downs on the Chicago one-yard line, pinned the Bears to their goal line, then hunted down their scrambling punter in the end zone for a safety. Chicago 20, Cleveland 2.

The Rams now were 1–4, and remarkably some observers saw hope for the team—or at least were charitable. "Good old Hugo Bezdek," John Kieran wrote in the *New York Times*, "is having a hard time with the newcomers on the circuit, the Cleveland Rams. But Hugo may get them rolling before the snow flies."[23] He did not, least of all against the defending champion Green Bay Packers, who would prove to be the most lethal of all Ram killers in coming years. Coached by the legendary Earl "Curly" Lambeau and powered by future Hall of Fame receiver Don Hutson and star fullback Clarke Hinkle, the Packers drilled the Rams on two consecutive weekends—35–10 at League Park and 35–7 at Green Bay City Stadium.

Between those losses the Rams slimmed down their squad to only 20 players, shipped journeyman player and assistant coach Brumbaugh off to the Dodgers, and reinstalled local boy Stan Pincura at quarterback, perhaps in hopes of reviving the razzle-dazzle play of 1936. The newspapers seemed to approve. "Under Bezdek," George Strickler wrote in the *Chicago Tribune* as the Rams arrived to play the Cardinals at Comiskey Park, "Cleveland has played better football than is generally expected of a new team in the league, but its won and lost record, 1 and 6, reads about as had been anticipated."[24] As proof, the Rams lost to the Cardinals and fell to 1–7. Nevertheless Marshman asserted that he and his stockholders were "absolutely" satisfied with their head coach. "We feel that Bezdek has done as well as could be expected with the material we have," he said.[25]

Statistics told a grimmer story. To date the Rams had been outscored 149–54, with nearly half their offensive points coming against one team only, the Eagles. Meanwhile attendance at the Rams' two most recent home games, hosting marquee franchises the Bears and the Packers, totaled only 15,400—not much more than half the amount that the team had attracted to its season opener alone. The trend line was not positive, but Marshman kept a brave public face. He said he had expected to lose money in his first year, he acknowledged the team's lack of raw talent, and in a move that would be echoed by a successor Rams ownership group seven years later, he asked newspapermen, fans, and others for tips on good player prospects from obscure colleges.

Such help would not arrive in time. Again taking on Clark's Lions, the Cleveland squad that the *Times'* Kieran shortly would deride as the "shorn Rams"[26] posted an early 7–0 lead but fumbled twice to set up two Detroit touchdowns, and lost 27–7. Similarly the Rams would have eventual league champion Washington down 7–0 at halftime before succumbing 16–7. It was a frosty battle on the snowy field of League Park that previewed the epic championship game years later, but it was witnessed by only 3,500 frozen fans—a sum that a decade later would drop to just 1,500 in Marshman's pained memory; the sight of nearly 20,000 empty seats in intimate League Park must have been too much to bear.

The Rams' debut season in the NFL came to a merciful end with a 15–7 setback to the merciless Bears. With the victory the Bears clinched the Western Division title, but the best that could be said of the Rams was that they had scored at least once on every opponent they faced in their first season. It was a slim thread of hope to cling to in the offseason. Knowing the team had escaped the AFL at a good time provided additional comfort. Cleveland's nemesis the Boston Shamrocks, disputed league champions the previous year, stood by helplessly in 1937 as NFL franchises picked their roster clean of star players. Boston dropped to 2–5, went out of business, and were succeeded as league champions by the undefeated Los Angeles Bulldogs, who prefigured the rise of West Coast sports franchises. By the end of 1938 the so-called second AFL was out of business.

Happy with their place in the NFL, the Rams were encouraged by the play of Drake, NFL president Carr's first-round selection on their behalf. The United Press named the fullback to its All-Pro second team, behind Green Bay's Hinkle. Propped up by Drake's team-leading 333 rushing yards and 30 points, the Rams were described charitably in league material edited by the always pro–Cleveland Carr as having given "considerable trouble and plenty of fear to the division leading teams" in their last five games of 1937.[27] But the numbers showed they scored only 75 points in 11 games, the league's lowest,[28] while giving up an NFL-high 207 points in a season in which all teams averaged 142.[29] Despite Bezdek's avowals that he was building the run in order to pass, the Rams finished next to last in both categories.[30]

The Link Between Winning and Fan Support: NFL Teams (1937)		
	Winning Percentage	Total Home Attendance (Games)
Chicago Bears	.900	155,000 (6)
Washington Redskins	.727	140,000 (6)
New York Giants	.667	260,000 (7)
Green Bay Packers	.636	83,251 (6)
Detroit Lions	.636	105,735 (6)
Chicago Cardinals	.500	53,000 (4)
Pittsburgh Pirates	.364	140,000 (6)
Brooklyn Dodgers	.300	120,000 (5)
Philadelphia Eagles	.200	75,000 (6)
Cleveland Rams	.091	44,500 (5)
Pro Football Reference, Cleveland Plain Dealer		

In the NFL's early years, lower-division teams like the Rams seemed to be caught in a common quandary: They needed to win more games to build fan support, and they needed more fan support—and more revenue—so they could win more games. In the meantime the Bears, Redskins, Giants, and Packers dominated the league.

Adding to Marshman's and the owners' woes were the team's year-end average home attendance figures—at the absolute bottom of the league.[31] At the end of 1937, a year in which the NFL had its "greatest financial year"[32] to date, the Rams reportedly were set to lose $30,000 and would join only the Cardinals and the Eagles, compatriots in generally subpar attendance and on-field performance, in the ranks of unprofitability. Cities like Cleveland "need only a winning club to get out of the red," a newspaper account said brightly,[33] and the reasoning did seem accurate: Win more games and attract greater attendance; attract more attendance and become more profitable. But by an immutable law of mathematics, not every team could be a winner. The Rams somehow had to vault their way from the NFL's second division to the first in order to save the young franchise and prevent it from becoming another pro football failure in Cleveland. Marshman and his investors were prepared for the long haul, but how long could that haul possibly last before the money began to run out? The team would have to move fast.

With a final record of 1–10, the Cleveland Rams had been led to the slaughter in 1937. Clearly something would have to change in 1938.

Part II: Upstarts

Chapter 5

Race-Wrecking Rams

After a calamitous 1–10 season in their National Football League debut, the Cleveland Rams' head coach Hugo Bezdek and his sole star back Johnny Drake drifted in different directions in the offseason. Bezdek returned to his chicken farm in eastern Pennsylvania, while Drake went west and donned boots, a leather jacket, a constable's badge, and a Stetson hat and became a ranger and supervisor in the East Bay Regional Park in northern California. World War II still was a brewing European conflict, Adolf Hitler's Third Reich was a problem far away, and in Bezdek's and Drake's quiet contentment it is unlikely either was fully aware of changes stirring back in the big, snowy city of Cleveland. The Rams franchise, wracked by investors' impatience and their compulsion to immerse themselves in football affairs, was to undergo its first major upheaval.

Lead owner Homer Marshman declared that getting new—meaning, better—player "material"[1] was the team's chief and almost sole concern. He felt the pressure of the arms race for talent he was in with the other NFL teams. Competition was cutthroat, and the most successful and wealthiest teams—the Chicago Bears, Green Bay Packers, Washington Redskins, and New York Giants—commanded a huge edge in luring players. In 1938 the Rams again would turn over most of their roster as they had in their jump from the American Football League to the NFL, retaining only a dozen players who would surround Drake, their emerging star. Among those who made the cut were Bob Snyder, who would leave an important mark on the franchise as both a player and a coach, and center Chuck Cherundolo, a Bezdek favorite at Penn State. Founding Rams Harry "Horse" Mattos and Bill Cooper were gone, their brief NFL careers at an end. This left only Stan Pincura from the team's start in the AFL just two years earlier.[2] Co-founder Damon "Buzz" Wetzel's dream of bringing Ohio State alumni together in a winning pro football franchise was a distant memory; he now was fighting for grim survival in the NFL with players drawn from wherever he could muster them.

The 1938 player draft helped the Rams' competitive situation, though not in a way the Rams might have liked. The management trio of Marshman, Wetzel, and Bezdek initially had their hearts set on drafting "Whizzer" White, who as one of the nation's leading collegiate scorers in 1937 held the potential to transform the Rams' backfield immediately. But there was word that White had been offered a Rhodes Scholarship, and Marshman, a lawyer, confirmed through back channels that White indeed intended to study law in England instead of playing pro football. So the Rams, the last-place team holding the number-one pick, decided White was too much of a risk and passed on him in the draft, as did the Philadelphia Eagles and Brooklyn Dodgers.

The hapless Pittsburgh Pirates, however, drafting fourth, had no such qualms. Owner and horseracing savant Art Rooney gambled and drafted White any way, and when White told Rooney he intended to continue his academic studies, the Pirates owner doubled down and offered the then-richest pro football deal to date—an unheard-of $15,800 for a one-year contract in 1938.[3] It was more than double the $7,200 that Detroit Lions superstar Earl "Dutch" Clark would make that year as both a player and a coach.[4] White smartly signed, held off on his trip to the University of Oxford for one semester, and led the NFL in rushing in his rookie year.[5] Then, after taking 1939 off for his studies, he repeated the feat in 1940 when he left Yale Law School, the second time joining the Lions and again pacing all rushers.[6] In due time he became best known as Byron White, associate justice of the U.S. Supreme Court, and joined Sammy Baugh as a would-be Rams star whom fate swept from the franchise's grasp.

Having forfeited their chance at White, the Rams instead selected a power runner in the Bronko Nagurski mold to join Drake in the backfield— Corbett "Corby" Davis, a "human battering ram"[7] of an All-American fullback from Indiana. The Rams also benefited from a rare show of charity among the other NFL owners, who even then were striving in a nascent way to establish more competitive balance in the league. As one of five teams with the worst records, the Rams were allowed to make two supplemental draft selections for 1938—one after the first round, and one after the third. To their enduring fortune Arkansas end Jim Benton fell to their possession. Benton was not fast on foot but he was an early prototype of the tall, spider-like receiver who could pick up large chunks of yardage at a time and propel the NFL into the passing-oriented modern game. Only Green Bay's Don Hutson arguably would be better in Benton's era.

Marshman was reported to be "highly elated"[8] with the draft, but

Cleveland Plain Dealer sports editor Gordon Cobbledick was skeptical. He wondered about the enormous amount of talent the Rams would need to close the gap between them and the league's best teams, especially when the defending champion Redskins said they wanted five or six new backs and at least a half-dozen new linemen for the coming season. Indeed, in the 1938 draft the Rams had overlooked two future Hall of Fame players who could have filled a gaping need on the line: Alex Wojciechowicz and Frank Kinard.

Team leadership was thought still to be subpar as well. Rams investor Albert C. "Al" Sutphin, a local magnate in the ink and printing industry and a highly successful team owner in minor-league hockey, announced an interest in acquiring the football franchise outright because he had not been "very pleased with some of the operations of the club."[9] Though negotiations never went far, the Rams' future in Cleveland might well have been drastically different—in fact, they may have stayed in Cleveland—had Sutphin assumed majority control. His Cleveland Barons became a dynasty in the American Hockey League, winning nine regular-season titles and eight Calder Cup playoff championships[10] and drawing attendance that rivaled and often exceeded that of the Rams. For a midweek match in the dead of a 1938 Cleveland winter the Barons drew nearly 11,000—more than had attended three of the Rams' five home games in 1937.[11]

Meanwhile it seemed as if nearly every team in the league was bidding for Drake's services. The Chicago Cardinals offered three players straight up; the Bears, hearing of the offer from their crosstown rival, called Marshman and asked for an extension so that they too could be part of the negotiation; then the Detroit Lions said they would like to make a bid. Marshman and Wetzel likely had in mind their old AFL compatriots the Boston Shamrocks, who were picked clean of talent by NFL teams, in happily proclaiming that Drake was not going anywhere.

* * *

With 1938 came growing encroachment by the Rams' owners into matters best left to the football experts. Such a conflict between football and business leaders can tear a franchise apart and plunge it to the depths of league standings for years at a time. The job of the business side of a football team generally is to hire good football minds, pay salaries, manage the front office, market the team, and get out of the way. But some owners fancy themselves as knowledgeable sportsmen, and "too many times—and you can go back in time and look at the franchises that don't succeed—it's usually the sportsmen who don't make it," Joe Horrigan of the Pro Football

Hall of Fame noted. "They don't make business decisions; they make football decisions."[12] Such a fate would befall the Rams.

In March 1938, Edward P. Bruch, member of a prominent Cleveland manufacturing family and secretary of the Rams, was wintering in the Southwest when he was told of Bronko Smilanich, a promising ball carrier at the University of Arizona. Trouble began when Bruch traveled to the university's campus and stepped boldly on the practice field to scout the prospect himself. As many experienced football people knew, this was a fairly serious breach of protocol—an aggressive foray into collegiate territory. Smilanich's college class furthermore was entering its senior year, so Smilanich was not yet even eligible to turn pro. Bruch had made a brazen move as a representative of a pro sport then widely thought to consist of unscrupulous pirates out to plunder the purer college game, and for a middling product at that—nearly half of the sports editors and writers responding to a United Press poll that same year said they believed the top college

Edward P. Bruch (upper right) at a Rams game in Cleveland Stadium in November 1940. One of the so-called Downtown Coaches who owned and operated the team, Bruch caused a sensation when he attempted to scout an ineligible collegiate player in 1938 *(The Cleveland Press Collection, Cleveland State University Library)*.

team in the country was capable of defeating the best pro team in the land.[13] Not surprisingly, as soon as Arizona coach Orian Landreth became aware of Bruch's presence he had the Rams representative "ejected bodily, and with scant ceremony"[14] from both the field and the campus. The university then filed a grievance with NFL president Joe F. Carr.

Carr helped to smooth over the controversy on behalf of his favored franchise in Cleveland, but it all came to naught when Smilanich eventually was signed and played just two games for the Rams in 1939, catching one pass for 11 yards and rushing only once—for a loss of three.[15] It was apparent that some the Rams' directors not only were not especially politically savvy, they also were not NFL-caliber assessors of talent either. They were "downtown coaches,"[16] as the *Cleveland Press*'s Ben Williamson charged, ensconced as they were in the Union Club and assorted high-rise buildings around the city's office district rather than on grassy practice fields. And the Smilanich incident would not be the first or only time they would immerse themselves in football decisions.

Rams leadership in 1938 was drawn, as it had been since the team's founding in 1936, from Cleveland's elite circles of businessmen and sportsmen: lawyer Marshman, manufacturer Bruch, printing executive Sutphin, and department store executive Robert H. Gries. Joseph G. Fogg was an attorney and former football coach at the Case School of Applied Science, where Stephen Belichick, father of Bill Belichick, then was in the football program. Gregory S. McIntosh was an investment counselor. John A. Hayden served in the Ohio House of Representatives. Insurance executive Ellis W. Ryan one day would own a piece of the Cleveland Browns and join Marshman in selling the team to Art Modell. Elected president of this group in 1938 was, surprisingly, a Cleveland outsider, Thomas E. Lipscomb—a man who would shape the team's destiny in the front office, on the football field, and in the courtroom.

Lipscomb, then age 42, came from humble circumstances. Born in 1895 in Nashville, Tennessee to a hardware merchant who fathered eight children, Lipscomb played tackle for the Vanderbilt University football team, gained an Ivy League education at Yale Law, and left his family behind in the South for good after graduation to make his fortune in boomtown Cleveland. There he joined Thompson, Hine & Flory, a law firm whose fortunes were intertwined with the city's rise as a manufacturing and banking center. Sports, the law, and Vanderbilt would be Lipscomb's lifelong and nearly sole passions as he remained unmarried and lived alone at a social club on Cleveland's former Millionaire's Row. His elongated chin, flared ears, smiling but slitted eyes, and slightly chipped front teeth lent an air of affable but feral intensity, and he made no bones about his desire to raise the performance of the organization he now was leading. "I certainly don't believe in this idea of tossing the ball wildly all over the lot," he declared in a presumed swipe at Wetzel's razzle-dazzle offense of 1936, "but I am strong for a smart, well conceived offense, based on forward and lateral passing."[17] He seemed to hold particular contempt for the Rams' jumbo-sized but outmanned line. On an inspection tour with the coaching staff in the summer of 1938 he noticed the team's uniforms were practically spotless—except for the shiny seats of the pants which, he surmised wryly, must have been due to the players having spent most of the previous season on them.

Yet Lipscomb also made the still-puzzled-over call to open the Rams' 1938 season not in the city's premier sports venue of Cleveland Stadium, capacity 78,000, nor even in the Indians' League Park, which held 23,000—but instead at a high-school field seating just 15,500. Nothing seemed to better symbolize the Rams' futility in their early years than their sharing of Shaw Stadium in East Cleveland, if only briefly, with the Shaw High School Cardinals. Yet the Rams' decision to host two games there in 1938—against the Detroit Lions and the Chicago Cardinals—made some sense. Shaw Stadium just had been renovated and enlarged and was lavishly maintained, off limits to high-school practices but available for game-day use by colleges and other high schools. The stadium furthermore was among the best illuminated in Ohio, its lighting designed and installed by General Electric, whose NELA Park, one of the nation's first planned industrial research facilities, was just a mile-and-a-half away. And its capacity was well suited to the team's small but growing fan base. How soon the Rams might live up to their box-office promise by playing at Cleveland Stadium depended on the talent they were about to put on the field.

To that end, critical pieces came into place as the spring of 1938 faded to summer. Lipscomb enticed top draft pick Davis to sign, locked in Drake and Snyder to new contracts, and brought in a new player-coach from the Giants who would help to carry the team to its first era of respectability. Art "Pappy" Lewis, age 27, had a square jaw, thick black eyebrows, and a bristly thatch of dark hair topping his six-feet-three frame. Like Marshman and Wetzel he was a native of southern Ohio—from Middleport, on the Ohio River. And like Marshman he had attended Ohio University where he played alongside future Rams teammate Snyder. With a degree in political science and history, Lewis was said to be something of a shape-shifter as a player recruiter who could come on like a "sweet-talking hillbilly" or "as Slavic as Mom and Dad"[18]—whatever was warranted.

The home grandstand of Shaw Stadium in East Cleveland, Ohio, in the spring of 2014. The high-school field is a lingering piece of the Cleveland Rams' infamy, though the team hosted only two games there in 1938 in what was then a top-notch facility with state-of-the-art lighting *(James C. Sulecki).*

Lewis's hire was no minor appointment for Lipscomb and the other Rams directors. Increasingly disenchanted with Bezdek, who they now strongly suspected was not up to the pro game, the Downtown Coaches made a tantalizing promise to Lewis: He would become the Rams' head coach when Bezdek left, and that could be quite soon. Lewis responded eagerly. In June 1938 he drove 180 miles due north from his home in Parkersburg, West Virginia to Cleveland to proclaim that "there is only one mood for pro football—either you play it hard, or you don't play." As for those self-governing player committees that Bezdek had put in place to ensure player discipline, Lewis narrowed his eyes and said he was "confident that a couple of $50 fines slapped on players for excessive drinking will curb any tendency toward breaking training rules."[19] With Lewis on the scene, Bezdek was doomed and he knew it. Shortly thereafter, management asked Bezdek to resign and he refused. As at Penn State, he would hold on until the bosses forcefully removed him.

By the time the Rams reported for training camp at Baldwin-Wallace College—there would be no women's school in 1938 as there had been in

1937—word had leaked among the players about the potentially corrosive promise the Downtown Coaches had made to Lewis. Amid two-a-day practices and so-called "skull practice"[20] during cooling-off periods between, over meals at the training table, and after the 11 p.m. curfew in the college dormitories, player loyalties began to split—some for Bezdek, some for Lewis. It was precisely the type of distraction the fragile Rams did not need. They were in many ways a new team—"vastly improved"[21] from the previous season in Bezdek's own words. Drake was back, and Davis was in the fold. Snyder had returned and would throw seven touchdown passes in the coming season. Benton was about to have a breakout rookie year. And Marshman and Wetzel believed they had rounded up enough hefty linemen to ensure the Rams would not be pushed around as they had been in 1937. "You get the feeling these are going to be different Rams," Williamson wrote hopefully in the *Press*.[22]

The team would look different as well. Discarding the red-and-black color scheme of their two consecutive inaugural years because it was too similar to that of other NFL teams, the Rams went in favor of something entirely new: a striking match of blue helmets, blue jerseys with yellow numerals, blue socks, and gold pants with black stripes on the back. In time they "really embraced the yellow," said sports uniform historian Scott Sillcox. "They were ahead of their times to be bright and bold and beautiful."[23] The iconic Rams color scheme that would pace the sleek NFL uniform in the decades ahead was coming into place.

But even in their new colors, opening day on September 11, 1938, brought a familiar result for the Rams. The Packers' Hutson, well on his way to Babe Ruth–like fame as a pass receiver in his era, riddled Cleveland's defense for three touchdowns in a 26–17 Cleveland loss at Green Bay. Snyder countered with two touchdown passes of his own, one a 53-yard strike to tailback Ed Goddard, and the outcome was a considerable improvement over the 35–10 and 35–7 poundings Green Bay had laid on the Rams the previous season. But for the Downtown Coaches it was not good enough.

As was customary on Mondays after each loss, the Rams directors summoned Bezdek downtown and gave him advice on how he should have coached the game. More shockingly, they told him that Wetzel—co-founder of the franchise with Marshman—had been let go from the organization. Wetzel had lost control of the franchise he had conceived, designed, built, christened, and captained—and to the very businessmen he invited onboard as partners. Rams management had taken pains to let Wetzel down easy, assuring the press he had "resigned" and that he retained stock interest in the team, but it was obvious he had been fired over a "disagreement over policies with officers and Coach Hugo Bezdek."[24] Wetzel was a football man, loyal to his head coach, and he went down with the ship. But to add insult, moving into his former role as business manager was Mannie Eisner, one-time press agent for the team and Wetzel's assistant. Eisner would not last long in sports management.[25]

Nor, for that matter, would Wetzel. On the night of his firing he said his future plans were uncertain, and this much is known: While he instantly was credited with developing a "razzle-dazzle style" that "apparently whetted Cleveland fans' appetite for pro football,"[26] Wetzel never again served as an NFL executive. Instead he settled for a job far from the bright lights of big-league sports, as manager of a minor-league baseball team in the Cleveland Indians' farm system, following in his father's footsteps after all as the elder Wetzel might have wanted. When World War II arrived he joined the Navy and became an instructor on boxer Gene Tunney's staff, and in 1950 when the Rams returned to Cleveland to face the Browns for the NFL championship, the local newspapers took a moment to recall Wetzel's, Marshman's, and Lipscomb's roles in establishing "the first continuous pattern of pro football"—"unprofitable as it was."[27]

Wetzel left little trace in the sports world thereafter. His work in establishing an NFL franchise rarely is mentioned. By the early 21st century, Marshman instead almost universally received sole credit for having founded the Rams.

* * *

In September 1938, with escalating hostilities in Europe and British Prime Minister Neville Chamberlain calling for peace for his time, Clevelanders surely had more important news to follow than the machinations of a local pro football franchise, but the firing of Rams head coach Bezdek merited plenty of attention anyway. The dismissal of Wetzel as general manager, it was clear, would not be enough to satiate the do-it-now Downtown Coaches. Perhaps they were waiting for an embarrassing pratfall against the also-ran Cardinals to justifiably hang Bezdek, a "grand old figure of athletics."[28] If so they would not be disappointed. Under state-of-the-art lights in Shaw Stadium, in a cozy facility stitched in by neighborhoods less than seven miles from Cleveland's downtown, the Cardinals marched straight down the field on the evening's opening drive and scored a touchdown in only four plays. The Rams would not recover. Though they finally reached the end zone in the fourth quarter on a Corby Davis run, the point-after attempt was blocked and the Rams lost 7–6. Bezdek was called to a Monday meeting with the Downtown Coaches and told that the directors henceforth would suggest plays and substitutions via back Jules Alphonse. Team president Lipscomb, in fact, would sit on the bench himself and direct lineup changes. The Downtown Coaches were becoming actual field coaches.

Bezdek pridefully held on. On September 25, 1938, the Rams traveled to Griffith Stadium in Washington, D.C., to face the defending NFL champion Redskins. When Washington stretched its lead to 31–0 after three quarters, reserves were sent in to preserve a 37–13 win. The Rams dropped to 0–3 and a deplorable 1–13 under Bezdek. After the loss, within earshot of several Rams players in a Washington hotel lobby, Lipscomb erupted with "scathing criticism"[29] of Bezdek. The team president had ordered film to be taken of the game, and with this evidence he would show Rams players— and newspaper reporters as well, he said—everything that the Rams and Bezdek especially were doing wrong. The message was clear. "Debacle Angers Rams' President," blazed a headline in the *Cleveland Plain Dealer*. "Lipscomb to Swing Ax Unless Team Improves."[30]

And still Bezdek held on. But not for long. While the Rams were in eastern Pennsylvania to play an exhibition against the Allentown Bears, the Downtown Coaches gathered inside the imposing walls of the Union Club to agree on the next course of action. The die was cast. When the team returned, Bezdek was fired—summarily "relieved of his duties"[31]—only three games into the second of a three-year contract. As much as not winning games he had failed to "make the turnstiles click,"[32] opting to build his team slowly with the run rather than call for passes and "razzle-dazzle" that would be crowd-pleasing. As Rams management had promised, Lewis was hired as "temporary"[33] head coach, the youngest in the NFL at age 27.

The ouster of Bezdek, more than twice Lewis' age at 54 years, initially was attributed to the usual "virulent gridiron malady": "'fire the coachitis.'"[34] But far more damning accounts in Cleveland and other NFL cities emerged in the days and weeks afterward. George Strickler of the *Chicago Tribune* saw a "defeatist complex [that] prevailed under the reign of Hugo Bezdek."[35] "Dissension had hurt the squad," Arthur J. Daley agreed in the *New York Times*. "Most of the youngsters had been on winning teams in college. Defeat to them was more bitter than wormwood and gall."[36] A *Cleveland News* interview with Marshman a decade afterward starkly referred to "the revolt of 1938."[37]

In point of fact, the *Cleveland Press*' Williamson countered, at least 13 players—including virtually the entire starting 11—pleaded with the owners via telegram to hold off on firing Bezdek. Furthermore, Williamson said, the Downtown Coaches were putting Lewis in as uneasy a position as they had placed Bezdek by informing the new coach before he had led a single game about their intention to find his successor. No, the chief need of the Rams, Williamson asserted, was not to have replaced its head coach but to have found a strong-willed replacement for Wetzel in the general manager position who could "combine football savvy with the ability to block out downtown coaches in directors' huddles" while the football experts built a solid foundation for the franchise. What the Downtown Coaches most lacked, in short, was "cohesive organization by which the Rams can be directed."[38] They needed a tough manager who could manage themselves.

Williamson's sympathy did not exonerate Bezdek. For the second time in two years the old coach had been hounded, viciously, from a leadership post in which he had taken a semi-experimental approach to running a team. And again he had refused to listen to his bosses and leave under his own steam. Perhaps it was time for him to retire—and indeed he did, returning to the "life of a chicken fancier"[39] in Doylestown, Pennsylvania, except for one brief season as head coach and athletic director at the National Agricultural College near his home. By then he was well into his 60s.

With Bezdek out of the picture, the Cleveland Rams belonged to acting head coach Lewis. He soon would be seen as a miracle man.

* * *

It was a sunny Indian-summer afternoon on October 2, 1938, when the Rams franchise finally broke through with its first home victory in the NFL. As interim head coach Lewis prowled the sideline, the Rams played with a ferocity that was equal to the pent-up anger, shame, and frustration they suffered through 12 consecutive losses under Bezdek. Under blue skies and before 8,000 spectators on benches in the whitewashed grandstands of Shaw Stadium, Cleveland stunned future Hall of Famer Clark and the Detroit Lions with a come-from-behind 21–17 victory that was paced by two long and exciting touchdown passes. It was such a sweet win, such retribution for prolonged NFL disgrace and for Detroit embarrassing the Rams in their league debut in Cleveland Stadium a year before, that Drake recalled it fondly to a reporter nearly 20 years later.[40] On this day, for once, his running game would not have to bear a disproportionate load of the offense. Lewis well knew he had only eight games in which to impress the team's directors and to earn a permanent appointment as head coach, so he went to the passing-oriented offense that the fans wanted and the Downtown Coaches expected. He had two good arms in Ohio natives Bob Snyder and Stan Pincura and he pressed them into action, even as the Lions seized a lead of 10–7 at halftime and 17–7 at the end of the third quarter. The crowd had been electrified early on by a 42-yard touchdown strike from Snyder to Johnny Kovatch, so with 10 minutes remaining in the game the Rams again went to the air. Pincura dropped back at midfield and hurled a pass down the center of the field to Benton, who with three steps on his defender swept into the end zone for a 45-yard touchdown—the first of his pro career.

Cleveland had narrowed Detroit's lead to 17–14, and some in Shaw Stadium sensed there might be a different outcome on this day for the Rams. The Lions had possession deep in their own territory with four minutes remaining and were trying to pick up first downs and run out the clock when Clark fumbled on an end run and Benton recovered at Detroit's 14. Five plays later top draft pick Corby Davis crossed the goal line on a two-yard push, Snyder added the extra point, and the Rams were on the verge of an upset. The Lions were not yet ready to concede defeat, however, and were slicing downfield when Cleveland's Bob Davis finally intercepted a pass to ice the victory—and was promptly knocked out cold by the opposition. He had sustained a bruised midriff and a concussion, and two of his teammates were sent to a Cleveland hospital with injuries, but the Rams had convinced the Downtown Coaches that firing Bezdek was the right decision. For a week at least the cloud of losing lifted for the Rams—and importantly for Lewis there would be no Monday meeting with the team's directors.

But greater danger lay ahead. As always the Chicago Bears hauled in a human wall of a line with an average weight advantage of 33 pounds per man over Cleveland. If the Bears did not scare off the plucky Rams team, they likely did many of their fans. The Rams had departed Shaw Stadium forever for more spacious League Park in anticipation of a swell of ticket sales, but only a small and very Shaw-like contingent of 8,024 arrived for what was sure to be a car wreck of a game. Lewis had a plan, however. The Rams would fight toe-to-toe with the Bears, hold them in check, force turnovers, capitalize on what they sensed was a weakness in their pass defense, and show derring-do when rare scoring opportunities presented themselves. Their first chance came in the opening minutes when Pincura whizzed a pass over the Bears secondary and into the hands of end Ray Hamilton, who was tackled at the Chicago 10 but had not yet been stopped. In exploiting an NFL rule still then in place allowing for laterals to continue after a runner had been downed, Hamilton heaved the ball up to Alfphonse, who went the last 10 yards for a touchdown and a 7–0 Rams lead. Wetzel's razzle-dazzle offense rode again.

Cleveland struck again when Chicago's Carl Brumbaugh, a former

Ram, fumbled a punt in Chicago territory and into the hands of Carl "Moon Eyes" Littlefield, who scooped up the ball and took it 25 yards into the end zone. With the Rams leading 14–0, the League Park fans "almost fell out of the stands in excitement and joy,"[41] wrote the *Cleveland Plain Dealer*'s John Dietrich. A pounding 12-play drive by Chicago—all rushes—yielded a touchdown and narrowed the margin. But then several subsequent Bear passes misfired in the Rams' end zone, Cleveland made two dramatic interceptions, and Lewis inserted himself into the lineup near the end of the game to shore up a defensive stand and pounce on a fumble to seal a 14–7 victory. The Rams "are still rocking the world," Dietrich tapped out on his typewriter that evening in the *Plain Dealer* newsroom, lauding "another giant-killing performance" in a "show that ranks near the top in achievement against overwhelming odds."[42]

The Rams were only 2–3, but could Cleveland dare to dream its football miracle worker had arrived in "Pappy" Lewis? The media swarmed the new coach. Insouciant in an interview with the national Newspaper Enterprise Service, Lewis said he simply "loosened up our offense a bit. I kicked the backs back a yard and a half, so the interference could get in front of the play." The NEA concluded Lewis was "the country boy who outslicked the big time slickers ... the great Dutch Clark of the Lions and the famous George Halas of the Bears."[43]

In two short weeks he would do it again. On October 23, 1938, the Rams entered Wrigley Field certain that Chicago's tendency to play the receiver rather than the ball on pass defense could be exploited, so they came out firing. Snyder connected with Benton for a 45-yard touchdown just 90 seconds into the game and the Rams were up 6–0, then led 9–7 at the intermission. The Bears rallied to grab a 21–16 edge early in the fourth quarter until a pumped-up Corby Davis slammed off tackle and muscled into the end zone to put Cleveland ahead 23–21. The Chicago crowd began to cheer on the visitors, and whether it was in sarcastic derision of the Bears or in grudging admiration of the upstart Rams, Lewis chose to believe the latter, saying he thought the fans "couldn't help liking the way our kids were going." Chicago attempted two field goals in the final 45 seconds as darkness settled on Wrigley Field and missed both. The Rams had prevailed as a "miracle team."[44] Cleveland at last was a respectable 3–3.

Lewis went to a telephone at the LaSalle Hotel to relay the good news back to the bosses in Cleveland. After hooting and hollering on the other end, one of the Downtown Coaches inquired as to the whereabouts of the rest of the team. "Maybe you misunderstood me," Lewis replied cheerfully. "I said we beat the Bears, so where the devil do you think they are at a time like this? They're out celebrating—and I'm joining 'em just as soon as I get a shower."[45] The football world was shocked. At the halfway point of the season the race-wrecking Rams were threatening the dominance of the Bears, Packers, and Lions in the Western Division. In only their second NFL season they had swept a season series from Chicago, the first time the mighty Bears ever had lost twice to the same foe in one year.[46] Greatness seemed to await the Cleveland Rams.

But the fun could not last. The young Rams were playing on a limited mix of pure enthusiasm, adrenaline, and anger since the firings of Wetzel and Bezdek. They had caught the more seasoned Lions and Bears amid uncharacteristic streaks of mistakes and missed scoring attempts. They demonstrated real offensive firepower—especially in Drake, Benton, Davis, Snyder, and Pincura—but they still had weaknesses on their line. The remaining games of 1938 passed like a funeral procession. The Packers buried any hopes for a division championship in a 28–7 thumping at League Park, a loss even worse than the 26–17 setback Bezdek had suffered to start the season. The Lions blanked the Rams at the beginning of a week that would witness *Kristallnacht* in Germany as dark clouds gathered in the world outside of football. Then the Giants shut out the Rams too and sent Cleveland center Jack May to a New York hospital with a serious concussion. Even a late-season swing to sunny California could not rouse the morale of the 3–6 Rams. At L.A.'s Gilmore Stadium, on a site later to hold CBS Television City—and in a game that passed quietly as the Rams' first-ever in California—the now-independent Bulldogs, refugees of the Rams' old AFL, drilled Cleveland 28–7.

The Rams' season ended with a thud as they bowed to the Chicago Cardinals 31–17 before "a small party of friends and relatives"[47] at Comiskey Park, but not before they participated in the first-ever NFL game in New Orleans.[48] The unusual matchup came about only because Pirates owner Art Rooney postponed a meeting with the Rams earlier in the season due to injuries and a fire sale of players that had decimated his roster. The Big Easy, technically Pittsburgh's home field, really was a test of Southern interest in the NFL, yet only about 8,000 curiosity-seekers came to Tulane Stadium on December 4, 1938, to see Snyder toss two touchdown passes to Benton as the Rams won 13–7. The Rams concluded the season at 4–7—a triumph given their 0–3 start under Bezdek, but also a disappointment after Lewis had rattled off three straight wins against the Lions and the Bears. He would not be their head coach in 1939.

For a time the Rams thought they had their new ideal candidate in Cliff Battles, a star with the Redskins who might well have made a fine coach in Cleveland. He had been born in nearby Akron, was a Phi Beta Kappa student in college, had been scouted by an undergraduate student at Georgetown University named Daniel F. Reeves, and like White was eligible for a Rhodes Scholarship but passed up graduate school so he could play football. But complications in the Rams' negotiations arose immediately. Battles still was property of the Redskins, who were not going to let go of him without a fight. They demanded a high toll in exchange for his services: the Rams' first-round pick in the coming draft, and failing that, either Rams back Davis or the team's second-round pick. The Rams balked, but what likely killed the negotiation was news that Battles reportedly had told friends he did not like "the setup of the Rams' organization"[49]—almost certainly an indictment of the multi-headed Downtown Coaches and their incessant second-guessing. With this the deal was off.

But another surprising candidate came into view: Clark, the Lions' player-coach whose late-game fumble at Shaw Stadium weeks before had handed the Rams a surprise win. A quiet and independent type of coach, Clark had grown weary of Detroit owner George A. Richards, telling friends he often felt as if he were "Coach No. 2."[50] He was willing to take a chance on the Downtown Coaches, he indicated, so he traveled from his home in Pueblo, Colorado, to interview with Lipscomb and talk until nearly dawn about the Rams' many bright prospects for 1939. The team had rebounded from Bezdek's trio of opening losses in no small part because of its passing game, and rookie end Benton—the Rams' bonanza supplemental draft pick from the first round—led the league in yards per reception in 1938 with an average of 19.9 yards per catch, ahead even of the great Hutson.[51] The recent player draft also had been productive. In the first round, with the third overall selection, the Rams took Parker "Bullet" Hall, a back from the University of Mississippi. In the second they grabbed Gaylon Smith, a fullback from Southwestern University, and in the twelfth they selected Chet Adams, a native of Cleveland and a tackle from Ohio University. All three would be solid contributors to the Rams, with Smith and Adams going on to lend NFL savvy to the founding roster of the Cleveland Browns.

During their late-night chat, Lipscomb sized up the soft-spoken Lions coach, who looked positively scholarly in his eyeglasses when off the field. Signing Clark, a perennial winner and star of Detroit's 1935 championship team, would be an instant coup for Lipscomb and the Rams. He also would be good box office, thought by many to have "the perfect football face" as *LIFE* magazine enthused in its December 1936 issue. His helmeted profile, photographed in profile, had reminded *Detroit News* photographer William Kuenzel of a "Roman gladiator."[52] Entertainers Bette Davis and Bing Crosby prized reprints of Kuenzel's iconic image, likely not knowing Clark was nearly sightless in one eye from a congenital condition. Lipscomb offered Clark a two-year contract. Lewis would be removed from the head coach position and would become his assistant, he said. Pappy, in fact, had recommended Clark to the Rams' directors.

The Rams job was tempting to Clark. He had spent his entire NFL career with the Lions organization in Detroit and, before that, in Portsmouth, Ohio, when they were the Spartans. But this was a whole new opportunity. It was worth the change, and the challenge. He accepted.

"Luck to Them Both," the *Cleveland Press* editorialized. Clark's "football knowledge is unquestioned," and "we are glad Art Lewis will remain with the team." Lewis had been "rushed into the breach after the morale of the team had been all but ruined" by Bezdek, but Lewis had done "an excellent job for one of his years and inexperience…. We wish both these young men luck."[53]

The Rams' Lewis and Clark expedition had begun.

CHAPTER 6

The Rams' Lewis and Clark Expedition

The Cleveland Rams were so confident they were on the cusp of something promising in 1939 that they scheduled every one of their National Football League home games for huge Cleveland Stadium, the yellow-bricked, tarnished-aluminum wonder on the city's waterfront. Lying empty and locked on Sundays the autumn before, the stadium silently mocked the Rams as they played to small houses at Shaw High School in East Cleveland and at Cleveland's League Park. But now the team had notches on its belt marked *Chicago Bears* and *Detroit Lions*, vanquished foes in 1938 who could testify that the Cleveland franchise, after only two seasons with the big boys, was capable of holding its own in the NFL. The Rams' roster was studded with budding stars in backs Johnny Drake and Corby Davis; receiver Jim Benton; and rookie Parker Hall, a passer with great promise. And after several false starts the team was led by an experienced and championship-winning head coach in Earl "Dutch" Clark, who in turn was bolstered by a more than capable assistant in his predecessor Art "Pappy" Lewis. The Rams' aspirations at last seemed equal to the Stadium in which they seemed destined to play.

But when Clark, in a suit and sporting a jaunty fedora, took his Rams to the stadium field on September 6, 1939, for his debut game as Rams head coach—a preseason 28–0 triumph over the Ohio College All-Stars—he likely felt the implicit expectations of the structure's massive capacity. The crowd of 21,442 barely filled more than one-quarter of Cleveland Stadium's seats. Clearly, Clark intuited, it was going to take a lot more player talent and on-field success to come even close to filling that grandstand. Until that day, the largely empty stadium would echo with unfulfilled promise.

6. The Rams' Lewis and Clark Expedition

The ballpark's playing surface, furthermore, was inordinately enormous. Clark no doubt would have nodded in recognition with Babe Ruth's observation that "you'd have to have a horse to play outfield"[1] there. Staging a game in the center of such a huge structure "made the players feel as if they were performing before empty stands," Clark would say a few years later. Spectators were "just too far away, not only for themselves, but the players also."[2]

This was something quite new for Clark. University of Detroit Stadium, capacity 25,000 and home of his prior team the Lions, was more of his accustomed habitat. But his pro career had begun in a venue even more humble than a university field. In 1930 Clark graduated from small Colorado College and came east to Ohio, to a Depression-stricken shoe-manufacturing town hard against the charging waters of the Ohio River and a stone's throw from Kentucky. The Portsmouth Spartans' Universal Stadium was a brusquely art deco edifice of grand archways and graceful curves, of special grandstand boxes and obelisk-shaped light standards, but it held only 8,200 at its capacity. This did not deter the Spartans from tearing through the young NFL as one of the powerhouse teams of their era—runners-up to the Bears as league champions in 1932 before they broke through with their own title as the renamed Detroit Lions in 1935. Like future Ram Bob Waterfield, Clark wore number 7, became the highest-paid player in the league, and eventually was inducted into the Pro Football Hall of Fame. But never in his many circuits through the NFL had he played in a venue quite the size of Cleveland Stadium, nor had he been handed a shortage of talent such as he had inherited with the woebegone Rams.

Vowing Cleveland would not suffer again the ignominy of finishing last as it had in the team's inaugural year, Clark quickly executed several trades, including that of Ohio native Bob Snyder—the team's foremost passer as well as one of its top runners[3] in the team's first two NFL seasons—in exchange for center Bill "Red" Conkright. The Rams had assumed Snyder would not play in 1939, but indeed he did—as backup to passing legend Sid Luckman of the Chicago Bears. Three Chicago championships and six years later, Snyder would return to the Rams organization as a coach; and while Conkright was a solid contributor at center, letting Snyder go would not be Clark's last misjudgment of talent: A lack of quality drafts would come to be his undoing in Cleveland.

Clark in the meantime took good-natured ribbing about fumbling the ball away the previous season at Shaw Stadium to give the Rams their first-ever home victory, and he accepted sage advice from the locals on Cleveland's dire need to shut down Green Bay's star receiver Don Hutson. Yet he also bristled some at the media's perception of the Rams as a dark horse and countered that "we'll have a good scrappy team this year."[4]

To make doubly sure of success, Clark dispatched Lewis to the South to get several of the Rams' newly drafted players in the fold. Lewis's biggest prize was Hall, who would be voted the 1939 recipient of the league's newly created Joe F. Carr Trophy as the first of two most valuable players for the Rams in only eight seasons in Cleveland.[5] Hall, with a triangular face and hooded eyes, had suffered a crushed chest and a punctured lung in a car accident as a high-school sophomore in northern Mississippi, but he bounced back to become a dominating tailback at the University of Mississippi.

Joining Hall in the Rams backfield would be Gaylon Smith, a rookie fullback from Arkansas who seven years later, after a legal kerfuffle, would jump to the founding roster of the brand-new Cleveland Browns. "Gaylon the Great" resembled a "Roman emperor—harsh and imperious"[6] to the Memphis *Commercial Appeal*, but to the editor of a Rams press guide published after the team had moved to Los Angeles he looked more like "a husky, barrel-chested, stocky-legged footballer who can run 100 yards in about 10 [seconds] flat and who runs smack into and through tacklers like a regular battering ram."[7]

Continuing the team's haul from the South, Clark made possibly the best and most impactful assessment of talent in his Cleveland tenure when he signed the undrafted free agent guard/tackle Riley Matheson on a tip from a friend at the Texas School of Mines. Matheson, after a slow start with the Rams, came to evoke allusions of violent collision as he helped to power the team to its 1945 championship. He was among the most colorful players in the team's early era, picking up the nickname "Rattlesnake" after being bitten twice while hunting in the American Southwest. A Texas native who one day would come to operate a ranch in New Mexico and reportedly manhandle 1,000 hay bales a week in the offseason, Matheson showed up at the Rams' 1939 training camp in Berea, Ohio, wearing only tennis shoes, blue jeans, an open-necked shirt, either a "gallon hat"[8] or a "battered sombrero"[9] depending on the account most to be believed, and carrying a worn-out old bag, "the sole contents of which was one toothbrush."[10] On top of it all, Matheson bore heavy black eyebrows and a smiling face resembling a comedy mask in ancient Greek theater. "He was really a strange looking character," then–Rams president Thomas Lipscomb recalled. "I can remember Art Lewis asking him what position he played and Matheson replied: 'Oh, don't worry about that, coach. Just put me anywhere and I'll make you a good hand.'"[11]

Of the two coaches, one the new head coach and the other newly demoted, it was the assistant Lewis rather than Clark who greeted Matheson at camp. Lewis was the "loud one,"[12] the voice of management to the players. Clark in contrast was a quiet, thoughtful presence according to tennis commentator and Cleveland native Bud Collins, and a "handsome figure on the field"[13] in football pants and cleats, reticent enough to have prompted former boss and Lions owner George A. Richards to retain a public relations agent to curry more favorable press. Together Clark and Lewis became "one of the smartest coaching combinations" in the view of one out-of-town newspaper account.[14] With star running back Drake returning from his offseason job as a policeman at San Francisco's World's Fair, Chuck Cherundolo holding down center, and Lewis ready to jump back in as player-coach to support Chet Adams and Ted Livingston on the line, the Lewis and Clark duo began to whip its roster into shape. Hall, Benton, Smith, and Matheson were Southerners, and with Ohioan Snyder gone, the Rams increasingly were becoming more Cotton Belt than Corn Belt in derivation—an influence perhaps of president Lipscomb, a native Tennessean.

Earl "Dutch" Clark (left) and Art "Pappy" Lewis, pictured in 1941, were respectively the third and second head coaches of the NFL Rams. Lewis was the "loud one," Clark more quiet and thoughtful *(The Cleveland Press Collection, Cleveland State University Library)*.

Rams co-founder Homer Marshman brought on investors, including Akron tire magnate Leonard Firestone, $1,000 at a time, issuing convertible notes as he went. Firestone later joined Daniel F. Reeves as a partner in the Los Angeles Rams (*Donald Gries Collection*).

Never in fact would Lipscomb and the Rams' Downtown Coaches—the many investors who collectively could lay claim to no practical pro football experience—make their presence known more acutely to Rams coaches than they would in 1939, which was to be the second-to-last season in which they would hold title to the team. Lipscomb and the other Rams directors, who now included Akron tire magnate Leonard Firestone and iron-ore executive Elton Hoyt II, informed Clark and Lewis that in the coming season "interference from the club's directorate" would be "systematized."[15] This meant that each of the Downtown Coaches would advise the coaches on "various parts of the Ram machine"[16]—one telling Clark how to play the ends, for instance, while another advised on the tackles, and another provided counsel on the centers and guards, etc. "And," Lipscomb helpfully told Clark, "if you find our assistant end coach messing in with your guards and tackles, you tell him to go to hell!"[17] Former head coach Hugo Bezdek had endured Monday morning meetings and even Lipscomb sitting on his bench on game days, but Clark and Lewis would receive second-guessing on a daily basis. The Rams owners were Downtown Coaches indeed, and Lipscomb particularly seemed to be banking on a breakout year. As 1939 training camp began—just before Nazi Germany invaded Poland to drive World War II forward in Europe—he stood before a lunchtime gathering of the Cleveland Athletic Club to predict intrepidly that his Rams, now newly outfitted in golden-yellow pants and gold helmets, would enjoy a successful season. Perhaps he saw it as motivation for his team. But his faith would be tested.

The Rams opened with two losses and immediately they optioned the promising Matheson to the American Football League's Columbus Bullies, among whom the young guard could learn the intricacies of how to play defensive line in professional football. Quick coming off the line, Matheson nevertheless was "mousetrapped" so frequently and thoroughly by wily NFL lineman—lured across the line of scrimmage and into blocks as running backs whizzed through a hole he just had vacated—that players began calling him "Limburger."[18] One day soon he would return to Cleveland, and triumphantly.

In the meantime, on October 1, 1939, the Rams claimed their biggest victory to that time in a 27–24 come-from-behind win—their first ever against the Green Bay Packers, Western Division nemesis and eventual NFL champions that year. Clark was "jubilant"[19] as the Rams held Hutson to only one touchdown, then scored two of their own in the fourth quarter. The Downtown Coaches brimmed with happiness and relief as they invited their entire squad to a steak roast at Cleveland's most exclusive enclave for the wealthy, Kirtland Country Club.[20] Rams players, in adherence with the country club's as well as the team's dress code, likely attended wearing white shirts, ties, and dark blazers embroidered with the team's ram's-head logo and the words "Clev. Rams."[21] Clark characteristically had ensured that his Rams were well dressed, setting a policy often attributed to coaches of a later era that players wear collared shirts and jackets off the field and generally comport themselves more like gentlemen rather than like "pro grid bums"[22] as Lipscomb phrased it. If the Rams dressed and acted like champions, Rams management reasoned, they would become champions; and there were reassuring signs the franchise generally was pointed in the right direction.

With the team finally having broken through with defeats of its two biggest division rivals—the Bears and the Packers—over the previous 12 months, the Downtown Coaches sensed momentum. They took out newspaper ads for the team's upcoming home opener against the Bears and ordered the formation of a "Rams' 80-Piece All-American Band"[23] to add pageantry to the proceedings. Then they watched in horror as the Rams blew a lead gained on Drake and Benton touchdowns, fizzled in unseasonable early-October heat, and lost 35–21. A crowd of 18,209 had left more than three-quarters of Cleveland Stadium's seats empty.

The Rams then were up and down through the middle section of the 1939 season until they brought a 3–4–1 record to a match with Clark's former Lions that was billed with the intensity of a playoff game. The *Cleveland Plain Dealer* whipped up a "grudge battle"[24] against the Lions, who, it was suggested, had surrendered Clark to the Rams because he had not won a championship in several years and because his run-oriented offense was behind the times. Clark was so hungry to beat his former team, and with a potent passing attack which to that point had led the league in completions, that he asked the Lions to relinquish their rights to him as a player so he could suit up and play. But in return Detroit asked for the moon—Rams star passer Parker Hall—so Clark just "forgot about it"[25] and retired finally as a player.

On the day before the game, Cleveland mayor Harold Burton—future U.S. senator and associate justice of the U.S. Supreme Court justice and the same politico who had tossed out the first pass at the Rams' premieres in both the AFL and the NFL—raised the ante on the outcome by offering a newly fashioned Burton Trophy to be presented to the game's winner. "To an extent probably not true of a professional football team in any other city, the Cleveland Rams are something of a civic institution," Chads O. Skinner of the *Plain Dealer* noted. The team's directors were in it not for the money, he said, but for the communal good, because a winning, crowd-drawing team is "good for Cleveland, good advertising for Cleveland."[26] Another account underscored that "no team has played under much greater pressure than the Rams" would against Detroit, and that "in every respect, the battle will be a real money game."[27] The hopes and pride of a city—the future financial viability of professional football in northeastern Ohio, in fact—rested on the Rams' shoulders, and the team responded well to the pressure. After spotting Detroit a 3–0 lead, Cleveland surged back to claim the Burton Trophy by defeating the Lions 14–3 on two Hall touchdown passes, one to emerging star Benton. With 28,142 in attendance at Cleveland Stadium, the Rams at long last had "sold professional football to Cleveland,"[28] and had done so with an exciting offensive attack.

The publicity machine swung into high gear. Advertisements and pregame coverage blanketed local newspapers as the Rams had a chance at a season sweep of the Packers who, as the embodiment of big-time championship football, flew into Cleveland on a private plane. The Packers took the Cleveland Stadium field before 30,690, the largest pro football crowd in city history to that time, and battled the Rams to a scoreless first half. In the third quarter, from the Packers' 18-yard line, Hall fired a cross-field pass to big Jim Benton, who with nemesis Hutson draped on him in blanket coverage simply dragged both his defender and a game official across the goal line for the go-ahead touchdown. It was Hall's 90th completion of the season, breaking the NFL record of 81 set by Washington's Sammy Baugh two years earlier.[29] Vic Spadaccini, however, fatefully missed the extra point, and Green Bay countered with a touchdown late in the game to take a 7–6 lead, then challenged the Rams to score in the final two minutes. A 50-yard field goal try by Cleveland fell short on the final play and the Rams lost by one point. In the taut, closely fought loss, "pro football came of age in Cleveland," the *Plain Dealer* reported the next day.[30]

And when the Rams trounced the Philadelphia Eagles 35–13 in Colorado Springs the following week in the team's first-ever regular season game in the West, it was clear the franchise finally had arrived. Hall, a first-year tailback, set a new NFL record of 106 completed passes, the first time a professional passer had completed more than 100 passes in a season.[31] His favorite targets far and away were Benton and Spadaccini, major factors in the Rams finishing fourth in the league in scoring.[32] Hall in fact well earned his MVP award by playing as a double weapon, finishing second in passing yards (1,227) and fifth in rushing yards (458).[33] The Rams had crawled from the mire of losing with a 5–5–1 record, and as they said goodbye to Cleveland for the winter, "for the first time in a long history of attempts to establish the paid game here thousands of citizens will be waiting eagerly for another hello next fall," wrote the *Plain Dealer*'s Gordon Cobbledick.[34]

But just before Christmas an ominous report surfaced that the Rams' Downtown Coaches, sportsmen and civic leaders at heart but businessmen first and foremost, already had lost $100,000 in their three years of operation in the NFL. The team desperately could have used a home game against marquee powers the New York Giants or the Washington Redskins to make the turnstiles click and build much-needed revenue, but neither team would be coming to Cleveland in 1940. It would be the last season in which Clevelanders could feel confident about the Rams' future in their city.

* * *

Cleveland sports fans and the Rams' Downtown Coaches were at something of a standoff as 1940 dawned—the former holding out for more wins before anteing up their full-throated support, the latter waiting for better ticket sales before deepening their investments in the team. The Rams' 5-5-1 record in 1939, balanced as it was precisely on a cusp between winning and losing, was an apt symbol for this impasse. But even after the team doubled season-ticket sales year over year, Clevelanders soon were to discover that it would be NFL owners and not football fans in the nation's largest population centers who increasingly held the decisive advantage.

In 1939 the NFL had surpassed 1 million total attendance for the first time in its 20 seasons,[35] a major milestone in the league's growth. An NFL game also was televised for the first time that year, to approximately 1,000 sets in New York. Coming into bloom was what the *Plain Dealer*'s John Dietrich that year would enthuse as "the color and action that makes professional football a dazzling show for the spectator."[36] In 1940 the NFL's owners were aware of their league's rising popularity, and they were growing weary of potential ownership groups from then-minor-league cities including Buffalo, Baltimore, San Francisco, Los Angeles, and Miami showing up at their meetings in hopes of securing a franchise. In the owners' minds only cities with existing Major League Baseball franchises need apply. The cost of air travel to far-flung metropolises, furthermore, was prohibitively expensive. Round-trip airfare on American Airlines from, say, Cleveland to L.A. was $221.84[37]—nearly $3,800 in 2015 dollars.

To keep their league geographically taut and perceived as being in the big time, the owners voted to quintuple the entrance fee from $10,000 to $50,000 in hopes that they would "eliminate all but the most sincere and wealthiest franchise cities."[38] Cleveland's place in this exclusive fraternity was assured, or so Clevelanders thought. "Cleveland is unquestionably the

6. The Rams' Lewis and Clark Expedition 85

best spot in the nation for the development of pro football," Dietrich reassured his readership, noting the city's central place in a region of 1.5 million. "A winning pro team here would be a huge financial success."[39]

But such civic self-confidence increasingly felt unmerited. Cleveland no longer had its advocate and defender in former NFL president Joe F. Carr, who died in 1939. The Rams' Downtown Coaches were discovering the hard way that the NFL decidedly was not "one big happy family"[40] as Dietrich phrased it, and that other teams would not provide help in building a team for Cleveland. The Rams had done little to justify large crowds, Dietrich acknowledged, and predictably in 1940 the team continued to wallow near the basement as a box-office attraction. Only the Chicago Cardinals, who bore the unique and unfortunate handicap of sharing a market with the dynastic Bears, would draw less in average per-game attendance (15,714) than the Rams (16,750).[41] Rumors circulated for the first time that the Rams franchise might be sold if ticket sales did not pick up, and watching at least one their home games with keen interest that autumn was wealthy Cleveland businessman and prospective pro football owner Arthur "Mickey" McBride, later to bid for the Rams and ultimately to found the Browns.

But in a year when the Rams could have used all the luck they could get, they faced a snake-bitten 1940. First their streak of drafting and signing at least one new star each year—Drake in 1937, Davis and Benton in 1938, Hall in 1939—came to a thudding halt as first-round pick Olie Cordill, a halfback out of Rice, spent the better part of the season on the injury list. Coach Clark had had high hopes for Cordill—reports out of Texas were that he was a multipurpose weapon who could kick, block, run, catch passes, and defend—"but he got hurt right off the bat and then he got hurt again and he hasn't been much good to us," Clark told Cobbledick the day before Halloween.[42] Cordill in fact never would play again after entering the military following the 1939 season, and joining him among the injured that season were well-regarded center Bill "Red" Conkright and team captain and right guard Livingston. Furthermore the Rams now were on the league's radar and found they could not sneak up on powerhouse teams as they had the previous two seasons.

After an opening-day win over the Eagles followed by a 6–0 loss to the Lions, the Rams caught the Bears a week after the Chicago team was upset by crosstown rivals the Cardinals and took it on the chin at Cleveland Stadium, 21–14. On a gloriously warm and sunny day, the home team found one bright spot in a 25-yard touchdown pass from Hall to Dante Magnani, a promising rookie back out of St. Mary's College in California.

A week later the Rams faced a Packers squad still smarting from a humiliating 41–10 loss at home to the Bears and were throttled 31–14 at Green Bay. To compound matters, Hall was suffering through a sophomore slump. He had had a rookie year in which he set a new record for pass completions, beat out Hutson for the league's most valuable player award, and enjoyed side-by-side honors with legendary Cleveland pitcher Bob Feller. But in 1940 he was tight, failing to show the same precision and accuracy he had in 1939 and dropping to only 77 completions, third behind leaders Davey O'Brien of Philadelphia (124) and Sammy Baugh (111) of Washington[43]—both of whom kept pushing the ever-upward trajectory of passing in the NFL.

But coach Clark kept a stiff upper lip and insisted his team was better balanced and an improvement over the 1939 edition. As was their wont, the Rams had opened the season poorly and muddled to an initial 2–4 record, but then they rattled off signature games against three league powers at the end of the season that tantalized their winning-starved fan base. They neutralized the Lions 24–0 on touchdowns by Drake and Benton, and a week later they pulled off a 13–0 blanking of the New York Giants at the Polo Grounds that reversed a 28–0 drubbing they had received on the same field two years earlier. Then, as they had done the season before, they closed out their home schedule by surprising the Packers, this time with a 13–13 tie. Given the spate of injuries and bad luck the team had endured, a final record of 4–6–1 was a reasonably good achievement. Spadaccini, Cordill, and Livingston were replacement selections for the Pro Bowl game that season, and Drake was voted first-team All-Pro, easily pacing the league in rushing touchdowns and finishing second in total rushing yards behind only the estimable would-be Ram "Whizzer" White.[44]

In the offseason Drake was something of a "Hollywood cowboy"[45] as he worked as a stuntman and extra in Western movies, presaging the coming arrival of quarterback Waterfield and foreshadowing the Rams' future in California. And indeed there was a bit of Hollywood in the Rams already. The team's uniforms, with flashy yellow winging out along the top of their shoulder pads and blue piping contrasting with their matching yellow pants, surely must have caught the approving eye of Clarence "Fred" Gehrke, a speedy back who signed with Cleveland in 1940 as an undrafted free agent. Gehrke, with wavy hair and a feral expression and packing a lot of power in a lean five-foot-eleven frame, had been an all-around star athlete at the University of Utah and was the most outstanding tailback in the Rocky Mountain Conference in 1939. Perhaps just as importantly he was something of an heir to Rams founder Damon "Buzz" Wetzel in that he was as artistic off the football field as he was atavistic on it. An art and education major in college, Gehrke would observe that the Rams' distinctive horns could make as fine a decoration on helmets as on letterhead, and he personally would paint the NFL's first logo on his and all his teammates' helmets.

But that was years in the future. In 1940 Gehrke still was a backup to Hall in the Rams' single-wing offense and played in only three games. One report had him being released by the team midway through the season after showing "considerable promise but ... an inferiority complex about big-league competition."[46] Not quite yet ready for the NFL, he went back West, took a job as an aircraft illustrator in California, disappeared into World War II—"frozen" to his job in an airplane plant and "as forgotten as a spare tire"[47]— before returning to Cleveland in 1945 to play an important role in the Rams' championship and the visual feast the NFL game was to become.

In 1940 the Rams also made a key acquisition in back Jim Gillette, a star out of the University of Virginia. Gillette grew up in something of a rarity for the era: a multi-generation football family. His father had competed on the gridiron while he was in law school and attempted to teach his left-handed son how to throw a football with his right, to no avail. "You won't amount to nothing," the elder Gillette told him.[48] Gillette's football future was nearly derailed by a squirrel-hunting accident in his youth in which he took a gunshot wound to the hip,

Jim Gillette played for the Cleveland Rams in 1940 before joining the Navy to serve on a convoy ship in the North Atlantic during World War II. He returned in time to star in the 1945 NFL championship game. His son, Walker Gillette, also played in the NFL (*Walker Gillette Collection*).

an injury that in 1930s Virginia was allowed to heal on its own. Told he might never run again, Gillette persevered by extra-exercising the wounded leg. Gillette "was a tough man,"[49] his widow Marguerite would say many decades later with some understatement. After achieving success at the collegiate level he trained with the Packers but caught on with the Kenosha Cardinals, a high-caliber semi-pro outfit that played preseason and exhibition games against NFL teams. When Clark and the Rams finally plucked Gillette out of relative obscurity, the Cardinals and their fans were in a "gloom of despair,"[50] and Gillette made the most of his big-league opportunity by playing in four games for the Rams in 1940.

The war was about to scatter many of the Rams to other franchises and multiple branches of the military, but four players from the 1940 team—Benton, Gehrke, Gillette, and Matheson—would reunite in Cleveland in 1945 under a completely different Rams owner, general manager, and head coach to form the core of "sport's first spectacular postwar team."[51] However, much trauma and change lay in the intervening five tears. Industry and the nation's population base steadily were moving westward. Millions of civilians including Drake and Gehrke went to work in war-related industries to supply tanks, planes, and guns to America's allies as Nazi Germany carried on sustained bombing of England. President Franklin D. Roosevelt called on all male citizens between the ages of 26 and 35 to begin registering for the military draft.

With a nearly breakeven total record of 9–11–2 across the 1939 and 1940 seasons, the coaching tandem of Clark and Lewis had brought the Rams to the threshold of football respectability. A question for the franchise now was which would come sooner: success in Cleveland, or a departure from Cleveland. But just as much in doubt was whether the NFL would be in business at all, given looming war clouds in Europe. Events were gathering, both abroad and at home, that would change the direction of the Rams franchise forever.

CHAPTER 7

"The public be pleased"

War was coming. And in the well-upholstered quarters of Cleveland's exclusive Union Club, in the boardrooms and carpeted corner offices of downtown towers, on the tidy greens of Kirtland Country Club and in the chandeliered dining rooms of imposing Chagrin River valley homes on the city's wealthy East Side, the Cleveland Rams' so-called Downtown Coaches—the businessmen, sportsmen, and civic leaders who were the team's directors—came to a conclusion in early 1941: It might be best for the team, the city, and most importantly themselves if they were to sell the Cleveland Rams.

Stockholders in the franchise had ballooned to 45 men by New Year's Eve 1940[1] as the team's directors continued to cut in investors to keep the enterprise afloat. The list included Damon "Buzz" Wetzel and Hugo Bezdek, former Rams coaches long fired, but most others were prominent men in the local business community, many of whom feared a suspension of the National Football League due to the war and a resulting loss of their investments. They were encouraged that the previous year the Detroit Lions had sold for a commanding price of $200,000,[2] while Art Rooney recently had accepted an offer of $160,000[3] for the Steelers team he had founded in 1933. "I certainly hated to give up the franchise in the old home town," he told the *Pittsburgh Post-Gazette* on December 9, 1940, in what would be a nightmare scenario for 21st-century Steelers fans, "but it would have been poor business to refuse the proposition for a second division ball club at the terms that were offered."[4]

Rooney actually sold the Steelers to young millionaire Alexis Thompson, who was to have moved the team to Boston and changed their name to the Ironmen; then was to have taken his proceeds from that sale and joined Philadelphia owner Bert Bell in a franchise that would adopt the name Keystoners, split its home games between Pittsburgh and Philadelphia, and control the entire state of Pennsylvania. By spring 1941, however, Rooney had changed his mind about abandoning a full-time team in Pittsburgh, and before playing a single down as the Keystoners, the Rooney/Bell franchise moved to the Steel City and resurrected the Steelers, Thompson took the would-be Ironmen to Philadelphia and operated instead as the Eagles, and both franchises settled into stability that lasted well into the next century. In Cleveland the cash-strapped local ownership of the Rams surely took notice that qualified and willing buyers would pay top money for a second-division NFL franchise.

And understandably so. The NFL was starting to attract public attention for an almost outlandish new style of play. The Chicago Bears just had shocked the Washington Redskins 73–0 in the 1940 NFL championship game using the newfangled T-formation—placing a quarterback behind center as a special passing weapon and arraying three other backs in a row behind him in a T-pattern, so that the quarterback could turn away from the defense and execute hand-off or pitch-out feints and other misdirections in the backfield to freeze defenses for precious milliseconds. Potential new ownership groups were electrified and wanted a piece of the action. Show-business star Don Ameche headed up a syndicate of Los Angeles investors soliciting the NFL for an expansion franchise in Buffalo which eventually could be moved to L.A.—a request that was rejected because Chicago Cardinals owner Charles Bidwill yearned to move his own struggling team there if his fellow owners might one day allow it.[5] Thwarting Ameche later would come to haunt the NFL—and the Rams particularly—in L.A.

The Downtown Coaches, meanwhile, were taken aback by increasing player demands. Rudy Mucha, Cleveland's top draft pick in 1941, made noise that he might reject the Rams' offer of $150 per game and instead accept $175 to play in the rival American Football League. Rams team president Edward P. Bruch—who controversially had scouted the draft bust Bronko Smilanich on the campus of the University of Arizona three winters earlier—responded by harking back to the Rams' shaky founding in the AFL in 1936 and the banning of former Ram Gomer Jones from the NFL. He offered Mucha and other newly drafted players a cautionary message: Don't try it; you'll risk being banned from the NFL. Plus, the AFL just was not financially sound. "We started out in the American [Football] League, and we found it very unstable," Bruch recalled. "That was why we decided that if professional football is worth anything in Cleveland, we must get a franchise in the National [Football] League."[6]

The Rams' owners were unnerved more than anything by the coming war's potential to stick them with $100,000-plus in debt and with no football income in sight. They began to "look favorably" on an offer to sell the team.[7] So on April 8, 1941, Bruch announced the Rams had received a "substantial offer" from an "eastern group." Then he floated a shocking trial balloon: The Rams might move to Cincinnati or Boston. But, Bruch equivocated: "We would like to feel the pulse of the [Cleveland] public on the situation. If it is favorable we will continue next fall, but it would be silly to go on if we are not assured of both moral and financial support."[8] The threat was valid. Cincinnati had lost its NFL franchise in 1934 when the football Reds moved to St. Louis to merge with the Gunners, which then folded in 1935, coincidentally opening a tenth league slot that the Rams would fill in 1937. Now Powel Crosley, Jr., owner of the baseball Cincinnati Reds, reportedly was interested in buying a football team,[9] and with the Steelers remaining in Pennsylvania, Boston still was a pawn in the NFL owners' game as it had been since George Preston Marshall whisked the Redskins off to Washington in 1937.

On the issue of whether to sell the team, the Rams' Downtown Coaches were, as always, not in unanimity. Some pointed out that new football clubs typically suffered losses for several seasons before becoming established, and that more patience was merited. This likely set off an argument about how long "several seasons"[10] likely was to be—there had been four already, five dating to the team's founding year in the AFL—as well as a debate about whether baseball-mad Clevelanders ever would embrace pro football. It is perhaps telling that Al Sutphin, the Cleveland hockey and arena magnate, did not make a move to buy the team outright as was his announced interest three years earlier. His franchise the Cleveland Barons just had won the American Hockey League championship, so perhaps his time and attention were fully occupied, perhaps he was scared off by the impending war—or maybe he had decided that pro football in Cleveland just was not a sound investment after all.

In any event, though no qualified local ownership group had stepped forward, on the day after Bruch announced the Rams were up for sale and that they might move, a frenzy of civic mobilization began. The Cleveland Chamber of Commerce, the Cleveland Advertising Club, the Come-to-Cleveland Committee, and the Cleveland Convention and Visitors Bureau all lined up to convey their assurances that they would do everything in their power to keep the Rams in Cleveland. Otherwise, the *Cleveland Plain Dealer* declared in an editorial titled "We Want the Rams," the city would be impoverished by losing "something fine in sports and important."[11] The professional game had exceeded collegiate football in power, speed, and skillfulness, the editors said, "and it would be a civic loss if the Rams were taken to another city."[12] New NFL commissioner Elmer Layden, once of Notre Dame's famed Four Horsemen, came to town to speak in support of the Rams and to praise Ohio as the "cradle of professional football."[13] A Chamber of Commerce official phoned from a Western trip to note that Cleveland was "teeming with industrial activity, with employment at a new all-time high,"[14] which augured well for fan patronage in the coming season.

Within a few weeks civic support for the Rams coalesced and anxiety subsided. The Downtown Coaches issued a mea culpa for their lack of full-time promotion of the team, a failure that would be fixed in the coming season, they promised, if the team were to continue in Cleveland. Civic and political leaders vowed they would pull for the franchise, local businesses promised to increase season-ticket purchases for the coming season, and fans mailed in letters and cards requesting that the Rams be kept in Cleveland. As a result the prospective new ownership group apparently softened on its plan to move the franchise to Boston. With public affirmation of pro football in Cleveland in hand, the Rams' directors had a tantalizing offer on the table—one that could resolve their financial concerns in the most painless of ways. Perhaps, they dared to think, they could pull out a win-win: recoup their losses and keep the franchise in town. But who was in this "eastern group" that had stepped forward and seemingly out of nowhere presented a "substantial offer" of $150,000 to move the team out of town? Clevelanders were about to find out.

* * *

Daniel Farrell Reeves was first and foremost the son of a highly successful grocery magnate in an era when the "industrialization of food" meant the grocery trade was particularly big business. "He was not polishing apples," Joe Horrigan of the Pro Football Hall of Fame noted. "The grocery chains were huge then." The future Rams owner "understood franchising, he understood expansion, he understood how to operate as a mass employer."[15] It was good training for operating a pro football team.

For this he could thank his father James A. Reeves. The elder Reeves was born in Ireland, immigrated to the United States in 1890, and gained a foothold in New York City by peddling fruit from a small space he leased in front of a grocery store. "Eventually he was able to buy the store that he was in front of, and that led to more and more" stores in the New York area, said Dan Reeves, Jr., son of the Rams owner and grandson of James Reeves. "It was all the Irish connection that really helped make that happen."[16]

7. "The public be pleased"

The sale of New York City's Daniel Reeves Inc. grocery chain to Safeway provided Daniel F. Reeves with capital needed to buy the Cleveland Rams in 1941. Here, a promotional flyer from 1928 (*Dan Reeves, Jr., Collection*).

James Reeves partnered with his younger brother Daniel in a chain of stores that grew spectacularly from just one in 1903 to 35 in 1911. Then Daniel died suddenly, and in his memory James incorporated the chain in his brother's name to become Daniel Reeves Inc. A year later, 1912, he welcomed a son whom he too named Daniel. The younger Dan Reeves learned "through long association with his father" in the family business that "money invested wisely is bound to reap dividends and that successful management produces pleasing results."[17]

Reeves grew up in New York City wealth and Irish-American political influence that may have intimidated even the prosperous Cleveland country club set that initially funded the Rams. Reeves' family occupied a gracious limestone residence on Fifth Avenue directly across from the Metropolitan Museum of Art and Central Park. When Reeves was married in 1935 to Mary Carroon of Long Island, guests at their wedding included Alfred E. Smith, the former New York State governor and the Democratic Party's

Guests at the 1935 wedding of Mary Carroon and Daniel F. Reeves included a former Democratic presidential candidate, an ex–New York Supreme Court justice, and a one-time mayor of New York City (*Dan Reeves, Jr., Collection*).

presidential candidate in 1928; John H. McCooey, a New York Supreme Court justice associated with the powerful Tammany Hall political machine; and a former mayor and police commission of New York City. Reeves' best man was his brother Edward, a minority owner with George Preston Marshall in the Boston/Washington Redskins.

Indeed it was through Edward that Reeves acquired his first taste of pro football management. Dan Reeves was a capable football player at a private prep school in New Jersey, but as a 150-pound undergraduate at Georgetown University he was too light to play intercollegiate sports. Instead he spent his spare time doing amateur scouting of college players, during which he unearthed a halfback prospect, Cliff Battles, at West Virginia Wesleyan. Battles signed with the Braves/Redskins in 1932, won the league rushing title his rookie season and an NFL title in 1937, and went on to enshrinement in the Pro Football Hall of Fame. The young Reeves, his confidence much boosted, was hooked on football. He made a journey west to Los Angeles the same autumn he married Carroon and watched the University of Southern California team in action at the majestic L.A. Memorial Coliseum. "I was captivated by Los Angeles and by the glamour of football," he later recalled.[18] He remained an official of Daniel Reeves Inc., working in the quasi-independent investment office of his father's grocery chain, and became vice president of the Telenews Theater chain of newsreel theaters, during which he would meet a future business partner who would both enrich and bedevil his many years in football ownership. All the while he was making unsuccessful attempts to secure a financial interest in either the Steelers or the Eagles, putting out feelers that might gain him entrée to the exclusive circle of NFL owners. Owning a football team was "all he wanted, since he was a kid," said Reeves Jr.[19]

The paths of the eager young Reeves and the urgently divesting Cleveland investors were about to converge. Reeves knew his father's chain was about to merge its now commanding 750 outlets with the 3,700 operated by Safeway Stores, a grocery goliath that would acquire the Reeves stores and immediately close them as a threat to their market domination. News of the Safeway founder's resignation, and of negotiations between that company and Daniel Reeves Inc., was in the business news at the very time that Reeves' talks to buy the Rams were in the sports news. And sure enough the merger went through late in the summer of 1941, with the sale yielding $11 million[20] to Daniel Reeves Inc. just as the company's young namesake yearned to buy a seat on the New York Stock Exchange and a professional football team.

When the Rams' owners welcomed Reeves for negotiations in the spring of 1941—at one point during the talks he walked down to the city's lakefront to size up Cleveland Stadium, while at another he issued a statement from Palm Beach, Florida—Clevelanders would have caught fleeting glimpses of a smallish, slender, dapper man not quite 30 years old. Reeves' face was sharp and handsome with a high forehead, later likened to Frank Sinatra's. He dressed in tweeds and button-down-collar shirts, had a glib sense of humor, and always enjoyed a good time and a drink, frequently holding court at P.J. Clarke's bar on Third Avenue in midtown Manhattan. He favored daiquiris—rum in particular, like many of the men of his generation, in imitation of Ernest Hemingway and his hard-living ways—and he especially loved hanging out with sportswriters. He was a consummate New York cosmopolitan of the prewar era and likely held some indifference toward the nation's interior. Cleveland just as well could have been Cincinnati, Milwaukee, or St. Louis from his perspective as a potential sports-team owner—the important thing was that the Rams were up for sale. Reeves would not be buying into Cleveland, he would be buying the Rams, and he was part of a new breed of young millionaire owners, the youngest of his peers after only Dan Topping of the Brooklyn Dodgers to have bought his way into the NFL.[21]

At Reeves' side was business partner Fred Levy, Jr., age 39, also scion of a retailing fortune. Levy's father was a Kentucky Colonel and an expert merchandiser who owned a department store in Louisville and also was an early pioneer in motion-picture theaters, holding extensive interests in some of the most important production, distribution, and exhibition companies of the 1920s and 1930s. He was a long-time associate of the producer of early *Tarzan* films and later owned a chain of West Coast drive-in theaters, palling around part of the year with Hollywood celebrities including Al Jolsen and Sophie Tucker. The younger Levy shared his father's passion for film, presiding over the Photo Developing Co. of Cincinnati and Camden, New Jersey, an enterprise through which he came to call on Reeves the newsreel-theater executive. "I had a tough time selling Reeves on my photo-finish product," Levy recalled in 1941, "but I finally did and we've been associated in enterprises since."[22] Levy was slightly shorter than Reeves—like his business partner a natty dresser in pinstriped double-breasted suits, but older, heavier, jowlier. Like Reeves he enjoyed a good drink—in his case, Kentucky bourbon, which he would come to consume in considerable quantities in the press box at Rams games. And like his own father he longed to spend far less time in the cold East than in sunny California. "He is," Franklin Lewis of the *Cleveland Press* wrote later, "one of those California boosters whose admiration for the golden sunshine of the golden west is attached to a spring and all you have to do is mention California or oranges or [the] Rose Bowl..., and Levy uncoils to the attack."[23] Cleveland newspapermen later came to believe Levy had played no small role in convincing Reeves to move the team to Los Angeles.

On April 30, 1941, Reeves issued a statement from Florida that a potential deal hinged on "three important conditions" that were not publicly specified—one of them, the *Plain Dealer* speculated, being "the immediate transfer of the Rams" to Boston.[24] Some in the Cleveland ownership group likely were tempted to take the money and run and let Boston have the team. Indeed the Rams directors already had voted to accept Reeves' and Levy's initial offer of $150,000, but league politics came into play. The Redskins' Marshall was no fan of Boston as an NFL town. He had left that city four years earlier due to a lack of fan support and financial sustainability and found immediate and unqualified success in Washington, D.C. He had vigorously opposed the shift of Rooney's Steelers to Boston, and his view of the Rams potentially moving there was the same. It was the first but hardly the last time the league powers would impose their opinions on Reeves' business decisions.

On a more immediate and practical level attendant to the idea of the team moving, however, was the 1941 game schedule—it already was set, and changing it would be no mean feat in an era when NFL teams were tenants of Major League Baseball franchises and therefore not in control of their own playing venues. If the Rams were to move to Boston they would need to switch from the Western Division to the Eastern Division, leaving four teams in the West and six in the East, unbalancing the league, and playing havoc with the schedule. The NFL concluded that at best the Rams would need to play at least one more season in Cleveland before deciding definitively to move to Boston.

With Cleveland now on a one-year probation with the Rams, a number of minority team owners attempted again to persuade the majority bloc to turn down the offer. They argued that the schedule for the upcoming season would be the team's most favorable yet, with the Rams facing all of the league's four big powers—the Bears, Redskins, Green Bay Packers, and New York Giants—and being well positioned to enjoy the box-office bonanza that would result. The franchise was about to turn a corner, they argued. The majority owners—apparently Bruch, former team president Thomas Lipscomb, and Robert H. Gries especially—seem not to have fully agreed. Bruch announced he expected the team to be sold soon, and on June 11, 1941, a deal was consummated. In exchange for a sum that the *New York Times* said was "reliably reported at about $140,000,"[25] Reeves bought 60 percent of the Rams, Levy picked up 30 percent, and Lipscomb, Bruch, and Gries stayed on as members of the board of directors.[26] Lipscomb later provided legal representation to Reeves as he moved the team to Los Angeles, and Gries eventually partnered with Arthur "Mickey" McBride to found the Cleveland Browns. Homer H. Marshman, founder of the team along with Wetzel in 1936, cashed out and later would re-emerge as a Browns minority owner succeeding McBride's group.

Of immediate impact to Clevelanders was that the Rams were going to stay, at least for one more year. "Originally, we contemplated taking the Rams to Boston," Reeves confessed, but "after our visit here, which included a good look at Cleveland's huge stadium, we decided there was no reason why big-league football couldn't be put over in a big way."[27] *But for how long?* reporters wondered. Reeves responded with studied vagueness: "As long as Cleveland wants pro football, it shall have it, and I am confident the fans here are happy the team is staying in Cleveland."[28]

Reeves likely used the NFL's temporary grounding of the team in Cleveland to drive down final terms of the sale, reported variously as $140,000,[29] $135,000,[30] and even as low as $125,000[31]—and in any case less than the $150,000 he and Levy originally had offered and a good bit less than the $160,000 that Rooney had negotiated for the lackluster Steelers. Nevertheless the sale would pay back at least 12 times the $10,000 league entry price that Marshman had laid out just four years earlier, a harbinger of the rapid escalation in franchise values that awaited the exclusive fraternity of NFL team owners. Even with the Downtown Coaches' many losses both on the field and in the financial ledger over the ensuing four years, they recouped all of their investments and with a small profit to boot.

Yet the sale also spelled the end of a short, innocent era in which the Rams had been controlled locally in Cleveland as a civic treasure and as a living promotion for the city. Wetzel had seeded the team with local stars and originated an enduring franchise tradition of wide-open, exciting offensive play. The problem was that the Downtown Coaches, far more businesspeople than football people, paradoxically had approached each game as "a weekly social event"[32] and ran an outfit that "lacked cohesive organization."[33] "Everybody was a coach, and everybody second-guessed at the board meetings held the day after we lost a game," Marshman lamented later, as he watched McBride give free rein to his own football people and take the Browns to success in Cleveland that the early Rams only could have dreamed about. "Each one of us had a play that should have been used and had it been used would have won the game for us."[34]

Financial strains especially took their toll. Marshman brought on partners $1,000 at a time to keep the franchise moving, and periodically he and co-owner Dan Hanna personally loaned the club additional spots of $1,000. Other owners were thriftier, however, and there was a revolt when it was suggested that all stockholders should buy tickets for employees in their businesses in order to help spark attendance; most of the investors apparently were not *that* invested in the team. So when Reeves offered to buy the franchise, "everybody said 'grab it,'" Marshman said. "It meant a small profit for each of us."[35] Shaken by the coming war, the first ownership group in Rams history sold out just years before the NFL began its meteoric rise.

Four-and-a-half years after the sale of the team to Reeves, Lipscomb, aglow at a celebratory dinner on the eve of the Rams' first championship game, admitted that "in the early days of split ownership there was some confusion about running the team."[36] But there was no confusion now: Reeves was in charge. He was majority owner and president and had a great deal of confidence in his ability to manage both the football and business sides of the operation. A good many things were about to change on the Cleveland Rams.

* * *

"*The public be pleased.*"[37] The sprightly phrase peppers the inaugural edition of *Ram Rumblings,* a fan newsletter published by the Rams' new ownership group in September 1941, compliments of the house: "The Price—Your Perusal." The public-be-pleased sentiment in fact appears a remarkable 27 times in only four pages as the club's new slogan and a stark contrast to a philosophy that "the public be damned—often the way the pay-going public is treated," the newsletter claimed.[38] Reeves and Levy clearly deduced that the chief failing of the previous group of owners had been fielding a pro football team for their own personal entertainment rather than for the paying public's. There would be no such failing this time. The franchise needed wins both on the field and at the ticket office if the Rams were to stay in Cleveland, and more so if Reeves and Levy eventually were to convince their new NFL colleagues to allow them to move the team to another city. Reeves and Levy made immediate announcements and changes.

Hired as Rams general manager was Billy Evans, who once was the youngest umpire in the Major Leagues, then served as the GM of the Cleveland Indians as the first executive to carry that official title with the team.[39] Evans had no practical experience in pro football but had been well known in the Cleveland area for decades and was credited with signing such stars as Bob Feller and Hal Trosky. With his hiring Reeves and Levy had "won the wholehearted support of the city's football fans," the *Plain Dealer* editorialized.⁴⁰

But it was just as likely a shrewder motive was at work. Reeves and Levy were "outsiders," *Plain Dealer* sports editor Sam Otis noted, "strongly suspected when they first took over" of planning to move the franchise out of Cleveland. Otis thought hiring Evans "went a long way toward allaying this fear."⁴¹

The new owners set up team headquarters on the fifth floor of the commanding Union Commerce Building downtown. There, Reeves decamped—on the rare occasions he was in Cleveland—in an office overlooking Euclid Avenue, with a framed print of Rams coach Dutch Clark's iconic gladiatorial photo on the wall behind him. As was his nature, Reeves mingled with local newspapermen alongside Levy, Evans, and some of the Rams players at an introductory gathering at the Hotel Cleveland at which they lauded the city's potential as a football town and spun visions of big crowds and a league title. In buying the Rams, Reeves had explained formally in *Rams Rumblings*, he and Levy acquired "a standard product to sell." "Good football" was their "merchandise," Reeves said, and the "brand of football that the Rams will furnish this fall will have an appeal." Hiring Evans was "the first step to sell our merchandise," and Reeves was confident "you can always sell the public a good product provided you make the proper approach."⁴²

Turning their sights to Cleveland Stadium, Reeves and Levy agreed with previous ownership that an intimate fan setting for football was difficult to achieve with the gridiron placed in the center of the monstrous horseshoe that their new team seemed destined to occupy. The Stadium, the *Plain Dealer* wrote, had "few if any bad seats" but "too few good ones."⁴³ Reeves and Levy were considerably less charitable: Cleveland Stadium "has never been a popular or satisfactory place to watch a game of football," their newsletter said flatly.⁴⁴ Whereas Marshman and company had tried pushing the gridiron toward the park's southwest corner for the Rams' NFL debut in 1937, Reeves and Levy attempted at "considerable expense"⁴⁵ to move the field in the opposite direction—toward the northeast corner, along the third-base line, where there was greater warmth and protection from winds that whipped in from Lake Erie. The shift would be short-lived and still would not remedy the Rams' attendance problems—nor could it do anything about the city's always-tempestuous late-autumn and early-winter weather.

The new owners pressed on. To assure a better flow of up-and-coming talent to Cleveland, Reeves bought a controlling interest in the Jersey City Giants, champions the previous year of the minor-league American Football

Association, and selected as the team's head coach former Cleveland Bulldogs star Benny Friedman. Then Rams coach Clark prevailed on Reeves and Levy to offer the Chicago Bears $15,000 for draft pick Tom Harmon, who opted instead for an immediate career in radio, later to join the Rams in L.A. It was apparent, however, that that the new owners—cost be damned—were "willing to spend money to give Cleveland a title contender,"[46] the *Plain Dealer*'s John Dietrich wrote. To Reeves and Levy it was an investment in a franchise that they reckoned now was "worth from $200,000 upwards,"[47] an estimate that must have stuck in the throats of the Downtown Coaches who just had accepted a check from the out-of-towners for perhaps two-thirds that amount.

Nevertheless the pair of owners seemed astonished at the expense involved in running a modern-day pro football team. True sons of retailers, they conducted inventory of their newly acquired stock, then took to the pages of *Ram Rumblings* to note that it "costs real money" to operate a big-league football team.[48] They would need to invest, for instance, in 75 pairs of football pants at $14 each for a total of more than $1,000, a considerable sum for the immediate prewar era. Seventy-five pairs of football shoes at $9 each came to another $675. Helmets were $15 each—another $600. Fifty regulation footballs at $8.50 each would cost $425. And for inclement weather, a not-uncommon occurrence in Cleveland, 40 coats with hoods would need to be acquired at $10 each. And the list went on for the financial edification of Rams fans who might otherwise be inclined to question high ticket prices or the team's difficulty in reaching financial solvency: the cost of medical and training supplies, laundry and dry cleaning, training camp, travel and hotel expenses, and then of course players' and coaches' salaries, running a "high-pressure front office" in preparation for a three-month season. "For nine months everything is going out and nothing [is] coming in," *Ram Rumblings* noted to the team's fans. Worse, "if you have a loser nothing much comes in during the playing season" either.[49]

And they did have a loser, as Reeves and Levy soon were to discover—in good part because of the imminent world war.

"Ready, Rams!"[50] ran a banner headline over a full-page photo of the team in offensive formation in the September 3, 1941, edition of the *Cleveland News*, and the Rams made an auspicious showing for the new bosses against the Steelers. Everything seemed brand-new on this day. Forty newspapermen from Pittsburgh and at least a dozen Ohio cities packed the freshly opened press box at the Akron Rubber Bowl, then considered one of the finest football facilities in the nation. Commissioner Layden shared a front-row field box with Paul Brown, a high-school coaching legend in

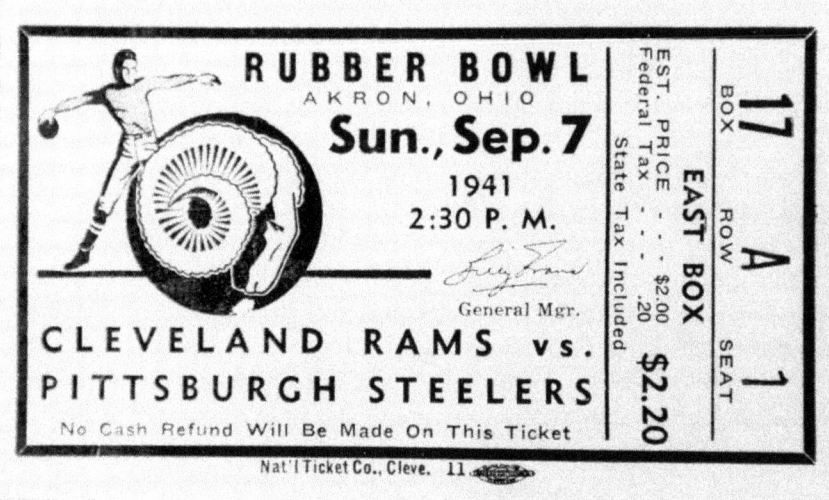

Daniel F. Reeves' first game as owner of the Cleveland Rams was a 1941 exhibition win over the Pittsburgh Steelers at Akron's Rubber Bowl. In attendance were NFL commissioner Elmer Layden and up-and-coming collegiate head coach Paul Brown (*Donald Gries Collection*).

the state and new head coach of the Ohio State Buckeyes. Brown a year later would win a national collegiate championship that would propel him to the professional ranks, so not surprisingly, he and Layden were observed to be "inseparables nearly all afternoon."[51] The Rams continued with their new blue-and-yellow color scheme that would define their image for decades to come. Even the regulation footballs—at $8.50 each—were new, and as they bounced into the stands they were swallowed up by the crowd, finally delaying the game until coach Clark took to the public address system to promise he would autograph a ball if it just were passed back down to the field for the duration of the game. It was.

Second-year back Dante Magnani riddled Pittsburgh on the opening kickoff as he scurried 93 yards for a quick score. Levy turned to Reeves, clapped him on the back so hard that he almost knocked the majority owner off his feet, and shouted jubilantly, "Is it this easy?"[52] Alas it was not. The Rams won 17–13 but the *Akron Beacon Journal* noted ominously that Rams star passer Parker Hall "was not at his pitching best,"[53] overshooting his targets repeatedly for only seven completions on 21 attempts. Hall had good reason for his middling performance. Long-limbed end Jim Benton briefly had left the pros that year to coach high-school football in Arkansas, while equally effective receiver Vic Spadaccini—coming off his best season ever—

now was in the military and playing for the Second Air Force Bombers of the Pacific Coast Service Football League,[54] never to return to the NFL. Olie Cordill, Cleveland's first-round draft pick the previous season, also had been yanked into the armed forces as the United States continued rearmament over mounting hostilities in Europe. The *New York Times* opined that "Uncle Sam has virtually wrecked the Cleveland Rams' backfield."[55]

All around the Rams it was a time of great change, some of it somber. The Rams were playing their last season in the increasingly outmoded wing offense as Clark boned up on and plotted an imminent switch to the Bears' feared T-formation offense. Art "Pappy" Lewis was in his final season with the team after being relegated to serving as an assistant on the team, following his flash-in-the-pan wins over the Bears and Packers as temporary head coach in 1938; near season's end he would announce he was leaving to coach at Washington and Lee College in Virginia, "reversing the trend of college coaches entering the pro ranks."[56] Power back Corby Davis returned to the team after a stint as a high school coach and made little impact, nor did Gaylon Smith, who suffered injuries after he was installed at fullback. Mucha, who ultimately passed on the AFL to sign with the Rams, came up short filling the vacancy left behind by Spadaccini, while tackle Riley Matheson, back after his year in Columbus and no longer mousetrapped by opposing linemen, broke his arm in the last game of an otherwise All-NFL season.

Only star running back Johnny Drake remained from the Rams' NFL debut in 1937, and he stepped up his pass receptions with 211 yards on 16 catches, but his yards-per-carry rushing average was well below what it had been in 1939 and 1940. He retired at the end of the season having played as many as 55 minutes of 60-minute games on a losing club, leaving the Rams a completely transformed organization, literally top to bottom, from the one he had joined four years earlier. He took a battering in his career, playing "too hard for his own good," wrote Franklin Lewis of the *Cleveland Press*,[57] but he was rewarded with a brand new car from the fans in appreciation at "Johnny Drake Day," which—much to the team's shame—resulted in a 14–0 blanking by the Detroit Lions amid boos from the 10,554 at Cleveland Stadium.

The fans' animus was merited. Following their defeat of the Steelers and a win over the Chicago Cardinals, the Rams lost every one of their remaining games to finish a hugely disappointing 2–9. It was the team's most lackluster showing since their disastrous debut year under Bezdek, and it was Clark's worst season ever in football. To goose ticket sales, entertainer Bob Hope, a native Clevelander and a future Rams investor with

Reeves, was summoned from Hollywood in early October for a promotional stunt as he donned a Rams helmet and sent a ceremonial opening kickoff "a scant 10 yards."[58] The Bears went on to drill the Rams 48–21 before 23,850 at Cleveland Stadium, but the game at least was good for the ticket office— with Hope on the card, it was the biggest gate the Rams had drawn to that time in Cleveland.

By the time the team faced a rematch with the Bears in Chicago, Clark was a defeated man, telling reporters "they'll probably beat us 100 to 0 and set a new National League scoring record."[59] The score was 31–13. But the Rams actually reached rock bottom in mid-November when the Giants, in retribution for a 13–0 home loss the year before, handed them the most lopsided defeat in their young history, 49–14. Rams end Johnny Wilson recalled an ardent reserve player being sent into the game, poking his head into the huddle, and yelling, "Come on, let's go! We'll kill 'em!"[60] Rams center Bill "Red" Conkright, thoroughly frustrated, punched him in the mouth.

Yet Cleveland apparently, and remarkably, had passed its audition with the team's new owners. Reeves announced just before Halloween that the Rams would be staying for the foreseeable future. "I will admit we were on the fence for a while," he said, "but we have made our decision."[61] Within a month the club's officials reported that the Rams' financial losses for the season would be slight. Reeves, flashing his characteristic wit, asked: "Where else could a team have lost nine in a row and still keep from losing enough dough to fill the United States mint?"[62] But foreboding omens loomed for those who looked more closely. *Plain Dealer* sports editor Otis asserted that "Cleveland football fans should be grateful" the Rams were staying and suggested the city still needed to prove it deserved a team. He said that it was up to local fans to "show [their] appreciation by generously patronizing" the Rams in their remaining two home games.[63] But they did not. Attendance barely surpassed 15,000—*total*—on the final two afternoons of the season.[64] The *Plain Dealer's* Gordon Cobbledick was reduced to seeing hope for the future in the fans' booing: It meant, he thought, "that somebody cared."[65]

In a year when Americans attended more NFL games than ever[66]— and in an era when major college teams could draw 50,000 fans or more per game while NFL teams were "lucky" to draw 25,000[67]—the Rams finished with the lowest per-game attendance in the league at 15,242, a nine-percent drop from the previous season.[68] The Cardinals, the next nearest, drew nearly 1,000 more fans per game, while the Giants averaged nearly 36,000 per contest and Washington more than 33,000. The Redskins notably built their attendance on season tickets, selling 15,200 and banking $155,000 by late September; the Rams by contrast were proud to report in early August that they had collected $4,000 in advance ticket sales.

As the *Cleveland Press*' Lewis noted, in the Rams' first five NFL years they "had some good players, some inefficient players. Some of the time they had teams good enough to play close games with the league leaders."[69] If Clevelanders were going to support the Rams, they were going to do so cautiously, one game at a time, perhaps for several years more. But who could see very far into the future, through so much global uncertainty? Two weeks after the Rams ended the season "with a sickening thud"[70] in a blanking by the Cardinals at Cleveland Stadium, the Japanese bombed Pearl Harbor and the United States entered World War II. President Franklin D. Roosevelt went to Congress to decry the Japanese attack as one that would live in infamy, and on that same day the Rams hired a new assistant coach named Charles "Chile" Walsh to succeed Lewis. At age 38, Walsh was a moon-faced, portly football veteran with slicked-back hair. He was a California native, a graduate of Hollywood High School, and the younger brother of Adam Walsh, head football coach at Bowdoin College. In a small handful of years the Walsh brothers would unite in Cleveland to become architects of the Rams' first championship ever and agents in the franchise's shift to California.

In the meantime the war would decimate team rosters even as the NFL carried on. The years of 1942, 1943, and 1944 were about to present the most challenging test for the franchise ever as the Rams dodged the worst fates that the war—and the rest of the league—could throw their way.

CHAPTER 8

The War Year, the Lost Year

On the day after Christmas 1941, Earl "Dutch" Clark left an apartment he and his family maintained in Cleveland and headed to the Rams' offices overlooking the busy intersection of Euclid Avenue and East Ninth Street. As head coach, director, and vice president of the team he felt especially responsible for the Rams' disappointing 2–9 record in 1941. This surely was not how Daniel F. Reeves and Fred Levy, Jr., wanted their tenure as the team's owners to begin, and Clark was about to make a very important decision about his career. On a holiday Friday that might have kept many Clevelanders at or near home, he stayed busy by holing up in the Rams' offices on the fifth floor of the Union Commerce building and dictating letters to prospective players that urged them to sign with the Rams, or at minimum to respond in some way with their reaction to the proposed contracts the team had sent them. "The new owners are desirous of rebuilding the team and making it over into a pennant contender just as quickly as possible," he stressed earnestly—hopefully—in one of his letters."[1]

But Clark, the Rams, and indeed the entire National Football League now had stiff competition. The United States was at war with Japan and Germany, and across the country young men in their athletic primes were receiving recruitment letters of a different kind: from Uncle Sam. As a consequence, many NFL players already accustomed to multiple identities as both football players and offseason employees received military titles too. Chet Adams, for instance, was a railroad detective in the offseason as well as a tackle on the 1942 Cleveland Rams, and with the arrival of the war he became a captain in the military police. Howard "Red" Hickey, Rams end in 1941 who reported baseball as his off-season occupation, added the title of Navy lieutenant and served 13 months of sea duty as a gunner on a Liberty cargo ship. Fullback Gaylon Smith sold cars when not playing football and

With their roster decimated by the start of World War II, Rams management gathered in their offices in Cleveland's Union Commerce Building in mid–December 1941 to review scouting reports. From left: head coach Earl "Dutch" Clark, owner Daniel F. Reeves (at desk), assistant coach Charles "Chile" Walsh, and business manager Mannie Eisner *(Donald Gries Collection/Cleveland News, Cleveland Press Collection)*.

soon became a coxswain at the Naval Ammunition Depot in Hastings, Nebraska. Fullback Corby Davis, who had walked a beat as a cop at Cleveland amusement attraction Euclid Beach Park, became a Second Infantryman rifleman who was wounded in France and awarded a Purple Heart. World War II, in fact, sheared 20 to 30 percent of nearly every NFL team's roster,[2] so much so that the main question was not why so many players were in the military but why pro football was playing its regular schedule at all. The answer came in no small part from President Franklin D. Roosevelt, who encouraged professional sports leagues to carry on as a diversion for the millions of civilians working in the industries that supported the Allies' war efforts.

As the war escalated and players in their prime began to go off to war, NFL roster holes came to be filled temporarily by aging players who came out of retirement—backs like Bill Lazetich of the Rams, and Bronko

Cleveland Rams back Gaylon Smith (44) eludes a tackler at Akron's Rubber Bowl in 1942 thanks to a block by Warren Plunkett (58), as the New York Giants' Ed Hiemstra (29) and Emmett Barrett (11) give chase. Note Barrett's embryonic version of a facemask (*The Cleveland Press Collection, Cleveland State University Library*).

Nagurski of the Chicago Bears. Many active players participated in games while they awaited their call-ups or after they had been discharged before war's end. Others continued their playing careers while supporting the war effort at home, often because they were withheld from military service due to medical conditions, or family situations, or both. Rams star end Jim Benton, for instance, was rejected for Navy service not only due to a heart murmur but also because he had dependents at home.

World War II hit pro football especially hard, with the highest casualty rates of any professional sports organization in America. An estimated 638 NFL players,[3] including 60 from the Cleveland Rams,[4] served in the war—the equivalent of the 10 teams' active 35-man rosters in peacetime nearly twice over. Of those players at least 20 died, including Al Blozis, who filled in at tackle for the New York Giants in the 1944 championship game while on leave from the Army and perished soon afterward in battle just months before the close of World War II in Europe.

Even among players who survived, the war left an enduring mark in ways big and small. Halfback Jim Gillette, who had played briefly for the Rams in 1940 before returning in 1944 and helping to power the team to its 1945 championship, was a lieutenant on a Navy convoy ship that was torpedoed in the North Atlantic at a time when German submarines were to sink more than 600 vessels in American-protected waters.[5] An inveterate sleepwalker, Gillette wandered his ship at night and one morning was found curled up just feet from the ship's edge. Gillette's son Walker Gillette, who followed Jim into the NFL as a first-round draft pick in 1970, recalls his father later scratching walls as he sleepwalked in the family's home. Jim had "crazy dreams,"[6] said his widow Marguerite Gillette, and the war certainly made his nighttime worse. But the NFL kept its lights burning for the duration of World War II, and in part because of this perseverance pro football cemented its place in American culture and enjoyed a surge in popularity when peace returned.

None of this, of course, was of immediate comfort or benefit to Rams coach Clark and his new assistant Charles "Chile" Walsh in early 1942, just as America's early war efforts in the south Pacific began with disastrous results in a battle defeat by the Japanese. On New Year's Eve 1941 Billy Evans had resigned abruptly as Rams general manager and returned to baseball after only one football season because he and Reeves were "too far apart on 1942 salary terms."[7] Evans's departure opened up an opportunity for Walsh, who proved to possess superb player evaluation and recruitment skills that would bring the Rams to contending status at last in the NFL. By early spring 1942 he was "combing the country for players and doing a fine job of it"[8] in Reeves' view, and his scouting work soon was to net the Rams their first championship.

Walsh was born in Des Moines, Iowa, in 1903. At the age of five, about the time he picked up his nickname from other children, he moved with his family to Hollywood, which in 1908 was a "quiet little California town of about 150 families."[9] By age 13 he was a stocky kid organizing, coaching, and promoting a football team at Blessed Sacrament Parochial School. He was a fullback at Hollywood High School, then followed older brother Adam Walsh to the University of Notre Dame where he played end under coach Knute Rockne. In the late 1920s he came back east to coach at St. Louis University before briefly co-owning the short-lived Cincinnati Reds-St. Louis Gunners. When the NFL revoked the St. Louis franchise due to team debt and the Gunners folded in 1935, he wandered off to Florida to join a real estate and hotel management firm, only to be lured back to football in 1940 as an assistant coach for the Chicago Cardinals. The following year Reeves wooed him away from the Cardinals with a "fat contract,"[10] bringing him to the Rams to help Clark implement a modified version of the Bears' famed T-formation offense.

Walsh had plenty of "zip,"[11] according to Rams blocking back Warren Plunkett, and like assistant coach Art "Pappy" Lewis before him he did most of the talking for the Rams' quiet head coach. Walsh in fact was the team's great "orator," delivering a "rousing speech"[12] in October 1942 to guests of the Cleveland Touchdown Club during which he overshadowed a brief address by Clark by providing insights into the Bears' revolutionary offense, explaining enthusiastically that "the chief value of the T-man in motion as the Bears use it is that they force their opponents into a man-for-man defense and they have a marked superiority man for man over any team they play."[13] Attendees may have been left to wonder who truly was leading the team, Walsh or Clark.

Walsh, in fact, was about to implement the Rams' own version of a man-to-man, personally taking it upon himself to rebuild the team player by player and offset the massive advantage the league's powerhouses held over second-division teams like Cleveland. He scoured college football programs across the country for top-flight talent and set his sights on a postwar period when the Rams would have durable long-term success. By his own admission one of the "impractical dreamers,"[14] he foresaw a day when the NFL might play in covered stadiums that protected the game from inclement weather and extended the season so owners could pay players better salaries. He dared even to envision a time when pro football might play on weekdays as well as on Sundays.

8. The War Year, the Lost Year

None of Walsh's bright vision was evident in the Rams' training camp in August 1942, however. The U.S. government just had warned college students that a "youth draft"[15] might be imminent. Reeves and Levy had "made a determined effort to strengthen the club, but soon ran into the war," the *Cleveland Plain Dealer* noted. "A host of fine talent was lined up on paper, but most of it disappeared into the armed forces."[16] One example was 1942 first-round pick Jack Wilson, a halfback from Baylor who enlisted in the service and did not play until 1946.

Another was "Indian" Jack Jacobs, a six-feet-one, 186-pound Native American back whom the Rams selected out of Oklahoma in the second round in 1942. Jacobs was "a great runner and passer" and "the only player I've ever seen that could kick 70 yards in the air," recalled Woody Strode,[17] who played for the Rams in their first post–Cleveland season. Strode was a teammate of Jacobs on the March Field Fliers, a service football team in California, and remembered a typical outcome of a Jacobs punt being that "the ball would just hang in the sky, [giving] us time to get downfield. And I don't remember any fair catches being allowed; I think we just nailed the receiver."[18] On September 27, 1942, Jacobs threw two touchdown passes and booted several "miraculous punts"[19] as the Rams defeated the Lions in Detroit for the first time in their history. In only eight games that season Jacobs tossed six touchdown passes, tied Smith in fielding the most interceptions on the team, and was leading the league in punting[20] with a 42.3-yard average when he was called into the Air Corps. Three years later he would return to the Rams in a cameo role during their 1945 title season, then go on to play for the Redskins and Packers before leaving the NFL after the 1949 season. But as a highly promising rookie in 1942 he was unavailable to Cleveland for several wartime years.

Former Rams star Johnny Drake had retired for good, turning down a generous $10,000 offer from the Philadelphia Eagles to return to football. Vic Spadaccini, Rudy Mucha, and Hickey all were in the service. Even Rams minority owner Levy now was in the military, at a base in Dayton, Ohio. Still, the Rams retained a solid core of players who would lead the team to a respectable 5–6 record and third place in the Western Division. Parker Hall, the Rams' league MVP in 1939, returned for another season, "entrenched"[21] as the team's quarterback and slowly learning the Rams' new modified T-formation system and the nearly 100 plays in their growing playbook. He would show a tendency to scramble out of the pocket until finally he was hit so hard that his helmet was knocked off; Plunkett, charged with blocking for Hall, looked down at the quarterback and told him plainly, "Stay in the pocket and that won't happen."[22] After the season ended, Hall enlisted in the Navy and would play only one more season of pro football, with the new San Francisco 49ers of the All-America Football Conference.

Other stalwarts of the 1942 club included Benton, Adams, Davis, Smith, and fan favorite Riley Matheson. But none perhaps carried the team that year more than Dante Magnani. Smallish at five-foot-10 and 170 pounds, with a chiseled face and dark wavy hair, Magnani was a "fireball"[23] who paced the Rams in rushing yards and scoring and finished behind only ends Benton and Ben Hightower in receiving yards.[24] On September 13, 1942, in a season opener against the Cardinals at a neutral site in Buffalo, Magnani tore off a gain of 71 yards, one longer than any rush from scrimmage in the NFL the previous season,[25] and was pulled down just short of the goal line. The Rams failed to punch the ball in and lost 7–0, but Magnani, in his last year of playing until 1946 because of military service, was off to an All-NFL season.

A week later in Akron the Rams went on a passing rampage against the Eagles as Johnny Wilson hauled in a 45-yard touchdown pass from Hall and Jack Boone grabbed a 48-yard scoring throw from Jacobs as the Rams downed Philadelphia 24–14. It was the last Rams game that Reeves would see for some time; that same day the team's majority owner received word he was to report to the Air Corps training station in Miami and be sworn in as a second lieutenant. With both Reeves and Levy in the service, Walsh effectively was in charge.

The Rams suffered their customary losses to league powers the Chicago Bears, Washington Redskins, and Green Bay Packers, with a U.S. Army War Show fittingly tearing up the turf at Cleveland Stadium just before the Bears did much the same to the home team. The Rams fell to a record of 2–4 as the war news continued: Chicago's George Halas announced he was re-entering the Navy to bring the tally of NFL owners in the service to six, now also including Dan Topping of the Brooklyn Dodgers, Alexis Thompson of the Eagles, and Wellington Mara of the New York Giants along with the Rams' Reeves and Levy. Questions about the league's immediate future grew louder.

As the season steamed into its second half, Magnani again picked up the Rams with the team's sole touchdown in a 7–3 win over the Cardinals in Cleveland Stadium. Levy was on leave and on hand the following week to see his team shut out the Dodgers in Ebbets Field 17–0. With a mark of 4–4 and three games to go, the Rams were poised for their first winning record in six NFL seasons, but their usual nemeses Green Bay and Chicago stood in the way. Given the Packers' dominance of the era, they had had some trouble with the scrappy Rams in three prior meetings in Cleveland, outscoring them by only four total points and walking away with a tie and two very hard-earned—even lucky—wins. Cleveland figured its time was due. Not this time; not yet. Don Hutson, in the midst of a record-setting MVP year in which he was "nearly impossible to stop,"[26] caught three touchdown passes as Green Bay dominated in Cleveland Stadium 30–12. The Bears similarly dispatched the Rams handily with an epic 47–0 win at Wrigley Field.

But the Rams closed out the season at home on November 15, 1942, with an uplifting 27–7 victory over Detroit, sweeping the season series from the Lions in what would turn out to be Clark's final victory as an NFL head coach. Hall, in his last appearance in Cleveland as a member of the Rams, threw three touchdown passes, one to Magnani. Still, the game was played before an embarrassingly small assembly of 4,039—only five percent of the capacity of cavernous Cleveland Stadium. A few days later *Plain Dealer* sportswriter Gordon Cobbledick wondered why "the Rams are ignored," why they seemed to have "no appeal except to small groups of loyal followers."[27] Not surprisingly the team would schedule no more regular- or postseason games in Cleveland Stadium until their 1945 championship match three years later.

Still, there were small signs of hope. At the end of the season Adams and Magnani joined former Ram Chuck Cherundolo as selections to play in the All-Star Game against the league champion Redskins. Matheson, the undrafted lineman who once showed up at training camp with only a worn-out bag and a toothbrush, was the first Cleveland player since Drake in 1940 to be named first-team All-Pro by the Associated Press. The Rams may have been a hardscrabble team, but the Bears, even as they had throttled Cleveland in two meetings that season, made particular note of two emerging stars on their roster: Magnani and Benton.

* * *

Dutch Clark had enough. Enough losing. Enough frustration. Reeves and Levy wanted him back as head coach for the 1943 season, but after the holidays Clark allowed his contract to expire and returned home to Colorado Springs. Then on March 10, 1943, he sent word to the *Plain Dealer* that he had "advised Mr. Reeves not to consider renewal of my contract due to uncertain conditions. Possibilities elsewhere seem greater."[28] It was cryptic, but Clark definitely was through. He never was much of a believer in the pro game; he thought most players peaked in their junior years in college and rarely improved after that. He confided to friends that he "found the coaching job irksome"[29] and greatly missed his playing days with the

Portsmouth Spartans and Detroit Lions. But perhaps as much as anything he despaired of the Rams ever truly challenging the Bears and Packers for the Western Division title. With a final overall record of 16–26–2 he bowed out of the Rams' head coaching position under his own power rather than be removed against his will as his predecessors Art Lewis and Hugo Bezdek had been. He recommended Walsh as his replacement, then departed for military service. Beyond his pickup of free agent Matheson, his "ultimate failure in Cleveland came down to his inability to draft good players," wrote Clark biographer Chris Willis.[30] Like Lewis and Bezdek—indeed like Rams founder Damon "Buzz" Wetzel before them—Clark never coached in the NFL again.

Yet Clark may have been as astounded as anyone when, less than three years after his resignation, the Rams swept both the Bears and the Packers on their way to the Western crown as they were powered in no small part by the player scouting of Clark's own hand-picked replacement, Chile Walsh. In marked contrast to Clark, Walsh had a distinct eye for talent, and while he was in fact technically elevated from assistant to head coach in the first of many such internal promotions in Reeves' long career as Rams owner, he never actually coached a single down. The ink on his one-year contract was dry for not quite three weeks when Reeves and Levy asked him to represent them at the NFL meeting in Chicago on April 5, 1943. There, he dropped a bombshell on league: The Cleveland Rams were going to suspend operations for the duration of the war.

Reeves certainly was aware that attendance at college football games in 1942 was down a full 25 percent from the pre–Pearl Harbor season of 1941,[31] and that fan support for baseball's Cleveland Indians had plummeted the previous season by 300,000 tickets, the largest drop of any team in the Major Leagues[32] due in good part to star pitcher Bob Feller's enlistment in the Navy. Reading the mood of the customer from his lieutenant's post at an Air Corps facility near Syracuse, New York, the public-be-pleased Reeves likely thought that if the Indians, the number-one sports attraction in Cleveland, could suffer a drop in attendance, the Rams' fate could be much worse. Surely his peers in the NFL would follow his lead in seeing the wisdom of suspending operations in wartime. They did not. The other owners, a powerful few of whom were a good bit older than Reeves and had nursed the young league through the depths of the Depression, voted to continue steadfastly through the war. Even the hard-hit Philadelphia and Pittsburgh franchises merged that year to create a team informally called the Steagles, bringing to temporary fruition the all–Pennsylvania squad that Art Rooney and Bert Bell had envisioned in December 1940.

There were dark insinuations that the Rams franchise had yet to put up sufficient earnest money to be competitive, that they were riding on the coattails of the more successful franchises, and that the dilettante Reeves was impatient and petulant, hoping to bring to a temporary halt a competitive game that clearly he was losing. The other owners would not be "stampeded" into sidelining their teams along with the Rams, an official at a competing club said under condition of anonymity, because "it is a long time before any money has to be placed on the table to indicate you mean serious business. You can play cards for a long time as long as every draw in the game is a free one."[33] Recurrent rumors spread that the Rams were for sale or would be moved, to either Cincinnati or Baltimore. "If the Rams do quit Cleveland," an April 1943 Associated Press story warned, "they will be leaving very fertile soil where, after the war, someone else will reap the harvest."[34]

The league indeed was evolving rapidly. Helmets now were mandatory for all players. A new substitution rule just implemented would allow for the creation of separate offensive and defensive units and special teams, a move toward platooning that would reserve players' energy through a game and increase its speed and excitement. And potential new ownership groups were stirring. Arthur "Mickey" McBride, eventual founding owner of the Cleveland Browns, failed in an attempt to buy the Rams from Reeves in 1942. Ted Collins, manager of star singer Kate Smith and soon-to-be owner of the expansion Boston Yanks, followed him in 1943, also to no avail. Walsh was left to shoo off rumors and prospective buyers until Reeves and Levy issued a definitive statement that they were "not interested in offers of any kind for the purchase of the [Rams] franchise."[35] *Plain Dealer* writer John Dietrich saw reassurances in the team's dormancy and in Walsh having said "nothing of shifting the Cleveland franchise to some other city" that "Reeves and Levy do not intend to desert Cleveland without making another try here."[36] But sports editor Sam Otis sensed a lack of long-term commitment, writing presciently that he was "not optimistic" there would be a Cleveland Rams team after the war.[37]

With the Rams halting operations in 1943, the NFL held a dispersal draft of eleven of Cleveland's current and newly drafted players. Like orphans sent to foster homes, Rams players temporarily joined other teams. Matheson, Hightower, and guard Roy Stuart went to Detroit. Tackle Joe Pasqua, end Joe Gibson, and center Bill "Red" Conkright joined Washington. Tackle Jake Fawcett was shipped to Brooklyn, while Adams joined the Packers. Steve Pritko, a newly drafted end who would rank among the heroes of the 1945 title season, was assigned to the New York Giants. And Magnani and Benton joined the Bears.

Benton's 13 receptions with Chicago in the 1943 season would be far and away the lowest of his stellar career,[38] but he and quarterback Sid Luckman "formed a deadly combination in key situations"[39] for the Bears. Teamed with Magnani and former Ram Bob Snyder, Benton helped power Chicago to the 1943 championship game in which the Bears trounced Washington 41–21 at Wrigley Field. There, Benton caught a 26-yard scoring pass from Luckman, while Magnani grabbed two—one for 36 yards, the second for 66 yards—as the touchdown total of the two exiled Rams matched that of the entire Redskins offense. Snyder added five extra points as three onetime Rams accounted for a total of 23 points, more than half the champion Bears' total. It was abundantly apparent that the talent the Rams been assembling for its skilled positions could well be championship-caliber—*if* management surrounded its skilled players with a solid supporting cast as the Bears had done.

Rams ownership quickly realized its error in suspending operations. On September 21, 1943, only weeks into the team's exiled season and just five months after Walsh told the league the Rams would be mothballed for the duration of the war, he announced the team would resume play in 1944. "As things have turned out," Walsh said as he shuffled before newspaper reporters, "the other clubs have been able to carry on."[40] The Cleveland media was quizzical. "Prize for the worst guess of the year must go to the owners of the Cleveland Rams, who thought that there would be no professional football this year, and that if there were the cit[i]zens would ignore it,"[41] Cobbledick wrote.

Sensing good times ahead, Reeves on December 9, 1943, bought out Levy and became sole owner of the franchise, beginning a short, rarified period in which he would have total control of a football team as he had wanted since he was a boy. Reeves and Levy remained friends and business associates, but once the team was in Los Angeles, Reeves would become so financially strained that he would have to cut Levy and other investors back into ownership shares—a compromise that his son Dan Reeves, Jr., said was "the beginning of the end"[42] of his father's idyllic period as a pro football owner. But that was several years away. For now Reeves was sole captain of his ship, and he appointed Walsh as his number-two with full latitude to rebuild the team in his own continued military absence. The Cleveland Rams were back and, as soon would be evident, they were on a quest for vengeance.

Part III: On the Up and Up

CHAPTER 9

Twenty Months to a Title

It was the spring of 1944, just weeks before the Allied invasion of Normandy and the beginning of the liberation of Europe, and the Cleveland Rams franchise felt set upon by the "open animosity"[1] of the rest of the National Football League. With $100,000 in financial losses to date since buying the team in 1941,[2] Rams owner Daniel F. Reeves realized that discontinuing play for the 1943 season because of the war had been a mistake and he wanted back in for 1944. The other NFL owners agreed to the team's return but, by the Rams' accounts, seemed to have a desire to see the Rams pay for their one-year lapse in operation—perhaps even for their lack of faith in the league's capacity to survive the war. Their severity would provoke the Rams into a near-manic quest for survival and success.

The owners' initial preference was that Cleveland remain "out of the picture for this year—and probably for good," as the *Cleveland Plain Dealer*'s Alex Zirin described it.[3] With the Yanks starting up as the first NFL franchise in Boston since 1936, and with two teams again to merge because of wartime-depleted rosters, the league would have been comprised of an even 10 teams, five in each division, without the Rams. Allowing Cleveland back into the fold would upset the balance of the league's schedule.

NFL commissioner Elmer Layden nevertheless approved Cleveland's re-entry—but he gave the Rams a provisional schedule that would have had them playing three games in Akron and only one in Cleveland. Rams general manager Charles "Chile" Walsh resisted: The Rams already were struggling to build a fan base in Cleveland, he argued; hosting only one home game in 1944 after taking all of 1943 off would mean the team practically was disappearing in its home city, and this might spell doom for the franchise. Layden was sympathetic and pivoted to a second option: The Rams could merge with the Steelers just as the Philadelphia Eagles had done the year before in creating the so-called Steagles—an expeditious creation meant to benefit two war-torn rosters. With a Rams-Steelers merger (the Cleve-Pitts?), *two* games could be played in Cleveland. Walsh again objected vigorously. A Cleveland-Pittsburgh union was nearly as unthinkable for the Rams then as it would be for generations of Browns and Steelers fans to come. Layden, running out of options, figured Pittsburgh owner Art Rooney already had been amenable to a merger, so for the 1944 season he matched the Steelers with the Chicago Cardinals as the Eagles returned to stand-alone status. The so-called Card-Pitts, jocularly known as the Carpets, would go on to a record of 0–10 that season as "perhaps the most hapless football team in league history."[4]

But Cleveland was not off scot-free. In payment for allowing the Rams to return to the league as a self-contained Cleveland franchise, Layden would have no choice but to turn them into a "roving"[5] franchise in 1944—that is, essentially to make them a road team in a year when traveling conditions were arduous because of the ongoing war. This too was unacceptable to Walsh, and a "stormy"[6] meeting broke out in Philadelphia and continued into 3:30 a.m. on the morning of April 23, 1944. The league's final offer was that the Rams could remain intact in Cleveland but would play only three of their ten regular-season games at home. Walsh continued to haggle for more, and negotiations remained deadlocked until he finally asked Layden to make a ruling. The commissioner replied that a majority vote would carry.

Cleveland was outvoted 10 to one—unanimously stonewalled by the rest of the league. The up-and-coming Rams would play only three of their regular-season games in Cleveland in 1944. It felt like a punishment, and Walsh was angry and defiant. "We got the crumbs off the table," he grumbled. He vowed the Rams were in the NFL to stay, and promised furthermore that "in one year after the war we'll have a fighting, slashing, smart team capable of giving anyone a run for their money."[7] Walsh would be true to his word, and months ahead of schedule: By the end of the following season, only four months after the conclusion of World War II and 20 months after the league's other owners were surprised to see them return, the Rams would be NFL champions.

But first they had to overcome long odds. Walsh had only ten players and 111 days to field a team in time for the season opener[8] with no particular short-term relief from the 1944 player draft. In a repeat of 1937, when as an expansion team they received the tenth and final selection in a draft that could have landed them eventual Hall of Famer Sammy Baugh, the Rams in their re-entry to the NFL again selected last. As a consequence they again missed out on a chance to take a future-legend quarterback in the first round—the NFL rights to Otto Graham instead went to Detroit, and Steve Van Buren was the property of Philadelphia.

Walsh was philosophical and set his sights longer term for the Rams. He decided not to worry about missed chances at blue-chip players and the wartime draft's numerous 4-Fs—the graduating seniors who could be counted on to play immediately due to their low military classifications but who likely were not the highest-caliber players. Let the upper-division teams take this second-tier talent, he reasoned; they needed it most immediately to "maintain their station."[9] Instead he focused on finding and securing high-quality, lesser-known prospects who were likely to be available after the war—players like Bob Waterfield, a non–All-American quarterback who had missed the 1943 collegiate season because of military service, then returned to the University of California, Los Angeles for one more season. To track down such scarce talent, Walsh traveled through the South, West, and "Big Ten territory"[10] and employed scouts around the country, one of whom turned up at a UCLA game in California. Jane Russell, a Hollywood actress who married Waterfield during his college years, recalled the two of them meeting with "a small gray-haired man who was a scout for the Cleveland Rams."[11] Walsh also offered to anyone in the general public a $50 bonus for turning up an "acceptable player"[12] available for 1944 and was deluged with replies from around the country. Many came from women and girls who recommended players with no more than high-school experience, none of whom panned out.

Nevertheless Walsh believed he had found some "sleepers"[13] as he headed into the 1944 draft. First he selected Tony Butkovich, an All-American fullback from Purdue and the leading Big Ten scorer in 1943,[14] never knowing the young Marine had died in battle on the south Pacific island of Okinawa just a day before. (Weeks in fact would pass before even Butkovich's parents were notified of their son's death.) In the second round Walsh took Gil Bouley, a tackle from Boston College who would join the team in 1945 and remain a mainstay of the Rams' line through 1950. And in the fifth round, with the 42nd overall pick, Walsh selected Waterfield. Although some pundits on the West Coast had told Walsh the passer was "temperamental"[15] and something of an erratic performer, Waterfield would go on to join first-round picks Graham and Van Buren in the Pro Football Hall of Fame. The *Plain Dealer*'s Gordon Cobbledick was well pleased with the Rams' direction and told a doubting city as much. "The rest of you can do as you like," he wrote, "but I'm putting in my order for a couple of season tickets for the first postwar campaign of the Cleveland Rams."[16]

First, however, the team would need a leader on its sideline. Walsh, the would-be head coach whose promotion after Earl "Dutch" Clark's resignation was thwarted by the Rams' suspension of play in 1943, now decided to focus solely on his duties as general manager. So the Rams, after six NFL seasons of employing the likes of old college hand Hugo Bezdek and pro veterans Art "Pappy" Lewis and Clark, opted for a unique direction: a head coach who had experience at both the pro and college levels—and for a time, simultaneously.

Aldo T. "Buff" Donelli briefly led the Steelers in 1941 but also somehow managed to hang onto his day job as head coach at Duquesne University. In the morning he tutored the college Dukes to what would be an undefeated season; in the afternoon he grabbed a bite to eat, hopped in his car, and traveled across town to pilot the Steelers to an opposite result: an unbroken string of losses. When Sunday, November 9, 1941, arrived he faced a dilemma: take a two-day train ride to California to lead the 6–0 Dukes against St. Mary's in the Bay Area, or make a short jaunt east as the 0–5 Steelers visited the Philadelphia Eagles. Donelli—a "smallish" man with dark eyes and a nose whose contours were altered by "innumerable knees and elbows and headguards, and maybe a fist or two"[17]—chose the train ride to California with the Dukes, and left leadership of the professional Steelers to his assistant. Layden was incensed and forced Rooney to fire Donelli, thus ending the coach's short tenure as the only man since 1933 to lead college and NFL teams simultaneously.

Yet this was but one of two "singular footnotes"[18] in Donelli's biography: He also was a legend in soccer.

Donelli was born, like Rams founders Homer Marshman and Damon "Buzz" Wetzel, in Appalachia—in Morgan Township, Greene County, southwest of Pittsburgh, and near Pennsylvania's southwestern-most tip intersecting with Ohio and West Virginia. He was the fifth of an Italian miner's 11 children, of whom Aldo's younger brother Allen played halfback for the hometown Steelers. But it was Buff who turned out to be "a sportsman for many seasons."[19] Even though he knew soccer was "second fiddle"[20] to football in the coal-mining region of his birth, it was the sport he most loved. He acquired a reputation as a lethal goal-scorer and attracted a contract offer from the English Football League even as he pursued a football career as a Duquesne halfback and ambidextrous punter/kicker. His finest hours as a soccer player came in the 1934 World Cup tournament, when in a qualification game in Rome before Italian dictator Benito Mussolini and 10,000 spectators, he scored an astonishing four goals as the United States shocked Mexico 4–2 to enter the tournament bracket. Donelli and his teammates were eliminated the following game by eventual world champion Italy, but Donelli had scored another goal—the only American to do so in that year's competition. Again he was offered a lucrative pro contract, this time by one of the top Italian clubs, and again he turned it down, choosing instead a coaching career in red-blooded American football.

Donelli initially succeeded in the college coaching ranks as well as he had playing soccer. By 1941 his squads at Duquesne had accumulated a record of 29-4-2 in four seasons,[21] then the university suspended the sport for the duration of World War II. Out of work with both the Steelers and the Dukes, he caught on briefly as an assistant with the NFL's Brooklyn Dodgers, until Walsh, on the evening before the Fourth of July 1944—a month after D-Day, and weeks before an unsuccessful attempt on Adolf Hitler's life—enticed him to coach in Cleveland.

Donelli, standing five-feet-eight and at age 37 still trim at 165 pounds, told reporters that as coach of the Rams he would dispense with old-style play and shun "butting heads against the wall."[22] Instead he would spread the Rams' offense to weaken the solidity of the opposing defense, deploy the T-formation with a man in motion, sometimes send an end out for a pass, or a halfback, or two ends—all with an objective of making his system "as flexible as possible" and able to respond to any defense. "Speed afoot and quick reflexes are the most prized qualities that Donelli seeks in a player," the *Cleveland Press* reported.[23] He was pointing the Rams toward the future of pro football.

Donelli would meet with immediate if qualified success as the Rams once again finished one win shy of a .500 record. Two years on, with a championship trophy in their possession, the team would look back on Donelli's rebuilding of their franchise in 1944 as a key chapter in their "story of rags to riches,"[24] and it is true that only ten players were available when the Rams elected to resume play. But it was a solid core, especially on the line, with six holdovers from the 1942 squad[25] including star guard Riley "Rattlesnake" Matheson, back from his exiled year in Detroit and primed to power the Rams for four more seasons. Center Bill "Red" Conkright, like Matheson a stalwart presence with the Rams organization since 1939, returned from a season in Brooklyn and Washington for what would be his final campaign as a player before he became a scout and assistant coach for the team. Tackle Jake Fawcett came back from Brooklyn, and end Joe Gibson returned from Washington. And of course there was end Jim Benton, back in the fold after starring with the champion Chicago Bears in 1943.

By late summer Walsh had dipped repeatedly into his thick dossier of scouting reports and managed to sign 14 other players. It was such a sudden

The 1944 Cleveland Rams went 4–6 but were the nucleus of the championship squad the following year. On the line (from left): Steve Pritko, Jake Fawcett, Chuck Riffle, Bill "Red" Conkright, Riley "Rattlesnake" Matheson, Mike "Mo" Scarry, and Floyd Konetsky. In the backfield (from left): Mike Kabealo, John Karrs, Walt West, and Tommy Colella *(Donald Gries Collection/Cleveland News, Cleveland Press Collection)*.

abundance of newly recruited Rams that Walsh felt compelled to tell reporters, "We've got so many new players you can't tell what they're going to do."[26] The *Cleveland Press*, as a way of helping its readership keep tabs on the team's new makeup, ran a series of short player biographies called "Know Your New Rams."[27]

One of the featured players was Steve Pritko, an end drafted out of Villanova in 1943. When the Rams suspended play that year and prompted a dispersal draft, Pritko was shipped off to the New York Giants for his rookie NFL season. Back with the Rams, he was six-feet-two and a solid 207 pounds, with a square jaw, curly hair, and a physique that the *Press* told its readers was "Adonis-like."[28] He had been born in Pennsylvania to immigrant parents from Austria-Hungary who could not speak English, and he signed his father's twice-monthly $30 paychecks from the local slate quarry. But it seems that even with his master's degree from Columbia University and his experience teaching high-school English, history, algebra, and biology he never completely shook his immigrant origins. Seventy years after he joined the Rams, Marguerite Gillette, widow of teammate Jim Gillette, still remembered that Pritko "talked funny."[29]

Another important Rams signing in 1944 was Mike "Mo" Scarry. With a "big, round face" and "a prominent, determined jaw,"[30] he had made history in 1939 by participating in the nation's first televised football game ever: a matchup between Waynesburg and Fordham that was beamed to hundreds, and possibly thousands, of sets in the New York area.[31] Scarry mostly remembered that game for television cables that snaked along the sideline and repeatedly tripped the players. But in another contest, against Duquesne, he made such a vivid impression on Donelli that the coach signed him to the Rams as soon as he had been discharged from the U.S. infantry in North Africa. He succeeded Conkright as the team's center and locked down the middle of what was gelling into a championship-caliber line. Car-less and barely eking out a living, he would stretch his $325-per-game pay by taking the streetcar to and from practice, just a blue-collar guy with a slightly bent nose. It would be broken fully nine times by 1948.

Joining Scarry would be back and kicker Albie Reisz, an undrafted local from Lorain, Ohio, who would make a key play in the 1945 title game. But four other signings just before the start of the 1944 season had a particular impact on the Rams' emergence as a legitimate contender. First, Donelli acquired back Tommy Colella from the Detroit Lions in what the *Cleveland Press* thought was to that time "perhaps the most fruitful deal ever put over by the local club."[32] Originally drafted by Detroit out of Canisius College in 1942, Colella had been unhappy there as backup to star tailback Frankie Sinkwich, and he demanded a trade. In Cleveland he joined Reisz in tossing 12 of the Rams' 13 touchdown passes in 1944. He also was a great runner, finishing second in team rushing, just behind Walter West, with 208 yards and three touchdowns.[33] Colella's greatest asset was his speed—or his "jet,"[34] as Paul Brown was wont to call it when he later coached Colella to even greater heights with the Cleveland Browns.

Meanwhile, welcomed back to the Rams fold were two one-time nascent stars who had been swept away by wartime. Jim Gillette, the Virginia halfback who had played briefly for the team in 1940 before entering the Navy, rejoined as a runner and punt and kick returner and would put in a decisive performance in the 1945 championship game. Taking the other halfback spot across from Gillette was Fred Gehrke, who was on the Rams' roster briefly in 1940 in a mostly undistinguished role before he left to become an aircraft illustrator in California, finally to "acquire poise"[35] with the Los Angeles Bulldogs of the Pacific Coast Football League.

But the team's marquee returnee was end Jim Benton. As 1944 began, Benton was summoned to a pre-induction physical examination in Little Rock, Arkansas, and looked as if he might be sent off to war; but in a rare spot of positive war-related news for the Rams he was classified 4-F and deemed available to play. Initially he was evasive about whether he would return to the Rams; he managed a restaurant in Arkansas, and much like the NFL owners he initially feared there would be a shortage of available help that fall. But in time his concerns were answered and he reported to training camp at Hiram College in Ohio just days before the regular season opened.

With the Rams' roster nearly complete, the team was reported to look "hot"[36] in training camp—possibly the hottest in the league—as it prepared for a "gantlet"[37] of a schedule that would send them on the road for seven of their ten games as a possible "punitive measure"[38] for not having operated in 1943. The Rams did not know that forces that would jeopardize their future in Cleveland and would mount a legitimate threat to the NFL were gathering 300 miles away in Chicago.

* * *

The American Football League that had midwifed the Rams franchise was but one of many failed attempts to challenge the status quo in pro football. Since at least 1935, the NFL, with its finite number of teams and often-high bar of entry, had been viewed as prime for competition, and few felt this way as much as Arch Ward, *Chicago Tribune* sportswriter and a force behind Major League Baseball's and college football's all-star games. In 1944 he turned his sights to pro football and grew certain that it was time for a second league—an American League to balance the National League as in baseball—with the two playing off for a championship. It was a vision of what 20 years later would become the Super Bowl.

As Ward promoted the concept of a new rival league to the NFL to be called the All-America Football Conference, Arthur "Mickey" McBride became intrigued, began to feel as if owning a pro football team might be in his future. Nearly three decades earlier he had come to Cleveland when the father of Dan Hanna, Jr., one day to be a founding owner of the Rams, had hired him to be a "two-fisted newspaper circulation executive"[39] for his paper the *Cleveland News*. By October 1940, McBride's son was a freshman at the University of Notre Dame and the sole reason McBride attended a Fighting Irish football game—probably a 61–0 shellacking of Carnegie Tech.[40] If so, it was the first football game that McBride ever had seen.[41]

Exhilarated by the spectacle, McBride sped 250 miles back to Cleveland the following day so he could watch Clark's Rams in what probably was a 26–14 downing of the Chicago Cardinals. McBride became a football fan on the spot, but probably he also was puzzled by a sparse turnout that Sunday—only 13,363 in 78,000-seat Cleveland Stadium. This must have been due, he seems to have deduced, not to the game itself, which clearly was exciting, but to a lack of good marketing. Very soon he grew certain that "a sound team and proper promotion could transform Cleveland into a good football city."[42] So with an innovative business mind—he was among the first taxicab operators in the nation to test the possibilities of radio dispatching[43]—and secure in a diversified fortune he had made in real estate, radio stations, printing, and a race wire syndicate, he offered to buy the Rams from Reeves in 1942. It was his way of ensuring Cleveland would continue to have a pro football team among its civic treasures.

Reeves rejected the offer.

If McBride could not buy Reeves' team in Cleveland, he would start one that would compete with Reeves in the same market. When the AAFC was announced in Chicago in September 1944, just as the NFL was set to kick off its new season, McBride was identified as the owner of the league's new Cleveland franchise. He knew next to nothing about football, but very likely Creighton Miller—nephew of Four Horseman Don Miller, All-American halfback at Notre Dame, and eventually lawyer for the Browns and an organizer of the NFL's players' union—had "talked him into football, and gotten him interested," said Robert D. Gries, later a Browns minority owner with Art Modell.[44]

One can only speculate what course pro football history may have taken if McBride had succeeded in convincing Reeves to sell the team. The Rams franchise might well have stayed in Cleveland, with the on-field success and fan-friendly promotion that became hallmarks of McBride's Browns. The team might never have had to leave for Los Angeles (and then for St. Louis, and in time back to L.A.). The Browns might never have come into existence. NFL football on the West Coast might have begun with an expansion team rather than with the relocation of an Eastern franchise.

As it was, fateful wheels had been set in motion that soon would carry the franchise to L.A., and four days after the new AAFC was unveiled, the Rams were off to what would be their second-to-last season in Cleveland.

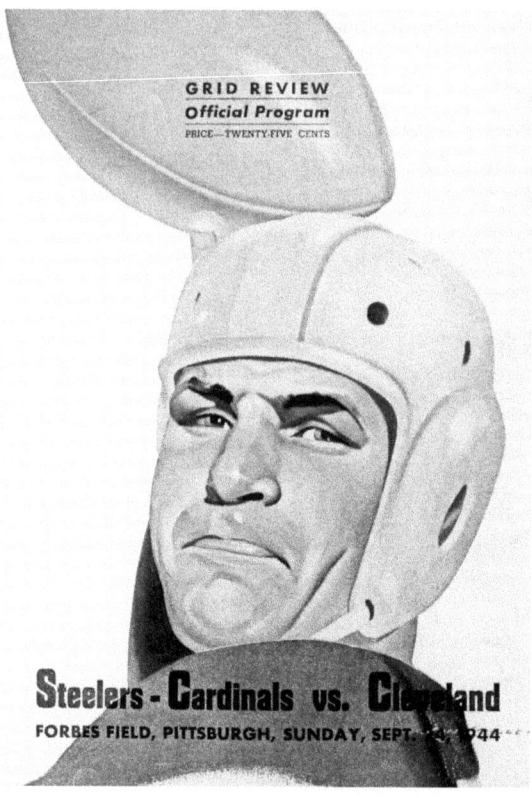

The Rams very nearly merged with the Pittsburgh Steelers due to a wartime shortage of players. Instead, Pittsburgh joined with the Chicago Cardinals to form the infamous Card-Pitts (or "Carpets"), whom Cleveland narrowly defeated 30–28 in 1944 *(Donald Gries Collection)*.

First they spoiled the Boston Yanks' NFL debut with a 9–0 exhibition-game victory at Cleveland Stadium, then they edged the woebegotten Card-Pitt franchise 30–28 in a contest in Pittsburgh in which Benton grabbed three touchdown catches, two on passes from Colella.

On October 8, 1944, Benton and the Rams faced the Chicago Bears at League Park, which once again had become the Rams' home field for regular-season games, with Reeves and his former partner Fred Levy, Jr., having quickly grown disinterested in attempting to make cavernous Cleveland Stadium habitable for pro football. In a steady all-afternoon rain that dampened attendance, new Ram Pritko suffered a broken nose on the game's third play and was knocked out cold, and Matheson at times was triple-teamed. But Benton made his former Bears teammates miss him as he scooped up a fumble early in the third quarter and rumbled 23 yards for a touchdown to lead Cleveland to a 19–7 victory. It was only the third Rams win in 13 chances against the Bears and their first since Art Lewis' triumphant phone call to the so-called Downtown Coaches in 1938. "The millen[n]ium practically has arrived," the *Cleveland Plain Dealer*'s John Dietrich wrote gleefully. "The long-downtrodden Cleveland Rams have become so great that they can make monkeys of the Chicago Bears."[45] At 2–0, the Rams—a franchise that "didn't even own a football" the previous spring[46]—were upsetting predictions.

A week later the Lions piled up 17 straight points in the first 18 minutes of play—even without the services of star Frankie Sinkwich, who was sidelined with appendicitis—before the Rams rallied furiously and won 20–17 in Detroit. Colella, overshadowed by Sinkwich during his time with Detroit, had the last laugh by tossing a nine-yard touchdown strike to Pritko. "Those unheralded and unpredictable Cleveland Rams"[47] remarkably were a perfect 3–0 and threatened the Green Bay Packers' hopes in the Western Division. Even Donelli admitted to surprise at the team's performance as he lavished praise on veterans Benton and Matheson for mentoring the team's younger and newer charges. Benton said he was enjoying himself immensely, and Matheson was said to be herding around his young fellow linemen "like a mother hen."[48]

But Cleveland fans had seen this film before: having their hopes raised early in the season, then dashed in the end as games turned ugly. Colella went on another tear in Green Bay, scoring on runs of 75 and 25 yards and throwing a 23-yard touchdown pass to Benton, but Gillette suffered a deep wound in his leg under circumstances that only could be described as "mysterious."[49] Donelli charged that the cleats of a Packer player caused the razor-like cut, but others were not sure. "I don't know whether it was a spike wound or one of the yardstick markers," Rams trainer Leroy (Tiny) Dippery said, "but there was a gash in his leg that reached almost from his ankle to his knee.... It was wide open and when I first viewed it I said to myself that I doubted if Jim would even play football again."[50] Gillette did return, and played well—but not until late in the season. The Packers outlasted the Rams 30–21 as Cleveland suffered its first loss.

Mayhem continued the following Sunday. It was a brilliant late-October afternoon in the so-called friendly confines of Wrigley Field, but "the play was so violent that even some of the Chicago fans were rooting for Cleveland,"[51] Dietrich reported, and afterwards the league promised it would begin sending observers to all games to report on excessive roughness and rules infractions that were not being caught or enforced by game officials. Benton caught a 13-yard pass from Reisz to deadlock the game at 21 until Chicago back Al Grygo took a handoff from quarterback Sid Luckman on a naked reverse and cruised 66 yards for a touchdown. The Bears triumphed 28–21 and Cleveland fell to 3–2.

The Rams traveled the following week to Washington, D.C., where President Franklin D. Roosevelt was only two days from re-election to his fourth and final term on a ticket that now included Harry Truman. At Griffith Stadium, Frank Filchock—foreshadowing the following year's title game—substituted for quarterback Sammy Baugh, and the backup's two touchdown throws in the second quarter were enough for 3–0–1 Washington to surge past Cleveland 14–10. The Rams had fallen to earth with a

3–3 record, but they were "tasting public favor for the first time and finding it pleasant."[52] An increasingly confident Walsh assured the local newspapers that he saw no real threat from the Browns and the coming AAFC.

But the taste of victory quickly turned sour when the Packers arrived to do what they had done so enduringly well for so long: bring Clevelanders' football hopes crashing around them. The *Plain Dealer*'s Dietrich believed "the strain of that week after week struggle against insurmountable odds finally caught up with the Rams"[53] as Cleveland was humiliated 42–7. Don Hutson tallied two touchdown receptions in what would be his last season as a genuine torturer of the Rams. To Cleveland's misfortune, his career in the Western Division (1935–1945) almost exactly paralleled the NFL Rams' era in Cleveland (1937–1945)—but after this loss the Rams would not lose to the Packers again until 1947. Reeves was in attendance on this day, on military leave from upstate New York for the only game he would watch in person in the 1944 season, and he claimed to be sanguine despite the afternoon's dismal results. "All our plans have been long range for after the war," he reassured Dietrich, in reference to Walsh's player strategy. "We didn't expect anything this season."[54] But he doubtless was less than happy with the gate: 17,166 at League Park. It was the league's second-lowest attendance that week, against a premier opponent, and on "an important day on the Rams' calendar"[55] when a solid turnout was essential for refuting a widespread claim that Cleveland would not support pro football. Cleveland's fans did not pass muster, and plans to rectify the situation no doubt whirred in Reeves' mind.

The Rams rebounded the following weekend with a 33–6 rout of the beleaguered Card-Pitt squad at Comiskey Park. Five Rams players logged touchdowns, including Colella on a 54-yard pass reception, and a recuperating Gillette on a 58-yard dash in his NFL scoring debut. At 4–4 the Rams' record again was level, and Walsh said he planned to reward Donelli with "one of the finest contracts in the game."[56] The *Cleveland Press* saw in the gesture a hint that Reeves was "willing to travel along whatever road is deemed necessary toward lifting the Rams to the topmost plane of the pro game."[57]

The Rams were poised to post their first-ever winning record, but standing in their immediate way were the Lions and a now-healthy Sinkwich, the league's eventual most valuable player that season. It was time to prove that the city "will support real topflight football," *Plain Dealer* sports editor Sam Otis wrote. "Let's all go!"[58] Few did. Only 7,452 fans were on hand in League Park on November 26, 1944, as the Rams held the lead through three quarters before relinquishing two touchdowns in the final quarter and falling 26–14. Consolation prize would have to be a .500 record, the Rams' first since Clark's 1939 squad went 5–5–1. But this chance eluded the Rams as well. The resurgent Eagles, now decoupled from the 1943 merger with the Steelers and in the midst of a lengthy Ram-killing era that would extend even into the Rams' championship season and beyond, ripped Cleveland 26–13 in Shibe Park. Though the Rams had begun the campaign at 3–0, they lost five of their last six games to finish 4–6 and complete their seventh straight non-winning season in the NFL. But all was not lost. Matheson and Benton were named All-NFL at season's end, and Benton finished second only to Hutson in receptions, receiving yards, and receiving touchdowns.[59] If not for the incomparable Hutson, Benton may have become the dominant pass receiver of his era and possibly a Hall of Famer.

The Rams assuredly had a solid nucleus on which Walsh could build after the war, but the league's handling of the team was troubling. Cleveland had been "sentenced"[60] to the league's hardest schedule in 1944 with games against the top four teams in the league (the Bears, Packers, Redskins, and Eagles) and seven road contests in a 10-game schedule. But the fact of the matter was, the *Plain Dealer*'s Otis wrote, "the Rams NEVER have had a respectable list of home games with which to attract real crowds[,] so naturally have not done as well at the gate as might be expected."[61] The record bears him out: From 1937 through 1944 the Rams played only 43 percent of their games as the home team,[62] and a handful of these were at the so-called neutral sites of Colorado Springs, Colorado, and Akron, Ohio—the latter nearly 50 miles from the Rams' home field of League Park. Compare this to the six home games afforded in a 10-game season in 1944 to the New York Giants, Washington Redskins, Detroit Lions, and Philadelphia Eagles. It was a pattern of league favoritism toward the more athletically and financially successful teams that would continue into the 1945 season.

Reeves and Walsh felt marooned in their mission to make pro football sustainable in Cleveland but remained undaunted in building a winning and financially successful franchise. They identified 200 prospective Rams—two-thirds of them still overseas, in the war—who either had been drafted by or had been recommended to the club, and they set out to sign every one that was interested in playing pro football. On December 16, 1944—the day the Third Reich began its last desperate operation of World War II with the Battle of the Bulge—Reeves and Walsh came through with their promise to Donelli and finalized a three-year contract at a reputed $15,000 per season. Regretfully for the Rams, it turned out to be money they never would spend: Donelli went into the Navy just four weeks later, his initial spadework in building a winner left unfinished, and the Rams again were on a search for their next head coach. Had the team not enjoyed instant success with Donelli's successor, they might forever have rued the bad timing of the coach's call-up. But other very promising developments were brewing.

On December 22, 1944, the *Plain Dealer* reported the Rams had signed "an experienced T formation quarterback"[63] out of the University of Illinois named Don Greenwood, who was freshly released from the Air Corps. Donelli personally had traveled to Champaign to persuade him to sign, and once Greenwood was switched over to fullback he would prove to be a valuable and versatile player in his brief but successful time with the Rams. Even more importantly, encapsulated in a single paragraph near the end of the article about Greenwood was notice that the Rams also were "said to be dickering with"[64] a star back out of UCLA who had been their third pick in the 1944 draft, a player who in fact would take over the Rams' quarterback position. That Californian, one year practically to the day later, would make NFL history in near-arctic weather conditions in Cleveland.

His name was Bob Waterfield.

CHAPTER 10

The Hero's Journey to Cleveland

Robert Staton Waterfield came of age in the 1920s and 1930s in a Western American paradise, then "lush with green fields and orchards and ranch-style houses with horses and dogs."[1] California's San Fernando Valley was nestled quietly between the San Gabriel Mountains to the northeast and the Santa Monica Mountains to the southwest—a world-within-a-city just a short distance over the mountains to the glamor of Hollywood and the splendors of Los Angeles. Yet it had rural comforts enough for Bing Crosby to sing in 1944 about settling down and never roaming again. "That's the country," Waterfield would tell a Cleveland reporter one day. "Climate, mountains, nice living conditions, no snow."[2] Many came and few left the San Fernando Valley, and Waterfield—save for a hot and miserable military stint in the South and one cold autumn in the Midwest that was to shape the course of his life and define his legacy—was among the many who stayed.

Waterfield was born on July 26, 1920, in Elmira, New York, but he remembered little of the place, his family having headed west when he was a toddler to the flat and nearly prairie-like Valley of the pre–Depression era. His father Staton "Jack" Waterfield became owner and manager of the Van Nuys Transfer and Storage Company and was an athlete in his own right, playing baseball in Van Nuys and taking young Bob with him to games. Jack had much of the healthy, chiseled look his son would inherit, but on St. Patrick's Day 1930, only 38, he died of an unexpected attack of what would be reported as acute indigestion. This left Waterfield's mother Frances, a handsome woman with bobbed hair and some of the reserved, thoughtful appearance of her son, to return to her job as a private nurse and raise nine-year-old Bob alone in a small English-style cottage on tidy, unbending Hartland Street in the flatlands of Van Nuys. The Waterfields

Bob Waterfield was exposed to sports at a very young age, here attending a Van Nuys, California, baseball game with his father, Staton "Jack" Waterfield (bottom center) in the mid-1920s. After the elder Waterfield died prematurely in 1930, Bob's mother Frances Waterfield raised Bob alone (*Buck Waterfield Collection*).

had an oversized lot that later would be subdivided for more housing, with plenty of space for Frances's gardening as well as for her young son and his dogs, and Bob hunted doves with his shotgun on then-open land just across the street.

The widowed Frances left a deep imprint on her only child, who was to grow to a tanned and athletic six-feet-one with wavy brown hair and striking green eyes. "My grandmother was a pretty phenomenal woman— a very, very strong woman," said Waterfield's adopted son Buck Waterfield. "She would say she would rather be around the men than with the 'cackling women.' I think a lot of my dad's love of the outdoors came from her. She taught my dad how to fish. 'Nana' was a huge influence on him."[3] Frances, in fact, doted on Bob. "She was the spitting image of her son, except for a shock of prematurely white hair, and brown eyes, instead of his green," remembered actress Jane Russell, Waterfield's girlfriend and then wife. "I

Bob Waterfield's life revolved around his mother Frances Waterfield's simple house on Hartland Street in Van Nuys, California. He returned here to live, at least for a time, after achieving stardom with UCLA; after winning the NFL championship in 1945; while constructing a new home in Sherman Oaks with his wife, actress Jane Russell; and after Frances died. The house still stood in early 2016 *(James C. Sulecki)*.

have never seen anyone so devoted to her son. He was her reason for living."[4] As Waterfield's football exploits and fame grew, Frances kept a scrapbook of his newspaper clippings, commendatory letters, congratulatory telegrams, and other odds and ends that her son rarely if ever stopped to reminisce about.

At Van Nuys High School, Waterfield was attractive to, and precocious with, many members of the fairer sex including Russell. He also was a highly skilled athlete and gymnast who wowed small crowds with his routines on the gymnastic bars at Santa Monica's original Muscle Beach. Sometimes, daringly, he performed handstands on the ledges of multi-story buildings. Years later, Buck Waterfield recalled, his father walked around the family house on his hands. But Waterfield also had spent many solitary afternoons in Frances's back yard. "My grandmother told me that when she encouraged him to play football, they had a tire in a tree and Dad would go and throw the football hour after hour after hour after hour," Buck Waterfield said.[5] Growing increasingly interested in football, Waterfield sometimes would disappear into L.A. so he could watch practice sessions of the University of California, Los Angeles football team and its sensational African American back Kenny Washington, of whom he became a fan and, later, a Rams teammate.

Waterfield was, however, a bit directionless as he moved through his late teens. He played one year of football at Van Nuys as a wispy 155-pound tailback, apparently demonstrating enough raw athletic talent to be given the business card of Raymond "Fido" Murphy, a West Coast scout for the Chicago Bears. "Me," Waterfield wrote in his spare communication style in a scrapbook, an arrow pointed toward the pasted-in card. "Passer?" Then, mysteriously: "Quarter."[6] After he graduated from high school at 16 he took a job in a Douglas Aircraft factory, then augmented his income in nearby Hollywood with bit acting roles that included working as a double for movie actor Michael O'Shea. "Playing college football was far from my dreams," Waterfield said, "not only because of my size, but because my father had died ... and I figured I had to get a job."[7]

Frances had other ideas. By 1940 Waterfield had grown to a solid 190 pounds and was offered a gymnastics scholarship to UCLA. "I thought school was behind me," he said, but "my mother didn't feel that way. She kept after me to get more education,"[8] so at the age of 19 he enrolled. Still, he sidled up to football in college as hesitantly as he had in high school. That autumn and winter when he had spare time he walked to the UCLA practice field and "kicked the ball around."[9] By springtime, no doubt at his mother's insistence and with her encouragement, he had gathered sufficient courage to attend the football team's practices.

As chance had it, UCLA had grown impatient with its eight-game winless streak against bitter crosstown rival the University of Southern California and was about to join many college and NFL teams—the Rams included—in retooling its wing offense to the sensational new T-formation. The Bruins brought in Bernie Masterson, a 29-year-old ex-quarterback who was Sid Luckman's predecessor on the Bears, to help with the transition. Masterson and UCLA head coach Edwin "Babe" Horrell knew well the importance of a multi-skilled quarterback in the T and began screening available players for leading candidates. Booming punts by Waterfield caught their eye.

Waterfield, it was said, "could pass a football 60 yards and kick it just as far."[10] His Rams teammates would come to call him "Waterbuckets"—then "Buckets," and eventually just "Buck"—because he could placekick a ball from the 50-yard line and strike a pail.[11] But he also would go on to launch punts that went as long as 91 yards. By the time he took his first college practice field he had become a conjunction of size, strength, speed, intelligence, athleticism, deeply rooted competitiveness, and skills developed through hours of solitary repetition. All he lacked was the opportunity to demonstrate his ability. More than four decades after that spring afternoon on which Masterson and Horrell first saw him punt, Los Angeles Times columnist Jim Murray would write that "man or boy, Bob Waterfield was the best football player you or I ever saw. What could be done with a football, he could do—run, pass, kick, tackle, bat down, catch. He had gifts that were not given to the rest of us."[12] Waterfield may have been a "loner," a "reserved, taciturn young man"—Russell herself came to call him "Old Stone Face"[13]—but inside, Waterfield burned to win.

Horrell and Masterson, finding an unexpected star in their midst, excitedly tried out Waterfield at left halfback and asked him to throw a few passes. Convinced of his innate ability, they moved him behind center and installed him as UCLA's new T-formation quarterback. Masterson "practically adopted" the younger player, becoming his mentor, giving him his "big push"[14] at quarterback and providing paternal guidance that Waterfield had not felt since the death of his father.

Waterfield's first test arrived in late September 1941, the same month that the Rams began their first season under new owner Daniel F. Reeves 2,400 miles to the east. Waterfield's college debut was a Friday-night home game for UCLA, played at the Los Angeles Memorial Coliseum, using a white football designed to increase its visibility under what was then still dusky, early-technology lighting. Stitched to Waterfield's dark jersey was "7," the number he wore on his football jersey like an amulet throughout his high-school, collegiate, and professional careers. Founding Ram Harry "Horse" Mattos had worn the numeral before Waterfield, but no Rams player would do so after him, and one day Denver Broncos star John Elway would tell Buck Waterfield that his father was one of the reasons he also wore number 7.[15]

Waterfield in his premiere at quarterback tossed several long completions with a distinctive wrist-snapping motion and also pitched out, ran, blocked, and punted as sideline newspaper cameras flashed in the night. By halftime the Bruins could battle only to a scoreless tie with conference rival Washington State, but then as the third quarter was drawing to a close, Waterfield lined up behind center, waited for a man in motion to pass behind him, took the snap, rolled right, feigned a pitchout, and with an almost sidearm flick whipped a pass on the run to catch a receiver in the flat and score the game's go-ahead touchdown. He served as holder on UCLA's decisive point-after attempt and the Bruins won 7–6. Bob Waterfield, it seemed, was on his way.

But UCLA was not yet a top football attraction in California, even with previous seasons' rosters that had included the likes of Kenny Washington and future baseball legend Jackie Robinson. The Bruins traveled to Stanford to match their new offense against T-formation pioneer Clark Shaughnessy. After helping George Halas install the T on the Bears, Shaughnessy had moved west, brought the same formation to Stanford, and carried a team that won only one game in 1939 to a 10–0 record and a Rose Bowl victory in 1940. Shaughnessy's success continued as Stanford drilled the Bruins 33–0 and brought Waterfield swiftly back to earth. While Waterfield and Shaughnessy later were to team up in Los Angeles on a run to the NFL championship game in 1949, Waterfield had to take his lumps as his first college season rolled on, losing by sizeable margins to California, Oregon State, and Santa Clara.

The Bruins finally dragged a 4–5 record into their annual matchup with hated USC, and with the Trojans suffering a rare losing season, UCLA had a chance to defeat their rivals for the first time ever. Instead they tied 7–7. For many UCLA fans it felt like a victory. But to Waterfield it very likely left a churning sensation in his stomach. He wanted only to win.

* * *

By this time Waterfield was well into in a tempestuous relationship with Russell, swearing fealty to the future starlet but occasionally wandering off to other young women. Russell likewise saw other men through the early years of her relationship with Waterfield. The two had begun dating in high school; Russell said she felt "like a bird hypnotized by a green-eyed snake, and the snake won."[16] Waterfield and Russell were engaged until she became pregnant in 1942, underwent a painful abortion, and broke up with Waterfield, telling him they "had nothing in common. He loved football, hunting, and fishing, while I loved artistic things—music, reading, talking."[17] Russell in fact was quite religious, and came from a spiritual family, while Waterfield was much more grounded in the temporal world.

"There was a real love-hate relationship between those two," Buck Waterfield said. "They couldn't be away from each other, but they couldn't be together either."[18] Russell was troubled by Waterfield's unexpected eruptions when the two had differences of opinion. Eventually, with the help of a psychiatrist, she came to attribute Waterfield's aggression to his player mindset. "A quarterback's whole strategy is to throw the opposition off guard," Russell wrote as if in realization. "Never let them know what your plan is. Your best defense is a good offense. Attack!"[19]

In fact, Waterfield's sleight of hand and his ability to flummox the competition soon became his calling card. The Bruins opened the 1942 season with two losses including a razor-thin 7–6 opener to Texas Christian University. Russell had remained close enough to the quarterback to send him a telegram reading "Congratulations on fine game" and signing with a pet name he had given her: "J R Luke Waterfield."[20] Suddenly Waterfield and UCLA began to blossom. The Bruins blitzed Oregon State 30–7 and blanked California 21–0, with Waterfield in the latter game unleashing what became his trademark play: a naked reverse in which he wheeled into the end zone in one direction as the rest of his team—and the defense—went the other. "It wasn't the play that was called," remembered Mike Marienthal, a guard on the team. "He just did it. He stood in the end zone and held up the ball to show us."[21]

UCLA won four of its next five games before facing USC for a shot at the Pacific Coast Conference championship and the school's first-ever appearance in the Rose Bowl. Could the Bruins defeat a Trojans team against whom they were 0–5–3 all time? Actor Mickey Rooney knew a player on the UCLA team and he and Ava Gardner, both fans, would be among the nearly 90,000 expected in the L.A. Coliseum. The Bruins' players were confident because "we had Waterfield," said Bruin halfback Ed Tyler. "He could do it all—run, pass, kick, play defense. He was the No. 1 quarterback on the West Coast."[22]

With the game off to a scoreless battle, the Bruins started to mix up their T-formation offense with double-wing-formation plays. Then Waterfield took off on a 15-yard sprint that brought the ball to USC's five-yard-line, fullback Ken Snelling punched the ball in from the two, and UCLA went into halftime with a 7–0 lead. Waterfield stood out again in the third quarter when he fired a 41-yard pass to end Burr Baldwin for a touchdown and a 14–0 lead. He also contributed on defense with an interception and a shoestring tackle to save a touchdown, and UCLA hung on for a 14–7 victory. At long last the Bruins had defeated USC and secured their first invitation to the Rose Bowl.

Sportswriting eminence Arch Ward reported that UCLA believed it was Waterfield—not Georgia's Heisman Trophy winner and future Detroit Lions star Frank Sinkwich, who had ankle injuries; nor his teammate future Pro Football Hall of Famer Charley Trippi—who would be the "man to watch"[23] in the New Year's Day matchup in Pasadena. An L.A. newspaper carried a large photograph of Waterfield in his characteristic punting pose—

arms raised, kicking leg at head-level, eyes gazing skyward. Frances Waterfield clipped a copy and placed it in her scrapbook with a penned notation: "This is swell, isn't it. I'm collecting them from all the neighbors."[24] UCLA's first trip to the Rose Bowl unfortunately was a long afternoon for Waterfield, who threw an interception in the fourth quarter to set up a Bulldog touchdown then watched as his punt was blocked and knocked out of the Bruins' end zone for a safety. UCLA bowed to Georgia 9–0. After the game, Rooney and Gardner threw the Bruins players a consolation party in the Cocoanut Grove ballroom at the celebrity-thick Ambassador Hotel in L.A., and "that was the end," Waterfield's teammate Tyler remembered. "By spring, everyone was off to war."[25]

Events indeed took a more serious and life-setting turn for Waterfield in 1943. He finally reunited with Russell, whose career as a movie star and a sex symbol took wing with her appearance in Howard Hughes' *The Outlaw*, a notorious film that was embargoed for several years—ironic given Russell's religious background. And on Easter Sunday of that year, with two friends in tow, the couple eloped in Las Vegas in a private and joyless wedding ceremony that "couldn't have been less romantic," Russell wrote.[26] Shortly afterwards, Waterfield's ROTC class was sent to officers' candidate school at Fort Benning, Georgia, for his first extended period away from Russell and southern California, and his need to have Russell near him became more apparent. "After he arrived in Georgia we would get frantic phone calls: 'Get me out of here, get me into the air force, anything, I can't stand this,'" Russell wrote.[27] Russell, by this time a high-profile celebrity, "hailed as the 'sexpot of the century,'"[28] joined Waterfield in the Georgia heat—causing a bit of a local stir—as he rose to first lieutenant while playing on the 176th Infantry's football and basketball teams. When he injured his knee and received an honorable discharge, he returned posthaste to UCLA anxious to complete a degree in physical education and resume his football career after a year's absence.

And resume football he did. While the Bruins went only 4–5 in 1944—without him the season before they had gone 1–8—Waterfield rose to the football world's attention on New Year's Day 1945 as the most valuable player in the annual East-West Shrine Game at San Francisco's Kezar Stadium. Waterfield's "towering and lengthy punts that kept the East bottled up during the last three quarters of the game"[29] were especially lauded by observers—those, anyway, who had watched him more than they had his movie-starlet wife. A radio executive in attendance at a post-game players' party later admitted to Waterfield that he "wasn't as interested in watching you shake hands as I was in looking at that lovely Mrs. Waterfield beside you."[30]

But the ever-confident Waterfield now was certain—after his failure in the previous year's Rose Bowl—that he could compete on a very large stage. On this same afternoon, a Rams scout approached Waterfield and offered him a pro contract. "Robert was very pleased," Russell wrote, "but the stone face said, 'I'll think about it.' When he did sign, it was for more than any other new player was getting at the time."[31]

It was indeed an outlandish salary—$7,500 for the coming season—and payment that Reeves and Rams general manager Charles "Chile" Walsh were happy to make because the duo finally had unearthed a real star for the Cleveland Rams. "We ain't giving out the terms of the contract," Walsh told reporters, "but he's married to Jane Russell, the movie star, and that didn't make signing him any easier."[32] The *Cleveland Press*' Franklin Lewis, a self-styled voice of the average fan who had shared a backfield at Cleveland's Glenville High School with 1920s–1930s NFL star Benny Friedman, was incredulous and took Walsh and Reeves to task for "throwing their money around." Reflecting on the Rams' hardworking early stars and their relatively low salaries, he wrote: "When you think that Parker Hall and Johnny Drake, two of the best backs ever to play in the National [Football] League, got top

In 1943, Bob Waterfield's ROTC class at UCLA was summoned to officers' candidate school at Fort Benning, Georgia, where he played on the 176th Infantry's winning football team. His wife, actress Jane Russell, joined him in Georgia, causing a local stir. When Waterfield injured his knee, he received an honorable discharge and returned to UCLA to finish school (*Buck Waterfield Collection*).

money around here with contracts that were under $7,000, it is a trifle shocking to discover that new college recruits, weighed down with clippings, are being signed for that much money!"[33]

Regardless of what the Cleveland newspapers thought, Waterfield was in the big time, and "the big time meant being away from home again," Russell wrote. "We weren't thrilled about that. Cleveland was as cold as Georgia was hot."[34] Russell again joined Waterfield, this time in an efficiency apartment on Cleveland's Euclid Avenue. The two lived in the Hotel St. Regis, an eight-story brick edifice that at one time had been a grand home to residents including a Rockefeller of the Standard Oil Company and the president of the old Cleveland Spiders pro baseball team. But since then, the building had been remodeled into apartments, and Waterfield and Russell shared a pull-down bed and cooked on a "tiny stove on top of the fridge."[35] Russell would attend some of the Rams' games in Cleveland, "sit in the stands, and say [in a soft voice], 'Come on, Robert!' She didn't want

In addition to playing football, Bob Waterfield also immediately was placed on the basketball team for the 176th Infantry at Fort Benning, Georgia. As always wearing his distinctive number 7, Waterfield at six-feet-one was the shortest of the team's core players (*Buck Waterfield Collection*).

to call attention to herself," recalled Marguerite Gillette, widow of Waterfield's Ram teammate Jim Gillette.[36] Russell remembered "keeping warm with the help of something from a flask, and root[ing] for our guys, who were slipping and sliding around on the ice. This was a new experience for Californians."[37]

For Waterfield and Russell, the autumn of 1945 would become a brief and novel departure from home, and one more career obligation in extreme conditions to be endured before Waterfield could return, a triumphant hero, to enchanting southern California. But for Clevelanders it was to be both the peak and the valley—and the concluding year—of the Rams' storm-tossed decade in the city of their birth.

CHAPTER 11

A New Power Rises in the West

Nineteen forty-five was a pivotal year, an influential "year zero"[1] as the historian Ian Buruma called it, that shaped a postwar world whose outlines would endure for decades to come. So, too, would 1945 be for the Cleveland Rams. Life for the franchise—indeed, the life of the National Football League at large—never would be the same thereafter.

Just weeks after ringing in a hopeful New Year, the Allied Powers discovered the horrors at Auschwitz and liberated that concentration camp; by early spring they had done so at Buchenwald too. The Nazi regime was on the retreat, and as the Allieds grew increasingly confident victory was at hand the river of American servicemen coming home widened. They would return eager to forget what they had seen on the battlefield and "hungry," as Joe Horrigan of the Pro Football Hall of Fame put it, "for rest and relaxation and distraction."[2] The NFL was ready. A quarter-century of often-Pleistocene football and experimentation since the league's founding in 1920 was drawing to an end. Excitement and interest in the jet-age T-formation offense had been sparked at many if not most of the league's franchises, and rosters quickly were replenishing with postwar players who had sufficient speed, agility, and intelligence to forge an exciting new game. The 1945 edition of *Street and Smith's Football Year Book* declared simply that "professional football has arrived."[3]

No city could claim to be more firmly at the center of pro football's immediate postwar ascendancy than Cleveland. Organizing and gathering momentum there just as the American Century was nearing its midpoint was a pair of franchises that, in Horrigan's words, would be "two of the most entertaining football teams in the country for a very long time"[4]—the Rams and the Browns.

Cleveland's entry in the new All-America Football Conference made

11. A New Power Rises in the West 143

news first in 1945. Browns franchise founder Arthur "Mickey" McBride initially had made a handshake deal with the University of Notre Dame's Frank Leahy to become Cleveland's first head coach, but with two sons enrolled at South Bend, McBride was told to back off. At a loss for a second candidate—McBride still was relatively new to football—he strode one night into the sports department of the *Cleveland Plain Dealer* and asked John Dietrich for his opinion as to whom he thought was the best football coach in the country. Dietrich, midwife to the name "Rams," once again made a call that would ring through football history. He answered without hesitation: Paul Brown.

And so on February 8, 1945, in Arch Ward's office at the *Chicago Tribune*, the former Ohio State coach signed a five-year deal to lead the new AAFC team. Brown initially favored the name "Panthers" because it suggested motion and had connotations of sleekness and speed,[5] but that brand had been taken in 1926 by Cleveland's short-lived entry in the American Football League. The team instead became the Browns, and almost immediately Brown attracted the highly talented Otto Graham, who had rejected the Detroit Lions' drafting rights and signed instead with the AAFC. Graham was far from alone in favoring the upstart league over the NFL; by the start of the 1946 season, 95 players with NFL experience—about 30 percent of all NFL veterans—had joined the AAFC.[6]

Meanwhile the Rams had their own head coach to hire. Aldo "Buff" Donelli, abruptly summoned into the service in January 1945, left behind his lone season with the team and his freshly signed three-year contract and shipped out of Pittsburgh with a group of Navy trainees. Rumors circulated that Rams general manager Charles "Chile" Walsh had approached Chicago Bears coach Luke Johnsos with the $15,000 he was prepared to pay Donelli in 1945, then raised the stake an additional $5,000 per year; and further that Walsh had sweetened the deal by noting that Johnsos could live in California year-round by operating out of the large Los Angeles branch office of his full-time employer, a paper company. Walsh, the *Chicago Tribune* reported, "mentioned the possibility of his Cleveland team operating in Los Angeles after the war."[7] The Rams' desire to move to California had become an open secret. But Walsh denied making an offer to Johnsos, saying he only had "sounded out" Johnsos as to his availability.[8] Further, he called "unfounded" any report that the Rams might move to Los Angeles. "Cleveland is our home, and we intend to stay there," he asserted on March 6, 1945.[9]

Six days later, on March 12, 1945—10 months to the day before Rams owner Daniel F. Reeves would request permission to move the Rams to

California—Walsh just had returned to Cleveland from a suspiciously long visit to the West Coast followed by a face-to-face conference with Reeves in Rome, New York, and he still was denying the California rumor "with some vehemence." "For one thing," he explained, increasingly impatient with Cleveland reporters, "we have a five-year lease on League Park." Raising some suspicion was the fact that he appeared to be "non-commi[t]tal"[10] about the new AAFC's forthcoming occupancy of the much larger Cleveland Stadium, which would leave the Rams in the city's smaller venue even as they were the more established big-league team. How Walsh could be unconcerned about such a slight was something local writers could not understand. Worry in Cleveland about the Rams' possible departure had been mildly chronic since Reeves bought the team in 1941, but now concern was becoming acute.

Walsh had little time to answer such rumors. He had only six months to field a capable head coach who could mentor a young team, and who better to fill that role than his own brother—an experienced collegiate coach and, like the general manager himself, an alumnus of California's Hollywood High School. Chile persuaded his brother to join him in Cleveland, and on March 14, 1945, Adam Walsh, age 43, signed a five-year contract to become rookie head coach of the Rams. The announcement merited a top-of-the-page banner headline in the *Chicago Tribune* sports section.

Adam Walsh was about a year older than Chile and something of a counterbalance to his younger brother's intense and often scowling presence. With sandy slicked-back hair, a raspy voice, and round wire-rim eyeglasses, Adam Walsh was a "pleasant, unobtrusive personality who makes friends and gains respect easily," Dietrich wrote in the *Plain Dealer*.[11] A former head coach and athletic director at Santa Clara University, Walsh held a degree in mechanical engineering and carried something of the cerebral air of one who had served as an assistant at Yale and Harvard before arriving at Maine's Bowdoin College to mentor a multitude of Phi Beta Kappa players. At Bowdoin, Walsh took a program that had scored only two touchdowns and won one game in two years and transformed it into a powerhouse that won or tied for a conference title seven times in eight seasons. But he was no elite. Just after high school he entered the workforce for two years to earn money to attend Notre Dame, where he roomed with eventual NFL commissioner Elmer Layden. He captained the 1924 Four Horsemen team and spurred the Fighting Irish to a perfect season and victory in the Rose Bowl. With Bowdoin football on hiatus for the duration of the war, he left behind an assistantship at Notre Dame and took a flyer on the NFL. He was a student of the pro game even while coaching at the college level, often

11. A New Power Rises in the West

attending games in New York, Boston, and Chicago; and he was a pioneer in his own right, deploying the T-formation at Bowdoin a year before Clark Shaughnessy did so at Stanford. In taking charge of the Rams he would go all out with the T offense that had begun tentatively with former head coach Earl "Dutch" Clark and continued in modified form under Donelli.

Some of the springtime thunder of the Walsh signing was stolen by a dispatch from the Rams' new rival in the AAFC. On March 31, 1945, Browns owner McBride called a news conference to announce he had taken in four partners including Dan Sherby and Robert H. Gries, the latter for his NFL experience as a member of the Marshman syndicate that had owned the Rams for five years. "We are not in this just to make money," McBride said. "We are interested in all sports, and in the city of Cleveland, where all of us have lived a long time."[12] The statement was true especially of Gries, whose family had settled in Cleveland in the 1830s and would continue to invest in pro football for decades to come as a gesture of civic support. For McBride, the declaration was a transparent shot at Reeves' out-of-town ownership and a reference to continuing whispers about the Rams' impending move. A few weeks earlier he had launched as well as broadside on the Rams' losing tradition. "The people of Cleveland will support only the best," he proclaimed. "You can't fool 'em, and we know we will have to have outstanding players and a winner from the start."[13]

The competition was real. The Rams no longer had the Cleveland market to themselves, and they continued amassing talent that would make them durably competitive for years to come. The franchise in fact was at the dawning of its greatest era, one in which it would play for the NFL title four times in seven years and five times in the 11 seasons spanning from 1945 through 1955.[14] Chile Walsh was its chief architect, and he unquestionably was on a hot streak. His discovery of Waterfield in 1944 would prove to be critical to his legacy, alone exceeding all the drafts Clark had directed in his four years heading the Rams. Yet Walsh built on that find, taking Elroy "Crazylegs" Hirsch in the first round of the 1945 NFL draft and Tom Fears in the eleventh. Hirsch was a halfback and receiver who never came close to playing for the Cleveland-based franchise, instead jumping to the AAFC's Chicago Rockets immediately after the war before joining the Rams in Los Angeles. Fears too caught on with the Rams on the West Coast after extending his career with UCLA. The trio of Waterfield, Hirsch, and Fears powered the Rams to the 1951 NFL championship over, coincidentally, Cleveland. Each player ultimately was enshrined in Canton, Ohio—three Hall of Famers selected by Walsh over the course of just two drafts when the Rams were based in Cleveland.

Even with Hirsch and Fears in reserve, Walsh added plenty of firepower that could be put to immediate use in Cleveland. In the 1945 draft's second round the Rams picked up Milan "Mike" Lazetich, a lineman from Michigan who would anchor the guard spot opposite Riley "Rattlesnake" Matheson. Lazetich, younger brother of former Ram Bill Lazetich (1939, 1942), was nicknamed "Sheriff" because he once had worked as a deputy lawman in Montana.[15] He was "a wild one, small but fierce," recalled his nephew Pete Lazetich, who played defensive end for the San Diego Chargers and Philadelphia Eagles in the 1970s.[16] Another big pickup for the Rams' line was a trade for tackle Eberle "Elbie" Schultz, a five-year veteran of the Philadelphia Eagles, the Pittsburgh Steelers, and the war's two conjoined teams the Steagles and the Card-Pitts. With Waterfield in the fold, Walsh was able to trade two expendable quarterbacks to the now-standalone Steelers because, he said, he was tired of seeing Schultz tear apart the Rams' linemen. Joining Schultz at the other guard spot was rookie Gil Bouley, selected ahead of Waterfield in the 1944 draft. Adam Walsh's New England connections likely helped Bouley. After talking with Leahy, who had coached Bouley at Boston College, the Walsh brothers offered the lineman the "fantastic sum" of $6,000 a year. "I was told by a friend I better take it before they changed they minds," Bouley said.[17]

With that the Rams' line was complete. Team captain Mike "Mo" Scarry held down center, putting in his second and last season with the Rams before jumping to the Browns. At the guards were Lazetich and Matheson, the latter in his sixth season with the Rams and about to have another All-NFL year both on the offensive line and as a "crack diagnostician of opponents' plays" on the defensive side.[18] At the tackles were Bouley and Schultz. And at the ends were Jim Benton, the sixth-year Ram veteran who soon would put in a performance for the ages, and Steve Pritko, a third-year player with experience on both the New York Giants and the Rams.

In the backfield the so-called G-men of Fred Gehrke and Jim Gillette at halfback and Don Greenwood at fullback were arrayed around Waterfield, multi-talented centerpiece of Adam Walsh's T-formation offense. Tommy Colella, a star with the 1944 team, backed up Gehrke at halfback. Albie Reisz, Cleveland's leading passer the season before,[19] now was a reserve behind Waterfield. The Rams, long a shallow team with few star-caliber players, suddenly enjoyed a depth of talent and the luxury of moving Greenwood—signed as a free-agent quarterback by departed coach Donelli—over to fullback. Greenwood would win three league championships in as many seasons for the Rams and the Browns but would be a short-timer in pro football. "Football is transitory," he said; a job he had obtained at

Thompson Products (later TRW) in Cleveland "comes first, [and] football is second."[20]

Most of the 1945 Rams players would come together as utter strangers. Among the 11 starters, four—Waterfield, Lazetich, Bouley, and Greenwood—were absolute rookies. So too was backup fullback Pat West, picked up in the 1944 draft. In fact, as of late November 1945, 17 players, about half the Rams' roster, were in their first year of pro football.[21] Among the so-called veterans, Gillette and Gehrke had signed and played sporadically in 1940 but were in only their second full NFL seasons because of their wartime service. So was end Floyd Konetsky, drafted in 1943. Colella was in his fourth year, two spent largely as a backup in Detroit, and as the season wore on, other experienced Rams players from years past returned including Howard "Red" Hickey and Rudy Mucha (1941) and Jack Jacobs (1942). But only Matheson, Benton, and Schultz could be said to have had significant experience as starting players in the NFL heading into the 1945 season.

The task of shepherding this rich but disparate collection of skills and experience—this "small nucleus of seasoned veterans and a large bunch of ambitious rookies," as Dietrich described it[22]—fell to coach Adam Walsh and his experienced staff. George Trafton, then considered one of the "legendary linemen of the NFL,"[23] played for years with the Bears before becoming line coach for the 1944 NFL champion Green Bay Packers. Bill "Red" Conkright had relinquished his playing role to Scarry so he could concentrate on scouting and coaching. And Bob Snyder was in the midst of a long, illustrious career that had taken him from Ohio University to the old American Football League's Pittsburgh Americans, from a charter role on the NFL Rams to journeyman T-formation quarterback and placekicker for the Bears. Along the way he threw touchdown passes to Benton, backed up legendary quarterback Sid Luckman on three champion Chicago teams, and coached briefly at Notre Dame. He was to mold Waterfield for the Rams as surely as another Bears alum, Bernie Masterson, had mentored Waterfield at UCLA, and in a few years in L.A. he would succeed Adam Walsh as head coach.

Overseeing it all was Adam Walsh, the right coach for the right team and time. Hugo Bezdek and his laissez-faire style of directing players had been exactly the wrong prescription in the Rams' inaugural season in 1937, but in 1945, with the franchise maturing, Walsh was the ideal choice. Player dissent and a defeatist attitude sank Bezdek's less talented but similarly green roster; but Walsh, fortified by his turnaround success at Bowdoin, well knew that with a young team he had to "keep peace in the family and build team spirit."[24] He would have a high degree of motivation as well—

New Cleveland Rams head coach Adam Walsh (kneeling, lower right) led the team's 1945 training camp at Bowling Green State University with a skilled, scholarly manner. He later said he had a hunch about this collection of players, which notably included quarterback Bob Waterfield (third from left, bottom row), halfback Jim Gillette (third from left, top row), and end Steve Pritko (far right) *(The Cleveland Press Collection, Cleveland State University Library).*

he knew that a losing performance on the field would reflect poorly on his brother the general manager—and he would inveigle results from his players like the skilled politico and minority leader in Maine's House of Representatives he one day would become.

By the time the Rams made it to their new training-camp site at Bowling Green State University, nearly all of the important pieces were in place: a T-formation offense, Matheson holding down a solid line, Benton the star of an elite receiving corps, and Gehrke pacing a speedy backfield. But "nobody expected the Rams to be more than ordinary. They didn't know about Waterfield,"[25] said Nate Wallack, who handled public relations for the Rams and, later, the Browns. Waterfield had spent the summer of 1945 as an extra for Warner Brothers in Hollywood but no doubt he repaired periodically to an empty football field to "kick the ball around"[26] as he had at UCLA. It took a kindred soul in a quarterback/kicker like Snyder to "discover"[27] Waterfield. Snyder gave him a tryout at Bowling Green, and suddenly the Californian was the Rams' go-to placekicker even though he had no game experience at any level of football. This was a pivotal coaching decision that would reverberate all the way to the championship game in December.

Adam Walsh was new to the Rams organization, but he had a hunch about this collection of players—that they were potential champions in the making—that he dared not utter, perhaps not even to his brother, for fear of inviting overconfidence and bad luck. By the close of camp in late September 1945, atomic bombs had been dropped on Hiroshima and Nagasaki and VJ Day for the United States and its allies had been declared. World War II was over. The boys were coming home. And the Cleveland Rams—at long last—were ready for the big time.

* * *

In their 10-game championship season of 1945 the Rams would play only four times as the home team—the seventh time in eight seasons that they were a majority road squad. Every other NFL franchise in that same span enjoyed a higher number and percentage of home games on a head-to-head basis save for the benighted Chicago Cardinals,[28] who were doomed to share a town with the dynastic Bears. The Rams were "always hounded by that crushing road schedule," Dietrich recounted later[29] in conducting a postmortem on the Rams' departure. And while the Rams would play home-and-home series against their divisional foes the Bears, Packers, and Cardinals, they would meet the Lions only once, in a pivotal showdown for the conference championship—on the road, naturally, in Detroit.

But first came a set of preseason contests in September 1945 that previewed to the football world that the Rams franchise finally had arrived. In yellow-and-royal-blue jerseys and yellow helmets, with each Armed Forces veteran on the team also sporting sleeve emblems representing the area of the service from which he had been honorably discharged, the Rams took the field at Buffalo War Memorial Stadium to neatly dispatch the Pittsburgh Steelers 21–0. Gehrke jetted for a 54-yard touchdown on his first carry and sealed his lock on the left halfback spot. "Though they won handily, it cannot be said that the Rams looked like world beaters," Dietrich wrote, his eyes having seen far too many early-season hot streaks and late-season fizzles, "but they showed plenty of promise."[30] Exactly how much promise he could not have guessed.

Five days later the Washington Redskins arrived for their first game in Cleveland since their blizzard-muffled win eight years earlier in front of

Inequity in Scheduled Regular-Season Home Games 1937–42, 1944–45		
	Games Played as Home Team	Share of Total Schedule
New York Giants	52	59%
Detroit Lions	48	56%
Washington Redskins	47	55%
Brooklyn Dodgers-Tigers*	40	53%
Philadelphia Eagles	44	51%
Chicago Bears	42	49%
Green Bay Packers	42	49%
Pittsburgh Pirates-Steelers	41	48%
Boston Yanks**	9	45%
Cleveland Rams	37	43%
Chicago Cardinals	32	37%
*1937–42, 1944 only		
**1944–45 only		
National Football League		

Unbalanced schedules common to the NFL in the 1930s and 1940s meant the Cleveland Rams played the fewest home games of any team except for the Chicago Cardinals. Perhaps not coincidentally, the Rams and Cardinals franchises both have been based in three different states through their long histories.

a few thousand frosty spectators at League Park. This time it was a different venue and outcome: The Rams blanked Washington 21–0 before an "astonished gathering"[31] of 17,398 at Cleveland Stadium, and even though the win meant nothing in the regular-season standings, it was the Rams' first victory ever over the Redskins and a preview of the title game three months later.

"Bob is doing a terrific job," Chile Walsh wrote in a letter sent to Waterfield's mother, Frances, back in Van Nuys, California:

> His first appearance in Cleveland last night against Washington was so outstanding he captured the football fans of the City of Cleveland.
> I am sure you will be happy and proud to know the modest, courteous manner in which Bob has conducted himself has won him the affection and admiration of his team mates, the coaching staff, the Press, and our entire organization.
> Bob is truly a great performer and we expect him to develop into one of the League "greats."[32]

Walsh's take on how maturely Waterfield carried himself was confirmed by one of the linemen charged with protecting him. Bouley recalled one missed blocking assignment that caused Waterfield to be "creamed. We came back to the huddle and all he said was, 'Come on, guys, try to hold them out a little longer.'" Bouley remembered that the quarterback was "always the gentleman"—"a good teacher who would take the time to show people their assignments. He was patient."[33]

Waterfield also was multi-dimensional—so much so that the Rams sent him to tee up the opening kickoff for an exhibition game at League Park and collectively caught their breath when a New York Giant pasted him just after he had sent the ball off safely. Though Waterfield would pass, run, punt, placekick, and play defense, and the Rams would defeat the Giants 38–23, his time on kickoffs was one and done.

On September 23, 1945, Reeves was released from the service, three years to the day after he had entered, and he finally got an in-person glimpse of Waterfield and the reconstituted team that his money and Chile Walsh had assembled. Reeves, something of a superstitious man, may have attributed the Rams' 17–7 loss to the Eagles to his own unexpected and sudden presence at the Akron Rubber Bowl. Though Philadelphia was an emerging powerhouse, the afternoon was a rare dud for the Rams. Colella, nursing bruised ribs from practice and told he should sit out a game, missed a tackle on Philadelphia's star halfback Steve Van Buren "and was in the Walsh doghouse ever after," wrote Herman Goldstein of the *Cleveland News*. There Colella would stay, receiving spotty playing time. "The coaching staff had no confidence in Colella," Goldstein wrote. "I remember sitting near Snyder, Rams' backfield coach, who was telephone observer in the press box. Late in a close game, Colella started from the bench to the field and Bob yelled into the phone, 'Don't send him in, he's a fumbler.'"[34] Colella would turn in a decent season but would leave the Rams the following year and find new life with the Browns.

Still, the exhibition loss was barely a speed bump for the Rams. On September 30, 1945, Cleveland rolled right into the regular season with its third 21–0 decision of the young campaign, a win over the Cardinals at League Park that was sparked by touchdowns from Waterfield, Pritko, and Gillette. Cleveland's defense limited Chicago to only 25 total rushing yards as the Rams jumped to a 1–0 opening record. After the game Hollywood starlet Jane Russell joined husband Waterfield at a get-together for Rams players and sportswriters. Russell, Benton said later, "probably got more attention than the team did on the field," but she was game for the men's fawning. "Bob introduced her to all of us. Bob got a lot of good press after that," Benton said.[35]

A matchup with the Bears before 19,580 at League Park on October 7, 1945, would be the young Cleveland team's first real test in the regular season. The Rams were playing their second straight home game and would go on the road for six of their next seven. The game was billed as a quarterback duel between young Waterfield and the veteran Luckman, but with Benton out, Waterfield lost his number-one target. Instead it was the Bears who had the shakes, fumbling away the ball twice in the first quarter and exceeding the Rams in first downs without scoring. Waterfield was involved in all Rams scoring, running the ball in from the eight, tossing a 25-yard touchdown strike to Pritko, booting a field goal, and kicking two extra points. The Rams toppled the Bears 17–0 in the first shut-out of Chicago by any team in six years—a streak going back 59 games.[36]

Cleveland's record stood at 2–0, and many in the sporting world, including members of the team's own staff, were astounded if a bit skeptical. "Those kids have one of the youngest outfits in the game—their average [age] is 24 years and I've never seen a more jittery bunch of boys than those Rams," Leroy (Tiny) Dippery, the team's trainer, told the *Norfolk Virginian-Pilot*. "They're on edge for every game."[37] But games three, four, and six—come-from-behind victories, all—would prove the young Rams' mettle and set the course for their championship finale.

County Stadium in Green Bay was a lion's den for the Cleveland franchise. On the sunny but cool afternoon of October 14, 1945, the Rams entered with an all-time record of 1–12–1 against Ram-killing receiver Don Hutson and the defending-champion Packers, with Cleveland's only victory coming six years earlier in Clark's first year as Rams coach. Benton scored on an arcing 17-yard pass from Waterfield, a photo of which prompted one of the Gillettes to ink the word "Beautiful!" on the family's copy of the *Cleveland Press* sports page.[38] But as the sun cast long late-afternoon shadows, the Packers held a 14–6 advantage and looked as if they would continue their dominance of Cleveland. Then the Rams caught fire. Colella scored on a nine-yard pass from Waterfield, who kicked the extra point, and it was a one-point game. Green Bay turned over the ball on a fumble, Greenwood went in from the one, and the Rams were ahead 20–14. Then Reisz picked off a Green Bay pass and took it 61 yards to the five-yard-line, from which Colella, in a "long awaited rejuvenation,"[39] plunged in for the final touchdown and a 27–14 Rams win. Up in the press box, a previously tense and quiet Chile Walsh leaped to his feet. "It's happened!" he shrieked. "It happened right here in Green Bay!"[40] The Rams, 3–0, were not dark horses anymore but true title contenders.

Still the young team was jittery amid its success. The Rams blew a three-touchdown lead on the Chicago Bears the following week in Wrigley Field to fall behind 21–20, then rallied with three straight unanswered touchdowns by Greenwood, Benton, and Colella to win 41–20 and extend their record to 4–0.

The national media began to swarm. Wallack received a request from *LIFE* magazine to publish a story about Russell and Waterfield, but with Russell's studio in Hollywood hesitant to disappoint male fans with details of her marriage, Wallack went to the Hotel St. Regis apartment where the couple was staying temporarily in Cleveland to explain his problem. The publicity, he explained, would be good for the team. Luckily, Russell again was game. "I'll cooperate with you on anything that's good for Robert and [the] Rams," she told Wallack.[41] A photographer arrived to capture the couple at home in the St. Regis and at League Park, with Russell at the latter daringly holding a staged placekick for her fully uniformed husband. The celebrity duo and their homespun lifestyle in Cleveland would be introduced to a national audience in the *LIFE* issue dated December 17, 1945—the day after the Rams had been crowned champions.

Not everything went to a Hollywood script, however. Cleveland's sole setback of the regular season was another thumping by the Eagles as Philadelphia took to the air and plugged the Rams with four straight touchdowns at Shibe Park. At 38,149 the crowd was the largest the Cleveland Rams franchise ever had played to up to that time,[42] and the young team's jitters resurfaced. When the Eagles' Don McDonald took a 21-yard pass into the end zone late in the game for Philadelphia's fourth consecutive score and a commanding 28–7 lead, the Rams' West slashed across the field, tracked down the receiver, and speared him from behind just shy of Shibe's outfield wall. McDonald sprang up and began throwing fists at West as he was pinned against the wall, while players from both sides ran to the end zone, there to be followed by a swarm of fans, and finally joined by mounted policemen who arrived to "quell the disturbance."[43] The Rams lost 28–14 and fell to 4–1 and into a first-place tie with the Lions in the Western Division. Nevertheless the ever-confident Rams—an embodiment of their supremely optimistic general manager Chile Walsh—announced that should they win the Western Division, which by league rotation would host the 1945 playoff, they would hold the championship game at expansive Cleveland Stadium.

With that, the Rams left Philadelphia, traced a path along the Hudson, and went "into hiding"[44] at New York's Bear Mountain to prepare for a big game against the New York Giants, the local idols of Reeves' youth. On November 4, 1945, reporters in the nation's media capital were shocked by the upstart Rams and the young wonder that was Waterfield. New York jumped to a 17–7 lead at halftime before a hometown throng of 46,219, and Reeves—noting his team's tendency to lose when his wife sat with him to watch a game—sent Mary Reeves to a seat elsewhere in the Polo Grounds. "She is a lovely wife and a lovely mother," he said, "but when it comes to football, she is anathema."⁴⁵ Sure enough, with Mrs. Reeves seated a safe distance from the man who wrote the paychecks, Gehrke put in touchdown runs of 10 and 35 yards in the second half to propel Cleveland to a 21–17 victory. The Rams were 5-1 and deadlocked with the Lions for first in the West.

Gehrke was the hero of the New York game, but it was a magical escape and two-yard touchdown run by Waterfield with the Rams' backfield otherwise pinned by the Giants that really caught the media's attention. In a replay of his naked reverse against California in college, Waterfield faked to Greenwood then "kept the ball himself and sauntered almost leisurely around left end and over the goal line for a touchdown."⁴⁶ It was, the *New York World Telegram and Sun*'s Joe King believed later after watching game film, a "Houdini" play that "almost defied detection in celluloid and actually did fool everybody on the field." Walsh, the "rookie coach" with "the kiddie team," had to be "a rube" for entrusting his team to a rookie quarterback like Waterfield, King wrote, but "Adam had all his buttons."⁴⁷ The *New York Daily News* ran a flattering story on Waterfield and Russell that was headlined "Rams Zoom to Pro Peak Through Cutie and QB."⁴⁸ Oscar Fraley, a decade still from writing his book *The Untouchables*, asserted in a United Press International dispatch that Waterfield was "the wonder and the hope of the National Football League."⁴⁹

The Rams finally returned home from their four-game road trip on November 11, 1945, amid a controversial decision by team management. "There was a tremendous ticket demand" for the Rams' rematch with the Packers, Wallack recalled, and it was suggested that the game should be moved to Cleveland Stadium. Chile Walsh refused; he had his lease with League Park, and he believed playing in a smaller park ensured advance sales of tickets as a safeguard against attendance-dampening rain and snow—always a threat in Cleveland. "Besides," Wallack said, "he was stubborn." Instead Walsh inexplicably elected to erect along the baseball park's famed 32-foot right-field wall a battalion of temporary bleachers—and "I mean temporary," Wallack said, "strictly lumber"⁵⁰ due to a lingering wartime shortage of steel. Walsh was treading on unfamiliar ground: With the opening of 78,000-seat Cleveland Stadium 14 years earlier, this would be the only time extra seating ever had been installed at League Park for a football game and the first in nearly 20 years for any sporting event at all.

The decision, Dietrich would write just after the Rams had departed for L.A., was "a decisive blunder."⁵¹ The Rams could have seated 50,000 comfortably at the larger stadium just three miles away. Instead the team attempted to accommodate a flash crowd that "virtually fought their way into League Park"[52]: 27,531 who paid admission, plus 300 servicemen and 530 civilians who had complimentary passes, all totaling 28,361[53]—more than 20 percent over the facility's seating capacity of 23,000. (And who knows how many walked away from the unattractive prospect of being seated on provisional benches.) Not surprisingly, the temporary bleachers collapsed near the end of the first quarter, sending several hundred otherwise "wildly"[54] cheering fans to the ground, injuring 31, and sending displaced spectators to seats in the permanent stands or to wander the playing field so they could watch the game from the sidelines.

The Rams won handily 20–7, as a suddenly defanged Hutson finally was shut down and in fact quit flat out on a couple of pass routes near the close of the game, to the great satisfaction of the Rams and their fans. It was a huge day in Cleveland football history—the Rams' first home victory ever against the Packers, with the promise of a breakthrough in the Western Division. Walsh had assured the public the temporary stands were sturdy and suitably sized for the number of tickets sold, but with many disappointed patrons demanding their money back after the game, and the city's building commissioner soon thereafter attributing the accident to "purely a case of overcrowding,"[55] Dietrich believed "the confusion of that afternoon cost the Rams thousands of patrons, permanently."[56] In two short months Clevelanders would have far deeper motivation for antipathy toward the franchise.

The Rams juggernaut on the field rolled on in spite of it all. Cleveland made short work of the Cardinals on November 18, 1945, at Comiskey Park, winning 35–21 to push their record to 7–1. And still Chile Walsh was hectored by all the excitement that seemed to be building around the AAFC, which was due to begin play the following season. "Look at me!" he exclaimed at a guest appearance before the Cardinals' Quarterback Club in Chicago. He noted he was 20 pounds overweight, did not have time to exercise, had bags under his eyes, was "tied" to his desk. "I'm trying to run the Rams—and someone wants to know what I think of the new league." Instead he "almost snapped the buttons off his vest"[57] with pride in the newfound success of his Rams team. If Reeves was going to transfer the franchise to L.A. and enable the Walsh brothers to return to their home state of California, the move could not come soon enough for Chile Walsh—nor, possibly, for Waterfield. Winter was stealing in, and the Rams' final games would be played around the frosty Great Lakes—a novel experience for the California quarterback.

Thanksgiving 1945 was a historic day for the Rams. Waterfield was nursing bruised ribs from the Chicago game and was unable to lift his throwing arm, and he had had only four days to recover for a hugely significant game against the Lions. With Cleveland at 7–1 and Detroit at 6–2, at stake was nothing less than the Western Division title and a berth in the NFL championship game. Temperatures in the mid-20s were forecast and were certain to make every tackle even more painful than usual. "The hell with it," Waterfield told Dippery, the team's trainer, on the morning of November 22, 1945. "Just tape me up and give me a shot." Wrapped into a "partial mummy,"[58] Waterfield went out into the cold, snow, wind, and hostile crowd of 40,017 in Detroit's Briggs Stadium and joined Benton in a passing display for the record book.

"Adam Walsh told us we had to protect Bob," Konetsky recalled. "Nobody laid a hand on him that day."[59] Instead Waterfield put on what old warhorse Snyder called "the greatest exhibition of guts I've ever seen,"[60] connecting with Benton on 10 receptions for a staggering 303 yards and easily shattering the single-game mark of 237 set by Hutson two years earlier. Benton's record would stand for 40 years. Well into the 21st century it would still rank in the top four of all time.[61] Yet Benton tallied only one touchdown that day, a 70-yard strike in the second quarter. Otherwise the Rams amassed a 28–7 lead on touchdowns from Gehrke, Waterfield, and Pritko before a furious 14-point Detroit rally in the fourth quarter and a failed last-second onside kick caused the Lions to fall just short. The Rams held on to win 28–21 and were—at long last—Western champions.

The victors posed jubilantly for a photographer's flash in their Briggs Stadium clubhouse. Adam Walsh doffed his fedora joyfully as a mob of players lifted him above a boisterous human pyramid. Chile Walsh—ebullient, his nose and cheeks still red from the cold, a pair of binoculars slung around the lapels of his ample dark overcoat—anchored a corner of the frame. Benton, his golden Rams helmet still perched on his head, stood tall in the shadowy background looking subdued and almost somber in light of the day's performance. "Up to this season," Dietrich wrote, "guessing the winners in the National Football League was just about the easiest bit of prognostication in the realm of sports. No matter how much new material the lower rung teams had gathered, it was a pretty fair bet that in the western division the victor would be either the Green Bay Packers or Chicago Bears, and in the eastern section, either the Washington Redskins or the New York Giants."[62] Only the Lions in 1935 ever had busted the monopoly. No more. Cleveland gave hope to all the other would-be champions.

Reeves treated his Rams to dinner at the Statler Hotel in Detroit, then the club returned 170 miles to Cleveland on the sleek Mercury train as management and coaches rode in one Pullman car and Rams players and their wives traveled in another. Ralph Ruthstrom, backup fullback and a working musician in the offseason, entertained the celebratory players' car with a saxophone that he still was blowing as the train approached Cleveland and disgorged its happy passengers in Union Station. "That," Marguerite Gillette, Jim's widow, recalled 70 years later with a sly smile, "was a party."[63]

Cleveland Rams: Western Division Champions. It had a nice sound to it. But the team had one more regular-season game to play—a perfunctory afternoon, as it turned out, with a spot in the championship game already clinched. Attention instead was focused on a halftime celebration of fan favorite Matheson. With boxing legend Jack Dempsey as a guest of honor, the Rams presented Matheson with a 14-karat-gold wristwatch and a $1,300 certified check with which, he was told, he could buy a truck for his farm. Cleveland then put away the Boston Yanks 20–7 before 18,470, to complete their regular season at 9–1—the best mark in the NFL that season and the first winning record in the franchise's history. A successful season as foretold for nearly a decade at last had arrived, but it was the last game the Rams would play at League Park; by the end of the following summer the Cleveland Indians also would abandon the ballpark for good and leave the historic site as a slowly deteriorating practice field for the Browns.

For now, the edgy young Rams had to wait to see who their opponents would be in the NFL championship game, but one player felt it was not necessary to wait even that long. Gillette was so certain Washington would prevail over the Giants and clinch the Eastern crown the coming weekend that he confidently predicted the Rams then would defeat the Redskins for the NFL title simply "because we've got a better ball club."[64] Sure enough, Washington downed New York before a capacity crowd at Griffith Stadium that included General Dwight D. Eisenhower to reach its fifth NFL championship game in nine years, and the first in which it would face a team other than Chicago.

So it was official: On December 16, 1945, the Rams and the Redskins would face off in Cleveland Stadium in the 13th annual NFL title game. The Rams would be only the sixth team to play in such a game, and Cleveland only the sixth city to host one.[65] "We put the championship seats on sale," Wallack remembered, "and immediately we sold 30,000 and we had another week to go before the game. The weather was beautiful. It looked as though we'd sell out the Stadium."[66]

* * *

The two-week layoff between clinching the Western Division and playing for the NFL title allowed the Rams plenty of time to reflect on their implausible 1945 season. Benton's 1,067 receiving yards, powered by his 303-yard performance against Detroit, comfortably surpassed Hutson's 834 for most in the league[67]—especially remarkable considering Benton had missed one game. Waterfield easily paced the circuit with an average of 18.1 yards per pass completion and scored six touchdowns out of eight attempts on his now-famous naked reverse play.[68] Gehrke and Gillette, on a dangerous passing team that also led the league in rushing offense, finished one-two in the NFL in average yards per carry, with Greenwood close behind at seventh.[69] Not surprisingly, Waterfield, Benton, Matheson, and Gehrke filled four of the 11 spots on the list of all-league selections as selected by *Pro Football Illustrated*. Scarry and Pritko made the second team.[70]

Witness to the unexpected Cleveland Rams spectacle were an average of 32,544 fans per game on the road—supercharged by big crowds in Philadelphia, New York, and Detroit, but an average of only 19,402 at home in League Park.[71] This was in a season when the NFL averaged 28,482 total patrons per game.[72] But in Cleveland's defense, the first two of the team's four home games had been played on the inaugural weekends of the season, before the suddenly successful Rams had a chance to establish an identity and attract a long-skeptical Cleveland public. The *Plain Dealer*'s Dietrich likely spoke for many when he wrote just before the season's start that "having gone too much for unrestrained optimism in some other seasons, I no longer trust my judgment about the Rams."[73] The third home game came seven weeks into the campaign with the overflow Packers contest at League Park that could well have been moved to larger Cleveland Stadium and driven the attendance number higher. The last contest was the season-ender against the Yanks, a noncompetitive hybrid squad of the Boston and Brooklyn clubs that was played after the Rams already had clinched the division.

Hindsight might suggest that at this point the team's move due to low attendance was a fait accompli, but at least one first-hand account indicates otherwise. One "point is now clear," Dietrich wrote in mid–November 1945. "The fans are going for pro football."[74] The Rams, he and others hoped and thought, finally were turning a corner with the ticket-buying public in Cleveland. Nevertheless a charge that the city was indifferent to an exciting championship Rams football team was levied for years to come, even as the subsequent financial success of the Browns beginning immediately the following season proves Dietrich's contention that Cleveland in late 1945 was a sleeping giant for pro football that was about to be awakened.

This much is certain: The city's warmth for the Rams was well evident when more than 800 supporters turned out on the cold night of

11. A New Power Rises in the West 159

CLEVELAND RAMS
1945 PLAYER ROSTER

No.	Player	Pos.	Ht.	Wt.
7	Waterfield, Bob	B	6'1"	191
10	Nemeth, Steve	B	5'10"	172
11	Matheson, Riley	G	6'2"	210
12	Jones, Harvey	B	6'	182
15	Harding, Roger	C	6'2"	196
16	Zirinsky, Walter	B	5'11½"	187
17	Liles, Sonny	B	5'10"	196
18	Gehrke, Fred	B	5'11"	190
19	Koch, George	B	6'1"	200
20	Ruthstrom, Ralph	B	6'4"	208
21	Jacobs, Jack	B	6'	190
24	Gillette, Jim	B	6'1½"	186
26	Winkler, Joe	C	5'10"	200
27	Roisa, Albie	B	5'10"	172
29	Lasetich, Milan	G	6'1"	215
30	Pritko, Steve	E	6'2"	210
31	Mergenthal, Arthur	G	5'11"	215
33	Shaw, Bob	E	8'3"	251
34	Colella, Tom	B	6'	187
36	West, Pat	B	6'1"	200
38	Kosetsky, Floyd	E	6'	198
39	Scarry, Michael	C	6'	220
40	Schultz, Eberle	T	6'4"	260
41	Lanz, Les	T	5'11"	227
42	Bouley, Gil	T	6'2"	233
43	Eason, Roger	T	6'2"	220
44	Hamilton, Ray	E	6'4"	210
48	Sikich, Rudy	T	6'1"	219
49	Benton, Jim	E	6'2"	206
53	Hickey, Howard	E	6'2"	205
64	Levy, Leonard	G	6'	260
65	deLauer, Bob	C	6'1"	218
66	Greenwood, Don	B	5'11½"	191

DAN REEVES, Owner
CHARLES F. WALSH, General Manager
WILLIAM H. JOHN, Business Manager
NATHAN WALLACE, Publicity Director
ADAM WALSH, Head Coach
BOB SNYDER, Backfield Coach
GEORGE TRAFTON, Line Coach
BILL CONKRIGHT, Player Scout
LEROY DIPPERY, Trainer

Testimonial Dinner

Honoring

THE CLEVELAND RAMS

Western Division Champions
National Football League

☆

December 12, 1945
Hotel Carter, Rainbow Room
Cleveland, Ohio

MENU

FRUIT COCKTAIL

✻

QUEEN OLIVES and ICED CELERY

✻

ROAST TURKEY WITH CARTER STUFFING

✻

CANDIED SWEET POTATOES

✻

BUTTERED GREEN PEAS

✻

HEAD LETTUCE WITH THOUSAND ISLAND DRESSING

✻

NEAPOLITAN ICE CREAM AND COOKIES

✻

COFFEE

PROGRAM

PRESIDING
STANLEY B. COFALL
Chairman, Special Events Committee
The Cleveland Chamber of Commerce

TOASTMASTER
CHARLES A. OTIS

MESSAGES OF APPRECIATION
GOVERNOR FRANK J. LAUSCHE
MAYOR THOMAS A. BURKE, JR.

INTRODUCTION OF RAMS PLAYERS
AND OFFICIALS
CHARLES F. WALSH
General Manager, Cleveland Rams

GUEST SPEAKER
ELMER LAYDEN
Commissioner, National Football League

NATIONAL ANTHEM

✻

Music by Shaw High School Band, Jack Horwitz
Orchestra and Lamplighters—Barber Shop Quartet

TESTIMONIAL DINNER

Sponsored by the
Special Events Committee of
THE CLEVELAND CHAMBER OF COMMERCE
with the cooperation of

CLEVELAND ATHLETIC CLUB
CLEVELAND ADVERTISING CLUB
CLEVELAND ROTARY CLUB
CLEVELAND KIWANIS CLUB
CLEVELAND TOUCHDOWN CLUB
CLEVELAND LIONS CLUB
CLEVELAND BASEBALL COMPANY
THE ARENA
ALLMEN BASKETBALL COMPANY
KNIGHTS OF COLUMBUS
NOTRE DAME CLUB OF CLEVELAND
CLEVELAND JUNIOR CHAMBER OF COMMERCE
OPTIMISTS CLUB
MAX ROSENBLUM
CLEVELAND PETROLEUM CLUB
CLEVELAND PRESS
CLEVELAND PLAIN DEALER
CLEVELAND NEWS
and
RADIO STATIONS WTAM, WGAR, WHK, and WJW

Jim Gillette's personal program from a celebratory dinner held for the Western Division champion Cleveland Rams on December 12, 1945. Teammates signing the program included Fred Gehrke, Steve Nemeth, Pat West, and George Koch, the latter with a dedication to "Red Hot Jim" *(Walker Gillette Collection)*.

December 12, 1945, to pack a testimonial dinner at the swank Rainbow Room of the Hotel Carter in honor of the team's success. Roast turkey with stuffing, candied sweet potatoes, and buttered green peas were served while the state's governor, the city's mayor, various team officials, and NFL commissioner Layden took turns at the podium praising the Rams players as they sat on a tiered dais "squirming a bit from adulation."[75] Former team president Thomas E. Lipscomb lauded departed coach Clark's foundational work in the Rams' formative prewar era. Players signed one another's dinner programs as if sensing some type of ending was at hand. Rookie George Koch for instance wrote a dedication to "Red Hot Jim"[76] Gillette—a prophetic inscription for a running back who would count among the biggest stars of the championship game.

In the days leading up to the title match the Rams generally were three- or four-point favorites, even after having failed in all five previous regular-season tries against Washington—it was thought that Cleveland had played the tougher schedule in twice defeating both the Bears and the Packers. Redskins quarterback Sammy Baugh was tending to a rib injury aggravated in the division-clinching contest against the Giants. Waterfield too still had sore ribs, but also had some analgesic in just having signed a three-year contract nearly tripling his annual salary from $7,500 to $20,000. Reeves and Walsh likely felt they had to keep the quarterback moving in the same direction as his wife, who was paid a stratospheric $50,000 that year to make the picture *Young Widow*. Reeves was investing heavily in the team as local sports writers had predicted and hoped, and the Rams' $128,000 payroll now was 25 percent higher than the next highest team's,[77] even as the owner continued to underwrite financial losses that included $40,000 in 1945.[78]

Rams vs. Redskins was a spectacle few wanted to miss. Coach Brown, at work assembling his first Browns squad and with a special eye on Rams talent, planned to attend the title game. Donelli could have; he was honorably discharged from the Navy just the day before. Sid Gillman, a founding Ram on the 1936 team and a budding Pro Football Hall of Fame coach, was in town to speak to alumni about the Miami University team he now led. Indians pitcher Bob Feller would be there, sending his best wishes to Waterfield as one hard-throwing Cleveland sports star named Bob to another. Marguerite Gillette would be there too—she had taken the train all season to wherever the team was playing. Russell would not be in attendance; she was homesick for California and "disillusioned and depressed" by the Rams' carousing and hard play both on and off the field, so she returned home for Christmas to let Waterfield "do his thing."[79] She would be thronged there by 100,000 returning servicemen who were stranded on the West Coast for the holidays.

A record gate and a crowd of 45,000, 50,000, possibly even 55,000 was expected at Cleveland Stadium for the 1945 NFL championship game. However, a familiar Cleveland gremlin arrived ahead of the Redskins: severe winter weather. And arctic winds that blew in off Lake Erie were about to cast their influence on a title game that would go into history as being among the coldest and strangest ever played.

CHAPTER 12

"An even zero": The Title Game

Cleveland Municipal Stadium rose on landfill on the city's ragged northern shore in 1931, six years before the birth of the Cleveland Rams in the National Football League. The old ballpark started to come down on December 17, 1995, precisely a half-century after the Rams greeted their first dawn as NFL champions, when fans of the Cleveland Browns tore out seats in protest of a second pro football team departing the city. In its 64 years of existence between, the Stadium stood like a stolid, weather-beaten sentinel on the Lake Erie lakefront, its concrete, steel, yellow-brick, and aluminum composition harboring cold year-round, the so-called "ventilated superstructure"[1] of aluminum louvers in its upper-deck wall permitting winter winds from Canada to whistle through the horseshoe and sluice around its riveted-steel pillars like a perpetual ghostly presence. "Windy, cold—worse than Chicago," Virginia native Walker Gillette remembered of the place, where he played a road game in 1970 as a wide receiver for the San Diego Chargers. "Everybody says Chicago is cold, but that stadium on that water was *cold*."[2]

It was the frigid dampness that particularly devastated player, spectator, and stadium alike. Winter winds jetting across Canada picked up moisture from the watery archipelago of the Great Lakes before they had had a chance to freeze, then reached landfall at Lake Erie's southern shore. A frequent result was one big blast of cold, wind, and wet—lake-effect snow. And it could arrive capriciously, unannounced. The temperature in Cleveland had soared to 50 degrees Fahrenheit[3] the weekend before the Rams front office put tickets on sale for the 1945 World Championship Playoff of the National Football League, and more than 30,000—nearly 40 percent of the Stadium's 78,000 capacity—were sold immediately. Very much in jeopardy was the NFL playoff-game attendance record of 48,120 set in 1938 at Manhattan's Polo Grounds.[4]

12. "An even zero": The Title Game

Cleveland Stadium, upper left on the city's lakefront in this December 1937 aerial photo, not surprisingly was subject to strong winter winds and lake-effect snow. The game-time temperature for the 1945 NFL Championship Game was an "even zero" degree Fahrenheit *(National Archives and Records Administration/Wikimedia Commons)*.

But by the morning of Monday, December 10, 1945, six days before the game, the temperature in northeastern Ohio plummeted to the low 20s, and snow that by nightfall would accumulate as much as a foot-and-a-half on the city's hilly east side began to descend. Traffic was snarled, salt trucks were dispatched, and it looked as if repeated bouts of snow would continue all week, right up to that Sunday's championship game. Civic leaders slipped and slid their way through city streets for the team's mid-week testimonial dinner, where Rams head coach Adam Walsh assured the gathering of more than 800 that his players would be on their game even if they had to play on "skates, skis, or sleds."[5]

Indeed an ability to get the Stadium in decent condition by game day was very much in question. To keep the turf as dry as possible and prevent it from freezing, the Rams cornered the market on straw in northern Ohio by ordering 9,000 bales at a cost of $7,200—nearly the equivalent of Rams quarterback Bob Waterfield's entire salary for the 1945 season—then asked the Stadium's groundskeepers to spread it on the field and cover it with a tarpaulin.⁶ But another 18 inches of snow continued to fall in Cleveland as the week wore on.

Then the questions began: How best to remove the snow and the tarp to prepare for the game? How to sweep up the straw? And who would do it? The Rams were willing to pay whatever was necessary to get the field ready, but they had insufficient manpower. They approached Cleveland City Hall, which in turn prevailed on the city's street commissioner, who argued that his crew was preoccupied with its primary job: clearing the city's roadways. So a few days before the game, 50 workers from the United States Employment Service—hired by the city at the Rams' expense—arrived to hand-shovel snow off the tarpaulin and move it to the grandstand walls. Meanwhile another 50 hastily recruited workers, mostly from the city's trash-collection department, roamed the stands with brooms and shovels, brushing off snow, pushing it out of aisles, and dumping it under seats. The Stadium's parking area would be left as it was; officials assumed most spectators simply would walk down to the snowbound lakefront rather than risk it by car.

With the extreme cold and snow, the Rams practiced inside the 107th Cavalry Armory in Shaker Heights, while the Redskins, arriving via train with their 110-piece marching band, went through a brief workout at the Central Armory. Other preparations proceeded apace.

The Cleveland front office contacted a downstate Ohio farm and arranged for delivery of a ram to be dubbed Swifty Jr., heir to the sheepish mascot of the Rams' disastrous 1–10 NFL debut season in 1937.

Waterfield planned to wake before dawn on game day to study his playbook and prepare for his biggest test to date. Once diffident about football, he now was finding he could not envision life without the game and was making plans to extend his career as a coach when his playing days were over. This would be his first contest at Cleveland Stadium, and his last as a Cleveland player.

Waterfield's star receiver Jim Benton was recovering from the flu, gradually gaining strength from a bug that had classified him as a doubtful starter days earlier.

Reeves, as ever superstitious about his wife's presence at games and eager to ensure the team's luck, laughed good-naturedly at a reporter's suggestion that she be "air-expressed to Los Angeles"⁷—the choice of her proposed destination being uncomfortably ironic as events would transpire—but he still arranged for her to be seated far from him in the Stadium.

12. "An even zero": The Title Game

Unaccustomed to Cleveland cold but characteristically fashionable, he would don a beaver fur cap for the game.

On Saturday, an evening flurry of snow descended as tens of thousands of bearers of tickets, paid and complimentary, turned into bed steeled for the next day. The game-day forecast called for a temperature of 15 degrees or less.

When December 16, 1945, finally dawned, the lakefront was even colder than the weathermen had predicted—a numbing eight degrees below zero at 6:30 a.m. when the Stadium's floodlights were switched on.[8] At 7:00 a.m., with only six and a half hours until the 1:30 p.m. kickoff, a crew of about 250 men and high-school boys took pitchforks and flatbed trucks onto the field and began removing straw at the rate of 25 bales per minute,[9] ringing the grandstand, sidelines, end zones, and bench areas with soft tuffets laid hard against the brown and dusty-white turf. This was completed by 11:00 a.m. Then the grounds crew lined and marked the field; yet it froze despite all the effort. "There's nothing that could have been done about it. Nothing at all," Stadium groundskeeper Emil Bossard lamented. "The field just up and froze on us, pure and simple."[10] Rams fullback Don Greenwood, who would injure his shoulder in the game, later observed that the playing surface felt "just like a paved road."[11]

Up in the "slightly heated"[12] press box, a fireman was charged with the task of wiping frost off windows so reporters could see the action on the field. Harry Wismer of the ABC radio network bundled up in double overcoats, scarves, and a stocking cap as he prepared to describe the game to a live national audience. Some 50 reporters, "high among the icy crags"[13] of the Stadium, elbowed for indoor space, as others were relegated with no small complaint to outside seats that were set up with makeshift planks as writing tables.

Media covering the 1945 NFL Championship Game at Cleveland Stadium were housed in a "slightly heated" press box or else relegated to outside seats set up with makeshift planks as writing tables. For their troubles they received blue-and-gold press pins festooned with the Rams logo and the words "N.F.L. World Championship Playoff: 1945" *(Donald Gries Collection)*

And then the fans began to arrive: a ragtag army under blankets and draped in "parkas, varicolored earmuffs, arctics, stadium boots, flying suits, ski troop uniforms"[14]—many with flasks in their pockets. The first hard snow had stopped ticket sales cold, and more than 3,000 of the 35,305[15] who bought seats in advance were no-shows who elected instead to stay next to their radios and their fireplaces. But the hardy 32,178[16] who arrived witnessed the first-ever pro football playoff game in Cleveland. And with the Stadium only about 40 percent full, they huddled in seats closest to the field to stay warm and to get a better view.

Though game-day attendance was a disappointment after high expectations—speculation would build as to how much better the day's take could have been if not for the damnably cold weather—this was the most-attended pro football game ever to that time in Ohio,[17] and it exceeded the throngs that would gather at three of the next five NFL championship games including the 29,751 who watched the epic Rams-Browns showdown in 1950 in the same stadium.[18]

Wrote Franklin Lewis for the *Cleveland Press* of the 1945 title game: "The 32,178 customers who laughed at the gale were just about half as many as even ordinary weather would have attracted. As it was, the crowd was a terrific surprise to all parties."[19] Dick McCann, reporter for the *Times-Herald* in Washington, a city that supported the Redskins far more faithfully than Cleveland had the Rams, agreed. "Pro football is definitely here to stay when you can get 32,178 men, women and children to sit through the Polar temperatures they had to endure," he wrote. "And, by the way, if this isn't a good sports town, then it's full of a lot of fools."[20] At the very least it was a town that came to act foolishly, or at least to stay warm; one expert observer said that "he had never seen so many inebriates in crowds even three times as large as the one on the frigid lake front," reported Chads O. Skinner in the *Cleveland Plain Dealer*.[21]

Below the grandstand, in the home clubhouse, some Rams players insulated themselves with their alternate blue game jerseys before tugging the day's yellow game jerseys over their shoulder pads. Among the favored accessories were gloves and chemically treated heat pads, and once the game had begun, players on both benches huddled under hooded and high-collared coats and gathered up straw from the sidelines to use as cover for their legs and feet. This would create instantly striking images of the type to which stateside audiences unfortunately had become accustomed—of American can-do innovation in the face of privation. "It wasn't so bad for those of us playing because we didn't platoon," recalled Mike "Mo" Scarry, Rams center and captain, "but the guys on the sideline froze."[22]

12. "An even zero": The Title Game

Official program for the 1945 NFL Championship Game—just the 13th such playoff in NFL history and a record-setter to that time for gross gate, net gate, and radio broadcast rights despite the extremely cold weather in Cleveland Stadium *(Walker Gillette Collection)*.

Not long before game time, Rams coach Adam Walsh caught wind that the Redskins planned to wear basketball sneakers to gain better traction on the hard frozen field. The Rams had come equipped only to play in cleats, so Walsh went over to Washington's locker room and pleaded with coach Dudley DeGroot to do the same. DeGroot agreed—with fateful consequences. Washington owner George Preston Marshall would hear about DeGroot's "gentleman's agreement,"[23] and at halftime would express his vehement displeasure to DeGroot as he quietly made plans to fire the coach after the completion of the game and the season.

By kickoff the temperature had nudged up to "an even zero"[24] and the sky was beginning to clear. Scarry, the Rams' captain, trotted to the center of the field for the coin toss attired in his yellow helmet, yellow jersey with royal-blue trim, white pants with one blue and two yellow vertical stripes, yellow socks with three horizontal blue stripes, and a blue warm-up with "RAMS 39"[25] in yellow lettering on the back. Texas native Sammy Baugh wore the Redskins' burgundy helmet, gold pants, and jersey and hose of burgundy and gold, no doubt cursing his second wintry game in Cleveland in three visits. Members of the game's officiating crew bounced on their feet to stay warm as referee Ronald Gibbs tossed a coin. Umpire Harry Robb, once a member of the legendary Bulldogs in nearby Canton, returned from a dugout run to retrieve a pair of gloves as he remembered "how much your nose and hands and ears hurt" in such weather.[26]

Washington won the toss and elected to receive, and at last the game was on.

DeGroot, knowing star quarterback Baugh's ribcage was smarting, asked long-time backup Frank Filchock to be ready at a moment's notice as he planned to feed the ball repeatedly to burly fullback Frank Akins to start the game. On the first play Akins burst through the right side of the line, tore ahead for eight yards—and was swiftly delivered with a broken nose. "After that [he] was stopped," the *Washington Post* reported.[27] Akins would remain in the game but at reduced capacity as the Rams signaled they would not be run on this day.

The Redskins punted, and Cleveland's rookie wonder Waterfield took his position behind center and began a long drive from the closed end of the Stadium toward full daylight at midfield. With the temperature reaching six degrees above zero[28] and the Rams' yellow jerseys looking brilliant in the full sunshine of the patchily snowy field, Waterfield dropped back and heaved a wobbling pass to Benton along the left sideline for a 30-yard gain. Suddenly the Rams were threatening at Washington's 14-yard line and driving toward the straw-barricaded bleachers that decades later became the

Browns' Dawg Pound. After three short gains it was a critical fourth-and-three from the seven, and the Rams went for it. Cleveland's Riley "Rattlesnake" Matheson stepped back from his left-guard position and vaulted over to take on end Doug Turley as tackle Elbie Schultz slanted in, and halfback Jim Gillette hit the left hole looking as if he had daylight—a first down if not a touchdown. But Matheson failed to hold his block and Turley laid a shoulder into the legs of the leaping Gillette, who crashed to the field as he practically ate chalk on the five-yard line. The Rams were a yard short, and Washington took over to set up the most controversial and decisive play of the game.

The Redskins, as was the custom of the era, immediately played for field position from their hemmed-in position and lined up for a punt. But Baugh, halfway into his own end zone, mishandled the snap. As the Rams' Floyd Konetsky crashed in on him with outstretched arms, Baugh heaved a wounded duck to no one at the 10-yard line, taking an intentional grounding penalty and moving the Redskins half the distance back to their own goal line, to roughly their own two.

Washington again lined up in punt formation, just to the left of the goal post, with end/placekicker Joe Aguirre backed up to the padded part of the post as he dropped into his stance. Baugh now was in the rear of the end zone just a few yards in front of a heap of straw bales, but this time he had a play up his sleeve. The snap shot back and Baugh again bobbled the cold ball at knee-level before he hurriedly unloaded a hard, powerful pass to his left. In bright sunshine the ball smacked improbably off the center of the crossbar and skittered back to a corner of the end zone untouched. "We had no idea what was going on," recalled Jerry Sulecki, 10 years old at the time and seated with his father in the north grandstand behind the Redskins' bench. "The game stopped, and suddenly they put two points on the scoreboard for the Rams."[29] By existing league rules the officials correctly had ruled the play a safety, but it would be the last NFL game in which such a call would be made; at the vehement off-season insistence of Washington's owner, the so-called Baugh/Marshall Rule would decree any forward pass thrown from the end zone and striking the goal posts forevermore to be an incomplete pass.

Nearly two decades later, Washington end Wayne Millner, Baugh's intended receiver as he streaked on a sideline route, insisted that "never was there a surer touchdown pass" and "there was no one within a mile of me"[30] until a gust of wind carried the ball into the crossbar. A review of game film shows he indeed was open but with Waterfield just a few steps behind him in relatively tight coverage as the aborted play wound down.[31]

Had Baugh indeed been able to deliver the ball to Millner, the speedy Waterfield may well have had the speed to catch the receiver.

Regardless, the tally was Rams 2, Redskins 0—but Washington was poised to retaliate. The Rams were on their third consecutive stalled series in the second quarter when Waterfield attempted to thread a pass to Steve Pritko as the Rams end was swarmed by maroon jerseys. Washington's Ki Aldrich intercepted, and the Redskins took over near midfield. Filchock now had replaced Baugh, who clearly was in pain while lifting his arm to pass. From the Rams' 38-yard line, Filchock found Steve Bagarus at the 15, and the halfback—already two steps ahead of Waterfield—screeched to a stop at the 10 as Waterfield tried to wrestle him down, swung out of his grip, and glided into the end zone, leaving his Ram defender prone on the sideline.

Aguirre kicked the extra point, and it was Redskins 7, Rams 2.

Cleveland reclaimed the lead just before halftime when Waterfield faded back, and with Milan "Mike" Lazetich and Pat West barely holding off two onrushing Redskins, launched a high arc straight over the middle and into the hands of Benton, who was a comfortable distance ahead of the Redskins' Les Dye. Benton traced a snowy path down the center of the field and into the end zone to complete a 37-yard touchdown strike, running through the goalposts as if through the gates of victory with Dye flailing and sliding into the end zone in his wake.

The point-after attempt by the Rams' novice placekicker was not nearly as easy and spelled the ultimate difference in the game. After a long count, two Redskins stormed the Rams' backfield and descended on Waterfield—placekicker for only the eleventh regulation game of his young life. They dive-bombed past him as the kick was partially blocked, but somehow the ball still went up end-over-end, struck the crossbar with considerably less force than had Baugh's pass, hung for a moment, and—as if offered a slight push by fate's hand—landed safely on the other side.

Rams 9, Redskins 7.

Cleveland hounded Filchock on the ensuing series, sacking him twice and intercepting a pass as the Rams headed into halftime with a two-point lead and some swagger. But Walsh knew the Redskins hardly were down for the count and looked to prevent his young team from getting overconfident. "You guys haven't shown me a helluva lot," he charged in the team's acrid locker room.[32] Out on the Stadium field, Santa made a sleigh-borne halftime appearance as bleacher spectators huddled against a scoreboard wall for protection from the biting lake winds.

The Rams received the second-half kickoff and again marshaled a drive that brought them quickly to the Redskins' 44 on runs by halfbacks Gillette and Fred Gehrke. Gillette then ran straight ahead from the shadows of the backfield untouched as Waterfield paused for two or three beats and unloaded a fluttering pass that found the receiver in full stride and broad sunlight at the Redskins' 15. Gillette pulled in the ball over his left shoulder and cruised into the end zone with Aldrich diving at his feet. This time, Waterfield's PAT was no good as it pulled right, but the Rams were ahead by eight points, 15–7.

Then it was nerve-wracking time for Cleveland. In the Stadium's upper deck a large water main sprang a leak and turned a concrete spectator ramp into a veritable toboggan slide. Elsewhere a number of increasingly numb fans were getting the bright idea to set straw afire in the stands. Chester Sulecki, a local restaurateur attending the game with a vendor's complimentary tickets, forbade his son from getting too close to one of the fires for fear the boy would burn himself.

The Redskins pulled to within one point late in the third quarter with a touchdown as Bob Seymour, wide open, nursed a Filchock pass into his hands and high-legged his way through straw bales bordering the end zone. It was Rams 15, Redskins 14. Meanwhile, exhaustion seemed to be settling in for the Rams. Rushes went for just a few yards at a time whether by Gillette, Gehrke, or Greenwood, the latter of whom was hampered by his sore shoulder and was platooning with West. A long pass to Gillette in the wind-swept Stadium fell short. Another long attempt, to Benton, was bobbled and fell incomplete. A heave by Waterfield found no one open and bounced into the end zone.

The Redskins had several chances to pull off an upset as the game straggled into the fourth quarter. Their first opportunity came when an ill-advised lateral by West deep in Washington territory bounced off Gillette's arm and landed instead in Aldrich's hands as he clambered along the snowy sideline. West seemed destined to be the goat of the game when Filchock bounced right back with a short pass to Dye, who caught the ball in heavy traffic and bounded down his left sideline with Roger Harding, Matheson, and Waterfield taking chase. But Waterfield cut an angle of pursuit, and as he and Harding crashed into each other attempting to push Dye out of bounds, he caught Dye's shoe at the 32 and brought him down. It was a touchdown-saving tackle. Four players later, with Baugh holding, Aguirre—ironically nicknamed "Hot Toe"[33]—on this frigid day attempted what would be a go-ahead and potentially game-winning 31-yard field goal. The wind-tossed kick went up and looked to have made it inside the left upright. Field judge Bill Downes, standing in the end zone, shaded to his right to field the ball, then motioned.

No good.

The Rams and their fans erupted in relief.

But more than six minutes remained. Cleveland again could not get a drive started, and with the sunshine gone, punted the ball away. Rams owner Reeves barely could sit in the press box, nor could he bring himself to look at the field. The Redskins drove into Cleveland territory, and Aguirre again lined up for a potential game-winner. This time the kick was far short and landed at the seven. The exhalation of relief among Cleveland fans joined the winter winds. About two minutes still remained, however, as the Rams quickly went three-and-out. But Waterfield, the wunderkind from California, booted a 54-yard punt that sailed deep into Washington territory and pinned the Redskins at their own 15. This, as the *New York Times* reported, "sealed the Redskins' doom."[34] Reeves, the Rams, and their fans finally dared to believe they might just win.

Lined up behind center about five yards into the Stadium's baseball infield with a long field to go and not much time left on the clock, Filchock was pressured immediately as Howard "Red" Hickey barreled around the Redskins' right end. Filchock fired into a sea of Rams jerseys—Albie Reisz, Gillette, and Waterfield—and Reisz, a local kid from Lorain, Ohio and the team's backup quarterback, came up with an interception to ice the game. Two plays later, Waterfield dove into the scrum to make it official.

Rams 15, Redskins 14. The Rams were NFL champions. The hardscrabble, expansion, hapless, second-division, perpetually losing Cleveland Rams were … improbable World Champions.

Rams fans who had negotiated their way down from the grandstand and swarmed the sidelines in the game's closing minutes now stormed the field, ripped up a goal post under the benign gaze of nightstick-wielding city policemen, ringed the Cleveland players on the field, lifted Waterfield to their shoulders and carried him off the field, asked him to sign autographs—which he did for just a short time. "We're all going to freeze to death," he finally said.[35]

Reisz was among the first to push past fans who jammed the dugout door and reach the Rams' locker room. "We're champs. THE CHAMPS!" he roared.

"Hell yes, we're the champs!" West shouted.[36]

Benton, characteristically laconic and a veteran of many losing Rams teams, simply yelled: "Wow! Whadda you know. After all these years, we made it."[37]

Reeves could not believe it either. He was convinced the Redskins would erase the Rams' one-point margin. "Well they did it," he said. "I've

12. "An even zero": The Title Game 173

been used to losing for so long I wasn't counting on anything until it was all over."[38]

In the post-game commotion a very intoxicated fan pushed his way into the Rams' locker room, telling police, "Scram, I own this club."[39] The police ejected him, for it surely was Reeves who held title to the team. With reporters from across the nation as his audience, Reeves "intimated"[40] that League Park's 23,000 capacity might be expanded by 10,000 the following season to accommodate what was certain to be a much larger fan base in Cleveland and bigger paydays for the team. It looked as if the Rams were going to stay after all, as Reeves fended off persistent rumors about the following season—that the Rams would train in California, that Paul Brown would coach the Rams instead of the Browns...

But Walsh was Reeves' man, soon to be named the NFL's coach of the year. Walsh bellowed to his players, "You were great all the way!"[41] He said he knew as much all the way back at training camp in Bowling Green, and he wandered the clubhouse exclaiming his praises until he finally took each player by the hand to extend his personal thanks. He declared Waterfield—the only pure quarterback to take his team to an NFL title as a rookie[42]—to be the "greatest T-formation quarterback in the country."[43] He praised Gillette for rushing 17 times for 101 yards, alone nearly tripling the Redskins' total rushing output of 35 yards.[44] The Redskins, Walsh said, had "overshifted a bit at times"—focused in no small part on the ailing Benton, who ended up with nine passes for 125 yards and a touchdown[45]—"and that's why we made such good use of Gillette."[46]

As the celebration wound down, Walsh finally grabbed a folding chair and tilted it contentedly against the yellow-tiled clubhouse wall, with coffee in one hand, a cigarette in the other, and snow still wedged to the heel of his coach's football cleats. "Just say that I knew the size of their hearts," he said to a lingering reporter. The young Rams, he said, were the much better team, the game's tight margin notwithstanding, "and on a good field, we'd have won with ease."[47] He revealed he had made Cleveland his permanent residence and that he looked forward to working soon on the Rams' team for 1946.

The locker room slowly cleared out. Waterfield, among the last to leave, approached Walsh. "I'm shoving off for California tonight, coach,"[48] he said. With a teammate as his passenger (either guard Sonny Liles or center Bob Delauer; accounts vary), Waterfield would jump that night into his new Ford coupe, head to Cincinnati, then catch Route 66 to begin the long westward trek that would get him to the West Coast by Christmas Eve. There, staying in his mother's house in Van Nuys and triumphantly bearing foot-

"You were great all the way!" shouted Cleveland Rams head coach Adam Walsh (far right) to his victorious players in the team's Cleveland Stadium locker room after the Rams defeated the Washington Redskins 15–14 to win the 1945 NFL championship. From left, the three stars of the game accounting for all of Cleveland's scoring: halfback Jim Gillette, quarterback Bob Waterfield, and end Jim Benton *(The Cleveland Press Collection, Cleveland State University Library).*

ball's greatest boon, he would receive numerous congratulatory telegrams— one from the NFL office notifying him he had been named the league's most valuable player, another from the Touchdown Club in Washington, D.C., inviting him to stand before guests including General Dwight D. Eisenhower to receive a trophy as pro football's outstanding player of the year. In such an adulatory glow he would spend what his wife Jane Russell years later remembered as "perhaps the best Christmas we ever had."[49]

"It's been a great year," Waterfield said to Walsh. Then: "It's a little hard to say goodbye."

"Bob," Walsh replied, "it's going to be an even greater year, next year."[50]

* * *

12. "An even zero": The Title Game

Yet all around was persistent evidence that pro football was, in the end, a business, often shorter on sentiment than on a healthy interest in the bottom line. Elsewhere in Cleveland Stadium, away from the Rams' jubilant locker room, the day's receipts were being tallied up and it was a bonanza for all. Reeves just had presided over an NFL-record gross gate for a championship game of $164,542.40, which easily set a new high mark of $5.11 per attendee.[51] After the taxman took his 19-percent share, the game delivered a record net gate of $133,005.43. Radio broadcast rights kicked in another $13,081.81, also a new record.[52]

Reeves' take after expenses was not bad either. Though an accusation was made at the time by the press and would persist a half-century later that Cleveland's city fathers had "tripled the regular [Stadium] rental fee for the game"[53] and thereby hastened the team's exodus, Rams general manager Charles "Chile" Walsh in fact made a statement a week after the game that a claim of "gouging" by the city had been "just a little joke."[54] He said the team actually was "more than happy" to pay $10,000 in Stadium rental when the customary fee in the NFL would have been a full 15 percent of the gross gate—$24,681. Cleveland had not tripled the rent as charged; in fact, it was something of the opposite—the rent was a bit more than a third of what it could have been. As it was, the city stood merely to break even after paying to help get the Stadium in shape—but with a world championship, who really was counting?

The players, too, were happy. Drawing from a record players' pool, each Ram received $1,469.74.[55] "That was big money back then," said Marguerite Gillette, Jim's widow.[56] It was sufficient to entice Gillette—as well as Gehrke, West, and Pritko—to agree to return to the Rams for another season.

Still, the new All-America Football Conference remained the wolf at the door. McCann speculated that a league with newborn franchises in Miami and Los Angeles received a huge "boost" from the "subzeroed" playoff game and soon could be staging their own playoffs in "lovely weather"[57]—an observation that surely favored heretical talk of expanding the NFL beyond the Mississippi River. On the morning after the title game the league's owners met in Commissioner Elmer Layden's suite at the Hotel Cleveland to discuss a franchise spot vacated when Dan Topping, owner of the Brooklyn Dodgers and baseball's New York Yankees, bolted the NFL and took his team and Yankee Stadium to the AAFC. And deepening the NFL's concern was Rams star lineman Matheson's revelation that he had received an enticing offer to jump to the fledgling Cleveland Browns as line coach at nearly twice the salary the Rams had paid him in 1945. Reports quickly followed that the AAFC had approached assistant coach Bob Snyder as well as nearly all of the Rams' starters: Benton, Pritko, Scarry, Gehrke, Gillette, and Greenwood; and linemen Schultz, Lazetich, and Gil Bouley. Only Waterfield seemed to be off-limits, possibly because of his stratospheric new contract.

It was unsettling news, but Cleveland newspapermen and sports fans had every reason to believe they soon would be witness to two championship-caliber pro football teams: the Rams, who would host six games at League Park with finally, in their ninth NFL season, a favorable home schedule; and the Browns, who would play seven games at Cleveland Stadium in their inaugural year. "Could be," the *Cleveland Press* speculated, "that the city will own two pro football champions at this time next year."[58] But a darker view held that the two franchises were bent on a deadly showdown, with neither side giving "any indication that it believes there is room in Cleveland for two football teams," the *Plain Dealer*'s John Dietrich wrote.[59]

Some chose to focus on the positive indicators. Browns owner Arthur "Mickey" McBride offered to meet with Rams management to avoid scheduling conflicts between the two leagues, with his Browns potentially playing some night games or even sharing the Stadium with the Rams. The Browns and the Rams might even meet one another in a non-league exhibition game, it was reported, provided the Rams stayed—and an NFL franchise would not pull up stakes entirely and move to another city immediately after it just had won a championship, would it? Reeves himself had said that League Park might be expanded.

On New Year's Day the *Plain Dealer*'s poet laureate James E. Doyle rhapsodized about a "completely joyous" sports year ahead in 1946:

> Here's hoping for a year of slams
> All grand again for Cleveland's Rams,
> And may that Waterfield kid's arm
> Stay full of fire that's four-alarm.
> I ask, too, that the Cleveland Browns team
> Will be a wow, a go-to-town team—[60]

The Rams and the Browns were about to duke it out for the local fan's interest and discretionary dollar, with Clevelanders the winner. They soon were to discover how wrong they were.

Part IV: Up and Gone

Chapter 13

"The public be damned"

On Tuesday, January 8, 1946, a telephone rang in the New York City office of Cleveland Rams owner Daniel F. Reeves. More than three weeks had passed since he had returned home from Cleveland and the 1945 National Football League championship game, an almost indescribably cold event that left an indelible mark on him and the other team owners. They were about to debate whether to close the coming regular season one week earlier than they had in 1945 "so that there would be no repetition" of the arctic debacle that had "cut down the crowd" and made the frozen field in Cleveland "not conducive to good football."[1] It was but one of many steps that two decades later would carry the league to staging its championships at neutral, warm-weather sites.

On the line for Reeves now was Bob Yonkers, a sports reporter from the *Cleveland Press*. *What does he want?* Reeves wondered. *Aren't all the Cleveland newspapers on strike?* They were, and the strike was in its third day, silencing postwar Clevelanders' primary source of information. A story on January 5 that the newly established Browns had offered to cooperate with the Rams' front office in avoiding game-scheduling conflicts in Cleveland was the last that local newspaper readers would read of pro football—of anything—for four-and-a-half weeks. With labor unrest widespread in postwar America, the pressmen's union had stopped the presses of the city's three dailies—the *Plain Dealer*, the *Press*, and the *News*. Nonetheless Yonkers had received a tip, and as a thoroughgoing reporter he was seeking a confirmation or a denial regardless of whether the *Press* would have the means to print it. The rumor—and Yonkers was "reasonably certain"[2] this was about to happen—was that the Cleveland Rams, newly crowned NFL champions, were about to be transferred to Los Angeles. If true, this was big news—national news. *What about it?* Yonkers asked Reeves.

The Rams owner steeled himself. He liked to socialize with sportswriters as a rule, but now he had to be careful. "I'm well aware of the rumors," he told Yonkers. "I've seen them in the papers here and I've been asked about them a dozen times. But as far as I'm concerned they're not true. The Rams definitely will stay in Cleveland. In fact, I will have a statement to make before the end of the month that will dispel all rumors for once and for all."[3] Yonkers inquired as to why Rams general manager Charles "Chile" Walsh might have been in Los Angeles convening with civic and sports figures the previous three days. Reeves assured him Walsh was lining up exhibition games for the coming autumn, which Yonkers found a bit strange considering Walsh two months earlier had agreed to a preseason rematch with the Redskins in L.A.; how many more exhibition games on the very distant West Coast were there likely to be? This explanation seemed no more plausible than another that had emanated from the team: that Walsh's mother was seriously ill, which turned out not to be true.

In short, Yonkers wrote, Reeves "vehemently denied that he was even contemplating the move."[4]

But Reeves need not have bothered, for his declaration would be rendered largely mute by Cleveland's newspaper strike. The presses moreover still would be idle three weeks later when he was to have made his end-of-the-month statement. Cleveland papers in fact would not be back on the streets until February 6, 1946, and by then, Reeves' champion franchise was gone from Cleveland. But Reeves did not know this for certain on January 8, because still standing between him and his ultimate goal of basing the Rams in Los Angeles were the headstrong owners of the NFL.

For several years Rams general manager Chile Walsh had "denied with some vehemence the assorted rumors that the Rams might be moved elsewhere"[5] even as he and Reeves made quiet inquiries into the availability of stadiums in at least two other cities and the willingness of at least one prospective head coach to live in L.A. But now the NFL was about to hold its owners meeting in New York, and Reeves had every intention of surfacing his intent, of capitalizing on the opportunity to request permission once and for all to enact his "long-range plan"[6] to move his franchise to California. Winning the 1945 NFL title finally had given him leverage and elevated him to a level of league-wide esteem necessary to improve his circumstances. He would lay out his evidence for the need to leave: most damningly the city's lukewarm response at the box office and his $40,000 in financial losses during a championship season, not to mention Cleveland's unpredictable and even inhospitable weather. What was more, the move would be in everyone's best interest as the NFL needed to establish a foothold in

California before the All-America Football Conference's San Francisco 49ers and well-funded Los Angeles Dons, the latter founded by entertainer Don Ameche, could play their first games there.

But privately, a clincher for Reeves probably was the very real likelihood his team would be cast into the shadow of the new Browns and their perch in Cleveland Stadium, at best as co-tenants and peers and at worst as diminished NFL champions. The enormous Stadium had been a major reason Reeves elected to keep the Rams in Cleveland rather than move them to Boston forthrightly as he originally had planned. But now it looked as if he would be penned into the older, smaller, and less remunerative League Park when the Rams at last were a winner. Instead it was Browns founding owner Arthur "Mickey" McBride with his local political clout and decades of business relationships that had sewn up the Stadium. So Reeves turned his sights instead to the distant horizon—beyond the industrial Great Lakes and the Midwestern prairies and the Rocky Mountains—to the even larger Los Angeles Memorial Coliseum and southern California's Mediterranean climate and booming postwar population.

The team's performance on the field was peaking at just the right time. Reeves had watched as his brother Edward Reeves and co-owner George Preston Marshall transferred the Redskins from Boston to enjoy immediate success and fan embrace in Washington, D.C., as they won the NFL championship in 1937. Reeves envisioned a similarly quick payback in Los Angeles. "We have no problem that a winning team won't cure, and after the war we are pretty sure we will have it," he had said on one of his rare visits to Cleveland in 1945.[7] This turned out to be quite true, and at the time his confidence was reassuring to locals, but he had not said explicitly that he expected to have a winning team in *Cleveland*. The Rams practically were a Californian-led franchise already, with quarterback Bob Waterfield and the brothers Walsh—general manager Chile and head coach Adam Walsh—having been reared in the Los Angeles area. Even Waterfield's movie-star wife Jane Russell was well associated with L.A. and would be held accountable for the team's move by some Clevelanders for years to come.

On Saturday, January 12, 1946, at New York's Commodore Hotel, Reeves made his proposal and confirmed with dismay his hunch about his fellow owners. Bristling with no votes on the proposed move was the core of the league's power structure: George Halas of the Chicago Bears; Marshall of the Redskins, still smarting from his championship-game loss in what he doubtless thought was unjust fashion; and Tim Mara of the New York Giants—all concerned team travel to the West Coast would be prohibitively time-consuming and expensive.[8] This was, after all, the end of an era dominated by train travel, with flying still restricted to small-capacity planes at a large ticket price. Also opposing the Rams' transfer was the Chicago Cardinals' Charles Bidwill, but only because he hoped California would be his own team's new home. (More than 40 years later the Cardinals finally would land in Arizona following long stints in Chicago and St. Louis.)

When the vote was taken, two more voices had been added to the opposition and Reeves' motion went down to defeat 6–4. Spiriting the Rams all the way to Los Angeles would be "financial lunacy,"[9] the majority ruled. Most of the franchises of the era already were awash in red ink, and moving was not necessarily a cure-all. Indeed in a few short years the Eagles, en route to the 1948 NFL championship, would lose twice as much money as the 1945 Rams had[10]—and in a city more than twice the size of Cleveland.[11] Yet somehow they would manage to remain in Philadelphia. No, the owners said, laying on an additional expense of travel to and from California would exacerbate the established league's financial troubles just as it faced very real competition. Leave financial extravagance to the AAFC owners, they said. The new league's profligates in their folly had set up franchises in far-flung San Francisco, Los Angeles, and Miami and would use *airplanes* to transport their players; soon enough they would reap the financial whirlwind and fold, thus ending their threat to the NFL.

Reeves was incensed. The NFL's old guard had held him down for too long, had hung him out to dry when he alone disbanded operations in 1943 because of the war, then had made his reentry to the league especially difficult. The nation's future, it was clear to him, was in the West. How could his fellow owners not see this? They were stuck in the East, and in the past. "You call this is a *national* league?" he groused. "I suppose Texas doesn't interest you, either?" It did not. Even Reeves' backup plan—to take the Rams to the Cotton Bowl in Dallas[12]—was rejected, but he would not be bullied. He stormed out of the meeting proclaiming: "Consider the Cleveland Rams out of the National Football League."[13]

Behind the scenes, things were "very contentious" between Reeves and the other NFL owners, "to the point where they were going to throw him out of the league, and he was going to sue them," said Joe Horrigan of the Pro Football Hall of Fame. Reeves was not especially reverent toward his fellow owners, and "from most accounts" he was "not an easy guy to deal with."[14] Years in the future, after the Hall of Fame was established in Canton, Ohio, but before his own enshrinement there, Reeves would write a letter to newly installed director Dick McCann and jokingly request a job be reserved for him "as Assistant Curator—as I would enjoy painting mustaches on some of the busts entrusted to your care."[15] This was characteristic

Reeves, his son Dan Reeves, Jr., suggested. Through the decades of his clashes with fellow Rams owners as well as with the rest of the league, Reeves always maintained an outlook of "'I'm going to enjoy life. I'm not going to let these people get me down.' So maybe that's what the other owners didn't like about him—that he was much too carefree."[16] But Reeves was dead serious about the Rams leaving Cleveland, and "timing with them was everything—not only with the [newspaper] strike, but with the AAFC coming in. All the things worked in their favor," Horrigan said.[17]

Craig R. Coenen noted in *From Sandlots to the Super Bowl* that without a rival league to serve as his foil, Reeves may well have been ignored by the other owners. His only options would have been to sell the team or remain in Cleveland, and neither was agreeable to him. He was living his lifelong dream; he was just in the wrong city. But suddenly with the advent of the AAFC he had new leverage. The other owners could not countenance one more of their brethren defecting as Dan Topping had, establishing his football New York Yankees in fabled Yankee Stadium and providing the startup circuit with instant credibility. Leaving the nation's western flank open to the incoming 49ers and Dons could be further madness, and in Cleveland, Paul Brown's squad did indeed look to be an authentic threat. The NFL was surrounded. Halas, Mara, Marshall et al. concluded that compromising with the brash young Rams owner could be accommodated by ascribing the move to his intense desire to be in L.A. Siting a team two-thirds the width of the American continent from the next nearest NFL city had nothing to do with the AAFC, the party line went. Rather, Reeves—incited by Fred Levy, Jr., an admirer of golden California (and eventually a partner again with Reeves in L.A.)—long had wanted to take the team west. This would be the message to the public.

The owners reassembled and told Reeves he could go ahead and move his franchise, provided he would pay each visiting team $5,000 above the league guarantee as a way of covering travel expenses.[18] Also, he had only until April 15—three months—to secure a stadium in Los Angeles; otherwise the Rams would be transferred to Cincinnati,[19] just as a competitive bid to Reeves' in 1941 had aspired to do. The NFL still was leery of establishing an outpost west of the Mississippi.

Reeves eagerly agreed. He would get his way. The AAFC would get a brush-back pitch. And the Cleveland Rams—only 27 days removed from winning a championship in the city of their founding—were history.

* * *

Much of the media seemed startled by the announcement that a championship franchise would be transferred to a different city so quickly, even amid rumors that had swirled around the Rams. As the ensuing years would reveal, all of the previous winners of NFL playoff games to that time—the Chicago Bears, New York Giants, Detroit Lions, Green Bay Packers, and Washington Redskins—were growing deep roots in their respective home cities. The last NFL champions to leave for another town had been the 1923 Canton Bulldogs, and they transferred just 60 miles to the north to merge rosters with the football Indians and win the 1924 title in, coincidentally, Cleveland.[20] The Rams by contrast planned to move *in toto* to a new home nearly 2,400 miles away. "Dan Reeves was still the Rams' owner in Los Angeles, so it was basically the same franchise," Rams tackle Gil Bouley noted. "We just moved."[21]

Journalists of the time did not fully buy Reeves' story of a long-smoldering love for L.A. The *New York Times* instantly interpreted the Rams' announcement as a "bomb" tossed at the competing league, as "another solid belt at the All-America, which already has a club in the Coast metropolis."[22] John Keeshin, owner of the AAFC's Chicago Rockets, wryly said he was glad the NFL had followed the new league's "leadership" in moving west and that he could understand why the Rams were willing to leave Cleveland when the new Browns looked so formidable. "It wouldn't do to have the National [Football] League's championship club running second in its own town," he taunted.[23] But Reeves had a dry retort of his own, noting that by leaving Cleveland wide open for the AAFC, the Rams "certainly haven't done [the Browns] any harm if they can live up to our standard."[24]

For Clevelanders there would be no Rams-Browns duel in the "completely joyous" year of 1946 after all, as James E. Doyle rhapsodized in the New Year's Day edition of the *Plain Dealer*.[25] For Cleveland it alone would be the Browns, unproven representatives of a rival new league just as the Rams had been a decade earlier. "It's regrettable that the city has lost a winner," Dan Sherby, a partner in the new team, reassured the community, adding brightly: "I see no reason to go into mourning about it. We are prepared to spend every cent necessary to building a champion."[26] But many Cleveland sports fans initially were downcast, "disappointed,"[27] with their collective reaction muffled as much by the cold January that now kept them indoors as by the shutdown of local newspapers. Had it been only a month since they had hoisted Bob Waterfield to their shoulders and swarmed the Rams' locker room door in rhapsody? Where could they turn to understand the team's move, to register and process their disaffection?

For Clevelanders suddenly bereft of newspapers by the pressmen's strike, there was an immediate void. With the city's first television station still a year in the future, most Clevelanders turned to radio; but with its limited local news programming and fleeting nature, radio was of little use in aiding understanding and crystallizing public reaction to the team's move. Newspapers then were "everything," Horrigan said, "your lifeblood." With radio, "if you didn't hear it, you didn't hear it." By contrast "the newspaper was on your table, it was in everybody's home, in your business. That's how you got your information."[28] Newsprint shortages prevented most out-of-town newspapers from sending additional copies to Cleveland. As a stopgap the *Press* assembled daily page proofs, ran them off on flatbed presses, and posted them in their own offices, while makeshift news summaries were sent out via telephone to industrial plants and government agencies.[29] But beyond these there were no widely circulated print news reports. A front page was pasted up with the headline "Cleveland Loses Rams' Franchise to Los Angeles"[30] but never saw the full light of day because the January 14, 1946, paper never was printed and distributed. Nor, for that matter, was a phantom January 11, 1946, edition with a Yonkers story headlined, "Reeves Denies Rams Will Move to Los Angeles"[31]—an alarm bell rendered nearly silent.

Indeed what the strike silenced most dramatically was the virtual public square that newspapers provided. "To stop the newspapers strikes at the very lifeline of the people," the *Press* editorialized with some apology once the presses were rolling again.[32] Reeling out such a lifeline would have been sports columnists including John Dietrich and Gordon Cobbledick of the *Plain Dealer* and Franklin Lewis of the *Press*, all of whom had covered the Rams for years and published much-sought-after views. They would have jumped into the service of the reading Cleveland public, among whom 20 percent had ranked "sports" as the area of coverage after "news" that was missed most during the newspaper strike.[33] They would have crafted opinion pieces to help shape and articulate a communal point of view. Instead the city was left without a forum at the very moment of its fourth blown chance at sustained NFL football following failures by various Tiger, Indian, and Bulldog outfits.

News and analysis of the Rams' departure finally did arrive of course, but with local newspapers it was a full month later. Whether Reeves intentionally timed the move to coincide with the news blackout is uncertain—Browns owner Art Modell would use the cover of yet another Cleveland newspaper strike 17 years later to fire the popular Brown[34]—but for the defecting Rams the timing of the newspaper shutdown "was perfect," Horrigan said. "It kind of softened their escape."[35] Without news "and the accompanying expression of opinion," the *Press* editorialized, "there are evidences of public and quasi-public functionaries operating in a very different manner from what they normally do against the background of the printed page."[36] If the story of the move had received immediate and wide circulation—especially Reeves' prevarications with Yonkers, and the subsequent revelation that rumors about the team leaving town long denied by Reeves and Chile Walsh in fact were true—then public contempt for the Rams may well have been deeper, more widespread, and longer-lasting.

As it was, the new Browns quickly were positioned as a way to "forget" the Rams,[37] and the previous football franchise in town began to go down the memory hole: the bad *and* the good, at first slowly and with some spite, and then with increasing rapidity. In April 1976, just three decades after the Rams' championship and subsequent departure, well-known Cleveland sports writer and editor Hal Lebovitz received a letter that began, "When I was a kid growing up in Cleveland, I would have sworn that the Cleveland football team was the Cleveland Rams. My friends in Kentucky tell me I am crazy."[38] In December of that same year another letter arrived containing mixed recollections: "I claim we had a pro football team in Cleveland about 1936 called the Cleveland Buckeyes, with famous players from Ohio State University. If I remember correctly we had such men as Quarterback Stan Pincura."[39] In point of fact it was the Rams who featured Ohio State stars including Pincura; the Cleveland Buckeyes were a Negro League baseball team that, like the Rams, had won a championship in 1945.

In January 1980, with the Super Bowl about to pit the Rams against the Pittsburgh Steelers—two once-woebegone franchises that might have merged because of a wartime player shortage in 1944—Lebovitz was compelled to set the record straight. He had been urged by a younger colleague who was too young to remember the Rams in Cleveland but was much interested "to read about the team, how it came to be, how it did, why it was transferred to Los Angeles." In response Lebovitz penned a lengthy column titled "Remember the Cleveland Rams?"[40]—but alas, not many readers apparently had. By the early decades of the 21st century even the 1924 Cleveland Bulldogs would rouse a bit more recollection and nostalgia in some city quarters than would the 1945 Rams.[41]

In January and February 1946, however, the Rams' abandonment of Cleveland was raw and unexpected. It was "a shock at first,"[42] said Marguerite Gillette, widow of Ram halfback Jim Gillette. Center Chet Adams, a native Clevelander who had been out of football since 1943 because of the war but still was contractually obligated to the Rams, wrote to Chile Walsh that the team's move west probably would please many players "while irritating native Clevelanders."[43] The Cleveland Chamber of Commerce, which had persuaded Reeves and his mysterious "eastern group"[44] to stay in town in 1941 rather than move to Boston, dispatched its leader in 1946 to say that he was "terribly disappointed and sorry" and believed Reeves had "made a mistake."[45]

Reactions were more barbed by February 6, 1946. With Cleveland's newspapers finally back on the street, a month's worth of accumulated vitriol flowed. The *Plain Dealer*'s Cobbledick took particular exception to the way the deal had gone down. When "Danny Reeves"—as he and other local writers came to call the youthful, diminutive owner—took Yonkers' call in early January and assured him the Rams would play in Cleveland that fall, "he knew, of course, that this was not true. He had already made arrangements for the transfer to the west coast." Cobbledick invited readers to consider whether Reeves' failure to answer Yonkers' questions honestly was a "diplomatic denial" or a "bald-faced lie."[46]

The *Press*'s Lewis likewise used the word "lies."[47] The boxers and their handlers he had covered, he suggested, almost were expected to exhibit some mendacity, "but in the higher forms of sportive life, such as baseball, football and basketball, you look for caviar, and when you are served bologna ... well, you begin to wonder whether vegetarians might have the right idea, after all."

The entire move—both as engineered by Reeves and as sanctioned by the NFL—was odious to the fiery Dietrich, who had the best front-row view of the Rams' decade in Cleveland as their preeminent correspondent and one-time confidant. The league had done the Rams and their home city and state, situated in "very lush football territory," no favor when it "haughtily refused to give Cleveland a sensible and attractive schedule that would stir up the fans and keep them coming," he wrote. The marquee Giants never once played a regular-season game in Cleveland. The Redskins came one time, in 1937, and did not return until 1945; in the eight years between "all we knew about Sammy Baugh was what we read in the papers." The departure of the Rams came "without warning and without explanation and apology"—and furthermore it was characteristic of a league whose "policy always has been every man for himself and the devil take the hindmost."[48]

For the NFL as a whole it really was "the public be damned,"[49] Dietrich continued, as he threw back in Reeves' face the "public must be pleased"[50] promotional material the Rams owner had issued when he first bought the team in 1941. And perhaps the bitterest irony for Dietrich was that Reeves and Chile Walsh came to deem 78,000-seat Cleveland Stadium far too big for the team's fan base and decided instead to play in League Park, which at 23,000 capacity was the smallest venue in the league. Then they turned around and moved to L.A. so they could take up residence in the Coliseum and its capacity of more than 100,000. "Why in thunder," Dietrich asked, recalling the disaster of the collapsing temporary stands at over-capacity League Park on November 11, 1945, "didn't they have the same foresight here last fall, and give the people [of Cleveland] a chance to see?" The Rams at Cleveland Stadium, Dietrich concluded, "could have been a gold mine."[51]

Such harsh judgment almost certainly reassured Walsh and Reeves of the wisdom in their decision to leave Cleveland. And in fact, about the same time the first truckload of Rams equipment and office records arrived in L.A., so—not surprisingly—did a suggestion that "folks back in Cleveland considered the Rams a bunch of jerks," *Los Angeles Times* sports writer Braven Dyer reported. Reeves and Walsh and the NFL at large obviously would not have challenged such an account as they collectively hoped to win public favor for their controversial decision. Dyer said word was "that the Cleveland sports writers looked upon [the Rams] as champions only because the war had reduced the entire National [Football] League to mediocrity, and that they were generally regarded with contempt by discerning fans who were glad to see them move to Los Angeles."[52] But, Dyer wrote, "don't you believe it!" Before "perception was colored by peeve," such writers as Lewis and Jack Clowser of the *Cleveland Press* and Ed McAuley, Herman Goldstein, and Ed Bang of the *Cleveland News* had written glowingly of the Rams. Bang had stated simply: "Cleveland has the greatest team in the world." No, Dyer wrote; a perception that the Rams "were not highly regarded in and by Cleveland" was a "myth, strictly manufactured on an assembly line basis."[53]

However, newfound antipathy toward the team after it had moved well could have been anticipated. Football fans in Cleveland had been dealt an unwinnable hand: The Rams' recent success actually expedited their departure rather than cemented their place in the city as might reasonably have been expected. "In past years the league refused to sanction a transfer because we were not a leading team," Reeves said the day he announced the franchise's departure. "By winning the championship, we opened the door."[54] It was a paradox: Lose, and the Rams remain in Ohio as a failing second-division team; succeed, and the team leaves. The locals suddenly realized they had had a lose-lose proposition with Reeves' Rams. "Cleveland wins a big-league title for the first time since Woodrow Wilson missed out with the League of Nations" in 1924, Doyle wrote in the *Plain Dealer*, giving voice to an imaginary Rams fan, "and—bingo! You look around and the champs are gone. I knew there'd be a catch some place!"[55]

Said Horrigan: "I do think that the team was beginning to get a strong foothold, that it was one that could have worked" in Cleveland. When the Rams left, he said, "there was a void. People were just catching on" to the Rams as well as to pro football in general[56] as the popularity of the Browns soon would prove. Adding to the pain of the Rams' move was a realization that machinations had been at work for some time right under Clevelanders' noses, as some had suspected—prominently the *Plain Dealer*'s sports editor, Sam Otis, who wrote in 1943 that he was not optimistic about the team's future in Cleveland following the war. The *Press*'s Lewis revealed that "long before such commercial matters as pay roll deficits became a major part of the Rams' operation, Reeves and Levy were talking of removing their football team to Los Angeles," and added: "There also was some fancy needling by Chile Walsh, the Rams' general manager, who likes California and who does not like Cleveland, and particularly the sports writers herein."[57] After Walsh was quoted in L.A. in early 1947 saying he was pleased to have realized two of his "greatest ambitions" in life—to win an NFL championship as a general manager and to "bring National League football to Los Angeles, my home city"[58]—it could have been deduced that the Rams' move had been predetermined, with the Browns' start-up serving as convenient cover.

Whatever the master plan may have been, Chile Walsh seems to have departed Cleveland with barely a look over his shoulder as he left the responsibility of offering solace to the city to his older brother. In the glow of a title just four weeks earlier, Adam Walsh, the Rams' head coach and gentle scholar, had declared he was taking up permanent residence in the city. Now he was reduced to saying with some apology that "we did not find any fault with anything or anybody in Cleveland." Rather, the team was moving "because of the belief our chances were better out in Los Angeles."[59]

Apology not accepted. The Rams would be known as the "Scrams"[60] in Cleveland newspapers for years to come, and they had not seen the last of heartbreak in Cleveland.

* * *

Not everything about the Rams' bright new future in California was under the immediate control of the team's management. Reeves and Walsh—with Cincinnati nowhere on their itinerary as a temporary way station—were dead set on L.A. and were prepared for the possibility that the Rams might need to take up short-term residence in either of two L.A. venues that were, in a twist of irony, even smaller than Cleveland's League Park: Wrigley Field, capacity 21,850; and Gilmore Stadium, with seating for

18,000.⁶¹ But true fulfillment of Reeves' so-called long-range plan hinged on getting into the mighty Los Angeles Memorial Coliseum, which at the time was an Olympic and college facility that was as off limits to pro football as the NFL was to African American players. Gaining access to the Coliseum would vault the Rams immediately from the league's smallest venue to the largest,⁶² with ticket sales from the stadium's plentiful capacity paying for expensive transportation between the West Coast and the rest of the NFL. Reeves instructed his attorney in L.A. to open negotiations immediately to lease the Coliseum, bringing the Rams face to face with both an unexpected barricade and their own unique place in sports history.

Chile Walsh arrived in L.A. directly from cold Cleveland to act as Reeves' proxy while the owner remained in New York. Walsh and the attorney would work to convince the city's Coliseum Commission to allow pro football to be played there for the first time in 20 years—since Red Grange and the Chicago Bears came for an exhibition game in early 1926, drew a remarkable 75,000 spectators, and left major tenant the University of Southern California feeling threatened and "lobbying successfully to ban pro football from the Coliseum."⁶³ That was then—but now pro football was on the ascendance with the American public, the NFL was on the city's doorstep (as was the AAFC), and all it seemed Walsh needed to do to secure the stadium was to write a $5,000 "clincher" check,⁶⁴ which he happily did. As the *New York Times*' Arthur Daley noted, it seemed "inconceivable that [Reeves] would dare move his champions out to the Coast unless he was pretty certain that he'd be able to place them in the only stadium which could make the transfer a paying proposition."⁶⁵

But when Walsh appeared before a public hearing at the Coliseum at which he expected the Commission to sanction the Rams' request, he met with an obstruction he had not anticipated: a trio of African American sports reporters who were determined to reintegrate the NFL for the first time since 1933. This coterie of writers from black newspapers—Halley Harding, sports editor of the *Los Angeles Tribune*; Abie Robinson, sports editor of the *Los Angeles Sentinel* and the *California Eagle*; and Herman Hill, West Coast editor of the *Pittsburgh Courier*—had agitated at every available opportunity for the integration of sport leagues in America. They were in attendance to argue that the Rams should be prevented from presenting "lilywhite pro football"⁶⁶ in the publicly owned Coliseum. Behind the scenes they and other activists had built a cagey argument based on *Plessy v. Ferguson*, the 1896 U.S. Supreme Court decision upholding the constitutionality of segregation under the "separate but equal" doctrine. If all-white teams could play at the Coliseum, they reasoned, the city

13. "The public be damned" 189

The Rams' dash to Los Angeles was predicated on the team's gaining access to the publicly owned L.A. Memorial Coliseum, a collegiate facility then off limits to pro football. The Coliseum Commission opened its doors to the Rams on the condition that they sign at least one African American player, which they did, igniting the re-integration of the NFL (*James C. Sulecki*).

would need to build a "separate" stadium for taxpaying African Americans.[67]

Los Angeles officials might well have offered a second-rate field somewhere else in the booming city, as impractical as that would have been, and been done with it. But the city was anxious about this first chance at major-league sports and wanted it to be free of legal entanglements, so that the way might be smoothed for other franchises and leagues eyeing a move to the West Coast. Coliseum representatives leading the hearing were favorably disposed to ask the Rams whether they might, in fact, integrate their team. After Walsh had outlined the team's hopes and plans for the Coliseum and had taken his seat, L.A. County supervisor Leonard Roach asked whether anyone else in attendance had something to say either for or against pro football and the Rams. This was Roach's cue to the trio of sportswriters, who had alerted Roach in advance of their intentions.

Harding, spokesman for the group, rose. He was a highly vocal man in his mid–30s, articulate and well-traveled—a former multi-sport athlete who once had played for the Harlem Globetrotters and served as manager for pitching great Satchel Paige.[68] His hope was to appeal to the sympathies and a sense of fairness among those at the hearing. He invoked the name of his old teammate Frederick Douglass "Fritz" Pollard of the Akron Pros and other African American pioneers in the NFL. He noted Los Angeles's long history of racial tolerance and integration among its collegiate, service, and minor-league sports teams—what ex-Ram Woody Strode came to call an enlightened environment of "hanging loose" in Southern California[69] where African Americans were comfortable enough to believe they were equals with whites. But he also accused the NFL of Jim Crow football and said he found it "singularly strange"[70] that no NFL team had signed former University of California, Los Angeles star Kenny Washington—football hero to many Angelenos but relegated to playing for the minor-league Hollywood Bears of the Pacific Coast Football League. Finally, Harding reminded the assembled that African Americans just had fought for American freedom overseas in World War II and that it would be only fitting that they would enjoy those same freedoms at home.

When Harding was finished and had been seated, "you could have heard a rat piss on cotton," Robinson said.[71] The Rams' Walsh was, without a doubt, flabbergasted. Clearly he had not fully shaken pesky sportswriters when he departed Cleveland. He "turned pale and started to stutter," Hill recalled. "He denied any racial prejudice with the Rams or the NFL. He even went to the league's rule book."[72] But Harding and Hill countered that the NFL's segregation rule was unwritten.

NFL Stadium Capacities, 1945–1946			
Los Angeles Coliseum	101,296*	Forbes Field, Pittsburgh	40,000
Cleveland Stadium	78,000	Griffith Stadium, Washington	33,500
Briggs Stadium, Detroit	53,433	Shibe Park, Philadelphia	32,500
Comiskey Park, Chicago	49,500	State Fair Park, Milwaukee	30,000
Polo Grounds, New York	48,700	City Stadium, Green Bay	24,800
Wrigley Field, Chicago	41,500	**League Park, Cleveland**	**23,000**
Fenway Park, Boston	41,000		
*Most accounts of the era reported 103,000			
1946 L.A. Rams Press Guide			

The Cleveland Rams by their own choice had played all of their 1945 regular-season games in League Park, then the smallest facility in the NFL. When the incoming Cleveland Browns of the All-America Football Conference commandeered Cleveland Stadium, the Rams vaulted to the even larger Los Angeles Coliseum. The Rams and the Browns together then paced pro football attendance for years to come.

Roger Jessup, a member of the Coliseum Commission, stood and asked whether the Rams might bar Washington from their team. "Of course not," Walsh replied. Jessup pressed his point. "I just want you to know," he said, "if *our* Kenny Washington can't play, there will be no pro football in the Los Angeles Coliseum." The Rams' attorney stepped in and reassured Jessup and the entire assembly that the team would be open to trying out Washington or any other qualified African American player.

Said Hill, triumphantly: "We won our case, then and there."[73]

But so, really, had Walsh. In agreeing to integrate his team he had closed the loop on Reeves' master plan for the Rams—the *Los Angeles* Rams.

Back east, Reeves had made a habit of riding to an out-of-town newsstand in Times Square each day to pick up Los Angeles newspapers as he anticipated imminent residence there. On a wintry New York sidewalk he realized it was real: L.A. and its Coliseum were his. A decade earlier he had seen his first USC game and was "captivated by Los Angeles and by the glamour of football."[74] Now it would be his very own team taking the field at the gladiatorial Coliseum, home of the 1932 Olympics. Joyful, he stepped over to Times Square's telegraph station and wired Walsh a new long-term contract.

Transferring the team would not be without its personal conflicts for Reeves, however. His wife Mary hesitated at making the move west, and his parents openly questioned the wisdom of extending a branch of their New York family to the West Coast. Reeves, in fact, rarely had spent more than several days at a time in Cleveland during his first five years of Rams

Rams owner Daniel F. Reeves, rarely one to spend time in Cleveland, embraced the L.A. lifestyle after moving into this French chateau in Bel Air, California. In the team's early L.A. years he occasionally hosted Rams personnel, some of whom played indoor football in the house's large living room (*James C. Sulecki*).

ownership, typically taking the last train out of New York that would allow him to arrive in time for kickoff, and the first possible train out of the city after the game was over.

But now Reeves eagerly swapped his apartment on the Upper East Side with actor Basil Rathbone, who was then at the height of his fame from a series of *Sherlock Holmes* films. Reeves headed west and took up residence in the actor's sprawling French chateau in the Bel Air hills, just above that leafy neighborhood's famed country club and UCLA. There he often hosted many of his players as his wife raised roses and orchids, and he commuted four miles to the Beverly Hills office of his Daniel Reeves & Co. investment firm. The L.A. Coliseum was but 15 miles away—no more long-distance train rides on game days. Reeves loved the sun and sported a deep tan, ditching his New York suits for golf shirts, khakis, and cardigan sweaters and happily playing golf at Bel Air Country Club with celebrities including Dean Martin. Having almost been held hostage in Cleveland by the high cost of transportation, he came to flaunt cross-country flight as airfares progressively became less expensive. He frequently returned to New York to stay at the Stanhope Hotel, down Fifth Avenue from his parents' residence, and once flew coast to coast with a friend, restaurateur Dan Tana, just to buy him a drink at P.J. Clarke's, his favorite Manhattan watering hole. On other occasions he flew Waterfield—unfailingly loyal to Reeves and the Rams franchise throughout his playing and coaching career—to the East Coast for lunch, then returned him to California the same afternoon.[75]

Twenty-one years after arriving in Los Angeles, Reeves was inducted into the Pro Football Hall of Fame for criteria that included becoming the "first post-war NFL owner to sign an African American."[76] But Reeves hadn't "set himself up as Harriet Beecher Stowe," as the estimable Los Angeles sportswriter Jim Murray noted.[77] Signing Washington was a business move. "I doubt we would have been interested in Washington if we had stayed in Cleveland," Ohio native Bob Snyder, then a Rams assistant and later head coach, said.[78] Strode, Washington's friend and former UCLA teammate who was signed by the Rams essentially to be Washington's roommate, described the team's move more astringently: "They didn't take Kenny because of his ability. They didn't take me on my ability. It was shoved down their throats."[79]

Washington, one of the collegiate game's best in the 1930s, by 1946 already had undergone two knee operations and was in the twilight of his playing career—as was Strode. But "the Rams were smart in signing Kenny," Strode wrote, asserting that the Rams "almost folded" when they started play in California, and that "without Kenny they probably would have."[80] Strode's charge is credible given the financial losses Reeves and the Rams suffered in their early years in L.A. that dwarfed their deficits in Cleveland. Every pro football franchise save for the NFL's Bears (and interestingly, Cleveland in the AAFC) was a money-losing enterprise in 1946.[81] But in that one year alone the Rams hemorrhaged a staggering $161,000 in Los Angeles—practically double the $82,000 Reeves had lost in *all four seasons* of his ownership in Ohio.[82] In 1947 the toll leaped to $201,500, and in 1948—Washington's last as a player—the Rams franchise was awash in red ink at $253,300.[83] At least "with Kenny on the roster," Strode said, the Rams "were assured of drawing X number of people"[84]—Kenny Washington fans, African Americans, and miscellaneous curiosity seekers.

Nevertheless when the Rams went back east in October 1946 to face the Packers for an early-season game in Milwaukee, Washington and Strode were treated not as marquee attractions but as second-class citizens sent to stay with "a nice, Negro family there—not at the hotel where the team was quartered."[85] But the color line, importantly, had been broken. With Washington and Strode signed to the Rams that spring, coach Brown of the AAFC's Browns in August 1946 invited to camp and then signed Marion Motley and Bill Willis, rounding out the so-called "Forgotten Four"[86] who re-integrated pro football a year before Major League Baseball would do the same.

The stage then finally was set for Jackie Robinson. A former football teammate of Strode and Washington at UCLA, Robinson had been signed to the baseball Brooklyn Dodgers organization in late October 1945 when the Rams still were in Cleveland. Robinson would spend 1946 with the Dodgers' triple-A affiliate in Montreal before general manager Branch Rickey—also a part-owner of the AAFC's Brooklyn Dodgers—was emboldened to bring him up to the majors for the 1947 season. "Branch Rickey once told Marion Motley, 'Had I not had the experience of seeing you and Bill Willis play in a contact sport without incident, I might not have had the confidence to bring Jackie Robinson up into the majors,'" Horrigan said.[87]

As the color line slowly was encroached, absolutely smashed was a geographical barrier that had constrained major-league sports—a collective hesitation to move west that Reeves later ridiculed as having been overcome only by proving "to the Easterners that the Indians were no longer dangerous out here."[88] Once the NFL had "broken out of its east-midwest cocoon,"[89] baseball's Brooklyn Dodgers moved to L.A. and the New York Giants settled in San Francisco. Westward migration and the racial integration of pro sports were underway, and Reeves' decision to move the Rams from Cleveland was a falling domino that had helped set each in motion.

For Washington and Strode, being instrumental to the change became a struggle. Both were mistreated by other players, sometimes by their own teammates. Strode, a 210-pound end, barely caught any passes; instead he was placed on defense and sent up against 250-pound-plus linemen. "I think the Rams' brass was hoping I'd get killed out there," he wrote.[90] Washington and Strode were but "tokens"[91] in their short-lived NFL careers, and while both players—Strode especially—would be welcomed and find success in Hollywood, integration would creep slowly through the NFL for years to come.

For Reeves and Chile Walsh, it was a dream fulfilled. The Rams had arrived safely in Los Angeles. Their often-awkward Cleveland phase—of Ohio roots and humble Midwestern beginnings, of Damon "Buzz" Wetzel and Hugo Bezdek and Downtown Coaches, of Art Lewis and Earl "Dutch"

Clark and Aldo "Buff" Donelli, of Johnny Drake and Parker Hall, of League Park and Shaw Stadium, of lake-effect snow and the forbidding cold of Cleveland Stadium—was over. When the champion Rams shed their losing past and moved 2,400 miles to the western edge of the American continent, they transformed, like so many others who saw in the West the possibility of a new beginning, into an almost completely different identity: from also-rans in a smoky industrial town to a glamorous Sun Belt team that was the toast of Hollywood, a burgeoning city's first major-league sports team, "distinctly L.A."[92]

The Cleveland Rams were no more. They had become the Los Angeles Rams.

CHAPTER 14

"The Cleveland Rams ceased to exist"

By the summer of 1946, in a glow of postwar optimism and almost perpetual Pacific sunshine, the Rams were set up in Los Angeles with offices in Beverly Hills and in the swanky Hotel Alexandria downtown, and training camp soon to start at Compton Junior College. With swagger the Rams issued their *1946 Guide for Press and Radio,* the cover of which was embellished with "L.A. Rams Football Club: 1945 World Champions"[1] and a punting Bob Waterfield—right leg at head level, arms spread-eagle, eyes gazing skyward. Inside were confident biographies of Rams players including Chet Adams, a multiple All-National Football League pick for the Rams before he had entered the service. But Adams was not actually in the Rams fold. The Cleveland native was a Ram on the lam, signing instead with the fledgling Cleveland Browns and arguing that the Cleveland half of the entity with which he had signed his contract took precedence over the Ram half, thereby freeing him from obligation to Rams owner Daniel F. Reeves. It was a semantic contention Reeves would challenge in United States District Court, with bad blood developing between two franchises that were destined to clash for the NFL championship three times in the coming decade.

The controversy began almost as soon as the Rams had departed Cleveland. Browns head coach Paul Brown, an Ohio native bolstered by the fortune of owner and Cleveland civic booster Arthur "Mickey" McBride, was aggressive in signing the best players he could find. He was determined, he said, to build a winning team, saying he "never was in agreement with the cynics who branded Cleveland a poor sports town"[2]—an implicit indictment of the Rams' short and somewhat lackluster efforts to ignite interest there. He made it clear he would not raid the Rams' roster as long as they were in Cleveland, but it was said that "when they became the Los Angeles Rams, it was another story."[3]

On February 7, 1946—only three-and-a-half weeks after Reeves' announcement that he was vacating Cleveland and less than two months removed from the Rams' championship—the Browns purloined Don Greenwood, the Rams' workhouse fullback. Married and with a child, Greenwood had established a home in Cleveland and had secured a prized offseason position as personnel director with a local engineering firm. He wanted to stay in Cleveland, and he also wanted a chance to play for coach Brown.

Next to jump was Tommy Colella. In the 1945 title game he had expected to platoon with starting halfback Fred Gehrke but instead was left sitting, frozen, on the Rams bench as Waterfield's backup Albie Reisz was summoned and would make what would be a game-sealing interception. The Rams' coaches had lost confidence in Colella, calling him a "fumbler"—an insult that surely propelled Colella to sign with Brown and thrive under the pedagogical coach's "patience, tact and encouragement."[4]

In short order the Browns also plundered the Rams' clubhouse for center and former team captain Mike "Mo" Scarry, who defected for a big jump in salary; back Gaylon Smith; and assistant coach Bill "Red" Conkright, a Rams mainstay since 1939. Five players and one coach in all, the former Rams were to bring "a degree of a winning attitude"[5] to the Browns and contribute to the new franchise's earliest championships.

But it was the signing of Adams that incited Reeves to take legal action.

Adams had met with coach Conkright while passing through Cleveland en route from one military camp to another, committing to a roster spot on the Rams when his service was up. But then the Rams departed Cleveland, Conkright defected to the Browns, Adams was discharged in June 1946, and suddenly "agents of the Browns sought 'by offers of more money and argument and persuasion' to get Adams to breach his contract with the Rams,"[6] according to a front-page report in the *Cleveland Plain Dealer*. The Browns succeeded, but Adams was "undisturbed" by all the fuss he caused. He had received offers from several AAFC teams, he said, and his mind already was made up. "I signed my contract with the Rams when they were a Cleveland organization, and did so because I wanted to play in my home town," he said. "I still do and have no intention of reporting to Los Angeles because my contract stated I signed with a Cleveland team." Adams' home and offseason job both were in Cleveland, he said, and furthermore, "my wife says she won't go to the coast."[7]

But Reeves was not about to let go. In July 1946 he filed a petition in

U.S. District Court in northern Ohio with the intent of getting Adams committed to the Rams' roster in Los Angeles. To ensure this would happen, he engaged two high-powered attorneys as representation. Luther Day of the prestigious firm Jones, Day, Cockley & Reavis was described in a federal district court opinion as "possibly the greatest trial lawyer in Ohio's history."[8] His father had been a justice on the U.S. Supreme Court, and his family was deeply active in Republican politics. Thomas E. Lipscomb, of Thompson, Hine & Flory, was a former Rams president who had stepped to the podium at the team's civic testimonial dinner just the December before to praise the Rams as hometown heroes.

With this legal firepower at his disposal, Reeves went full bore. In August 1946 the Rams subpoenaed Brown, Conkright, and Adams to provide deposition statements at the same Bowling Green State University training camp where the Rams had begun their championship run just a year earlier. Back in Cleveland, McBride was required to report to Jones, Day's offices in a downtown office building that formerly headquartered the Rams—lingering reminders of the old franchise were all around—so he could present paperwork the Browns had in their possession about the Adams signing: contracts, letters, telephone messages, Conkright's expense accounts, and more.

At stake was more than Adams. Smith, a back who joined the Rams in 1939 and played for four seasons before entering the service, also intended to jump to the Browns. He admitted to signing with the Rams the previous winter, but that was with the *Cleveland* Rams, he noted, and Rams general manager Charles "Chile" Walsh had said nothing then about the team moving to L.A. "I can't just pull up stakes and move 2,500 miles," protested the Arkansas native, who had secured a postwar job and home in Ohio. "I decided if I couldn't play football in Cleveland, I wouldn't play at all."[9] Walsh accused the Browns of "tampering" with Smith and argued in the press that "legally and morally, both [Adams and Smith] are obligated to play for the Rams." He was confident "the court decision in the Adams' case should settle both."[10]

U.S. Federal Judge Emerich B. Freed of the Northern District of Ohio indeed did settle the issue—in the players' and the Browns' favor. Freed was something of a bookend to Reeves' senior attorney. Whereas Day had come from a prominent and long-established family in Ohio, Freed was an immigrant from Hungary; and while Day's father had served Republican presidents William McKinley, Theodore Roosevelt, and Warren G. Harding, Freed had been nominated for his judicial post by Democratic president Franklin D. Roosevelt. After three days of testimony, Freed rejected Day's and Lipscomb's contention that "Cleveland Rams" was a trade name for Reeves and that players therefore were required to play wherever he decided to move the team. Rather, the Rams were a *Cleveland* home team, Freed maintained, with no obligation for its members to play in Los Angeles. Furthermore, "the Cleveland Rams ceased to exist as of the date of the transfer of their franchise to Los Angeles," Freed ruled, meaning "Adams' obligations under the contract became impossible of performance."[11] Adams and Smith were free to join the Browns, leaving Day with a rare loss in court, and tagging a distinct reversal of fortune on Lipscomb and the Rams organization he had served faithfully for years in Cleveland.

Ceased to exist. Hearing the ruling must have brought a jolt of remorse to Cleveland fans who still cherished their rare NFL title—but who no doubt also had been amused a week earlier when the now–Los Angeles Rams were "outplayed in virtually every department"[12] by the College All-Stars in an exhibition game. "Ceased to exist," James E. Doyle mocked in the sports pages of the *Plain Dealer.* That was "precisely what most of the rest of us thought, after getting the returns last Friday night from Soldier Field in Chicago, where the All-Stars fell on the Rams."[13]

Party to that 16–0 exhibition-game upset was back Jim Gillette, who had been a standout in the 1945 title game but against the collegiate players twice allowed touchdown jaunts by Ram draft selection Elroy "Crazylegs" Hirsch, the second on a pass thrown in his direction by future Hall of Famer Otto Graham. Worse, Gillette now competed in a crowded backfield that included veteran Jack Banta, just acquired from the Philadelphia Eagles, and Kenny Washington, an African American signed by the Los Angeles organization as a condition for playing in the L.A. Coliseum. Gillette ended up taking the field only three times with the Los Angeles Rams, who sold his contract to the Boston Yanks less than a week before the start of the regular season. But Gillette would exact his revenge. Late in the season he would erupt for two touchdowns as the Yanks, on pace to finish 2-8-1, humbled the Rams 40–21 at Fenway Park and effectively ended his former teammates' bid to repeat as Western Division champions. "This," Gillette wrote in a letter to his father back in Virginia, "made my day."[14]

Most of the other Rams—21 players from the team's 33-man roster for the 1945 championship game—made the transition to California,[15] including eight of the team's 11 regular starters: backs Bob Waterfield and Gehrke, ends Jim Benton and Steve Pritko, tackles Gil Bouley and Elbie Schultz, and guards Milan "Mike" Lazetich and Riley "Rattlesnake" Matheson. Chile Walsh still was general manager, and Adam Walsh still led a coaching staff that included Bob Snyder and George Trafton. Only Gillette, Greenwood, and Scarry were gone among the team's starters; but with additions including Washington and Woody Strode, nearly a third of the Rams now originated from the West Coast[16]—especially L.A.'s two college football powerhouses, UCLA (Strode, Washington, and Waterfield) and Southern California (Banta, Pat West, Bob Delauer, Jim Hardy, and Bob Hoffman).

When the former Cleveland Rams took the field on the evening of Friday, September 6, 1946, for an exhibition-game rematch with the Washington Redskins in their first home game ever at the Los Angeles Memorial Coliseum, the contrast of home venues less than nine months apart was striking: the steely posts and lattices of the grandstand in Cleveland Stadium traded for the Coliseum's open bowl and graceful Mediterranean arches; industrial smokestacks replaced by towering palm trees; and the icy shores of Lake Erie swapped for the Pacific Ocean 15 miles in the distance. Just as startling would have been attendance of 68,188—more than twice the brave turnout of 32,178 that shivered through the title game in Cleveland. The only familiar sight was the Rams' 16–14 victory, which was practically identical to their 15–14 decision the December before.

But something of a miracle also had occurred that very same night back in Cleveland: 60,315 fans had materialized at Cleveland Stadium to witness the Browns' All-America Football Conference debut, a 44–0 thrashing of the Miami Seahawks. It easily was the largest assembly ever to that time for pro football in Ohio,[17] and the *Plain Dealer* noted that "many of the fans, after watching [Edgar] Special Delivery Jones and Lou Groza, seemed far less disappointed that the Rams had left town than they were several months ago."[18] The Browns, controlled by local business interests, had made the fans' transition from the Rams far easier by borrowing a tactic from the departed team's early Cleveland days: stocking their roster with familiar names as a gambit to coax instant ingratiation with the locals. More than half of the 1946 Browns were from Ohio, the Rams, or nearby colleges[19]—many from The Ohio State University, where Brown previously had coached and from which Damon "Buzz" Wetzel had drawn heavily to found the Rams a decade earlier.

"Local Pride" was how the *Plain Dealer* editorial page hailed the Browns upon their debut. "Cleveland had its taste whetted for big time football by the great squad of Rams which last year led the rival league. But just as the public was getting acquainted with the team," the paper noted, "it moved to far-off California."[20] As the relocated Rams finished with a middling 6–4–1 mark and failed to defend either their league or division crowns, the Browns went 12–2 and captured their first of four straight AAFC titles. As if in spite, three ex-Rams combined to account for a quarter of the Browns' 55 touchdowns in the team's explosive inaugural season—Greenwood (six), Smith (five), and Colella (three).[21] Cleveland fans quickly began to forget their departed NFL champions. While in 1946 the Rams played to one 60,000-plus regular-season house in L.A., the Browns played to *four* in Cleveland.[22] The Rams had moved out of Cleveland "convinced pro football would not draw in the Ohio metropolis," Edward Prell noted in the *Chicago Tribune* in 1952, and "they were wrong about that—but right in their confidence Los Angeles was a lush field for the sport."[23]

The Browns and the Rams in fact would rank among pro football's top drawing cards for years to come. When the Rams set a pro football record attendance of 86,080 in 1949, smashing the Browns' previous tally of 82,769 the year before,[24] the press speculated that should the two teams ever meet—Cleveland then still was in the AAFC—the country might not have a stadium large enough to accommodate all the interested ticket-buyers. Still, Reeves would incur losses totaling $825,000 between 1946 and 1949 as a down payment for establishing the Rams in L.A. In the same span in Cleveland, McBride's Browns would lose a fraction of that amount: $165,000.[25]

Was Cleveland merely a sleeping giant for pro football during the Rams' decade there? Had the Rams departed a season too early? David George Surdam in his book *Run to Glory and Profits* noted Reeves was unlucky in a sense to have won a championship just before a postwar attendance boom: In 1945 the country, and Cleveland, were just about—but not quite ready—to give their full attention to NFL football. The Rams furthermore had had their consistently unfavorable schedule, playing most of their games on the road and rarely hosting the league's top teams in Cleveland—a handicap that finally would be rectified for the champions in 1946. Of the Rams' move, Surdam wrote, one is "entitled to speculate, therefore, whether Reeves' decision was premature."[26]

If Reeves had stayed, it does seem likely that both franchises would have had a hard go of it in Cleveland. As successful as McBride's AAFC franchise immediately became, local interest even in the Browns' multiple championship teams of the late 1940s waned a bit as their dominance of the junior league continued. Announcement of the team's impending move to the NFL came just as ticket sales to their 1949 AAFC championship game against the San Francisco 49ers were "creaking along at an unhappy pace." Going to the NFL was seen to "promote" the Browns to the "big league." "Now we can see the [Chicago] Bears, [Green Bay] Packers, Eagles, and Rams," the *Press*' Franklin Lewis rejoiced in voicing a prevailing view among local fans. "No more [Chicago] Hornets, [L.A.] Dons, [Brooklyn–New York] Yankees."[27] A place in the NFL—not the AAFC or the AFL—was what a majority of Cleveland football fans seemed to want, and this desire for big-league football certainly could have played to Reeves' advantage had he elected to stay. Other NFL owners faced with comparable competition might simply have decided to stand their ground and outlast their AAFC rivals, as in fact Reeves did—but in L.A. rather than in Cleveland.

Beyond a hypothetical battle for Cleveland between the Rams and the Browns is a less-considered strand of the story: that the Rams were nearly as much agents as victims of the Browns' founding, which ultimately was seen to drive them from the city. Certainly the team's organizational instability and mediocrity on the field in the short era of the so-called Downtown Coaches—the coterie of sportsmen, businessmen, and lawyers who argued on Sundays about play calling then second-guessed coaches on Mondays—hobbled the franchise in its formative years and invited competition. Then Reeves, in his refusal to sell the Rams to McBride, sent the taxicab magnate off to seek a spot in the AAFC. Reeves further seemed to exacerbate the Rams' tenuous situation in Cleveland with a bit of youthful impatience in shutting down operations for the 1943 season, then announcing a return just months later instead of gutting out the war as, say, Art Rooney of the Pittsburgh Steelers would do. Finally Chile Walsh refused to play regular-season games in Cleveland Stadium in 1945 just as the Rams' success and fan popularity began to grow. Indeed, right from the start, a stronger and more vocal commitment from Rams management to keeping the team in Cleveland rather than a passive allowance of persistent rumors that they might skip town may well have defused McBride's reason to found the Browns. Ultimately more of the Rams' destiny had been in their control than some accounts might allow, and the team served to sharpen Cleveland's appetite for pro football even as it opened the door to competition from McBride.

The Browns, fired into existence with a spark of local rivalry, almost inexorably found their fates locked up with those of the Rams through the remaining years of the 1940s and into the 1950s. Rams founding owner Homer H. Marshman told a *Cleveland News* reporter in 1947 that "the Browns inherited all that we did and I wish them luck. They are doing it the right way while we just played and never did take it seriously."[28] By contrast the Cleveland Rams, after eight losing years, one championship, and a controversial move, had "ceased to exist" in the conclusion of Judge Emerich Freed, and even with the contested loss of a few key players to the Browns it seemed to be what Reeves wanted in the end: to jettison baggage in Cleveland so that he might pursue his California dream. If so, mission accomplished. But even Reeves may not have foreseen such a swift burial in Cleveland and rebirth in L.A. for his franchise, nor certainly that the city he had left behind and its NFL representatives thereof would come to haunt him for years to come. In the wake of the Rams' departure from Cleveland, the Rams unwittingly had sown the seeds of their own failure in two coming NFL championship games—blemishes in what otherwise would be the most glorious period in their history.

* * *

This much is certain: Reeves' Rams were the "enemy"[29] and "bitter rivals from the West Coast"[30] when they returned to the city of their founding on Christmas Eve 1950. Their opponents were the Browns, and the prize was an NFL championship. It was not auld lang syne; it was not home days. Cleveland was not yet fully over the Rams having "unceremoniously departed the city for the warmer climate of Los Angeles" five years earlier. With damning praise the *Plain Dealer* noted to a municipality turning into Browns Town that the departed team at least had established the first pattern of sustainable pro football in Cleveland, "unprofitable as it was."[31]

Unlike the Rams, the Browns had been a raging success in Cleveland from the start—the AAFC's sole champions across four consecutive seasons and, after the rival league had folded, the only franchise to join the 49ers and the Baltimore Colts in admittance to the NFL. In the Browns' inaugural season in the senior league they secured a berth in the title game with an upset playoff victory over the New York Giants, at whose hands they suffered their only two regular-season losses. The AAFC may not have been on a par with the NFL, but the Browns certainly were. The old-line league was flabbergasted.

The Rams, meanwhile, had taken their own adventurous path to the 1950 title game. On December 10, 1946, nearly one year to the day since the championship in Cleveland, Adam Walsh resigned abruptly as head coach. Rejecting lucrative offers from other pro as well as college teams and returning to Bowdoin College, he became the fifth straight Rams head coach—after Hugo Bezdek, Art Lewis, Dutch Clark, and Buff Donelli—to finish out his coaching career at the college rather than the NFL level. But his one championship in just two seasons and .750 overall win percentage (15–5–1) rank among the best, if highly abbreviated, coaching stints in pro football.[32] His brother Chile Walsh, general manager and architect of the roster that brought Cleveland its 1945 title, left the Rams organization the following month, stepping down—or being bought out of his contract by Reeves over several disagreements, as at least several accounts had it—to go into private business. He never returned to the NFL, though draft picks and signings he made in Cleveland would help to fuel the team's success for years to come. With Reeves he had been the most influential factor in moving the team from Cleveland, and he left satisfied he had won a championship and brought NFL football to his home region of southern California.

Bob Snyder, charter Ram from the team's inaugural NFL year and the man who made Waterfield into a placekicker for the 1945 championship season, took over as the franchise's sixth head coach in ten seasons. He filed a single-season record of 6–6 in 1947 and was fired in 1948 in favor of Clark Shaughnessy just before the Rams were to board a charter flight for an exhibition game in Hawaii. Yet in his one otherwise unspectacular season Snyder partnered with Gehrke to make NFL history. Reeves always had been eager to make his team look better, and "that got me thinking about the helmet," said Gehrke. He was a former art and education major who spent much of World War II in a California plant on the design team for the P-61 Black Widow fighter plane, breaking down plans and blueprints so aircraft could be brought to life on an assembly line. In 1947, a few years removed from Cleveland, he made a pen-and-ink sketch of ram's horns and showed it to Snyder. The coach said he could not quite visualize what the design would look like and asked Gehrke to create a sample. "So I took one of those gosh-awful brown leather helmets and painted it blue," Gehrke recalled, "then made a free rendering of a ram's horns in gold."[33]

Gehrke's unique vision was a curlicue design that originated over the player's brow and wound around the helmet's ear holes until it culminated just past the player's temple: a nautilus of a design that could be spotted easily from the grandstand and—more importantly as events would transpire—by television cameras. It was the first fully designed helmet in pro football, initially painted by Gehrke's own hand for $1 per helmet. In due time nearly all NFL teams would have logos of their own—and yet, "I don't think [the Rams] were really trying to create a logo," said Joe Horrigan of the Pro Football Hall of Fame. "They were trying to create a look."[34] A ram, Horrigan believed, carried negative connotations of a goat, which to Reeves especially had additional baggage as a holdover from the team's founding in Cleveland. A stylized charging ram by contrast was sleek and fast, something a player wanted to be, and a great new look for a team in a new city. When Snyder and Gehrke showed the sketch to Reeves they received his immediate approval. "I think they were trying to improve an image of what a ram was," Horrigan said.

And an improved image the Rams now had. Gehrke's iconic logo, introduced to an ovation on September 2, 1948, at a home exhibition game

14. "The Cleveland Rams ceased to exist" 205

The 1950 NFL Championship Game between the Cleveland Browns (in white) and the Los Angeles Rams as shown on ABC television. Some viewers of the 1951 telecast, a repeat match between the two teams, would say the Rams' horned helmets were the only features that distinguished them from the Browns *(Roger W/Flickr).*

against the Redskins, became the Rams' camera-friendly trademark. The competing Dons would top the Rams in average per-game attendance in both 1947 and 1948,[35] but they also lost money in even larger bundles than the Rams did—$1.425 million between 1946 and 1949, more than any other pro football team of the era[36]—and were dissolved after four seasons. The Rams by contrast had prevailed in L.A., and with their distinctive helmets they became the image-conscious football representatives of the entertainment industry's capital, as well as its go-to franchise when television or motion picture scripts called for real-world players. After a 6–5–1 season in 1948, the Rams went 8–2–2 in 1949 and made it back to the title game, where they lost 14–0 to the Eagles. This sharpened their hunger for a championship as they returned to Cleveland for the first time ever as representatives of Los Angeles.

In the 1950 NFL championship game at Cleveland Stadium the Rams faced weather conditions that ached with familiarity to Waterfield, Bouley, Lazetich, and coach Hickey—the only holdovers from the Cleveland-based team. A week earlier, before 83,501 in the Coliseum, the Rams beat the

Chicago Bears for the conference crown in 92-degree December heat. In Cleveland, skies were overcast, winds again howled off Lake Erie, game-time temperature was 29 degrees, and piles of snow ringed the frozen field. With the game televised on ABC television, attendance in the 78,000-seat stadium was only 29,751—several thousand fewer than the 32,178 who had witnessed the 1945 championship game in even harsher weather conditions. From the Rams to the Browns, some things in Cleveland, it seemed, had not really changed.

The Rams stormed the field in the same jersey colors they had brandished as Cleveland's representatives in 1945—yellow and royal blue—but now with Gehrke's gold ram's horns popping from blue helmets. On the first play from scrimmage Waterfield bulleted a pass to Glenn Davis, who caught the ball near the sideline and loped untouched into the end zone for an 82-yard touchdown. L.A. led 14–7 after one quarter, 14–13 after two, and 28–20 after three, and it looked as if the Rams might coast to their second championship in six years. But the Browns—in their distinctive white helmets and jerseys and pants with trim of dark-brown and orange, and determined to confirm their right to be in the NFL—kept bouncing back, twice on long touchdown catch-and-runs by Dante Lavelli. The game's final minutes held an uncanny resemblance to the close of the 1945 championship contest. After the Browns' Graham was leveled by Lazetich and fumbled on the Los Angeles 24, the Rams—as they had against the Redskins five years earlier—clung to a one-point lead and possession of the ball with only a few minutes to play. Once again they went three-and-out, and again Waterfield boomed a 54-yard punt that defied the Rams' opponents to score with a short clock and a long field. The Rams hoped to seal the victory and make it 1945 all over again.

But this time there was no pressure on the quarterback by Howard "Red" Hickey, who now stood on the sidelines as an assistant to Rams head coach Joe Stydahar; there was no interception by Reisz to ice the game. Starting with 1:50 remaining and the ball at the Browns' own 32-yard line, and with the Cleveland crowd chanting "go, go, go,"[37] Graham methodically drove his team downfield until Groza's field goal lifted in the wintry air and through the goal posts with 20 seconds remaining, staking the Browns to a 30–28 lead. The Rams mounted a furious comeback, but Warren Lahr came up with a Reisz-like interception to give the Browns an indelible place in history as newcomers who dared to flout the NFL's preeminence. The tables had been turned. The Rams, once upstart champs over the old-guard Redskins, in turn were shocked by the league's powerful new team. Strangers, enemies—now the vanquished—the Rams trod slowly off the field where five years earlier Waterfield had been hoisted triumphantly. The loss, the characteristically laconic Waterfield said, was "just one of those things."[38]

Celebrating Cleveland fans, in a repeat of 1945, ignited a bonfire in the grandstand, stormed the stadium field, engulfed their new NFL heroes, and made off with the goal posts as the evening hastened to Christmas Day. Cleveland, once a puzzlingly apathetic stop on the league circuit an hour's drive from the NFL's birthplace, was in the midst of a historic title-town era of pro football. The city collected six championship trophies in six years, beginning with the Rams in 1945 and continuing with the Browns' five titles from 1946 through 1950. How long, Cleveland football fans wondered, could the streak last?

Yet the Rams were nearly as successful as the Browns over the same period, deploying two future Hall of Fame receivers in Hirsch and Tom Fears and an exciting offense of long passes and high scoring that did team founder Wetzel proud. L.A. fans enjoyed an especially ebullient season in 1951 as the Rams again marched to the NFL championship game, which they would play—appropriately—before a television audience. Though only nine percent of Americans had TVs in their homes in 1950,[39] Reeves had electrified pro football that year by signing a deal with Los Angeles station KNBH and recruiting TV manufacturer Admiral Corp. as his sponsor. In this way he could televise all 15 of the Rams' 1950 games for $656,000— nearly double the $371,000 he had drawn in gate receipts the prior year.[40] The NFL's TV age had begun.

The Rams-Browns matchup on December 23, 1951, in fact became the first ever NFL championship game to be televised fully coast to coast.[41] With $75,000 in rights paid by the Dumont Television Network and transcontinental cable lines set up—but with a black-out in the host city of Los Angeles due to a less-than-capacity crowd in the 103,000-seat Coliseum—L.A. and Cleveland waged a closely fought battle as viewers studied their fuzzy black-and-white screens trying to decipher which team was which. Some said the Rams' horned helmets were the only features that distinguished the home team from the Browns, and indeed the game was deadlocked at 17–17 until about midway through the fourth quarter when Fears scored on a 73-yard pass play by quarterback Norm Van Brocklin. Waterfield added the PAT, and the Rams prevailed 24–17 to secure their first championship in Los Angeles. It would be their last NFL title on the West Coast in the 20th century.

After this high point, only one remaining echo of the Rams' past in Cleveland sounded in southern California. Sid Gillman, a charter member of the American Football League Cleveland Rams in 1936, became head coach in 1955 and led his team, as if by destiny, to face Cleveland for the NFL championship. But the Browns throttled Los Angeles 38–14 before 85,693 in the Coliseum in what would be Graham's farewell game and Cleveland's second downing of the Rams in three title games. The franchise that Reeves had allowed to sprout roots in Cleveland had come back to haunt him—but by 1955 only Gillman and Reeves remained from the Rams' days in Cleveland. Waterfield, Gehrke, Matheson, Benton, Bouley, Lazetich, Schultz, Pritko, Hickey, Pat West, Roger Eason, Ray Hamilton, even Dante Magnani, who had returned in the late 1940s—all had played for the Rams in Cleveland and followed the team to L.A., but all had retired as players and moved on to other lines either in or outside of pro football. The Rams were nearly a remade franchise in California, yet they slipped to depths of mediocrity unplumbed since their years in Cleveland. From 1956 to 1966 the team enjoyed just two winning seasons, and nearly a quarter-century passed between the Rams' 1955 title game and their appearance in a Super Bowl following the 1979 season.

Waterfield best personified the Rams' rise and fall in the mid–20th century. Winning the 1945 NFL championship and the most valuable player trophy as the team's sole star quarterback as a rookie in Cleveland would prove to be his single greatest moment in football. He and his wife actress Jane Russell were thrilled when Reeves moved the team to Los Angeles and its close proximity to their native Van Nuys. In 1948 they constructed a new home on a sunny mountainside in Sherman Oaks with a built-in pool and a commanding view of the San Fernando Valley at which they often hosted Waterfield's Rams colleagues and Russell's Hollywood friends. Waterfield and Russell had it all: youth, fame, and money enjoyed amid the splendor and familiarity of their native southern California. Buck Waterfield said his adoptive parents "really were the king and queen of L.A. at the peaks of their careers."[42]

But on the football field Waterfield no longer was the Rams' sole star under center as he began to share quarterback duties with Van Brocklin. Waterfield was the starter in the 1951 title win over the Browns, but he threw two interceptions on 24 attempts while Van Brocklin, in relief and on only six throws, picked up three more total yards and threw the game-winning touchdown.[43] Waterfield, according to *SPORT* magazine's Jack Sher, had become "no hero on his home grounds."[44] In 1952 the Rams' total home attendance would mount to 994,000, almost double the number any team had drawn up to that time,[45] but Los Angeles fans showed a "glaring lack of affection and appreciation" for Waterfield, Sher wrote. They were "quick to jump on him when he [had] an off day and razz him and arbitrarily label him an overrated egg-head."⁴⁶ Such was fan resentment drawn by a man who seemed to have everything, including a Hollywood-starlet wife.

But Waterfield's marriage to Russell had begun to show signs of strain, even as the two adopted and began to raise three children. In 1952 Waterfield developed a duodenal ulcer, an echo of the acute indigestion that had killed his father, and a doctor told him he was "psychologically unsuited"⁴⁷ for a career as a pro player because he assumed too much personal responsibility for his team's performance. "My father would watch game films, and he was pretty critical of himself," Buck Waterfield said. "If he couldn't be the best at what he's doing, why do it?"⁴⁸ Faced with the very real possibility his ulcer could "kill him if he didn't get out"⁴⁹ of football, Waterfield retired at the age of 32.

Russell enticed Waterfield to join her in a new Hollywood production company named Russ-Field, a vehicle for actors including herself and movie legend Clark Gable, but Waterfield "never really cared for the Hollywood scene," Buck Waterfield said.⁵⁰ The retired quarterback became a Rams assistant in 1958, then succeeded Gillman as head coach in 1960, tallying a total record of 9–24–1 with a rebuilding franchise. "Waterfield's case was particularly sad," Larry Bornstein wrote in *Football Digest*. By 1960 the Rams had endured "years of front office bickering and a series of bad trades." Waterfield, in short, was "handed a bad ballclub,"⁵¹ and he resigned before the end of his third season. When the press asked him what kind of coach he thought he had been, he replied: "Losing."⁵²

Russell, weary of her stormy relationship with Waterfield, left him in 1967 after nearly 24 years of marriage. "Those had been the good years and they were wonderful," Russell wrote, "but when everything went wrong, it went to hell in a basket."⁵³ Waterfield became a full-time scout for the Rams and was responsible for the drafting of future stars Roman Gabriel, Merlin Olsen, and Deacon Jones. Remarried, he spent much of his time among friends who knew and accepted him as just one of the guys, which in his humility he strongly encouraged, but according to a report in the *Los Angeles Times* he became "increasingly addicted to night life"⁵⁴ that hastened his deterioration. He died in 1983 after a lengthy illness, and his ashes were scattered by son Buck under pine trees near Waterfield's favorite hunting spot north of Los Angeles. Apart from his birth in upstate New York, a short military stint in Georgia, and one cold championship autumn in Cleveland, Waterfield had spent his entire life in southern California.

By the time of Waterfield's death the Rams were enjoying another surge of success and popularity, racking up 14 playoff appearances and a Super Bowl berth between 1970 and 1990. It was a second golden age of Rams football, in a sunny place where Reeves thought the team would remain forever—a location he believed had the "greatest football future of any city in America."[55] But the future that Reeves had dreamed of for his Rams in L.A. soon was about to become a major part of its storied past.

* * *

For 30 years Reeves invested his heart, mind, fortune, and reputation into the Cleveland/Los Angeles Rams. Such a peculiar preoccupation no doubt helped to inspire *Cleveland Press* columnist Franklin Lewis to note in 1949 that NFL owners were "businessmen who wouldn't keep a losing store open two weeks but who will, and do, pour hundreds of thousands of dollars into professional football and get back headlines, headaches and heckling."[56] To keep the Rams afloat through their early years in Los Angeles—through steep deficits through the late 1940s, a turning point in 1950, and modest profits beginning in the early 1950s[57]—Reeves took on a handful of investors to share the team's losses including oil man Ed Pauley; businessman Hal Seley; original partner Fred Levy, Jr., whom he had bought out in 1943; and comedian Bob Hope. "That was the beginning of the end," Dan Reeves, Jr., said. The other investors "were always unhappy with his decisions, and even though he owned 51 percent, they would make their unhappiness known." Coaches were a particular lightning rod of contention, especially to Pauley, "the lead dissident" among the minority investors whom Reeves Jr., suspected thought Reeves treated the team "like his own little kingdom."[58]

Amid such contention the league temporarily took over control of the franchise and at one point, according to Reeves Jr., offered his father the commissioner position. Reeves was not interested; managing a team was his first, last, and enduring passion. Seeking a resolution, the NFL put the Rams up for auction, and Reeves, with a winning bid of $4,778,422,[59] set up a Rams corporation in 1963 with seven new investors from the Los Angeles Angels baseball organization including singer Gene Autry and Leonard K. Firestone, whose initial involvement with the franchise dated all the way back to Cleveland in the late 1930s.

Through the decades Reeves steadfastly had built the Rams into an organization that was lauded for entering into football's earliest television contracts,[60] for developing the sport's first full-time scouting staff, and for giving career starts to future league legends Pete Rozelle and Tex Schramm, the former in public relations and the latter in publicity for the Rams. The franchise was the first to exceed attendance of 1 million in one season[61] and often shattered expectations of how many fans might attend a regular-season NFL game. At one 1957 contest alone, an upset of the 49ers in the Coliseum, the Rams attracted an astonishing 102,368 spectators,[62] very nearly filling the stadium's massive bowl.

But even the cunning Reeves could not control the business of the Rams forever. Player agents entered the business, and Reeves, the team's self-appointed general manager—a role he particularly relished, especially when he could deal directly with players—found the new layer of representation unrewarding. He died in 1971 of cancer, age just 58, returning in the end to New York City. After his death his family put the Los Angeles Rams up for sale. "He didn't want it continued after he died," Reeves Jr. said. "He didn't want us to have to deal with the player demands, the agents."[63] As James Reeves had cashed out of the grocery trade, so Dan Reeves exited pro football, and in each instance the family was enriched. By 2016 the Reeves family's sole claim on the team was, symbolically, a ram's-head logo for Dan Reeves, Jr.'s Reeves Ranch Vineyard near Santa Barbara, California, and a hope to see the franchise do well once again in Los Angeles.

The sale of the Rams in 1972, however, would set in motion a chain of events that temporarily would reverse Reeves' hard-fought journey from the Midwest to Los Angeles. By the time of Reeves' death the Rams—and the NFL in general—were runaway successes. Admitted to the league in 1937 for $10,000, then reclaimed by Reeves for less than $5 million in 1963, the Rams franchise by 1972 was worth $19 million, having increased in value an average of 21.5 percent annually since its entrance to the NFL—doubling in price about every 3.25 years.[64] Buying up this business juggernaut from the formerly Reeves-run corporation was Robert Irsay, a decade later to gain

After 30 years of possession, the Reeves family relinquished ownership of the Rams following the death of Daniel F. Reeves in 1971. Dan Reeves, Jr., memorialized his father's place in football history with a rendering of a ram's head for the logo of his Reeves Ranch Vineyard near Santa Barbara, California *(James C. Sulecki)*.

infamy for moving the Baltimore Colts to Indianapolis. But Irsay swapped the Rams for the Colts with Carroll Rosenbloom, who nurtured the L.A. team through a glorious 1970s period of six consecutive playoff appearances and robust attendance at the Coliseum.

Sadly for Los Angeles fans, Rosenbloom had begun making fateful arrangements to move the Rams out of the city and 35 miles south to the suburban reaches of Orange County. Then he died in a mysterious drowning accident in Florida and left control of the team to his widow, a former nightclub singer on her sixth marriage. After the 1979 season, Georgia Frontiere followed through with her husband's plans to vacate the L.A. Coliseum, a venue to which the team had been associated "as surely as Caruso belonged to La Scala,"[65] and the Rams took up residence in Anaheim Stadium. But unknown to the residents of southern California, Frontiere, a native of St. Louis, had her sights set on an even more distant horizon: the Midwest in which she and the team had originated.

While the Rams had reached (and lost) a Super Bowl, by the end of the 1980s the once-model organization was in a "death spiral."[66] Many L.A. football fans switched their allegiance to the Raiders franchise that was freshly arrived from Oakland. As Frontiere neared a deal to transfer their team to St. Louis, a small, booing crowd turned out in Anaheim on Christmas Eve 1994 to watch the 4–11 Rams fall in defeat to the Redskins—their opponents in so many pivotal moments in the franchise's history[67]—as they played their final game in Orange County. The 25,705 spectators in Anaheim Stadium that day could have fit inside a temporarily outfitted League Park in Cleveland in 1945. The Rams were about to go full circle: from also-rans to box-office sensations and back, and from the Midwest to the West Coast and back.

But this time no Rams player asked to stay behind. No federal judge ruled that *Los Angeles* trumped *Rams* in a player's contract. NFL teams now were Big Business, and highly lucrative player endorsement deals rendered offseason jobs unnecessary. Days before the Rams' final game in Anaheim the *Los Angeles Times'* Jim Murray wrote that "community identification is an important one to athletic teams. Otherwise you have traveling minstrel shows—Have Football, Will Travel." Football fans, he asserted, "don't paint themselves blue and gold and wear antlers on Mohawk haircuts for passing vaudevillians."[68]

But they do. St. Louisans fell nearly as hard for the carpetbagging Rams as Angelenos had, at least initially, when Frontiere's team enjoyed a Super Bowl–winning season in 1999 with their so-called "Greatest Show on Turf."[69] St. Louis fans cognizant of the Rams' beginnings in Cleveland—and there appear not to have been many—may have detected in 1999 a replay of 1945 as the Rams came off multiple non-winning seasons to shock the NFL with a phenom quarterback in Kurt Warner and a passing attack that wreaked the same sort of destruction that Waterfield-to-Benton had for Cleveland.

The Rams truly were a traveling show, but that show eventually lost its luster in St. Louis much as it had in Anaheim and Cleveland. Years passed in Missouri without a winning record or a postseason appearance. By the mid-2010s the team had slumped again to the depths of league attendance[70] and franchise value,[71] and in a repetition of the birth, ascendance, decline, and departure through which the team had cycled in both Cleveland and L.A., Rams ownership in the second decade of the 21st century agitated once again for a move—this time back to L.A., where the team now controlled by E. Stanley Kroenke might make a new start.

"NFL teams are not simply private enterprises," intoned one report in the *Los Angeles Times* as rumors swirled about a Rams departure from St. Louis in late 2015. "They are public trusts that are part of the fabric of a community."[72] But the question as to which side of the bargain really held the most sway—the private enterprise or the public trust—already had been settled. Pro football teams long had ceased to be local entities stocked with local and regional favorites as the Cleveland Rams of the 1930s and 1940s and the Cleveland Browns of the 1940s and 1950s had been. Now they were businesses that were national in scope, with players recruited from all over the country. And even with frequent use of public funds by NFL franchises, fans did not "own" their teams; businesspeople like Reeves and Frontiere and Kroenke did, and to no small degree they were free to move them where they liked. Fans had little more control of the on-field success of "their" teams than they had of the weather, but they often were held accountable. Fail to support a franchise through thick and thin—mostly thin, as was the case with the Rams in Cleveland and in St. Louis—and they could suffer the consequence of losing their team to another city.

As if to underscore the primacy of private enterprise over public trust, Kroenke on January 12, 2016—precisely 70 years to the day since Reeves had had his way at the Commodore Hotel in New York City, and over the protests of St. Louis civic leaders—received permission to move his Rams back to L.A. His team had not been adequately supported in its home city, he charged, echoing Frontiere and Reeves before him. Though a native Midwesterner, he would restore the Western inclination of the team, would undo what Frontiere had done, would place the Rams firmly back on the stupendous growth path that Reeves had set them on nearly three-quarters

In early 2016, an empty site in Inglewood, California, adjacent to the L.A. Forum awaited construction of a new stadium for the L.A. Rams. Until the stadium was built, the team was to play in the L.A. Memorial Coliseum—just as Rams general manager Charles "Chile" Walsh had arranged for the franchise in its previous move west 70 years before (*James C. Sulecki*).

of a century earlier. The move would at least double the valuation of the franchise.[73]

The Rams, it was said in Los Angeles, were "coming home,"[74] back to the L.A. Coliseum, and eventually to a new stadium in Inglewood just 15 miles from Reeves' former Bel Air home. But the Rams never truly can go *home*—to Cleveland, to the place of their origin. The Downtown Coaches, and World War II, and Reeves, and the Browns, and the westward sweep of the nation, and the rise of the NFL to become Big Business with near mythic status—all conspired to make certain of this. The Rams' provenance in Cleveland, however, remains, and even if it is often forgotten, it never can be taken away. The team began as the bright vision of an ex–Ohio State football star and a would-be newspaper artist, who humbly beseeched investment from Cleveland's business community as he happily recruited his old college chums as teammates and brainstormed with local reporters on a name that was just the right length for a newspaper headline. In 2016 the Rams returned not to Cleveland but to Los Angeles, as a multi-billion-dollar enterprise far, far removed from their humble roots but burrowed deep into American sports history as the only NFL team to be based in three different cities—*and* to have the audacity to win championships in them all.

Quite some time ago the Cleveland Rams ceased to exist, but their spirit—and their successors—still are very much alive in Los Angeles. Long live the Rams.

Appendix
What Became of Selected Individuals

Poignant or significant stories about select Cleveland Rams players, coaches, and owners.

Chet Adams, a lineman whose signing by the new Cleveland Browns incited an ultimately unsuccessful lawsuit by Los Angeles Rams owner Daniel F. Reeves, played pro football for 10 seasons—six in the National Football League (Cleveland Rams, Green Bay Packers, and New York Yanks) and four in the All-America Football Conference (Browns and Buffalo Bills). After leaving football in 1950 he worked full-time in construction until developing a double hernia, then in 1975 won the top prize in the Ohio Lottery awarding him $1,000 a month for life and allowing him to retire. He died in 1990 at age 75.

Jim Benton was a premier pass receiver for the Cleveland and L.A. Rams from 1938 to 1947, exceeded in his era only by Hall of Famer Don Hutson. Benton was holder of a record that stood for 40 years—making a blockbuster 10 catches for 303 yards in one game on Thanksgiving Day 1945, an accomplishment that in 2015 still ranked fourth all-time.[1] He won two NFL championships: with the Chicago Bears in 1943, to whom he was on loan while the Rams were inactive for one year due to World War II; and with the Cleveland Rams in 1945. He retired after the 1947 season, coached at Arkansas A&M, and distributed gas and motor oil to service stations in Arkansas. He died in 2001.

Hugo Bezdek, first head coach of the NFL Rams, was a former Major League Baseball manager and a future College Hall of Fame coach when he arrived in Cleveland. But he largely was a failure in pro football, taking the Rams to a 1–10 inaugural record in 1937 and 0–3 in 1938 before being fired. Nevertheless in 1946 he accurately predicted pro football would reach boom proportions. He became a farmer in Pennsylvania and returned to football briefly in 1949 as athletic director and coach at the National Agricultural College before dying in 1952, aged 68.

Earl "Dutch" Clark was inducted with the inaugural class of the Pro Football Hall of Fame for his play with the Portsmouth Spartans and Detroit Lions. His time with the Rams was as the franchise's first high-profile head coach and as the recruiter of Riley Matheson, a mainstay of the 1945 championship team. Unfortunately Clark never compiled a winning record in four seasons as a coach and left after the 1942 season, despairing the team never would get past division rivals the Bears and Packers. He briefly led the professional Seattle Bombers in 1944, then served as head coach and athletic director at the University of Detroit, before he died in 1978.

Tommy Colella, a native of Buffalo, New York and a graduate of the city's Canisius College, was a leading back for the Rams in 1944. He was demoted to Fred Gehrke's backup for the 1945 season but still finished as the fourth-leading rusher during the team's title run.[2] Feeling undervalued by Rams coaches, Colella jumped to the Browns as a star defensive back and won three AAFC championships between 1946 and 1948. He then was traded to Buffalo, where he scored a unique trifecta: playing for hometown football teams at the high school, college, and professional levels.

Bill "Red" Conkright anchored the Rams' line at center for the 1939–1942 and 1944 seasons, then made way for Mike "Mo" Scarry and became a scout and assistant coach in the team's 1945 title year. He jumped to the Cleveland Browns as a coach in 1946, then went through various pro and college stints before joining the Oakland Raiders in their third season in 1962. Conkright's time as head coach was short and unsuccessful—his record was 1–8—and he was replaced by Al Davis, who initiated an era of sustained success for the Raiders franchise. Conkright died in 1980.

Aldo "Buff" Donelli—perhaps best remembered for his exemplary play for the United States in soccer's 1934 World Cup—was head coach of the Cleveland Rams for just one season, 1944, in which he instilled an intricate T-formation spread offense with a man in motion and led the team to a respectable 4–6 mark. Rewarded with a three-year contract extension, he instead was called into the Navy where, near war's end, he received stateside duty as assistant football coach at Columbia University. Coincidentally discharged from the service the day before his old Rams played the Washington Redskins in the 1945 title game, Donelli spent two decades as head coach at Boston University and Columbia before retiring in 1967. He died in 1994.

Johnny Drake, a charter member of the NFL Rams and the franchise's first to score a touchdown in the league,[3] was a smash-mouth fullback and one of the few standouts on the team in its early years before he retired, battered and bruised, after the 1941 season. Hall of Famer Dutch Clark called him the best player he ever coached. Drake was a first-team All-Pro in 1940 and missed only one game in his five-year career. Upon retirement he was presented with a brand-new car by a grateful Cleveland public, then became a personnel executive in Detroit. He died in 1973 at age 56.

Fred Gehrke was a slight but speedy halfback who played briefly with the Cleveland Rams in 1940, served as a wartime aircraft illustrator, and returned to help pace the Rams to the 1945 title as the team's leading rusher.[4] He followed the team to Los Angeles, where for the 1948 season he designed and painted the team's iconic horned helmets—the first to carry a logo or insignia, an innovation for which the Pro Football Hall of Fame honored him with a Daniel F. Reeves Pioneer Award. He also served in the front office of the Denver Broncos, where he used pipe and netting to fashion the first kicking cage. He died in 2002.

Jim Gillette, a star halfback for the Rams in the 1945 championship season, was acquired by the Boston Yanks in 1946 before rounding out his career with the Green Bay Packers and Detroit Lions. He then retired to raise peanuts, corn, soybeans, cotton, and cattle in Virginia, where he often carried a photo from his playing days on the dashboard of his truck—proof he had played in the NFL. Gillette was followed into pro football by his son Walker Gillette, with whom he often watched NFL games on television, quietly breaking down plays and formations. Gillette died in 1990.

Sid Gillman was a founding member of the Rams franchise in the American Football League and scored the team's very first touchdown.[5] Though recruited as a player by former Ohio State teammate Damon "Buzz" Wetzel, Gillman's true aspiration was to coach. He climbed the collegiate ranks before owner Daniel F. Reeves recruited him to the L.A. Rams, whom he led to the 1955 NFL championship game. With the Rams, San Diego Chargers, and Houston Oilers, Gillman acquired legend as a master of the modern-day passing game and was inducted into the Pro Football Hall of Fame. He died in 2003.

Don Greenwood helped to power the Rams to the 1945 NFL championship, then seven weeks later became the first of his teammates to jump to the AAFC's new Cleveland Browns. There he won two more championships—a remarkable three titles in only three seasons—but suffered a shattered cheekbone in a game against the San Francisco 49ers in 1947. It was an injury he later said was uncalled-for and never healed, and he retired to go into coaching. In 1951 he resigned from the University of Toledo in protest of unnecessary roughness in a game against Bowling Green State University. He died in 1983.

Robert H. Gries was a founding investor in two NFL franchises, first with the Rams in 1936 and then with the Browns in 1946. He hosted Monday post-game lunches at the May Company, a downtown Cleveland department store that he managed at which the owners toted up expenses and pooled their money to make that week's payments. After Daniel F. Reeves bought the Rams in 1941, Gries joined Arthur "Mickey" McBride in founding the Cleveland Browns, a minority share of which still was held by Gries's son Robert D. Gries when Art Modell moved the team to Baltimore in 1995. The elder Gries died in 1966.

Parker Hall was the Rams' first-ever NFL most valuable player,[6] nudging out Packers legend Don Hutson as a rookie tailback in 1939. With emerging star Jim Benton as a target, Hall completed a record 106 passes, well surpassing Sammy Baugh's record of 81 in 1937.[7] In 1942, however, Hall struggled with the Rams' new T-formation offense and enlisted in the U.S. Navy after the season had ended. In 1946 he returned for one season with the AAFC San Francisco 49ers, then retired and went to work for a lumber firm in Memphis, Tennessee. He died in 2005.

Howard "Red" Hickey, acquired in 1941 to fill in at end when Rams great Jim Benton left briefly to coach high-school football, played on the 1945 championship team in Cleveland and continued on in Los Angeles through 1948 as a player and after that as an assistant coach. He became head coach of the San Francisco 49ers (1959–1963) where in 1960 he crafted an enduring legacy: the spread-formation shotgun offense. He instructed his quarterback to stand about five yards behind the line and spread his backs to the sides, hoping to gain an extra second or two to develop each play and propel the 49ers to upset the defending NFL champion Baltimore Colts. They did.

Gomer Jones was a marquee attraction of the original 1936 Rams, a Cleveland and Ohio State hero as a lineman who was drafted by the NFL's Chicago Cardinals but instead joined his former college teammates in the American Football League. He was banned from the NFL for joining a rival league, effectively ending his playing days, but he spent a long career at Oklahoma as a highly successful line coach and then as head coach and athletic director. He died at age 57 of a heart attack while in New York City, en route to an Oklahoma basketball game at Madison Square Garden.

Milan "Mike"/"Sheriff" Lazetich played college football in Montana; joined the Navy; was a rodeo rider, cowpuncher, and deputy sheriff in Montana; played another year of college football at Michigan—*then* reported to the Rams as an NFL rookie for the team's championship 1945 season. He anchored the team's line for six consecutive seasons in Cleveland and Los

Angeles before retiring due to health problems in 1950. He died in 1969 at only 47. His brother Bill Lazetich played for the Rams in 1939 and 1942, and his nephew Pete Lazetich was a member of the San Diego Chargers and Philadelphia Eagles in the 1970s.

Art "Pappy" Lewis was promoted from player-coach to head coach of the NFL Rams in 1938 after Hugo Bezdek was fired, and immediately the 0–3 team scored upset victories over the Detroit Lions, the Chicago Bears, and the Bears again. Then the Rams fell to earth with four straight losses and finished 4–7, and Lewis was demoted to assistant under newly hired head coach Dutch Clark. Lewis stuck around through the end of the 1941, then left for a collegiate coaching career that peaked with three nationally ranked teams at West Virginia. He was only 51 when he died in 1962.

Homer H. Marshman was a lawyer-businessman who founded the Rams with player-coach Damon "Buzz" Wetzel in 1936, then put up $10,000 to gain entry to the NFL in 1937. Marshman and a roster of Rams investors from Cleveland sporting and business circles—numbering 45 in total as of New Year's Eve 1940[8]—became fearful of the coming war and sold out to Daniel F. Reeves in June 1941. Marshman jumped back into pro football in 1953 as a minority owner of the Cleveland Browns, then sold to Art Modell in 1961—thereby achieving the distinction of having sold two pro football teams to New York buyers who eventually moved them out of Cleveland. Marshman died in 1989 in Palm Beach, Florida.

Riley "Rattlesnake" Matheson, the colorful and eccentric lineman whom Dutch Clark signed on a tip from a friend, showed up at his first training camp with just a bag and a toothbrush but went on to help power the Rams to the 1945 NFL title. He was first-team All-Pro five times[9] before rounding out his career with the AAFC 49ers and the Canadian Football League's Calgary Stampeders. A rancher in the offseason, Matheson became so frustrated with regulations in Idaho that he hauled a house trailer to Paraguay and set up a 10,000-acre cattle and lumber operation. He died there in 1987.

Max Padlow, an original 1936 Ram, played end for the NFL's Philadelphia Eagles before former Ohio State teammate Buzz Wetzel lured him to the American Football League for the 1936 season. There he joined future Hall of Fame coach Sid Gillman as a receiver on the Rams' so-called razzle-dazzle offense. But when the Rams entered the NFL in 1937, Padlow was banned for having jumped to the AFL. He played for the independent Cincinnati Bengals, then was offered reinstatement to the NFL in 1938, but never played again. Padlow, whom Gillman once called one of football's greats, died in an auto crash in 1971.

Steve Pritko, son of immigrants from Austria-Hungary, was drafted by the Rams in 1943, but when the team became inactive that season because of the war, he played 10 games instead for the New York Giants. Pritko returned to the Rams in 1944, won a championship in 1945, moved with the team to Los Angeles for 1946 and 1947, and jumped among the Boston Yanks, New York Bulldogs, and Green Bay Packers before retiring after the 1950 season. He served as an uncredited stand-in in the film *The Day the Earth Stood Still*, and was among the last surviving Cleveland Rams when he passed away in 2015 at the age of 94.[10]

Daniel F. Reeves was sole or majority owner of the Cleveland/Los Angeles Rams from 1941 until his death in New York City in 1971 at the age of 58. He took on multiple investors, then battled them for control until he outbid them and set up a new corporation, with new partners, in 1963. Reeves was inducted into the Pro Football Hall of Fame in 1967. At the time of his death the Rams were worth $19 million—about 135 times the amount he and Fred Levy, Jr., paid for the team 30 years earlier.[11] Reeves' son Dan Reeves, in honor of his father's ownership, incorporated a ram's head into the logo of his California winery.

Mike "Mo" Scarry, a battle-scarred center and team captain for the Rams, played in the first football game ever televised while he was in college, then broke his nose eight times in a pro career spanning two seasons with the Rams (1944–45) and two with the Browns (1946–47), winning multiple all-league honors and three championships along the way. After years of coaching in the collegiate ranks, he returned to the NFL as an assistant to former Browns teammate Otto Graham on the Washington Redskins; then joined the staff of ex–Brown Don Shula on the Miami Dolphins for a span that included the team's undefeated championship season in 1972. Scarry died in 2012 at the age of 92.

Bob Shaw, an Ohio State star drafted by the Cleveland Rams, was overshadowed as an end by Steve Pritko and Jim Benton on the 1945 championship team but went on to a measure of immortality five years later. His remarkable five touchdown receptions in a single game for the Chicago Cardinals in 1950 remained, into 2015, the most ever for an NFL receiver—tied only with Kellen Winslow and Jerry Rice.[12] Shaw is said to have helped pioneer the tight end position while with the Rams in L.A. in 1949, and was ends coach for the Baltimore Colts in 1958's so-called Greatest Game Ever Played. He died in 2011 at age 89.

Gaylon Smith played back for the Cleveland Rams from 1939 through 1942, departed for the military, then became an unexpected object of litigation when the L.A. Rams unsuccessfully attempted to force him and Chet

Adams to join their roster rather than that of the new Cleveland Browns. Smith won a championship with the Browns, scoring five touchdowns in the team's inaugural season in the AAFC,[13] then abruptly left football. He became a manufacturers representative and died in Cleveland in 1958. He was only 42.

Bob Snyder, a versatile passer and placekicker, was a founding member of the big-league Rams in 1937, throwing the franchise's first-ever NFL touchdown pass[14] in the team's sole victory of its inaugural season. He left to become Sid Luckman's understudy on the Chicago Bears, with whom he won three NFL championships, then returned to the Rams for their title in 1945—first as an assistant coach, shaping Bob Waterfield into a placekicker; then in 1947 as head coach, encouraging Fred Gehrke's vision of a horns-adorned helmet. Before Snyder's death in 2001 he turned down a $10,000 offer for the original drawing of Gehrke's revolutionary Rams helmet design; in 2015 the whereabouts of the artwork remained unknown to the Pro Football Hall of Fame.[15]

Adam Walsh, a member of Knute Rockne's Four Horsemen Notre Dame team and a seasoned college coach, was thrust into the NFL ranks by his younger brother, Rams general manager Chile Walsh. As head coach of the Rams he won the 1945 championship in his first season and was named the NFL's coach of the year, but he lasted only one more season in California before returning to the collegiate ranks at Bowdoin and then entering politics in Maine. In 1985, at age 83, he died on an eastbound cross-country flight from Los Angeles. Walsh is in the College Football Hall of Fame.

Charles "Chile" Walsh, assistant coach under Dutch Clark and then general manager of the Rams from 1944 through 1946, was more instrumental in the team's first championship and move to Los Angeles than anyone in the franchise outside of owner Daniel F. Reeves. He operated the organization while Reeves was in the military, drafted future Hall of Famer Bob Waterfield, hired his own brother Adam as head coach, fended off rumors of the team's impending move from Cleveland, and negotiated the deal that secured use of the L.A. Memorial Coliseum for the Rams. He left the team after the 1946 season, apparently in conflict with Reeves, and went into private business. He died in his hometown of Hollywood in 1971.

Bob Waterfield in just one year in Cleveland led the Rams to their first NFL championship as a rookie, the first pure quarterback to do so.[16] He followed the team to L.A.—in fact, as a resident of California and husband of movie star Jane Russell he was believed by some in Cleveland to have caused the move. In L.A. he won a second championship in 1951, splitting time at quarterback with fellow Pro Football Hall of Fame inductee

Norm Van Brocklin. He also was head coach of the Rams for several losing seasons as the team was rebuilding, but he never quite reclaimed the full singular glory he had achieved in his MVP season as a rookie in Cleveland in 1945. He died in 1983, and his famous number 7 no longer is in use by the Rams.[17]

Damon "Buzz" Wetzel, co-founder of the Rams franchise with Homer H. Marshman, eschewed a secure career as a syndicated cartoonist so he could become player-coach and then, after the team had joined the NFL, the general manager of the Cleveland Rams. When the team finished 1–10 in 1937 then opened the 1938 season with a loss to the Green Bay Packers, he was fired—though he did retain stock interest in the club until at least the end of 1940.[18] He became a manager in minor league baseball, served in the Navy in World War II, and died in Texas in 1985.

Chapter Notes

Preface

1. Dan Daly, *The National Forgotten League* (Lincoln: University of Nebraska Press, 2012), 200.
2. John Dietrich, "National Football League's Public Be Damned Policy Kept Rams from Building Large Following," *Cleveland Plain Dealer*, February 10, 1946.
3. Hal Lebovitz, "Hal Asks: Remember the Cleveland Rams?" *Cleveland Plain Dealer*, January 20, 1980.

Introduction

1. Arthur Daley, "Pro Football Musings," *New York Times*, January 15, 1946, 18.
2. Craig R. Coenen, *From Sandlots to the Super Bowl* (Knoxville: University of Tennessee Press, 2005), 112.
3. "NFC Championship Game Results," National Football League, accessed December 14, 2015, http://www.nfl.com/superbowl/results/championships. The only other team to break through was the 1935 Detroit Lions.
4. Steve Gietschier, "Go West, Young Rams," *The Sporting News*, January 23, 1995, 7.
5. Edward Prell, "Rams Beat Redskins, 15–14, for Pro Title," *Chicago Daily Tribune*, December 17, 1945.
6. Gietschier, "Go West, Young Rams."
7. Jack Clowser, "Rams Hand Bears First Shutout in Six Years," *Cleveland Press*, October 8, 1945.
8. Daley, "Pro Football Musings."
9. Edward Prell, "Rams Shift Franchise to Los Angeles," *Chicago Sunday Tribune*, January 13, 1946.
10. "Welcomes Rams' Move," *New York Times*, January 14, 1946.
11. Roscoe McGowen, "Cleveland Rams Transfer Eleven to Los Angeles," *New York Times*, January 13, 1946.
12. Bob Oates, *The Los Angeles Rams* (Culver City, CA: Murray & Gee, 1955), 15–16.
13. "Los Angeles Rams' Owner Dan Reeves Dies of Cancer," *The Palm Beach (Florida) Post*, April 16, 1971.
14. 14. Paul Jacobs, "Marshman's 1936 Pro Grid Vision Comes True," *Cleveland News*, November 4, 1947.
15. "Cleveland Rams Sold," *New York Times*, June 12, 1941.
16. McGowen, "Cleveland Rams Transfer."
17. *Ibid*.
18. Sid Feder, "Pro Football Rams Moved to Los Angeles," *Oregon Statesman*, January 13, 1946.
19. John Dietrich, "National Football League's Public Be Damned Policy Kept Rams from Building Large Following," *Cleveland Plain Dealer*, February 10, 1946.
20. *L.A. Rams Football Club: 1946 Guide for Press and Radio*. Los Angeles: 1946, 1.
21. The 1923–1924 Bulldogs won successive title in successive seasons, but the 1924 Cleveland Bulldogs were a "new" team—a merger between the Canton Bulldogs and the Cleveland Indians. "NFL Champions 1920–2014," Pro Football Hall of Fame, accessed December 18, 2015, http://www.profootballhof.com/football-history/nfl-champions-1920–2014/. John Maxymuk, "Chamberlin, Berlin G. (Guy)," in *NFL Head Coaches: A Biographical Dictionary, 1920–2011* (Jefferson, NC: McFarland & Company, 2012), 360.
22. Joe Horrigan, Pro Football Hall of Fame, in discussion with the author, May 7, 2015.
23. "Art McNally Named Pioneer Award Recipient," Pro Football Hall of Fame, accessed March 6, 2016, http://www.profootballhof.com/news/art-mcnally-named-pioneer-award-recipient/
24. James E. Doyle, "The Sport Trail," *Cleveland Plain Dealer*, February 6, 1946.
25. "NFL Single Game Receiving Yards Leaders," Pro Football Reference, accessed August

15, 2015, http://www.pro-football-reference.com/leaders/rec_yds_single_game.htm.

26. The Cleveland Rams' cumulative .412 record in 1937–42 and 1944–45 exceeds the Philadelphia Eagles' .333, the Pirates-Steelers' .264, and the Chicago Cardinals' .262. "Philadelphia Eagles Franchise Encyclopedia," Pro Football Reference, accessed December 18, 2015, http://www.pro-football-reference.com/teams/phi/. "Pittsburgh Steelers Franchise Encyclopedia," Pro Football Reference, accessed December 18, 2015, http://www.pro-football-reference.com/teams/pit/. "Arizona Cardinals Franchise Encyclopedia," Pro Football Reference, accessed December 18, 2015, http://www.pro-football-reference.com/teams/crd/.

27. Tom Reed, "How Moving a Franchise from Cleveland to L.A. Benefited the Browns and Fostered Social Change," Cleveland.com, accessed December 18, 2015, http://www.cleveland.com/browns/index.ssf/2014/02/cleveland_rams_browns_move_to_los_angeles.html, April 16, 2014.

28. Josh Katzowitz, *Sid Gillman: Father of the Passing Game* (Covington, KY: Clerisy Press, 2012).

29. Maxymuk 6, 102.

30. Hal Lebovitz, "Ask Hal," *Cleveland Plain Dealer*, April 16, 1976.

31. "Dante Magnani," *New York Times*, December 24, 1985, accessed December 18, 2015, http://www.nytimes.com/1985/12/24/sports/dante-magnani.html.

32. For instance, the Pro Football Hall of Fame's website attributed the drafting in 1941 of Rudy Mucha not to the Cleveland Rams but to the Cleveland Browns, who actually began play five years later. "The 1941 NFL Draft Picks," Pro Football Hall of Fame, accessed December 18, 1945, http://www.profootballhof.com/timeline/1940/the-1941-nfl-draft/

33. NFL franchises that have won championships in *two* different cities: the Colts (Indianapolis and Baltimore), the Raiders (Los Angeles and Oakland), and arguably the Bulldogs (Cleveland, Canton)—though the 1924 Cleveland championship was won with a Bulldogs team blended with the Cleveland Indians. "NFL Champions 1920–2014," Pro Football Hall of Fame, accessed December 18, 2015, http://www.profootballhof.com/football-history/nfl-champions-1920-2014/

Chapter 1

1. "Henry Wetzel," Baseball Reference, accessed November 15, 2014, http://www.baseball-reference.com/bullpen/Henry_Wetzel.

2. Gordon Cobbledick, "Plain Dealing," *Cleveland Plain Dealer*, February 17, 1938.

3. "Buckeye Gridder Hurt," *Cleveland Plain Dealer*, May 14, 1933.

4. "Gold Pants: An Ohio State Football Tradition," SB Nation Land-Grant Holy Land, accessed November 15, 2014, http://www.landgrantholyland.com/2013/6/3/4381740/gold-pants-an-ohio-state-football-tradition.

5. "He's a Touchdown Artist, Too," *Milwaukee Journal*, October 27, 1934.

6. Howard Barry, "Halas Will Root for Wetzel, but Not on Thursday Night," *Chicago Tribune*, August 27, 1935.

7. "Buzz Wetzel," Pro Football Reference, accessed January 6, 2016, http://www.pro-football-reference.com/players/W/WetzBu20.htm.

8. "Final Whistle Brings a Near-Riot as Pirates Beat Cardinals, 17–13," *New York Times*, October 21, 1935.

9. Chris Willis, *Joe F. Carr: The Man Who Built the National Football League* (Lanham, MD: Scarecrow, 2010), 239.

10. Ibid., 23.

11. "NFL 1920 Regular Season Standings," National Football League, accessed November 15, 2014, http://www.nfl.com/standings?category=league&season=1920-reg.

12. Willis, *Joe F. Carr*, 151.

13. Bob Oates, *The Los Angeles Rams* (Culver City, CA: Murray & Gee, 1955), 12.

14. Craig R. Coenen, *From Sandlots to the Super Bowl* (Knoxville: University of Tennessee Press, 2005), 7.

15. Ibid., 15.

16. Dixon Stewart, "Football Kills 32 in Most Disastrous Year," *Cleveland Press*, December 4, 1931.

17. Willis, 267.

18. Ibid., 163.

19. John Dietrich, "Rams Primed for Opening Kick-Off," *Cleveland Plain Dealer*, September 5, 1937.

20. Joe Horrigan, Pro Football Hall of Fame, in discussion with the author, May 7, 2015.

21. Willis, 271.

22. Coenen, 18.

23. Horrigan.

24. Coenen, 103.

25. "Two Seek Pro League Berths," *Milwaukee Journal*, February 9, 1936.

26. Hal Lebovitz, "Remember the Cleveland Rams?" *Coffin Corner* 7 (1985), Professional Football Researchers Association.

27. Paul Jacobs, "Marshman's 1936 Pro Vision Comes True," *Cleveland News*, November 4, 1947.

28. Lebovitz, "Remember the Cleveland Rams?"

29. "Cleveland News," Encyclopedia of Cleveland History, accessed November 15, 2014, http://ech.cwru.edu/ech-cgi/article.pl?id=CN1.

30. Bob Gries, *Five Generations: 175 Years of Love for Cleveland* (Shaker Heights, OH: Bob Gries, 2014), 239, http://issuu.com/thebraungroup/docs/gries-5generations/1.
31. "Buzz Wetzel and His 'Boys' Who Have Made Good," *Cleveland Plain Dealer*, March 22, 1936.
32. Lebovitz, "Remember the Cleveland Rams."
33. "Boston Refuses to Oppose Rams," *Cleveland Plain Dealer*, November 29, 1936.
34. Jacobs, "Marshman's 1936 Pro Vision."
35. Hal Lebovitz, "Old Pro Shuts Typewriter; Sports Scene Will Miss Him," February 2, 1964.
36. Andy Piascik, *The Best Show in Football: The 1946–1955 Cleveland Browns* (Lanham, MD: Taylor Trade Publishing, 2007), 12.
37. Lebovitz, "Remember the Cleveland Rams."

Chapter 2

1. Only three Rams players on the 1936 AFL team—backs Harry Mattos, Stan Pincura, and Bill Cooper—and coach and general manager Damon "Buzz" Wetzel were reported to make it to the 1937 NFL team (John Dietrich, "Rams Seek to Tame Lions at Stadium Friday Night," *Cleveland Plain Dealer*, September 5, 1937). However, Joe Horrigan of the Pro Football Hall of Fame made a distinction between a franchise as "a right to operate" and a team as "what you build" (in discussion with the author, May 7, 2015). The name Cleveland Rams and owner-investors including Homer H. Marshman and Robert H. Gries were common to both the 1936 AFL team and the 1937 NFL team, so from this perspective the Rams could be said to have begun as a franchise or organization in 1936. The NFL, however, dates the team's founding to entry to its own league in 1937.
2. Charles W. Lawrence, "Fans Just Can't Quit Baiting Umps," *Cleveland Plain Dealer*, October 12, 1936.
3. "Cleveland Pro Gridders Disband," *Cleveland Plain Dealer*, September 6, 1936.
4. "7 Former Ohio State Stars on Team Here," *Cleveland Plain Dealer*, September 26, 1936.
5. "1936 Cleveland Rams (AFL)," Pro Football Archives, accessed November 17, 2014, http://www.profootballarchives.com/1936aflcle.html.
6. Paul Jacobs, "Marshman's 1936 Pro Vision Comes True," *Cleveland News*, November 4, 1947.
7. "Rams to Exhibit Colorful Attack," *Cleveland Plain Dealer*, October 8, 1936.
8. Ibid.
9. Lawrence, "Fans Just Can't Quit."
10. "The Surprising and Unexpected Evolution of the Football Cleats," Sneaker Report, accessed December 21, 2014, http://sneakerreport.com/news/the-surprising-and-unexpected-evolution-of-the-football-cleat/7/
11. William M. Schaefer, Gridiron Uniform Database, e-mail message to author, November 22, 2014.
12. Lawrence, "Fans Just Can't Quit."
13. Jacobs, "Marshman's 1936 Pro Vision."
14. "Jack Graney, the First Player-Broadcaster," Society for American Baseball Research (SABR), accessed November 17, 2014, http://research.sabr.org/journals/jack-graney.
15. Lawrence, "Fans Just Can't Quit."
16. Including their six home games in the AFL, the Cleveland Rams played 19 of their 41 home games in League Park. The NFL Rams played 20 games in Cleveland Stadium, 13 in League Park, and two in Shaw Stadium. Statistics aggregated from newspaper accounts of all Rams games, 1936 through 1945.
17. "Rams Cut Prices for Home Games," *Cleveland Plain Dealer*, November 6, 1936.
18. A.F. Hinrichs, "Average Hourly Earnings in Manufacturing, 1933 to 1936," *Monthly Labor Review* 44 (April 1937): 828.
19. Lawrence, "Fans Just Can't Quit."
20. John Dietrich, "Laterals Fly as Rams Beat Syracuse, 26–0." *Cleveland Plain Dealer*, October 12, 1936.
21. Lawrence, "Fans Just Can't Quit."
22. Ibid.
23. Josh Katzowitz, *Sid Gillman: Father of the Passing Game* (Covington, KY: Clerisy Press, 2012), 58.
24. David C. Perry, "Cleveland: Journey to Maturity," in *Cleveland: A Metropolitan Reader*, ed. W. Dennis Keating, Norman Krumholz, and David Perry (Kent, OH: Kent State University Press, 1995), 18.
25. Ibid.
26. Erick Trickey, "Eliot Ness and J. Edgar Hoover," *Smithsonian* (September 2014): 81.
27. Carol Poh Miller and Robert A. Wheeler, "Cleveland: The Making and Remaking of an American City, 1796–1993," in *Cleveland: A Metropolitan Reader*, ed. W. Dennis Keating, Norman Krumholz, and David Perry (Kent, OH: Kent State University Press, 1995), 41.
28. In 2014 the NFL said women made up about 45 percent of its fan base. Mina Kimes, "Dear NFL, Women Matter..." *ESPN the Magazine*, accessed January 2, 2016, http://espn.go.com/espnw/news-commentary/article/11262500/espnw-why-ray-rice-light-punishment-bad-business-nfl.
29. Craig R. Coenen, *From Sandlots to the*

Super Bowl (Knoxville: University of Tennessee Press, 2005), 91.
30. Chris Willis, *Joe F. Carr: The Man Who Built the National Football League* (Lanham, MD: Scarecrow, 2010), 329.
31. *Ibid.*, 321.
32. *Ibid.*, xiv.
33. Coenen, 79.
34. Dietrich, "Laterals Fly."
35. John Dietrich, "Boston Irish Spank Rams Before 7,000," *Cleveland Plain Dealer,* October 19, 1936.
36. Katzowitz, 58.
37. "Beautiful Homes of Cleveland—Part 1," Cleveland Area History, accessed November 17, 2014, http://www.clevelandareahistory.com/2011_07_01_archive.html.
38. "Nails Ram Back for Loss on Jaunt with No Drivers License," *Cleveland Plain Dealer,* November 7, 1936.
39. "1936 New York Yankees (AFL)," Pro Football Archives, accessed November 17, 2014, http://www.profootballarchives.com/1936aflnewy.html.
40. "1936 Boston Shamrocks (AFL)," Pro Football Archives, accessed November 17, 2014, http://www.profootballarchives.com/1936aflbos.html.
41. Robert D. Gries, in discussion with the author, August 1, 2015.
42. John Dietrich, "Rams Win in Last Minute, Share Top," *Cleveland Plain Dealer,* November 9, 1936.
43. "Cleveland Rams Lead American Pro Grid Loop," *Lewiston Daily Sun,* November 11, 1936.
44. "Rams Balk, Game's Off," *Pittsburgh Press,* November 16, 1936.
45. James E. Doyle, "The Sport Trail," *Cleveland Plain Dealer,* November 30, 1936.
46. Hal Lebovitz. "Remember the Cleveland Rams?" *Coffin Corner* 7 (1985), Professional Football Researchers Association.
47. John Dietrich, "Rams Plan Game with Collegians," *Cleveland Plain Dealer,* November 18, 1936.
48. Lebovitz, "Remember the Cleveland Rams?"
49. Jacobs, "Marshman's 1936 Pro Vision."

Chapter 3

1. Chris Willis, *Joe F. Carr: The Man Who Built the National Football League* (Lanham, MD: Scarecrow, 2010), 233.
2. Craig R. Coenen, *From Sandlots to the Super Bowl* (Knoxville: University of Tennessee Press, 2005), 104.
3. Coenen, 84–85.

4. Hal Lebovitz, "On a Scale of One to 10?" *Cleveland Plain Dealer,* November 27, 1977.
5. Dan Daly, "Sammy Baugh, 1943: The Greatest Season?" The MMQB, accessed December 21, 2014, http://mmqb.si.com/2013/11/14/ammy-baugh-1943/
6. Willis, 355.
7. "20 Backers of New Rams Team Named," *Cleveland Plain Dealer,* February 4, 1937.
8. Hal Lebovitz, "Remember the Cleveland Rams?" *Coffin Corner* 7 (1985), Professional Football Researchers Association.
9. John Kieran, "The Eagles Are Screaming," *New York Times,* October 17, 1937.
10. Lebovitz, "Remember the Cleveland Rams?"
11. Willis, 163.
12. Lebovitz, "Remember the Cleveland Rams?"
13. Homer H. Marshman to Solon Holt, February 18, 1937.
14. Paul Jacobs, "Marshman's 1936 Pro Vision Comes True," *Cleveland News,* November 4, 1947.
15. Coenen, 95.
16. "Jay Berwanger, First Winner of the Heisman Trophy, 1914–2002," University of Chicago, accessed December 11, 2014. http://www-news.uchicago.edu/releases/02/020627.berwanger.shtml.
17. Coenen, 3.
18. *Ibid.*, 95.
19. *Ibid.*
20. "Hugo Bezdek," Baseball Reference, accessed December 11, 2014, http://www.baseball-reference.com/bullpen/Hugo_Bezdek.
21. Ben Williamson, "His Players Wanted Bezdek Kept; Rams' Owners Need Tough Manager for Selves," *Cleveland Press,* September 29, 1938.
22. Westbrook Pegler, "Nobody's Business," *Chicago Tribune,* December 11, 1932.
23. "Hugo Bezdek, Grid Coach, Ex-Buc Manager, Dies," *Pittsburgh Post-Gazette,* September 20, 1952.
24. George Strickler, "Bezdek, Once Maroon Star, Directs Rams," *Chicago Tribune,* October 29, 1937.
25. *Ibid.*
26. "Hugo Bezdek and the Razorbacks," University of Arkansas, accessed December 14, 2014, http://www.uark.edu/rd_vcad/urel/info/campus_map/446.php.
27. "Hugo Bezdek, Grid Coach."
28. "Managerial Maxims of Hugo Bezdek," *The Pittsburgh Press,* July 25, 1918.
29. "Hugo Bezdek Has Made Good," *The Spokesman-Review,* August 18, 1918.
30. "Managerial Maxims."

31. "Opinions Divide on Football Criticism," *New York Times*, January 20, 1922.
32. "Hugo Bezdek to Stick," *Lewiston Daily Sun*, December 5, 1922.
33. William T. Reedy, "Penn State Football Coach Address Penn Wheelmen," *Reading (Pennsylvania) Eagle*, January 24, 1926.
34. Ibid.
35. "Not His Brainchild, Says Hugo Bezdek," *Reading Eagle*, October 19, 1935.
36. Pegler, "Nobody's Business."
37. Henry McLemore, "Hugo Bezdek Recommends Drastic Changes in Rules," *The Pittsburgh Press*, December 29, 1930.
38. "New Student View on Football Noted," *New York Times*, December 29, 1931.
39. Pegler, "Nobody's Business."
40. "Penn State Ousts Bezdek from Post," *New York Times*, October 4, 1932.
41. Carl Shatto, "Hugo Bezdek Is Signed as Rams' Coach," *Cleveland Press*, May 25, 1937.
42. Shatto, "Hugo Bezdek Is Signed."
43. Ibid.

Chapter 4

1. John Dietrich, "40 Rams Report for First Grid Workout of Year," *Cleveland Plain Dealer*, August 3, 1937.
2. Gordon Cobbledick, "Plain Dealing," *Cleveland Plain Dealer*, September 1, 1937.
3. Dietrich, "40 Rams Report."
4. Cobbledick, "Plain Dealing."
5. John Dietrich, "Rams Seek to Tame Lions at Stadium Friday Night," *Cleveland Plain Dealer*, September 5, 1937.
6. Ibid. Mike Sebastian also appears to have been a member of both the 1936 AFL Rams and 1937 NFL Rams. ("1936 Cleveland Rams [AFL]," Pro Football Archives, accessed January 14, 2016, http://www.profootballarchives.com/1936aflcle.html. "1937 Cleveland Rams [NFL]," Pro Football Archives, accessed January 14, 2016, http://www.profootballarchives.com/1937nflcle.html.)
7. "Gomer Jones, Oklahoma Ex-Football Coach, Dies," *New York Times*, March 22, 1971.
8. "Padlow Is Reinstated by National," *Cleveland Plain Dealer*, September 28, 1938.
9. Joe F. Carr, ed., *Official Guide of the National Football League: 1937* (New York: American Sports Publishing Co., 1937), 44.
10. Dietrich, "40 Rams Report."
11. John Dietrich, "35,000 Expected to See Rams Open Season; Lions Favored," *Cleveland Plain Dealer*, September 10, 1937.
12. John Dietrich, "Rams Plan Surprise for Lions in Opener," *Cleveland Plain Dealer*, September 5, 1937.
13. Ibid.
14. "Rams Cut Price for Home Games," *Cleveland Plain Dealer*, November 6, 1936.
15. "NFC Championship Game Results," National Football League, accessed January 10, 2016, http://www.nfl.com/superbowl/results/championships.
16. "The Perfect Football Face," *LIFE*, December 28, 1936, 4.
17. Carr, ed., *Official Guide*, 45.
18. John Dietrich, "Detroit Outclasses Rams to Win Pro Grid Opener, 28–0," *Cleveland Plain Dealer*, September 11, 1937.
19. "Record & Fact Book: Team Records, Passing," National Football League, accessed April 22, 2015, http://www.nfl.com/history/randf/records/team/passing.
20. Roelif Loveland, "Ram Looks Sheepish in Debut to 25,000," *Cleveland Plain Dealer*, September 11, 1937.
21. John Dietrich, "Score on Fumble Beats Rams," *Cleveland Plain Dealer*, October 4, 1937.
22. John Dietrich, "Chicago's Husky Bears Rip Rams," *Cleveland Plain Dealer*, October 11, 1937.
23. John Kieran, "The Eagles Are Screaming," *New York Times*, October 17, 1937.
24. George Strickler, "Bezdek, Once Maroon Star, Directs Rams," *Chicago Tribune*, October 29, 1937.
25. John Dietrich, "Rams 'Satisfied' with Coach, Begin 1938 Rebuilding," *Cleveland Plain Dealer*, November 4, 1937.
26. John Kieran, "Red Hot from Green Bay," *New York Times*, November 21, 1937.
27. Joe F. Carr, ed., *Official Guide of the National Football League: 1938* (New York: American Sports Publishing Co., 1938), 43.
28. "1937 NFL Standings, Team & Offensive Statistics," Pro Football Reference, accessed January 2, 2015, http://www.pro-football-reference.com/years/1937/
29. "1937 NFL Opposition & Defensive Statistics," Pro Football Reference, accessed January 2, 2015, http://www.pro-football-reference.com/years/1937/opp.htm.
30. "1937 NFL Standings, Team and Offensive Statistics."
31. Winning percentages: "1937 NFL Standings." Total home attendance: George Kirksey, "Record 1,176,476 Watch National Pro Grid Games," *Cleveland Plain Dealer*, December 19, 1937.
32. Kirksey, "Record 1,176,476 Watch."
33. Ibid.

Chapter 5

1. John Dietrich, "Rams 'Satisfied' with Coach, Begin 1938 Rebuilding," *Cleveland Plain Dealer*, November 4, 1937.

2. "1938 Cleveland Rams (NFL)," Pro Football Archives, accessed January 14, 2016, http://www.profootballarchives.com/1938nflcle.html.

3. "Office Space," *Beaver County Times*, September 5, 2004.

4. "Leather-Bound Lions: Dutch Clark," SBNation, accessed February 1, 2015, http://www.prideofdetroit.com/2010/6/3/1498784/leather-bound-lions-dutch-clark.

5. "1938 NFL Leaders and Leaderboards," Pro Football Reference, accessed January 16, 2016, http://www.pro-football-reference.com/years/1938/leaders.htm.

6. "1940 NFL Leaders and Leaderboards," Pro Football Reference, accessed January 16, 2016, http://www.pro-football-reference.com/years/1940/leaders.htm.

7. Carl L. Storck, ed., *Official Guide of the National Football League: 1939* (New York: American Sports Publishing Co., 1939), 37.

8. "Rams Draft 3 All-Americans," *Cleveland Plain Dealer*, December 12, 1937.

9. "Sutphin Says He's Interested in Buying Rams," *Cleveland Plain Dealer*, January 15, 1938.

10. "Cleveland Barons," Encyclopedia of Cleveland History, accessed January 16, 2016, http://ech.case.edu/cgi/article.pl?id=CB3.

11. Pro Football Researchers Association, "1937 National Football League," Pro Football Researchers Association, accessed January 16, 2016, http://profootballresearchers.com/members-only/Linescores/1937Linescore.pdf.

12. Joe Horrigan, Pro Football Hall of Fame, in discussion with the author, May 7, 2015.

13. Dan Daly, *The National Forgotten League* (Lincoln: University of Nebraska Press, 2012), 136–7.

14. John Dietrich, "Only Social Error; Rams Didn't Know Arizona Star Is a Junior," *Cleveland Plain Dealer*, March 28, 1938.

15. "Branko Smilanich," Pro Football Reference, accessed February 1, 2015. http://www.pro-football-reference.com/players/S/SmilBr20.htm.

16. Ben Williamson, "His Players Wanted Bezdek Kept; Rams' Owners Need Tough Manager for Selves," *Cleveland Press*, September 29, 1938.

17. "Lipscomb Is Named President of Rams." *Cleveland Plain Dealer*, April 6, 1938.

18. Michael Oriard, *King Football: Sport and Spectacle in the Golden Age of Radio and Newsreels, Movies & Magazines, the Weekly & the Daily Press* (Chapel Hill: University of North Carolina Press, 2001), 153.

19. "'Play It Hard,' Is New Ram's Formula." *Cleveland Plain Dealer*, June 14, 1938.

20. Ben Williamson, "Pardon This Heat, but Drake Is Back on Range; and Here's How Indians Still Can Win It." *Cleveland Press*, August 16, 1938.

21. John Dietrich, "Rams Steam into First 1938 Drill," *Cleveland Plain Dealer*, August 16, 1938.

22. Williamson, "Pardon This Heat."

23. Scott Sillcox, "The Evolution of Colors," Los Angeles Rams video, 1:50, February 11, 2013, http://www.therams.com/videos/videos/Evolution-of-the-Rams-Colors/164595b6-f383-4af0-a9d1-141d1fba0c18.

24. "Wetzel Resigns as Ram Official," *Cleveland Plain Dealer*, September 15, 1938.

25. Thirteen years later, long after the Rams had moved to Los Angeles, Eisner still was in Cleveland, working in publicity and ad sales for a local radio station. "Air Checks," *Billboard*, August 11, 1951, 10.

26. "Wetzel Resigns."

27. "Rams Return to City Next Sunday as Enemy," *Cleveland Plain Dealer*, December 18, 1950.

28. Williamson, "His Players Wanted Bezdek Kept."

29. Ibid.

30. "Debacle Angers Rams' President," *Cleveland Plain Dealer*, September 27, 1938.

31. "Art Lewis Named Rams Head Coach," *Cleveland Plain Dealer*, September 28, 1938.

32. Williamson, "His Players Wanted Bezdek Kept."

33. Hal Lebovitz, "Remember the Cleveland Rams?" *Coffin Corner* 7 (1985), Professional Football Researchers Association.

34. "Art Lewis Named Rams Head Coach."

35. George Strickler, "Rams See Only Packers in Way of Championship," *Chicago Tribune*, October 25, 1938.

36. Arthur J. Daley, "Cleveland Coach Out to Upset Owen of Giants, His Ex-Mentor," *New York Times*, November 11, 1938.

37. Paul Jacobs, "Marshman's 1936 Pro Vision Comes True," *Cleveland News*, November 4, 1947.

38. Williamson, "His Players Wanted Bezdek Kept."

39. "Hugo Bezdek as a Player and Farmer," *Pittsburgh Post-Gazette*, June 11, 1942.

40. "Where Are They Now? Johnny Drake," *Cleveland Press*, February 9, 1954.

41. John Dietrich, "Rams Halt Bears' Closing Rush for 2d Straight Upset, 14–7," *Cleveland Plain Dealer*, October 10, 1938.

42. Ibid.

43. Harry Grayson, "Cleveland Boss Simply Gets His Interference in Front of Play," NEA Service, October 11, 1938.

44. John Dietrich, "Rival Fans Cheer for Rams as 'Miracle Team' Makes Comeback Stick;

Notes—Chapter 6

Lewis Praises 2 Ends," *Cleveland Plain Dealer*, October 25, 1938.
45. Arch Ward, "In the Wake of the News," *Chicago Tribune*, December 23, 1953.
46. "Cleveland Rams Coaching Staff," Game Program, World Championship Playoff: National Football League, December 16, 1945, 13.
47. George Strickler, "Cardinals Beat Rams, 31–17; Set Pair of Records," *Chicago Tribune*, November 28, 1938.
48. Daly, 133.
49. "Clark Signs for 2 Years with Rams," *Cleveland Plain Dealer*, December 17, 1938.
50. Ibid.
51. "1938 NFL Leaders and Leaderboards," Pro Football Reference, accessed February 15, 2015. http://www.pro-football-reference.com/years/1938/leaders.htm.
52. "The Perfect Football Face…," *LIFE* magazine, December 28, 1936, 4.
53. "Luck to Them Both," *Cleveland Press*, December 17, 1938.

Chapter 6

1. Jonathan Knight, *Opening Day: Cleveland, the Indians, and a New Beginning* (Kent, OH: Kent State University Press, 2004), 70.
2. "Ram Officials Shift Gridiron to Bring Game Closer to Spectators," *Cleveland Plain Dealer*, July 20, 1941.
3. "1937 Cleveland Rams," Pro Football Reference, accessed February 6, 2016, http://www.pro-football-reference.com/teams/ram/1937.htm. "1938 Cleveland Rams," Pro Football Reference, accessed February 6, 2016, http://www.pro-football-reference.com/teams/ram/1938.htm.
4. "Four Brilliant Rookies Playing with Cleveland Rams This Year," *Prescott (Arizona) Evening Courier*, August 31, 1939.
5. The other was quarterback Bob Waterfield in 1945. "Joe F. Carr Trophy (MVP) Winners," Pro Football Reference, accessed March 8, 2016, http://www.pro-football-reference.com/players/award_jfct.htm.
6. Vance Lauderdale, "Gaylon the Great," *Memphis Flyer*, November 4, 2008, accessed January 4, 2016, http://www.memphisflyer.com/AskVanceBlog/archives/2008/11/04/gaylon-the-great.
7. *L.A. Rams Football Club: 1946 Guide for Press and Radio*, 57.
8. Ibid., 40.
9. Bob Yonkers, "Outwitting Quarterback Gains Matheson Stardom," *Cleveland Press*, November 30, 1945.
10. "L.A. Rams Football Club," 40.
11. Yonkers, "Outwitting Quarterback."
12. Chris Willis, *Dutch Clark: The Life of an NFL Legend and the Birth of the Detroit Lions* (Lanham, MD: Scarecrow Press, 2012), 276.
13. Ibid.
14. "Rams May Be Big Factor in Pro Grid Loop," *Sunday Morning Star (Wilmington, Delaware)*, June 25, 1939.
15. "Eye on Packers, Rams Start Job," *Cleveland Plain Dealer*, August 6, 1939.
16. Ibid.
17. Ibid.
18. Yonkers, "Outwitting Quarterback."
19. "Chronicles of 1936, 1939 Seasons Through Former Press-Gazette Sports Editor's Eyes," Packers News, accessed March 14, 2015. http://archive.packersnews.com/article/20110128/PKR01/110128119/Chronicles-1936–1939-seasons-through-former-Press-Gazette-sports-editor-s-eyes.
20. Former Cleveland Browns owner Art Modell once resided in a home abutting Kirtland Country Club but reputedly was denied entry to the highly exclusive club because he was Jewish.
21. "1940 Press Photo Jerry Dowd, Chuck Cherundolo & John Drake of Cleveland Rams," eBay, accessed March 14, 2015, http://www.ebay.com/itm/1940-Press-Photo-Jerry-Dowd-Chuck-Cherundolo-John-Drake-of-Cleveland-Rams-/390961469059?pt=LH_Default Domain_0&hash=item5b071e9683.
22. Thomas E. Lipscomb, "Era of Pro Grid Bum Over, Says Lipscomb," *Cleveland Plain Dealer*, August 18, 1940.
23. "Band Pageantry to Mark Rams' Battle," *Cleveland Plain Dealer*, October 4, 1939.
24. Gordon Cobbledick, "'College Spirit' Blooms in Pro Camp; Rams Point for Grudge Battle with Lions," *Cleveland Plain Dealer*, November 14, 1939.
25. Willis, 278.
26. Chads O. Skinner, "C. of C. Cheers Grid Heroes; Rams and Lions Vie for Burton Trophy," *Cleveland Plain Dealer*, November 18, 1939.
27. "Rams Out to Do It for Clark," *Cleveland Plain Dealer*, November 19, 1939.
28. Carl L. Storck, ed., *Official Guide of the National Football League: 1940* [New York: American Sports Publishing Co., 1939], 33.
29. "Catching a Strike from Parker Hall…," *Cleveland Plain Dealer*, November 27, 1939.
30. John F. Huth, "Rams Dazzle 30,690 Even as They Lose, 7–6," *Cleveland Plain Dealer*, November 27, 1939.
31. "Ole Miss Football Greats Parker Hall and Bud Slay Pass Away," Ole Miss Football, accessed March 14, 2015. http://www.olemisssports.com/sports/m-footbl/spec-rel/021105aac.html.

32. "1939 NFL Standings, Team & Offensive Statistics," Pro Football Reference, accessed March 14, 2015. http://www.pro-football-reference.com/years/1939/#rushing_and_receiving.
33. "1939 Regular Season Statistics," NFL, accessed March 14, 2015, http://www.nfl.com/stats/player?seasonId=1939&seasonType=REG&Submit=Go.
34. Gordon Cobbledick, "Professional Football Is Over the Hump Here as Rams Make Good in Big Way," *Cleveland Plain Dealer*, November 27, 1939.
35. "History: 1931–1940," NFL, accessed March 14, 2015. http://www.nfl.com/history/chronology/1931-1940.
36. John Dietrich, "Clark Greets 40 Rams Wednesday," *Cleveland Plain Dealer*, August 11, 1940.
37. "American Airlines Timetable: September 24, 1939," DC3Airways.com, accessed February 11, 2016, http://www.dc3airways.com/flights/routes/american_airlines.htm.
38. Craig R. Coenen, *From Sandlots to the Super Bowl* (Knoxville: University of Tennessee Press, 2005), 113.
39. John Dietrich, "Rams Reach Turning Point of Campaign as They Face Lions," *Cleveland Plain Dealer*, November 1, 1940.
40. Ibid.
41. James Quirk and Rodney D. Fort, *Pay Dirt: The Business of Professional Team Sports* (Princeton: Princeton University Press, 1992), 341.
42. Gordon Cobbledick, "Clark Rates Rams Better than 1939 Club, Cites Injuries as One Reason for Slump," *Cleveland Plain Dealer*, October 31, 1940.
43. "1940 NFL Leaders and Leaderboards," Pro Football Reference, accessed March 14, 2015. http://www.pro-football-reference.com/years/1940/leaders.htm.
44. "1940 NFL Leaders and Leaderboards."
45. "Cowboy Drake Earns His Football Spurs," *Cleveland Plain Dealer*, December 26, 1940.
46. Franklin Lewis, "Gehrke Flies High as Airplane Artist, on Ground as Ram," *Cleveland Press*, November 1, 1945.
47. Ibid.
48. Walker Gillette, Jim Gillette's son, in discussion with the author, October 11, 2014.
49. Marguerite Gillette, Jim Gillette's widow, in discussion with the author, October 11, 2014.
50. Eddie McKenna, "Gillette Joins Cleveland; Cards Seek New Players," *Kenosha (Wisconsin) Evening News*, October 16, 1940.
51. Steve Gietschier, "Go West, Young Rams," *Sporting News*, January 23, 1995, 7.

Chapter 7

1. "Cleveland Rams Football Club Stockholders," December 31, 1940; document privately held by Donald Gries, Shaker Heights, Ohio.
2. Chris Willis, *Dutch Clark: The Life of an NFL Legend and the Birth of the Detroit Lions* (Lanham, MD: Scarecrow Press, 2012), 280.
3. Robert Dvorchak, "1940s Put Steelers to Tests That Nearly Break Them," *Pittsburgh Post-Gazette*, September 16, 2007.
4. "Rooney Tells How Big Deal Was Arranged," *Pittsburgh Post-Gazette*, December 10, 1940.
5. James Quirk and Rodney D. Fort, *Pay Dirt: The Business of Professional Team Sports* (Princeton: Princeton University Press, 1992), 341–2. The decision not to plant a flag on the West Coast in the early 1940s came to haunt the NFL as competition from Ameche's subsequent LA Dons of the AAFC threatened the Rams' very financial existence in their early years in California.
6. "Bruch Warns on Draft Jumping," *Cleveland Plain Dealer*, February 2, 1941.
7. Alex Zirin, "Rams Expected to Remain Here," *Cleveland Plain Dealer*, April 19, 1941.
8. "Civic Groups to Lead Ram Drive," *Cleveland Plain Dealer*, April 9, 1941.
9. "Cincinnati or Boston May Get Cleveland Rams," *Chicago Tribune*, April 9, 1941.
10. Ibid.
11. "Civic Groups."
12. "We Want the Rams," *Cleveland Plain Dealer*, April 9, 1941.
13. Zirin.
14. "C. of C. Official Is Rams Booster," *Cleveland Plain Dealer*, April 17, 1941.
15. Joe Horrigan, Pro Football Hall of Fame, in discussion with the author, May 7, 2015.
16. Dan Reeves Jr., son of Daniel F. Reeves, in discussion with the author, January 29, 2016.
17. Bob Yonkers, "Daniel Reeves, Owner, Cleveland Rams," Game Program, World Championship Playoff: National Football League, December 16, 1945, 7.
18. Bob Oates, "The New Hall of Famer," *Los Angeles Herald-Examiner*, February 7, 1967.
19. Dan Reeves Jr.
20. Bob Oates, *The Los Angeles Rams* (Culver City, CA: Murray & Gee, 1955), 20.
21. Craig R. Coenen, *From Sandlots to the Super Bowl* (Knoxville: University of Tennessee Press, 2005), 83.
22. George Peters, "Reeves and Levy Do Not Plan to Shift Grid Team," *Cleveland Plain Dealer*, June 12, 1941.
23. Franklin Lewis, "Levy, Ex-Partner in

Rams' Deal, Urged Removal," *Cleveland Press*, February 7, 1946.
  24. "Bidder for Rams Delays Decision," *Cleveland Plain Dealer*, May 1, 1941.
  25. "Cleveland Rams Sold," *New York Times*, June 11, 1941.
  26. John Dietrich, "Rams Will Remain in Cleveland, Is Decision of Club's Owners," *Cleveland Plain Dealer*, October 29, 1941.
  27. "Cleveland Rams Sold."
  28. Peters, "Reeves and Levy."
  29. "Cleveland Rams Sold."
  30. Paul Jacobs, "Marshman's 1936 Pro Vision Comes True," *Cleveland News*, November 4, 1947.
  31. James P. Quirk, *Pay Dirt: The Business of Professional Team Sports* (Princeton: Princeton University Press, 1992), 341.
  32. Jacobs.
  33. Ben Williamson, "His Players Wanted Bezdek Kept; Rams' Owners Need Tough Manager for Selves," *Cleveland Press*, September 29, 1938.
  34. Jacobs, "Marshman's 1936 Pro Vision."
  35. Hal Lebovitz, "Remember the Cleveland Rams?" *Coffin Corner* 7 (1985), Professional Football Researchers Association.
  36. John Dietrich, "Layden Praises Rams Before 800 at Fete," *Cleveland Plain Dealer*, December 13, 1945.
  37. *Ram Rumblings: Published by the Cleveland Rams Football Club* 1:1 (September 1941).
  38. "The Public Be Pleased—Slogan of Cleveland Rams," *Ram Rumblings*, 2.
  39. "Billy Evans," National Baseball Hall of Fame, accessed April 11, 2015, http://baseballhall.org/hof/evans-billy.
  40. "Billy Evans," *Cleveland Plain Dealer*, June 13, 1941.
  41. Sam Otis, "Brief News and Views on Sports," *Cleveland Plain Dealer*, December 31, 1941.
  42. "Reeves Will Take Active Part in Rams Management," *Ram Rumblings*, 3.
  43. "Ram Officials Shift Gridiron to Bring Game Closer to Spectators," *Cleveland Plain Dealer*, July 20, 1941.
  44. "Stadium Playing Field Drastically Changed," *Ram Rumblings*, 2.
  45. "Reeves Will Take."
  46. John Dietrich, "Rams Search for Shifty Halfback," *Cleveland Plain Dealer*, August 3, 1941.
  47. "Costs Real Money to Operate Big League Football Team," *Ram Rumblings*, 3.
  48. Ibid.
  49. Ibid.
  50. "Ready, Rams!," *Cleveland News*, September 3, 1941.
  51. Phil Dietrich, "Over 6,000 Latecomers Miss Magnani's Touchdown Gallop," *Akron Beacon Journal*, September 8, 1941.
  52. Bob Oates, *The Los Angeles Rams* (Culver City, CA: Murray & Gee, 1955), 14.
  53. Phil Dietrich, "Over 6,000."
  54. "Second Air Force 'Superbombers,'" Greater Northwest Football Association, accessed April 11, 2015, http://www.gnfafootball.org/2ndairsuperbombers.htm.
  55. "Backfield Is Wrecked," *New York Times*, February 27, 1941.
  56. "Art Lewis Named Coach at W.-L.," *Cleveland Plain Dealer*, November 15, 1941.
  57. Franklin Lewis, "Football Loses Real Star as Drake Retires," *Cleveland Press*, July 15, 1942.
  58. H.L. Samford, "Ram Game Sets Receipts Record," *Cleveland Plain Dealer*, October 6, 1941.
  59. Willis, 283.
  60. Dan Daly, *The National Forgotten League* (Lincoln: University of Nebraska Press, 2012), 200.
  61. Dietrich, "Rams Will Remain in Cleveland."
  62. Gordon Cobbledick, "Cleveland Boys, Mutryn and Lavelle, Lead Xavier to Upset of Eastern Eleven," *Cleveland Plain Dealer*, December 1, 1941.
  63. Sam Otis, "Brief News and Views on Sports," *Cleveland Plain Dealer*, October 30, 1941.
  64. "1941 National Football League," Pro Football Researchers Association, accessed March 13, 2016. http://profootballresearchers.com/members-only/Linescores/1941Linescore.pdf.
  65. Gordon Cobbledick, "'Somebody Loves Me,' Could Be Theme Song of Rams After Booing They Received at Stadium," *Cleveland Plain Dealer*, November 5, 1941.
  66. Anton, Todd and Nowlin, Bill. *When Football Went to War* (Chicago: Triumph, 2013), 8.
  67. Quirk and Fort, 7.
  68. Quirk and Fort, 341.
  69. Lewis, "Football Loses Real Star."
  70. John Dietrich, "Rams' Flat Pass Boomerangs, Cardinals Triumph, 7–0," *Cleveland Plain Dealer*, November 24, 1941.

Chapter 8

  1. Dutch Clark to Francis Logan, December 26, 1941.
  2. Todd Anton and Bill Nowlin, *When Football Went to War* (Chicago: Triumph, 2013), 13.
  3. Tony Barnhart, "The '40s: NFL Goes to

War," *Coffin Corner* 9:8 (1987), Professional Football Researchers Association.
  4. "Cleveland Rams vs. Washington Redskins, Cleveland Stadium," *Football Fanfare and Program*, September 7, 1945.
  5. "Discovering U-Boat 166," PBS Nova, accessed June 12, 2015. http://www.pbs.org/wgbh/nova/military/discovering-u-166.html.
  6. Marguerite Gillette, Jim Gillette's widow, in discussion with the author, October 11, 2014.
  7. "Evans Quits Pro Rams," *New York Times*, January 1, 1942.
  8. "Stadium Game Will Supplant All-Star Event," *Cleveland Plain Dealer*, April 2, 1942.
  9. Gordon Cobbledick, "Walsh's Remarkable Organizational Job Assures City of Powerful Postwar Ram Team," *Cleveland Plain Dealer*, November 5, 1944.
  10. "Rams Sign Walsh to Handle Line," *Cleveland Plain Dealer*, 1941.
  11. Chris Willis, *Dutch Clark: The Life of an NFL Legend and the Birth of the Detroit Lions* (Lanham, MD: Scarecrow Press, 2012), 285.
  12. "Walsh, Ram Aid, Is Orator, Too," *Cleveland Plain Dealer*, October 3, 1942.
  13. Ibid.
  14. Cobbledick, "Walsh's Remarkable Organizational Job."
  15. "Call to Arms to Hit Collegians," *Cleveland Plain Dealer*, August 28, 1942.
  16. "Rams Withdraw from Pro Football League for Duration," *Cleveland Plain Dealer*, April 7, 1943.
  17. Woody Strode, *Goal Dust: The Warm and Candid Memoirs of a Pioneer Black Athlete and Actor* (Lanham, MD: Madison Books, 1990), 126–7.
  18. Ibid.
  19. John Dietrich, "Jacobs' 2 Touchdown Passes Win for Rams, 14–0," *Cleveland Plain Dealer*, September 28, 1942.
  20. Dietrich, "Smith Alternates with Hall, Janiak at Fullback," *Cleveland Plain Dealer*, November 6, 1942.
  21. Willis, *Dutch Clark*, 285.
  22. Ibid.
  23. Henry Andrews, "Magnani Comes into Own as Ram Player," *Cleveland Press*, October 30, 1941.
  24. "1942 Cleveland Rams," Pro Football Reference, accessed June 12, 2015, http://www.pro-football-reference.com/teams/ram/1942.htm.
  25. "1941 NFL Leaders and Leaderboards," Pro Football Reference, accessed June 12, 2015, http://www.pro-football-reference.com/years/1941/leaders.htm.
  26. Willis, *Dutch Clark*, 287.
  27. Gordon Cobbledick, "Two Major Grid Games Draw 130,000 Fans, but Big Four Teams and Rams Are Ignored," *Cleveland Plain Dealer*, November 17, 1942.
  28. "Clark Asks Rams Not to Renew His Contract as Coach," *Cleveland Plain Dealer*, March 11, 1943.
  29. Willis, *Dutch Clark*, 173.
  30. Ibid., 288.
  31. "Football Attendance Drops 25 Per Cent," *Cleveland Press*, October 19, 1942.
  32. "Tribe Attendance Drop Is Largest," *Cleveland Plain Dealer*, October 3, 1942.
  33. "Cleveland Rams Drop from National Pro Grid League," *Daily Times* (Beaver and Rochester, Pennsylvania), April 7, 1943.
  34. "Layden Confident Pro Grid League Can Open Season," *Cleveland Plain Dealer*, April 6, 1943.
  35. "Cleveland Rams Not for Sale," *The Pittsburgh Press*, May 12, 1943.
  36. John Dietrich, "Rams Withdraw from Pro Football League for Duration," *Cleveland Plain Dealer*, April 7, 1943.
  37. Sam Otis, "Brief News and Views on Sports," *Cleveland Plain Dealer*, April 8, 1943.
  38. "Jim Benton," Pro Football Reference, accessed June 12, 2015, http://www.pro-football-reference.com/players/B/BentJi00.htm.
  39. Bob Carroll, "Mini-Bio: Jim Benton," *Coffin Corner* 17:2 (1995), Professional Football Researchers Association.
  40. "Rams Vote to Resume Play in 1944," *Associated Press*, September 21, 1943.
  41. Gordon Cobbledick, "Baseball Will Be Wise If It Continues Its Policy of Asking for No Favors," *Cleveland Plain Dealer*, November 16, 1943.
  42. Dan Reeves, Jr., son of Daniel F. Reeves, in discussion with the author, January 29, 2016.

Chapter 9

  1. Alex Zirin, "Rams Are in League to Stay, Walsh Says," *Cleveland Plain Dealer*, May 5, 1944.
  2. Ibid.
  3. Ibid.
  4. Todd Anton and Bill Nowlin, *When Football Went to War* (Chicago: Triumph, 2013), 29.
  5. "Rams Will Play Only Four of 13 Games at Home," *Cleveland Plain Dealer*, April 24, 1944.
  6. Ibid.
  7. Zirin, "Rams Are in League to Stay."
  8. "Here Is the Story of Rams' Rise to Championship," *Football Fanfare and Program*, "Cleveland Rams vs. Boston Yanks, League Park, Cleveland, Ohio," December 2, 1945.
  9. Gordon Cobbledick, "Rams Will Have Powerful Postwar Team If War Doesn't Last Too Long," *Cleveland Plain Dealer*, May 6, 1944.

10. Jack Clowser, "Walsh Returns, Hiding His Secrets," *Cleveland Press*, April 5, 1944.
11. Jane Russell, *My Path & My Detours, an Autobiography* (New York: Franklin Watts, 1985), 83.
12. Jack Clowser, "Rams Sign Two Halfbacks," *Cleveland Press*, April 15, 1944.
13. Clowser, "Walsh Returns."
14. "Sport: Okinawa's All-Americans," *TIME*, September 24, 1945, accessed January 4, 2016, http://content.time.com/time/magazine/article/0,9171,886603,00.html.
15. James E. Doyle, "The Sport Trail," *Cleveland Plain Dealer*, December 7, 1945.
16. Cobbledick, "Rams Will Have Powerful Postwar Team."
17. Cobbledick, "Donelli Gives Large Share of Credit for Rams' Success to Benton and Matheson," *Cleveland Plain Dealer*, October 18, 1944.
18. Robert McG. Thomas Jr., "Buff Donelli, College Football Coach, Dies at 87," *New York Times*, August 11, 1994.
19. Michael Lewis, "Aldo 'Buff' Donelli: The Man Who Ignited the USA-Mexico Rivalry in 1934," the *Guardian*, April 13, 2015, accessed June 15, 2015, http://www.theguardian.com/football/2015/apr/13/how-aldo-buff-donelli-drew-first-blood-in-usas-rivalry-with-mexico.
20. Ibid.
21. Thomas Jr., "Buff Donelli."
22. Isi Newborn, "Aldo (Buff) Donelli: Meet the Man Who Was Shamed into a Football Career, Whose Job Is to Rebuild Rams into a Pro Grid Power," *Cleveland Press*, August 21, 1944.
23. Ibid.
24. *L.A. Rams Football Club: 1946 Guide for Press and Radio*, 21.
25. "Rams to Open Training with 13 Veterans," *Associated Press*, August 11, 1944.
26. "New Men Dot Rams' Roster," *Milwaukee Journal*, August 10, 1944.
27. "Know Your New Rams: Steve Pritko," *Cleveland Press*, September 24, 1944.
28. Ibid.
29. Marguerite Gillette, Jim Gillette's widow, in discussion with the author, October 11, 2014.
30. Charles Heaton, "Scarry's Nose Broken 9 Times, but Reserve Coach Is Nostaglic About Pro(Boscis) Football," *Cleveland Plain Dealer*, February 2, 1948.
31. "First Televised Football Game Featured Fordham, Waynesburg in 1939," NCAA, accessed February 14, 2016, http://www.ncaa.com/news/football/article/2014-09-28/first-televised-football-game-featured-fordham-waynesburg-1939.
32. Isi Newborn, "Donelli to Receive 'One of Biggest Contracts in Football'—Walsh," *Cleveland Press*, November 22, 1944.
33. "1944 Cleveland Rams," Pro Football Reference, accessed June 12, 2015, http://www.pro-football-reference.com/teams/ram/1944.htm.
34. Herman Goldstein, "Pat on Back Pays Off with Colella," *Cleveland News*, October 9, 1947.
35. Jack Clowser, "Rams Sign Two Halfbacks," *Cleveland Press*, April 14, 1944.
36. James E. Doyle, "The Sport Trail," *Cleveland Plain Dealer*, August 14, 1944.
37. John Dietrich, "Rams Forced to Run Gantlet in Pro Grid League," *Cleveland Plain Dealer*, November 2, 1944.
38. Ibid.
39. Bill Levy, *Return to Glory: The Story of the Cleveland Browns* (Cleveland: World Publishing, 1965), 40.
40. "1940 Notre Dame Fighting Irish," Database Football, accessed June 13, 2015, http://www.databasefootball.com/college/teams/teamyear.htm?TeamID=75&Season=1940.
41. Levy, 40.
42. Ibid., 41.
43. "Yellow Cab Asks Cleveland Test of Radio Dispatching," *Cleveland Plain Dealer*, September 1, 1944.
44. Robert D. Gries, in discussion with the author, August 1, 2015.
45. Dietrich, "Rams Smash Bears, 19–7, to Send Pro Grid Title Hopes Soaring," *Cleveland Plain Dealer*, October 9, 1944.
46. Paul S. Underwood, "Rams Upset Pro League Predictions, *St. Petersburg Times*, October 14, 1944.
47. Jimmy Jordan, "Rams Threaten Packers' Hopes," *Tuscaloosa* (Alabama) *News*, October 16, 1944.
48. Cobbledick, "Donelli Gives Large Share of Credit."
49. Isi Newborn, "Gillette of the Rams—A Story of Irony and Grit," *Cleveland Press*, October 25, 1944.
50. Tom Fergusson, "Tiny Dippery, Rams' Trainer, Says Pro Champions Had as Much Spirit as Any College Team—Singles Out Gillette and Waterfield," *Norfolk* (Virginia) *Virginian-Pilot*, December 29, 1945.
51. Dietrich, "'Observer' Idea Is a Little Late for Rams," *Cleveland Plain Dealer*, November 3, 1944.
52. Cobbledick, "Rams' General Manager Cites Reasons for Not Fearing Threat of Pro Football Competition in Cleveland," *Cleveland Plain Dealer*, November 10, 1944.
53. John Dietrich, "Hutson Snares 2 Scoring Passes as Green Bay Blasts Rams, 42–7," *Cleveland Plain Dealer*, November 13, 1944.
54. Ibid.
55. Sam Otis, "Brief News and Views on

Sports," *Cleveland Plain Dealer*, November 12, 1944.
56. Isi Newborn, "Donelli to Receive."
57. Ibid.
58. Otis, "Brief News and Views on Sports," *Cleveland Plain Dealer*, November 26, 1944.
59. "1944 NFL Leaders and Leaderboards," Pro Football Reference, accessed June 13, 2015, http://www.pro-football-reference.com/years/1944/leaders.htm.
60. Dietrich, "Rams Forced to Run Gantlet."
61. Otis, "Brief News and Views on Sports," *Cleveland Plain Dealer*, April 25, 1944.
62. Statistics aggregated from the season-by-season database at "Standings," NFL.com, accessed January 3, 2016, http://www.nfl.com/standings.
63. "Greenwood of Illinois Signs Ram Contract," *Cleveland Plain Dealer*, December 22, 1945.
64. Ibid.

Chapter 10

1. Jane Russell, *My Path & My Detours: An Autobiography* (New York: Franklin Watts, 1985), 33.
2. Franklin Lewis, "Rams' Waterfield Intends to Become Football Coach," *Cleveland Press*, August 30, 1945.
3. Buck Waterfield, Bob Waterfield's son, in discussion with the author, September 27, 2014.
4. Russell, 48.
5. Buck Waterfield in discussion with the author, January 30, 2016.
6. Chicago Bears business card and personal notation in Bob Waterfield's scrapbook, ca. 1936; privately held by Buck Waterfield, Santa Maria, California.
7. David Condon, "In the Wake of the News," *Chicago Tribune*, August 2, 1966.
8. Ibid.
9. Ibid.
10. Rob Fernas, "Complete Package," *Los Angeles Times*, December 25, 1999, accessed October 25, 2015, http://articles.latimes.com/1999/mar/17/sports/sp-18189.
11. Buck Waterfield, September 27, 2014.
12. Fernas, "Complete Package."
13. Jack Sher, "The Bob Waterfield Story," *SPORT*, November 1951, 28.
14. Condon.
15. Buck Waterfield, January 30, 2016.
16. Russell, 46.
17. Ibid., 64.
18. Buck Waterfield interview, September 27, 2014.
19. Russell, 49.

20. Jane Russell in a Western Union telegram to Bob Waterfield, September 26, 1942.
21. Chris Foster, "UCLA's First Win Over Usc Was a Battle, but Don't Dare Call It a War," *Los Angeles Times*, November 13, 2012, accessed October 25, 2015, http://articles.latimes.com/2012/nov/13/sports/la-sp-1113-ucla-1942-usc-20121113.
22. Ibid.
23. Arch Ward, "U.C.L.A. Says Man to Watch in Rose Bowl Is Our Waterfield," *Chicago Tribune*, December 31, 1942.
24. Newspaper clipping and notation in Frances Waterfield's scrapbook, ca. 1940s; privately held by Buck Waterfield, Santa Maria, California.
25. Foster, "UCLA's First Win."
26. Russell, 75.
27. Ibid., 77.
28. Ibid., 81.
29. Wes Mathis, "Sensational Comeback in Final 12 Minutes Wins for West Shrine," *San Jose News*, January 2, 1945.
30. Tom Slater, Mutual Broadcasting System, to Bob Waterfield, January 18, 1945.
31. Russell, 83.
32. Steve Bisheff, *Los Angeles Rams: Great Teams' Great Years* (New York: Macmillan, 1975).
33. Ibid.
34. Russell, 83.
35. Ibid.
36. Marguerite Gillette, Jim Gillette's widow, in discussion with the author, October 11, 2014.
37. Russell, 83.

Chapter 11

1. Ian Buruma, *Year Zero: A History of 1945* (New York: Penguin, 2013).
2. Joe Horrigan, Pro Football Hall of Fame, in discussion with the author, May 7, 2015.
3. Craig R. Coenen, *From Sandlots to the Super Bowl* (Knoxville: University of Tennessee Press, 2005), 104.
4. Horrigan.
5. Ibid.
6. Coenen, 120.
7. Edward Prell, "Rams Offer Luke Johnsos $20,000 a Year," *Chicago Tribune*, March 6, 1945.
8. "Rams to Remain Here, Walsh Says," *Cleveland Plain Dealer*, March 13, 1945.
9. "Chile Walsh Denies Offer to Johnsos," *Cleveland Plain Dealer*, March 6, 1945.
10. "Rams to Remain Here."
11. John Dietrich, "Ram Coach Welds Rookies into Outstanding Team," *Cleveland Plain Dealer*, December 9, 1945.
12. "Brown Signs 2 Stars for New Grid Team," *Cleveland Plain Dealer*, April 1, 1945.

Sports," *Cleveland Plain Dealer*, November 12, 1944.
56. Isi Newborn, "Donelli to Receive."
57. *Ibid.*
58. Otis, "Brief News and Views on Sports," *Cleveland Plain Dealer*, November 26, 1944.
59. "1944 NFL Leaders and Leaderboards," Pro Football Reference, accessed June 13, 2015, http://www.pro-football-reference.com/years/1944/leaders.htm.
60. Dietrich, "Rams Forced to Run Gantlet."
61. Otis, "Brief News and Views on Sports," *Cleveland Plain Dealer*, April 25, 1944.
62. Statistics aggregated from the season-by-season database at "Standings," NFL.com, accessed January 3, 2016, http://www.nfl.com/standings.
63. "Greenwood of Illinois Signs Ram Contract," *Cleveland Plain Dealer*, December 22, 1945.
64. *Ibid.*

Chapter 10

1. Jane Russell, *My Path & My Detours: An Autobiography* (New York: Franklin Watts, 1985), 33.
2. Franklin Lewis, "Rams' Waterfield Intends to Become Football Coach," *Cleveland Press*, August 30, 1945.
3. Buck Waterfield, Bob Waterfield's son, in discussion with the author, September 27, 2014.
4. Russell, 48.
5. Buck Waterfield in discussion with the author, January 30, 2016.
6. Chicago Bears business card and personal notation in Bob Waterfield's scrapbook, ca. 1936; privately held by Buck Waterfield, Santa Maria, California.
7. David Condon, "In the Wake of the News," *Chicago Tribune*, August 2, 1966.
8. *Ibid.*
9. *Ibid.*
10. Rob Fernas, "Complete Package," *Los Angeles Times*, December 25, 1999, accessed October 25, 2015, http://articles.latimes.com/1999/mar/17/sports/sp-18189.
11. Buck Waterfield, September 27, 2014.
12. Fernas, "Complete Package."
13. Jack Sher, "The Bob Waterfield Story," *SPORT*, November 1951, 28.
14. Condon.
15. Buck Waterfield, January 30, 2016.
16. Russell, 46.
17. *Ibid.*, 64.
18. Buck Waterfield interview, September 27, 2014.
19. Russell, 49.

20. Jane Russell in a Western Union telegram to Bob Waterfield, September 26, 1942.
21. Chris Foster, "UCLA's First Win Over Usc Was a Battle, but Don't Dare Call It a War," *Los Angeles Times*, November 13, 2012, accessed October 25, 2015, http://articles.latimes.com/2012/nov/13/sports/la-sp-1113-ucla-1942-usc-20121113.
22. *Ibid.*
23. Arch Ward, "U.C.L.A. Says Man to Watch in Rose Bowl Is Our Waterfield," *Chicago Tribune*, December 31, 1942.
24. Newspaper clipping and notation in Frances Waterfield's scrapbook, ca. 1940s; privately held by Buck Waterfield, Santa Maria, California.
25. Foster, "UCLA's First Win."
26. Russell, 75.
27. *Ibid.*, 77.
28. *Ibid.*, 81.
29. Wes Mathis, "Sensational Comeback in Final 12 Minutes Wins for West Shrine," *San Jose News*, January 2, 1945.
30. Tom Slater, Mutual Broadcasting System, to Bob Waterfield, January 18, 1945.
31. Russell, 83.
32. Steve Bisheff, *Los Angeles Rams: Great Teams' Great Years* (New York: Macmillan, 1975).
33. *Ibid.*
34. Russell, 83.
35. *Ibid.*
36. Marguerite Gillette, Jim Gillette's widow, in discussion with the author, October 11, 2014.
37. Russell, 83.

Chapter 11

1. Ian Buruma, *Year Zero: A History of 1945* (New York: Penguin, 2013).
2. Joe Horrigan, Pro Football Hall of Fame, in discussion with the author, May 7, 2015.
3. Craig R. Coenen, *From Sandlots to the Super Bowl* (Knoxville: University of Tennessee Press, 2005), 104.
4. Horrigan.
5. *Ibid.*
6. Coenen, 120.
7. Edward Prell, "Rams Offer Luke Johnsos $20,000 a Year," *Chicago Tribune*, March 6, 1945.
8. "Rams to Remain Here, Walsh Says," *Cleveland Plain Dealer*, March 13, 1945.
9. "Chile Walsh Denies Offer to Johnsos," *Cleveland Plain Dealer*, March 6, 1945.
10. "Rams to Remain Here."
11. John Dietrich, "Ram Coach Welds Rookies into Outstanding Team," *Cleveland Plain Dealer*, December 9, 1945.
12. "Brown Signs 2 Stars for New Grid Team," *Cleveland Plain Dealer*, April 1, 1945.

10. Jack Clowser, "Walsh Returns, Hiding His Secrets," *Cleveland Press*, April 5, 1944.
11. Jane Russell, *My Path & My Detours, an Autobiography* (New York: Franklin Watts, 1985), 83.
12. Jack Clowser, "Rams Sign Two Halfbacks," *Cleveland Press*, April 15, 1944.
13. Clowser, "Walsh Returns."
14. "Sport: Okinawa's All-Americans," *TIME*, September 24, 1945, accessed January 4, 2016, http://content.time.com/time/magazine/article/0,9171,886603,00.html.
15. James E. Doyle, "The Sport Trail," *Cleveland Plain Dealer*, December 7, 1945.
16. Cobbledick, "Rams Will Have Powerful Postwar Team."
17. Cobbledick, "Donelli Gives Large Share of Credit for Rams' Success to Benton and Matheson," *Cleveland Plain Dealer*, October 18, 1944.
18. Robert McG. Thomas Jr., "Buff Donelli, College Football Coach, Dies at 87," *New York Times*, August 11, 1994.
19. Michael Lewis, "Aldo 'Buff' Donelli: The Man Who Ignited the USA-Mexico Rivalry in 1934," the *Guardian*, April 13, 2015, accessed June 15, 2015, http://www.theguardian.com/football/2015/apr/13/how-aldo-buff-donelli-drew-first-blood-in-usas-rivalry-with-mexico.
20. Ibid.
21. Thomas Jr., "Buff Donelli."
22. Isi Newborn, "Aldo (Buff) Donelli: Meet the Man Who Was Shamed into a Football Career, Whose Job Is to Rebuild Rams into a Pro Grid Power," *Cleveland Press*, August 21, 1944.
23. Ibid.
24. *L.A. Rams Football Club: 1946 Guide for Press and Radio*, 21.
25. "Rams to Open Training with 13 Veterans," *Associated Press*, August 11, 1944.
26. "New Men Dot Rams' Roster," *Milwaukee Journal*, August 10, 1944.
27. "Know Your New Rams: Steve Pritko," *Cleveland Press*, September 24, 1944.
28. Ibid.
29. Marguerite Gillette, Jim Gillette's widow, in discussion with the author, October 11, 2014.
30. Charles Heaton, "Scarry's Nose Broken 9 Times, but Reserve Coach Is Nostaglic About Pro(Boscis) Football," *Cleveland Plain Dealer*, February 2, 1948.
31. "First Televised Football Game Featured Fordham, Waynesburg in 1939," NCAA, accessed February 14, 2016, http://www.ncaa.com/news/football/article/2014-09-28/first-televised-football-game-featured-fordham-waynesburg-1939.
32. Isi Newborn, "Donelli to Receive 'One of Biggest Contracts in Football'—Walsh," *Cleveland Press*, November 22, 1944.

33. "1944 Cleveland Rams," Pro Football Reference, accessed June 12, 2015, http://www.pro-football-reference.com/teams/ram/1944.htm.
34. Herman Goldstein, "Pat on Back Pays Off with Colella," *Cleveland News*, October 9, 1947.
35. Jack Clowser, "Rams Sign Two Halfbacks," *Cleveland Press*, April 14, 1944.
36. James E. Doyle, "The Sport Trail," *Cleveland Plain Dealer*, August 14, 1944.
37. John Dietrich, "Rams Forced to Run Gantlet in Pro Grid League," *Cleveland Plain Dealer*, November 2, 1944.
38. Ibid.
39. Bill Levy, *Return to Glory: The Story of the Cleveland Browns* (Cleveland: World Publishing, 1965), 40.
40. "1940 Notre Dame Fighting Irish," Database Football, accessed June 13, 2015, http://www.databasefootball.com/college/teams/teamyear.htm?TeamID=75&Season=1940.
41. Levy, 40.
42. Ibid., 41.
43. "Yellow Cab Asks Cleveland Test of Radio Dispatching," *Cleveland Plain Dealer*, September 1, 1944.
44. Robert D. Gries, in discussion with the author, August 1, 2015.
45. Dietrich, "Rams Smash Bears, 19-7, to Send Pro Grid Title Hopes Soaring," *Cleveland Plain Dealer*, October 9, 1944.
46. Paul S. Underwood, "Rams Upset Pro League Predictions," *St. Petersburg Times*, October 14, 1944.
47. Jimmy Jordan, "Rams Threaten Packers' Hopes," *Tuscaloosa* (Alabama) *News*, October 16, 1944.
48. Cobbledick, "Donelli Gives Large Share of Credit."
49. Isi Newborn, "Gillette of the Rams—A Story of Irony and Grit," *Cleveland Press*, October 25, 1944.
50. Tom Fergusson, "Tiny Dippery, Rams' Trainer, Says Pro Champions Had as Much Spirit as Any College Team—Singles Out Gillette and Waterfield," *Norfolk* (Virginia) *Virginian-Pilot*, December 29, 1945.
51. Dietrich, "'Observer' Idea Is a Little Late for Rams," *Cleveland Plain Dealer*, November 3, 1944.
52. Cobbledick, "Rams' General Manager Cites Reasons for Not Fearing Threat of Pro Football Competition in Cleveland," *Cleveland Plain Dealer*, November 10, 1944.
53. John Dietrich, "Hutson Snares 2 Scoring Passes as Green Bay Blasts Rams, 42-7," *Cleveland Plain Dealer*, November 13, 1944.
54. Ibid.
55. Sam Otis, "Brief News and Views on

13. John Dietrich, "Pro Grid War Looms Here, but Ideal Solution Would Give City One Home Game a Week," *Cleveland Plain Dealer*, March 30, 1945.
14. "St. Louis Rams," Pro Football Reference, accessed August 9, 2015, http://www.profootball-reference.com/teams/ram/
15. L.A. *Rams Football Club: 1946 Guide for Press and Radio*. Los Angeles: 1946, 37.
16. Bill Scholl, "Lazetich—Charger with Song in His Heart, Football in Blood," *Cleveland Press*, November 1, 1974.
17. Joseph Hession, "Gil Bouley: 1945–1950," *Coffin Corner* 9:3 (1987), Professional Football Researchers Association.
18. "Good Luck, Riley," *Cleveland Press*, December 1, 1945.
19. "1944 Cleveland Rams," Pro Football Reference, accessed August 11, 2015, http://www.pro-football-reference.com/teams/ram/1944.htm.
20. Herman Goldstein, "The 'T' Man Comes to Town," *Cleveland News*, May 2, 1945.
21. Edward Prell, "Walsh Tells Why Pro League Can't Keep Rams Fenced In," *Chicago Tribune*, November 20, 1945.
22. Dietrich, "Rams Coach Welds Rookies."
23. Edward Prell, "Aug. 23 Homecoming for Ex-Bears Trafton, Snyder," *Chicago Tribune*, July 15, 1946.
24. Dietrich, "Rams Coach Welds Rookies."
25. Hal Lebovitz. "Remember the Cleveland Rams?" *Coffin Corner* 7 (1985), Professional Football Researchers Association.
26. David Condon, "In the Wake of the News," *Chicago Tribune*, August 2, 1966.
27. Gene Ward, "Rams Zoom to Pro Peak Through Cutie and QB," *New York Daily News*, November 11, 1945.
28. Statistics aggregated from the season-by-season database at "Standings," NFL.com, accessed January 3, 2016, http://www.nfl.com/standings.
29. John Dietrich, "National Football League's Public Be Damned Policy Kept Rams from Building Large Following," *Cleveland Plain Dealer*, February 10, 1946.
30. Dietrich, "Rams Bowl Over Steelers, 21 to 0," *Cleveland Plain Dealer*, September 3, 1945.
31. Dietrich, "Waterfield Stars as Rams Bag First Victory Over Redskins, 21–0," *Cleveland Plain Dealer*, September 8, 1945.
32. Charles F. Walsh to Mrs. S. E. Waterfield, September 13, 1945.
33. Hession, "Gil Bouley."
34. Herman Goldstein, "Pat on Back Pays Off with Colella," *Cleveland News*, October 9, 1947.
35. Richard Goldstein, "Jim Benton Dies at 84; Set Longtime Pass-Receiving Record," *New York Times*, April 3, 2001.
36. John Dietrich, "Rams Hand Bears First Whitewashing in 59 League Games, 17–0," *Cleveland Plain Dealer*, October 8, 1945.
37. Tom Fergusson, "Tiny Dippery, Rams' Trainer, Says Pro Champions Had as Much Spirit as Any College Team—Singles Out Gillette and Waterfield," *Norfolk* (Virginia) *Virginian-Pilot*, December 29, 1945.
38. Bob Yonkers, "Colella Sparks Winning Three-Touchdown Rally," *Cleveland Press*, October 5, 1945. Inscribed copy privately held by Walker Gillette, Franklin, Virginia.
39. Ibid.
40. Herman Goldstein, "Charles F. (Chile) Walsh," *World Championship Playoff: National Football League* Game Program, Cleveland Rams vs. Washington Redskins, December 16, 1945, 9.
41. Hal Lebovitz, "Remember the Cleveland Rams?" *Coffin Corner* 7 (1985), Professional Football Researchers Association.
42. John Dietrich, "Eagles Drop Rams into First-Place Tie, 28–14," *Cleveland Plain Dealer*, October 29, 1945.
43. Ibid.
44. Ibid.
45. Chads O. Skinner, "Wife of Rams' Owner Jinxes Team If She Sits with Him," *Cleveland Plain Dealer*, December 8, 1945.
46. William D. Richardson, "Giants Overcome by Rams, 21 to 17," *New York Times*, November 5, 1945.
47. Joe King, "QB Houdini's Back ... as Coach," *New York World Telegram and Sun*, October 21, 1961.
48. Ward, "Rams Zoom to Pro Peak."
49. Oscar Fraley, "Waterfield Makes Cleveland Rams Tough Club to Beat," (Beaver, Pennsylvania) *Daily Times*, November 6, 1945.
50. Lebovitz, "Remember the Cleveland Rams?"
51. John Dietrich, "National Football League's Public Be Damned Policy Kept Rams from Building Large Following," *Cleveland Plain Dealer*, February 10, 1946.
52. Dietrich, "Washington Redskins Install Special Grandstand Each Season; Rams May Adopt Same Set-Up," *Cleveland Plain Dealer*, November 13, 1945.
53. "Statement of Federal & State Tax Collected During November for Football Game at League Park," The Cleveland Baseball Club, November 1945; document privately held by Donald Gries, Shaker Heights, Ohio.
54. "31 Ram Fans Hurt at League Park as Temporary Stands Fall," *Cleveland Plain Dealer*, November 12, 1945.
55. "Walsh and Guion Differ on Crash," *Cleveland Plain Dealer*, November 13, 1945.
56. Dietrich, "National Football League's Public Be Damned Policy."

57. Prell, "Walsh Tells Why Pro League Can't Keep Rams Fenced In."
58. Harry Farrar, "Small Talk of Big Guy," *The Denver Post*, July 15, 1961.
59. Lebovitz, "Remember the Cleveland Rams?"
60. Steve Bisheff, *Los Angeles Rams: Great Teams' Great Years* (New York: Macmillan, 1975).
61. "NFL Single Game Receiving Yards Leaders," Pro Football Reference, accessed August 15, 2015, http://www.pro-football-reference.com/leaders/rec_yds_single_game.htm. As of 2016 the record was held, coincidentally, by another Ram, Flipper Anderson.
62. John Dietrich, "1945 Could Be Rough Year for National League 'Big Four,'" *Football Fanfare*, Cleveland Rams vs. Chicago Cardinals, September 30, 1945.
63. Marguerite Gillette, Jim Gillette's widow, in discussion with the author, October 11, 2014.
64. Phil Spartano, "Cleveland Rams Will Win Pro Title, Gillette Says on Visit to Utica," *Observer-Dispatch* (Utica, NY), December 6, 1945.
65. Coenen, *From Sandlots to the Super Bowl*, 88.
66. Lebovitz, "Remember the Cleveland Rams?"
67. "1945 NFL Leaders and Leaderboards," Pro Football Reference, accessed August 15, 1945, http://www.pro-football-reference.com/years/1945/leaders.htm.
68. *L.A. Rams Football Club: 1946 Guide for Press*, 59.
69. "1945 NFL Leaders and Leaderboards."
70. Forrest Kable, "All League Selections," *Pro Football Illustrated*, 1946 Edition.
71. "1945 National Football League," Pro Football Researchers Association, accessed June 12, 2015. http://profootballresearchers.com/members-only/Linescores/1945Linescore.pdf.
72. Coenen, *From Sandlots to the Super Bowl*, 102.
73. John Dietrich, "How Good Are the Rams? You Can Look for a 'Pennant' If They Beat Eagles Decisively Sunday," *Cleveland Plain Dealer*, September 18, 1945.
74. Dietrich, "Washington Redskins Install Special Grandstand."
75. John Dietrich, "Layden Praises Rams Before 800 at Fete," *Cleveland Plain Dealer*, December 13, 1945, 18.
76. "Testimonial Dinner Honoring the Cleveland Rams," Dinner Program, Cleveland, Ohio, December 12, 1945; Jim Gillette's personal copy, privately held by Walker Gillette, Franklin, Virginia.
77. Craig R. Coenen, *From Sandlots to the Super Bowl* (Knoxville: University of Tennessee Press, 2005), 130.

78. Edward Prell, "Rams Shift Franchise to Los Angeles," *Chicago Sunday Tribune*, January 13, 1946.
79. Jane Russell, *My Path & My Detours: An Autobiography* (New York: Franklin Watts, 1985), 85.

Chapter 12

1. "Cleveland Municipal Stadium," Ballparks.com, accessed September 20, 2015. http://football.ballparks.com/NFL/ClevelandBrowns/oldindex.htm.
2. Walker Gillette, Jim Gillette's son, in discussion with the author, October 11, 2014.
3. On December 8, 1945, the higher temperature in Cleveland was 50 degrees Fahrenheit and the low was 28. "Cleveland Weather History," Cleveland.com, accessed September 20, 2015. http://www.cleveland.com/datacentral/index.ssf/2008/09/cleveland_weather_history_find.html?appSession=431523366697702.
4. Craig R. Coenen, *From Sandlots to the Super Bowl* (Knoxville: University of Tennessee Press, 2005), 88.
5. John Dietrich, "Layden Praises Rams Before 800 at Fete," *Cleveland Plain Dealer*, December 13, 1945.
6. It would not be the last time such an insulation technique would be used for an NFL championship game—the Green Bay Packers spread hay on the field at City Stadium before their 1961 title match against the New York Giants. "Green Bay City Stadium Before NFL Championship Game," Wisconsin Historical Society, accessed February 26, 2016, http://www.wisconsinhistory.org/Content.aspx?dsNav=N:4294963828-4294955414&dsNavOnly=N:1135&dsRecordDetails=R:IM6661.
7. Chads O. Skinner, "Wife of Rams' Owner Jinxes Team If She Sits with Him," *Cleveland Plain Dealer*, December 8, 1945.
8. Skinner, "Grid 'Eskimos' Survive Zero Hour at Game," *Cleveland Plain Dealer*, December 17, 1945.
9. "Stadium Snow Licked, 50,000 to Hail Rams," *Cleveland Plain Dealer*, December 16, 1945.
10. John Wiebusch, "NFL Championship: A Look Back: A Long Winter's Day: The Improbable Saga of the 1945 NFL Championship Game," LATimes.com, accessed September 23, 1945. http://articles.latimes.com/1986-01-10/sports/sp-956_1_press-box.
11. Howard Preston, "Snuggies, Gloves Help Rams Win Title," *Cleveland News*, December 17, 1945.
12. Skinner, "Grid 'Eskimos.'"

13. Dick McCann, "Dick Mccann Says," (Washington, DC) *Times Herald*, December 17, 1945.
14. Skinner, "Grid 'Eskimos.'"
15. Edward Prell, "Rams Beat Redskins, 15–14, for Pro Title," *Chicago Daily Tribune*, December 17, 1945.
16. *Ibid.*
17. Edward Prell, "Cleveland Game Opens All-America Race Tonight," *Chicago Daily Tribune*, September 6, 1946.
18. "NFC Championship Game Results," NFL.com, accessed September 23, 2015. http://www.nfl.com/superbowl/results/championships.
19. Franklin Lewis, "Bits and Bites of Sports Chosen and Chewed," *Cleveland Press*, December 17, 1945.
20. McCann, "Dick McCann Says:."
21. Skinner, "Grid 'Eskimos.'"
22. Bill Scholl, "Scarry Tales of Browns' Glory Days," *Cleveland Press*, November 16, 1979.
23. Rich Tandler, "1945 NFL Championship Game: Cleveland Municipal Stadium," in *The Redskins from A to Z: The Games* (Midlothian, VA: Walking Encyclopedia Publications), 2002, 34.
24. Skinner, "Grid 'Eskimos.'"
25. *1945 NFL Championship.* (1945; Mount Laurel, NJ: NFL Productions, 2014), DVD.
26. Shelby Strother, "Postwar Classic," in *NFL Top 40: The Greatest Pro Football Games of All Time* (New York: Viking), 1988, 32–35.
27. Al Costello, "Redskins Lose Title Battle to Rams, 15–14," *Washington Post*, December 17, 1945.
28. Skinner, "Grid 'Eskimos.'"
29. Jerry Sulecki, in discussion with the author, June 14, 2014.
30. Arthur Daley, "Revisit to the Hall," *New York Times*, December 30, 1964.
31. *1945 NFL Championship*, DVD.
32. Wiebusch, "NFL Championship."
33. Strother, "Postwar Classic."
34. William D. Richardson, "Rams Top Redskins for Title," *New York Times*, December 17, 1945.
35. Wiebusch, "NFL Championship."
36. Alex Zirin, "Waterfield Signs 3-Year Contract with Rams for Reported $60,000," *Cleveland Plain Dealer*, December 17, 1945.
37. Jack Clowser, "In the Bag—Walsh Knew Size of Rams' Hearts," *Cleveland Press*, December 17, 1945.
38. Zirin, "Waterfield Signs."
39. *Ibid.*
40. Edward Prell, "Waterfield Is Man of Hour in Cleveland," *Chicago Daily Tribune*, December 18, 1945.
41. Zirin, "Waterfield Signs."
42. Another rookie passer to lead his team to a title was Sammy Baugh of the 1937 Washington Redskins, but he was a single-wing tailback. Dave Anderson, "Champion Quarterbacks Sooner and Later," *New York Times*, February 5, 2011, accessed September 28, 2015. http://www.nytimes.com/2011/02/06/sports/football/06anderson.html?_r=0.
43. Zirin, "Waterfield Signs."
44. Joseph S. Page, "1945 NFL—Of Cold and Crossbars," in *Pro Football Championships Before the Super Bowl: A Year-By-Year History, 1926–1965* (Jefferson, NC: McFarland & Company), 2011, 78–79.
45. *Ibid.*, 78.
46. Zirin, "Waterfield Signs."
47. Clowser, "In the Bag."
48. *Ibid.*
49. Jane Russell, *My Path & My Detours: An Autobiography* (New York: Franklin Watts, 1985), 85.
50. Clowser, "In the Bag."
51. The next highest gross per attendee to date was $3.51 at the 1943 championship game in Chicago. Coenen, 88.
52. Edward Prell, "Rams Beat Redskins, 15–14, for Pro Title," *Chicago Daily Tribune*, December 17, 1945.
53. "Dan Reeves Moves West," *Coffin Corner* 20:1 (1998), Professional Football Researchers Association.
54. Alvin Silverman, "Time Out," *Cleveland Plain Dealer*, December 25, 1945.
55. Prell, "Rams Beat Redskins."
56. Marguerite Gillette, Jim Gillette's widow, in discussion with the author, October 11, 2014.
57. McCann, "Dick McCann Says:."
58. Frank Gibbons, "1946 Promises to Be Bouncing Baby for Cleveland Sports Fans," *Cleveland Press*, January 1, 1946.
59. John Dietrich, "Pro Grid War Looms Here, but Ideal Solution Would Give City One Home Game a Week," *Cleveland Plain Dealer*, March 30, 1945.
60. James E. Doyle, "The Sport Trail," *Cleveland Plain Dealer*, January 1, 1946.

Chapter 13

1. "Elmer Layden Insists He Quit but Others Say He Was Ousted," *Pittsburgh Press*, January 13, 1946.
2. Yonkers, "Browns Aim to Make Fans Forget Departed Rams," *Cleveland Press*, February 6, 1946.
3. Bob Yonkers, "Reeves Denies Rams Will Move to Los Angeles," *Cleveland Press*, January 11, 1946 (page proof). Though printing and distribution of the *Cleveland Press* were shut down

at the time by a pressmen's strike, Yonkers's piece was among many others that were typeset into page proofs, run on flatbed presses, and posted about the newspaper's office ("Newspaper Black-Out Affected All Here," *Cleveland Press*, February 6, 1946.) These page proofs then were archived along with regular editions of the newspaper.

4. Yonkers, "Browns Aim."

5. "Rams to Remain Here, Walsh Says," *Cleveland Plain Dealer*, March 13, 1945.

6. Roscoe McGowen, "Cleveland Rams Transfer Eleven to Los Angeles," *New York Times*, January 13, 1946.

7. Dietrich, "Pro Grid War Looms Here, but Ideal Solution Would Give City One Home Game a Week," *Cleveland Plain Dealer*, March 30, 1945.

8. Craig R. Coenen, *From Sandlots to the Super Bowl* (Knoxville: University of Tennessee Press, 2005), 275.

9. "Dan Reeves Moves West," *Coffin Corner* 20:1 (1998), Professional Football Researchers Association.

10. The champion Eagles lost $80,000 in 1948. James P. Quirk, *Pay Dirt: The Business of Professional Team Sports* (Princeton: Princeton University Press, 1992), 71.

11. "Population of the 100 Largest Urban Places: 1940," U.S. Bureau of the Census, accessed October 24, 2015, https://www.census.gov/population/www/documentation/twps0027/tab17.txt. In the 1940 census, Philadelphia had more than 1.9 million people while Cleveland had close to 900,000.

12. "Dan Reeves Moves West."

13. Ibid.

14. Joe Horrigan, Pro Football Hall of Fame, in discussion with the author, May 7, 2015.

15. Daniel F. Reeves to Richard P. McCann, April 23, 1962.

16. Dan Reeves Jr. in discussion with the author, January 29, 2016.

17. Horrigan.

18. Steve Gietschier, "Go West, Young Rams," *Sporting News*, January 23, 1995.

19. Joe Horrigan, "National Football League Franchise Transactions," *Coffin Corner* 4 (1982), Professional Football Researchers Association, 15.

20. Besides the 1923 Canton Bulldogs, who merged with the Cleveland Indians to win the 1924 championship as the Cleveland Bulldogs, all other NFL champions before the 1945 Cleveland Rams played in the same city for at least one more season. This includes the 1924 Cleveland Bulldogs, as well as the 1921 Chicago Staleys who merely changed their name to the Bears in 1922. "NFL Champions," National Football League, accessed October 19, 2015, http://www.profootballhof.com/history/general/champions.aspx. See also—"Akron Indians Franchise Encyclopedia," Pro Football Reference, http://www.pro-football-reference.com/teams/akr/; "Chicago Bears Franchise Encyclopedia," http://www.pro-football-reference.com/teams/chi/; "Canton Bulldogs Franchise Encyclopedia," http://www.pro-football-reference.com/teams/cbd/; "Arizona Cardinals Franchise Encyclopedia," http://www.pro-football-reference.com/teams/crd/; "Frankford Yellow Jackets Franchise Encyclopedia," http://www.pro-football-reference.com/teams/fyj/; and "Providence Steam Roller Franchise Encyclopedia," http://www.pro-football-reference.com/teams/prv/; all accessed October 19, 2015.

21. Joseph Hession, "Gil Bouley: 1945–1950," *Coffin Corner* 9:3 (1987), Professional Football Researchers Association.

22. McGowen, "Cleveland Rams Transfer Eleven."

23. "Welcomes Rams' Move," *New York Times*, January 14, 1946.

24. McGowen, "Cleveland Rams Transfer Eleven."

25. James E. Doyle, "The Sport Trail," *Cleveland Plain Dealer*, January 1, 1946.

26. Yonkers, "Browns Aim."

27. Alvin Silverman, "Record 60,315 See Debut of Browns," *Cleveland Plain Dealer*, September 7, 1946.

28. Horrigan.

29. Bill Dvorak, "Newspaper Black-Out Affected All Here," *Cleveland Press*, February 6, 1946.

30. Yonkers, "Cleveland Loses Rams' Franchise to Los Angeles," *Cleveland Press*, January 14, 1946 (page proof).

31. Yonkers, "Reeves Denies Rams Will Move to Los Angeles." *Cleveland Press*, January 11, 1946 (page proof).

32. "The Presses Roll Again—," *Cleveland Press*, February 6, 1946.

33. Julian Griffin, "Poll Shows News Items Missed Most," *Cleveland Press*, February 6, 1946.

34. John Kroll, "When Art Modell Fired Paul Brown: How the Plain Dealer Reported It," Cleveland.com, accessed March 5, 2016, http://www.cleveland.com/browns/index.ssf/2012/09/when_art_modell_fired_paul_bro.html.

35. Horrigan.

36. "The Presses Roll Again—."

37. Yonkers, "Browns Aim."

38. Hal Lebovitz, "Ask Hal," *Cleveland Plain Dealer*, April 16, 1976.

39. Lebovitz, "Ask Hal," *Cleveland Plain Dealer*, December 12, 1976.

40. Lebovitz, "Hal Asks: Remember the Cleveland Rams?" *Cleveland Plain Dealer*, January 20, 1980.

41. In August 2014 the CLE Clothing store, 342 Euclid Avenue, Cleveland, carried merchandise featuring the Cleveland Bulldogs (1924 NFL champions), the Cleveland Spiders (a 19th-century Major League Baseball team), and the Cleveland Rosenblums (an early-20th-century pro basketball team), but nothing of the Cleveland Rams.
42. Marguerite Gillette, Jim Gillette's widow, in discussion with the author, October 11, 2014.
43. "Judge Upholds Chet Adams' Right to Stay with Browns," *Cleveland Plain Dealer*, August 30, 1946.
44. "Civic Groups to Lead Ram Drive," *Cleveland Plain Dealer*, April 9, 1941.
45. "Rams' Shift Is Surprise," *Zanesville (Ohio) Signal*, January 13, 1946.
46. Gordon Cobbledick, "'Diplomatic Denial or Bald-Faced Lie … Cases in Point … Not Limited to Sports," *Cleveland Plain Dealer*, February 9, 1946.
47. Franklin Lewis, "About Two Guys and Their Lies and Who Got Wise," *Cleveland Press*, February 8, 1946.
48. John Dietrich, "National Football League's Public Be Damned Policy Kept Rams from Building Large Following," *Cleveland Plain Dealer*, February 10, 1946.
49. Ibid.
50. *Ram Rumblings: Published by the Cleveland Rams Football Club* 1:1 (September 1941).
51. Dietrich, "National Football League's."
52. Braven Dyer, "The Sports Parade," *Los Angeles Times*, May 19, 1946.
53. Ibid.
54. Edward Prell, "Rams Shift Franchise to Los Angeles," *Chicago Sunday Tribune*, January 13, 1946.
55. James E. Doyle, "The Sport Trail," *Cleveland Plain Dealer*, February 6, 1946.
56. Horrigan.
57. Franklin Lewis, "Levy, Ex-Partner in Rams' Deal, Urged Removal," *Cleveland Press*, February 7, 1946.
58. "'Chile' Walsh Cuts Connections with L.A. Rams; Contract Settled," *Lewiston (Maine) Daily News*, January 22, 1947.
59. John Dietrich, "Greenwood, Ram Back, Eyes Berth with Browns," *Cleveland Plain Dealer*, February 6, 1946.
60. Frank M. Henkel, *Cleveland Browns History* (Charleston, SC: Arcadia, 2005), 9.
61. Prell, "Rams Shift Franchise." Gilmore Stadium once was the home of postseason NFL all-star games and, coincidentally, the site of the Rams' first-ever game in Los Angeles: an exhibition-game routing by the independent L.A. Bulldogs in 1938. Bob Gill, "The Bulldogs: L.A. Hits the Big Time," *PFRA Annual* 5 (1984), Professional Football Researchers Association.
62. *L.A. Rams Football Club: 1946 Guide for Press and Radio*. Los Angeles: 1946, 5.
63. Mike Penner, "History of Pro Football in Los Angeles," *Los Angeles Times*, March 17, 1999, accessed October 25, 2015, http://articles.latimes.com/1999/mar/17/sports/sp-18189.
64. Frank Neill, "Exclusive Use of Coliseum Given Rams," *The Deseret (Utah) News*, January 30, 1946.
65. Arthur Daley, "Pro Football Musings," *New York Times*, January 15, 1946.
66. A.S. (Doc) Young, "Dedicated Writers and Editors Paved Way for Integration of Major Sports," *Ebony*, October 1970, 58.
67. Alan H. Levy, "Jim Crows of a Feather: A Comparison of the Segregation and Desegregation Eras in Professional Baseball and Football," in *The Cooperstown Symposium on Baseball and American Culture, 2002*, ed. William M. Simons et al. (Jefferson, North Carolina and London: McFarland & Company, 2002), 163.
68. "'Halley' Harding, Noted Sportswriter, Dies at 56," *Jet* magazine, April 20, 1967, 54.
69. Woody Strode, *Goal Dust: The Warm and Candid Memoirs of a Pioneer Black Athlete and Actor* (Lanham, MD: Madison Books, 1990), 4.
70. Alexander Wolff, "The NFL's Jackie Robinson," *Sports Illustrated*, October 12, 2009, accessed October 25, 2015, http://www.si.com/vault/2009/10/12/105865272/the-nfls-jackie-robinson.
71. Ibid.
72. Young, "Dedicated Writers," 58.
73. Ibid.
74. Bob Oates, "The New Hall of Famer," *Los Angeles Herald-Examiner*, February 7, 1967.
75. Buck Waterfield in discussion with the author, January 30, 2016.
76. "Hall of Famers: Dan Reeves," Pro Football Hall of Fame, accessed October 25, 2015, http://www.profootballhof.com/hof/member.aspx?PLAYER_ID=178.
77. Jim Murray, "It's 4th and One for Washington," *(Fredericksburg, Virginia) Free Lance-Star*, September 29, 1970.
78. Charles K. Ross, *Outside the Lines: African Americans and the Integration of the National Football League* (New York: New York University Press, 1999), 82.
79. Strode, 142.
80. Ibid.
81. Mark Yost, *Tailgating, Sacks, and Salary Caps: How the NFL Became the Most Successful Sports League in History* (Chicago: Kaplan, 2006), 57.
82. Bob Oates, *The Los Angeles Rams* (Culver City, CA: Murray & Gee, 1955), 20.
83. Ibid.

84. Strode, 142.
85. Young, "Dedicated Writers," 60.
86. *Forgotten Four: The Integration of Pro Football*, documentary, directed by Johnson McKelvy (2014; New York: Epix, Ross Greenburg Productions), television show.
87. Joe Horrigan, *Forgotten Four*.
88. "Dan Reeves Proved Indians Were Gone," *Spartanburg (South Carolina) Herald-Journal*, April 18, 1971.
89. Prell, "Rams Shift Franchise."
90. Strode, 154.
91. Coenen, 123.
92. Emily Kaplan, "The NFL Wants L.A., but Is It a Requited Love?" The MMQB, July 23, 2015, accessed October 27, 2015, http://mmqb.si.com/mmqb/2015/07/21/nfl-los-angeles-st-louis-rams-stan-kroenke.

Chapter 14

1. *L.A. Rams Football Club: 1946 Guide for Press and Radio*. Los Angeles: 1946, 1.
2. Bob Yonkers, "Rams Aim to Make Fans Forget Departed Rams," *Cleveland Press*, February 6, 1946.
3. Bill Levy, *Return to Glory: The Story of the Cleveland Browns* (Cleveland: World Publishing, 1965), 59.
4. Herman Goldstein, "Pat on Back Pays Off with Colella," *Cleveland News*, October 9, 1947.
5. Andy Piascik, *The Best Show in Football: The 1946–1955 Cleveland Browns—Pro Football's Greatest Dynasty*, Lanham, MD: Taylor Trade Publishing, 26.
6. James H. Lanyon, "Reeves Sues Browns to Keep Adams on Los Angeles Roster," *Cleveland Plain Dealer*, July 20, 1946.
7. "Chet Adams Starts Football Work with Cleveland Browns Next Week," *Cleveland Plain Dealer*, July 25, 1946.
8. "The Beginning of the National Firm," Jones Day, accessed January 4, 2016, http://www.jonesday.com/principlesandvalues/firmhisory/beginningofthenationalfirm/
9. "Rams Seek Court Aid in Player Grab," *Brooklyn Daily Eagle*, July 24, 1946, 16.
10. "Tampering Says Walsh," *Chicago Daily Tribune*, July 24, 1946, 29.
11. "Judge Upholds Chet Adams' Right to Stay with Browns," *Cleveland Plain Dealer*, August 30, 1946.
12. Gordon Cobbledick, "Hirsch Leads All-Stars to 16–0 Victory Over Rams," *Cleveland Plain Dealer*, August 24, 1946.
13. James E. Doyle, "The Sport Trail," *Cleveland Plain Dealer*, August 30, 1946.
14. Walker Gillette, Jim Gillette's son, in discussion with the author, October 11, 2014.
15. "Cleveland Rams: 1945 Player Roster," *World Championship Playoff: National Football League* Game Program, Cleveland Rams vs. Washington Redskins, December 16, 1945; "1946 Los Angeles Rams (NFL)," Pro Football Archives, accessed November 29, 2015, http://www.profootballarchives.com/1946nfllarm.html.
16. Woody Strode, *Goal Dust: The Warm and Candid Memoirs of a Pioneer Black Athlete and Actor* (Lanham, MD: Madison Books, 1990), 151.
17. Edward Prell, "Cleveland Game Opens All-America Race Tonight," *Chicago Daily Tribune*, September 6, 1946, 27. An exhibition the week before was the previous record: 35,964 at the Akron Rubber Bowl. "1946 Cleveland Browns (AAFC)," Pro Football Archives, accessed November 29, 2015, http://www.profootballarchives.com/1946aafccle.html.
18. Alvin Silverman, "60,135 See Browns in Debut Here," *Cleveland Plain Dealer*, September 7, 1946.
19. Craig R. Coenen, *From Sandlots to the Super Bowl* (Knoxville: University of Tennessee Press, 2005), 280.
20. "Local Pride," *Cleveland Plain Dealer*, September 6, 1946.
21. "1946 Cleveland Browns," Pro Football Reference, accessed November 29, 2015. http://www.pro-football-reference.com/teams/cle/1946.htm.
22. "1946 Cleveland Browns (AAFC)," Pro Football Archives. "1946 Los Angeles Rams (NFL)," Pro Football Archives, accessed November 29, 2015, http://Www.Profootballarchives.Com/1946nfllarm.html.
23. Edward Prell, "Rams Champs at Gate in '52," *Chicago Daily Tribune*, December 17, 1952.
24. "Rams Break Pro Record, Draw 86,080," *Cleveland Press*, October 29, 1949.
25. Coenen, *From Sandlots to the Super Bowl*, 135.
26. David George Surdam, *Run to Glory and Profits: The Economic Rise of the NFL During the 1950s* (Lincoln: University of Nebraska Press, 2013), 106.
27. Franklin Lewis, "AAC Surrender Promotes Browns to Big League," *Cleveland Press*, December 10, 1949.
28. Paul Jacobs, "Marshman's 1936 Pro Vision Comes True," *Cleveland News*, November 4, 1947.
29. "Rams Return to City Next Sunday as Enemy," *Cleveland Plain Dealer*, December 18, 1950.
30. Harold Sauerbrei, "Browns Win World Title, 30–28," *Cleveland Plain Dealer*, December 25, 1950.
31. "Rams Return."
32. By sheer winning percentage Adam

Walsh ranks among the best head coaches of all time, but his total of only 21 games in the NFL leave him well short of the threshold for usual inclusion on such lists. "Coaches, Records, and Coaching Totals," Pro Football Reference, accessed November 29, 2015, http://www.pro-football-reference.com/coaches/.

33. Myrna Oliver, "Fred Gehrke, 83; Ram Player, Artist," *Los Angeles Times*, February 14, 2002, accessed November 29, 2015, http://articles.latimes.com/2002/feb/14/local/me-gehrke14.

34. Joe Horrigan, Pro Football Hall of Fame, in discussion with the author, May 7, 2015.

35. James P. Quirk, *Pay Dirt: The Business of Professional Team Sports* (Princeton: Princeton University Press, 1992), 62.

36. Coenen, *From Sandlots to the Super Bowl*, 135.

37. Harry Jones, "Groza's Field Goal Is Signal For Celebration," *Cleveland Plain Dealer*, December 25, 1950.

38. Ibid.

39. "Moving Image Section—Motion Picture, Broadcasting and Recorded Sound Division," Library of Congress, accessed November 29, 2015. http://memory.loc.gov/ammem/awhhtml/awmi10/television.html

40. "Rams Close $656,000 Deal for Television," *Cleveland Plain Dealer*, August 18, 1950.

41. "Impact of Television: Key Moments of the NFL on TV 1950–1978," National Football League Operations, accessed November 29, 2015. http://operations.nfl.com/the-game/impact-of-television/

42. Buck Waterfield in discussion with the author, January 30, 2016.

43. "1951 National Football League." Pro Football Researchers Association. Accessed November 29, 2015. http://profootballresearchers.com/members-only/Linescores/1951Linescore.pdf

44. Jack Sher, "The Bob Waterfield Story," *SPORT*, November 1951.

45. Jim Murray, "Rams Should Pack In Thoughts Of Move," *Los Angeles Times*, December 20, 1994, accessed November 29, 2015, http://articles.latimes.com/1994-12-20/sports/sp-10954_1_cleveland-rams

46. Sher, "Bob Waterfield Story."

47. Jane Russell, *My Path & My Detours: An Autobiography* (New York: Franklin Watts, 1985), 140.

48. Buck Waterfield, in discussion with the author, September 27, 2014.

49. Russell, 140.

50. Waterfield, September 27, 2014.

51. Larry Bornstein, "The NFL's Greatest QBs Have Been Only Average Coaches," *Football Digest*, October 1978, 74.

52. Russell, 210.

53. Russell, 239.

54. Rob Fernas, "Complete Package," *Los Angeles Times*, December 25, 1999, accessed November 29, 2015, http://articles.latimes.com/1999/mar/17/sports/sp-18189

55. Roscoe McGowen, "Cleveland Rams Transfer Eleven to Los Angeles," *New York Times*, January 13, 1946.

56. Franklin Lewis, "AAC Surrender Promotes Browns to Big League," December 10, 1949.

57. Bob Oates, *The Los Angeles Rams* (Culver City: Murray & Gee, 1955), 20.

58. Dan Reeves, Jr., son of Daniel F. Reeves, in discussion with the author, January 29, 2016.

59. "N.F.L. Puts O.K. on Sale of Rams to Reeves," *Chicago Tribune*, February 8, 1963.

60. In 1950 the Los Angeles Rams and the Washington Redskins became the first teams to reach agreements to broadcast all home and away games. "Impact of Television: Key Moments of the NFL on TV 1950–1978," National Football League Operations, accessed November 29, 2015, http://operations.nfl.com/the-game/impact-of-television/

61. Todd Anton and Bill Nowlin, *When Football Went to War* (Chicago: Triumph, 2013), 35.

62. "1957 National Football League." Pro Football Researchers Association. Accessed March 6, 2016. http://profootballresearchers.com/members-only/Linescores/1957Linescore.pdf

63. Reeves Jr.

64. Quirk, 62.

65. Jim Murray, "Rams Should Pack In Thoughts of Move," *Los Angeles Times*, December 20, 1994, accessed November 29, 2015, http://articles.latimes.com/1994-12-20/sports/sp-10954_1_cleveland-rams

66. "Top 10 Most Despised Owners: 7. Georgia Frontiere (Rams)," Real Clear Sports, accessed November 29, 2015, http://www.realclearsports.com/lists/top_10_despised_owners/georgia_frontiere_rams.html

67. The Redskins were the Rams' opponents when the Rams played their last game in Cleveland in 1945, played their first home game in Los Angeles in 1946, and debuted their iconic horned-logo helmets in 1948.

68. Murray, "Rams Should Pack In Thoughts of Move."

69. Neil Paine, "Revisiting The Greatest Show on Turf," FiveThirtyEight Sports, accessed November 29, 2015. http://fivethirtyeight.com/features/revisiting-the-greatest-show-on-turf/

70. In 2014 the Rams had the league's third-lowest average home attendance. "NFL Attendance—2014," ESPN, accessed November 29,

2015, http://espn.go.com/nfl/attendance/_/year/2014

71. In 2015 the Rams had the league's fifth-lowest franchise valuation at $1.45 billion. "The Business of Football: The List," Forbes, accessed November 29, 2015, http://www.forbes.com/nfl-valuations/list/#tab:overall

72. Sam Farmer, "Rams, Chargers, Raiders and relocation are focus of NFL's town hall meetings," *Los Angeles Times*, October 28, 2015, accessed November 29, 2015, http://www.latimes.com/sports/nfl/la-sp-nfl-la-town-meetings-20151027-story.html

73. Don Van Natta, Jr., and Seth Wickersham, "The Wow Factor," ESPN, February 11, 2016, accessed March 8, 2016, http://espn.go.com/espn/feature/story/_/id/14752649/the-real-story-nfl-owners-battle-bring-football-back-los-angeles

74. Clay Fowler, "Rams fans revel in team's return to Los Angeles area," *Los Angeles Daily News*, accessed March 6, 2016, http://www.dailynews.com/sports/20160115/rams-fans-revel-in-teams-return-to-los-angeles-area

Appendix

1. "NFL Single Game Receiving Yards Leaders," Pro Football Reference, accessed December 27, 2015, http://www.pro-football-reference.com/leaders/rec_yds_single_game.htm

2. "1945 Cleveland Rams," Pro Football Reference, accessed March 8, 2016, http://www.pro-football-reference.com/teams/ram/1945.htm

3. "1937 Cleveland Rams," Pro Football Reference, accessed March 8, 2016, http://www.pro-football-reference.com/teams/ram/1937.htm

4. "1945 Cleveland Rams."

5. John Dietrich, "Laterals Fly as Rams Beat Syracuse, 26–0," *Cleveland Plain Dealer*, October 12, 1936.

6. "Joe F. Carr Trophy (MVP) winners," Pro Football Reference, accessed March 8, 2016, http://www.pro-football-reference.com/players/award_jfct.htm

7. Chris Willis, *Dutch Clark: The Life of an NFL Legend and the Birth of the Detroit Lions* (Lanham, MD: Scarecrow Press, 2012), 279.

8. "Cleveland Rams Football Club Stockholders," December 31, 1940; document privately held by Donald Gries, Shaker Heights, Ohio.

9. "Riley Matheson," Pro Football Reference, accessed March 6, 2016, http://www.pro-football-reference.com/players/M/MathRi20.htm

10. "Top 3—Oldest Living Cleveland Rams," Oldest Living Pro Football Players, accessed December 6, 2015, http://www.oldestlivingprofootball.com/oldestlivingclerams.htm

11. James P. Quirk, *Pay Dirt: The Business of Professional Team Sports* (Princeton: Princeton University Press, 1992), 62.

12. "NFL Single Game Receiving Touchdowns Leaders," Pro Football Reference, accessed December 27, 2015, http://www.pro-football-reference.com/leaders/rec_td_single_game.htm

13. "Gaylon Smith," Pro Football Reference, accessed March 8, 2016, http://www.pro-football-reference.com/players/S/SmitGa21.htm.

14. "1937 Cleveland Rams."

15. Joe Horrigan, Pro Football Hall of Fame, in discussion with the author, May 7, 2015.

16. Dave Anderson, "Champion Quarterbacks Sooner and Later," *New York Times*, February 5, 2011, accessed September 28, 2015, http://www.nytimes.com/2011/02/06/sports/football/06anderson.html?_r=0. As the article notes, another rookie to led his team to a title was Sammy Baugh of the 1937 Washington Redskins, but he was a single-wing tailback.

17. "St. Louis Rams: Team Facts," Pro Football Hall of Fame, accessed March 8, 2016, http://www.profootballhof.com/teams/st.-louis-rams/team-facts.

18. "Cleveland Rams Football Club Stockholders."

Bibliography

About Travel. "What Is Lake Effect Snow?" Accessed September 20, 2015. http://cleveland.about.com/od/northeastohioweather/p/lakeeffect.htm.

"Adam Walsh Calls Legislative Signals." *Milwaukee Journal*, December 15, 1956.

"Adam Walsh Quits as Coach of Rams." *Milwaukee Journal,* December 10, 1946.

"Air Checks." *The Billboard*, August 11, 1951.

Anderson, Dave. "Champion Quarterbacks Sooner and Later." *New York Times*, February 5, 2011. Accessed September 28, 2015. http://www.nytimes.com/2011/02/06/sports/football/06anderson.html?_r=0.

Andrews, Henry. "'Dutch' Clark Named Coach of the Rams." *Cleveland Press*, December 16, 1938.

———. "Magnani Comes into Own as Ram Player." *Cleveland Press,* October 30, 1941.

———. "Parker Hall Is Honored by Writers." *Cleveland Press*, January 20, 1940.

Anton, Todd, and Bill Nowlin. *When Football Went to War*. Chicago: Triumph, 2013.

"Arch Ward, Tribune Sports Editor, Dies." *Chicago Tribune*, July 10, 1955.

"Art Lewis Named Coach at W.-L." *Cleveland Plain Dealer,* November 15, 1941.

"Art Lewis Named Rams Head Coach." *Cleveland Plain Dealer*, September 28, 1938, 16.

"Art Lewis Succumbs." *Beaver* (Pennsylvania) *County Times*, June 14, 1962.

"Art McNally Named Pioneer Award Recipient." Pro Football Hall of Fame. Accessed March 6, 2016. http://www.profootballhof.com/news/art-mcnally-named-pioneer-award-recipient/

"At Old Shibe Park." YouTube video, 9:56, posted by "John Smith." January 30, 2014, https://www.youtube.com/watch?v=la-yKe8bBc4.

"'Automatic Otto' Due to Retire from Pro Ball." *Daytona Beach* (FL) *Morning Journal*, December 8, 1954.

"Backfield Is Wrecked." *New York Times*, February 27, 1941.

Ballparks.com. "Cleveland Municipal Stadium." Accessed September 20, 2015. http://football.ballparks.com/NFL/ClevelandBrowns/oldindex.htm.

"Band Pageantry to Mark Rams' Battle." *Cleveland Plain Dealer*, October 4, 1939.

Barbash, Jack. "Unions and Rights in the Space Age." United States Department of Labor. Accessed October 18, 1945. http://www.dol.gov/dol/aboutdol/history/chapter6.htm.

Barnhart, Tony. "The '40s: NFL Goes to War." *Coffin Corner* 9:8 (1987), Professional Football Researchers Association.

Barry, Howard. "Halas Will Root for Wetzel, but Not on Thursday Night." *Chicago Tribune*, August 27, 1935.

Baseball Reference. "Hank Edwards." Accessed February 3, 2015. http://www.baseball-reference.com/players/e/edwarha01.shtml.

———. "Henry Wetzel." Accessed November 15, 2014. http://www.baseball-reference.com/bullpen/Henry_Wetzel.

———. "Hugo Bezdek." Accessed December 11, 2014. http://www.baseball-reference.com/bullpen/Hugo_Bezdek.

———. "1939 Mansfield Braves." Accessed February 3, 2015. http://www.baseball-reference.com/minors/team.cgi?id=9370cb08.

———. "Pittsburgh Pirates." Accessed December 17, 2014. http://www.baseball-reference.com/teams/PIT/

———. "Steve Gromek." Accessed February 3, 2015. http://www.baseball-reference.com/players/g/gromest01.shtml.

"Baseball Scribes to Honor Parker Hall." *Cleveland Plain Dealer,* January 29, 1940.

Bearak, Barry. "Where Football and Higher Education Mix." *New York Times*, September 16, 2011.

"Bears Crush Rams in Opener, 30–21." *Cleveland Plain Dealer,* September 16, 1939.

"Bears Crush Rams, 20–2, at Cleveland." *New York Times,* October 11, 1937.

"Bears Give Rams Stiff Test Today." *Cleveland Plain Dealer*, October 7, 1945.
"Bears' Passes Beat Rams, 15–7; Capture Title." *Cleveland Plain Dealer*, November 29, 1937.
Berelson, Bernard. "What 'Missing the Newspaper' Means." In *Communications Research: 1948–1949*, edited by Paul F. Lazarsfeld and Frank N. Stanton, 111–129. New York: Harper & Brothers, 1949.
"Bezdek Sought by Rams as Coach." *Cleveland Plain Dealer*, May 25, 1937.
"Bidder for Rams Delays Decision." *Cleveland Plain Dealer*, May 1, 1941.
"Billy Evans." *Cleveland Plain Dealer*, June 13, 1941.
"Birthday: Gregory S. Mcintosh." *Cleveland Plain Dealer*, July 20, 1937.
Bisheff, Steve. *Los Angeles Rams: Great Teams' Great Years*. New York: Macmillan, 1975.
"Bob Snyder, 87, Pro Football Player; Won Three NL Titles with Chicago." *New York Times*, January 8, 2001.
"Bob Snyder Will Coach Ram Backs." *Cleveland Plain Dealer*, July 15, 1945, 1-C.
"Bob Waterfield." *LIFE*, December 17, 1945.
"Bob Waterfield, Quarterback and All-Pro Star of the Rams." *New York Times*, March 26, 1983.
"Bob Waterfield, UCLA and NFL Rams Star." *Chicago Tribune*, March 26, 1983.
Bornstein, Larry. "The NFL's Greatest QBs Have Been Only Average Coaches." *Football Digest*, October 1978.
"Boston Refuses to Oppose Rams." *Cleveland Plain Dealer*, November 29, 1936.
"Boston Yanks Buy Gillette from Rams." *Lewiston* (Maine) *Daily Sun*, September 25, 1946.
Braunwart, Bob. "All Those A.F.L.'S: N.F.L. Competitors, 1935–1941." *Coffin Corner* 1:2 (1979), Professional Football Researchers Association.
"Browns Sign Greenwood; May Contact Other Rams." *Cleveland Plain Dealer*, February 8, 1946.
"Browns Sign 2 Stars for New Grid Team." *Cleveland Plain Dealer*, April 1, 1945.
"Bruch and Clark Get Guiding Reins of Rams in 1940." *Cleveland Plain Dealer*, December 16, 1940.
"Bruch Warns on Draft Jumping." *Cleveland Plain Dealer*, February 2, 1941.
Brulia, Tim. "A Chronology of Pro Football on Television: Part 1." *Coffin Corner* (26:3), 2004, Pro Football Researchers Association.
"Brumbaugh to Assist Bezdek at Cleveland." *Chicago Tribune*, June 13, 1937.
"Buckeye Gridder Hurt." *Cleveland Plain Dealer*, May 14, 1933.
Burick, Si. "Max Padlow Dead." *Dayton Daily News*, August 19, 1973.
Buruma, Ian. *Year Zero: A History of 1945*. New York: Penguin, 2013.
"Buzz Wetzel and His 'Boys' Who Have Made Good." *Cleveland Plain Dealer*, March 22, 1936.
"C. of C. Official Is Rams Booster." *Cleveland Plain Dealer*, April 17, 1941.
Calgary Stampeders. "Division All-Stars." Accessed December 5, 2015. http://www.stampeders.com/division_allstars.
"Call to Arms to Hit Collegians." *Cleveland Plain Dealer*, August 28, 1942.
"Cardinals Topple Cleveland." *New York Times*, November 1, 1937.
Carr, Joe F., ed. *Official Guide of the National Football League: 1937*. New York: American Sports Publishing Co., 1937.
_____. *Official Guide of the National Football League: 1938*. New York: American Sports Publishing Co., 1938.
"Carr Hopes Grid Star Remains in University." *The Milwaukee Journal*, April 1, 1938.
Carroll, Bob. "Johnny Drake." *Coffin Corner* 16 (1994), Professional Football Researchers Association.
_____. "Mini-Bio: Jim Benton." *Coffin Corner* 17:2 (1995), Professional Football Researchers Association.
_____. "Triumph of the T: 1940." *Coffin Corner* 18:1 (1996), Professional Football Researchers Association.
Case Western Reserve University. "Stephen Belichick." Accessed January 16, 2016. http://athletics.case.edu/sports/spartan_club/bios/belichick_stephen.
"Catching a Strike from Parker Hall…." *Cleveland Plain Dealer*, November 27, 1939.
"Chet Adams Starts Football Work with Cleveland Browns Next Week." *Cleveland Plain Dealer*, July 25, 1946.
"Chicago's Cards Win on Tinsley's Dash." *New York Times*, October 4, 1937.
Childs, Kingsley. "Fourth-Period Field Goal Downs Rams for Football Dodgers." *New York Times*, September 27, 1937.
"'Chile' Walsh Cuts Connections with L.A. Rams; Contract Settled." *Lewiston* (Maine) *Daily News*, January 22, 1947.
"Chile Walsh Denies Offer to Johnsos." *Cleveland Plain Dealer*, March 6, 1945.
"Chile Walsh Goes to Work on Tough Job." *Cleveland Plain Dealer*, December 14, 1943.
"Cincinnati or Boston May Get Cleveland Rams." *Chicago Tribune*, April 9, 1941.
"City to Get New Gridiron Club." *Cleveland Plain Dealer*, September 2, 1944.
"Civic Groups to Lead Ram Drive." *Cleveland Plain Dealer*, April 9, 1941.
Clark, Dutch. *Dutch Clark to Francis Logan*, Cleveland, Ohio, December 26, 1941.

Bibliography

"Clark Arrives to Study Grid Plans." *Cleveland Plain Dealer*, August 4, 1940.

"Clark Asks Rams Not to Renew His Contract as Coach." *Cleveland Plain Dealer*, March 11, 1943.

"Clark Gets New Line Material in Chicago Deals." *Cleveland Plain Dealer*, February 13, 1939.

"Clark Signs for 2 Years with Rams." *Cleveland Plain Dealer*, December 17, 1938.

Cleveland Area History. "Beautiful Homes of Cleveland—Part 1." Accessed November 17, 2014. http://www.clevelandareahistory.com/2011_07_01_archive.html.

"Cleveland Browns List 7 Stadium Games in All-America Circuit." *Cleveland Plain Dealer*, January 5, 1946.

"Cleveland Pro Gridders Disband." *Cleveland Plain Dealer*, September 6, 1936.

"Cleveland Rams." *Official National Football League Roster and Record Manual: 1941.*

"Cleveland Rams Are Favored Over Redskins in Pro Play-Off." *Milwaukee Journal*, December 16, 1945.

"Cleveland Rams Begin Training." *Pittsburgh Post-Gazette*, August 10, 1942.

"Cleveland Rams Drop from National Pro Grid League." *Daily Times* (Beaver and Rochester, Pennsylvania), April 7, 1943.

"Cleveland Rams Football Club Stockholders." December 31, 1940. Document privately held by Donald Gries, Shaker Heights, Ohio.

"Cleveland Rams Lead American Pro Grid Loop." *Lewiston* (Maine) *Daily Sun*, November 11, 1936.

"Cleveland Rams Not for Sale." *The Pittsburgh Press*, May 12, 1943.

"Cleveland Rams Sold." *New York Times*, June 12, 1941.

"Cleveland Rams Take Pro Crown." *Ellensburg* (Washington) *Daily Record*, December 17, 1945.

"Cleveland Rams to Have Strong Eleven." *Berkeley* (California) *Daily Gazette*, February 13, 1939.

"Cleveland Rams vs. Washington Redskins." Game Program. September 7, 1945.

"Cleveland Weather History." Cleveland.com. Accessed September 20, 2015. http://www.cleveland.com/datacentral/index.ssf/2008/09/cleveland_weather_history_find.html?

"Cliff Battles, 70, Football Player Who Gained Hall of Fame, Dead." *New York Times*, April 29, 1981.

Clowser, Jack. "Drake Turns Down $10,000 Grid Offer from Philadelphia to Stay on War Job." *Cleveland Press*, August 19, 1943.

_____. "In the Bag—Walsh Knew Size of Rams' Hearts." *Cleveland Press*, December 17, 1945.

_____. "Rams Hand Bears First Shutout in Six Years." *Cleveland Press*, October 8, 1945.

_____. "Rams Sign Two Halfbacks." *Cleveland Press*, April 15, 1944.

_____. "Rams Sign Waterfield, Best Back on Coast." *Cleveland Press*, June 26, 1945.

_____. "Walsh Returns, Hiding His Secrets." *Cleveland Press*, April 5, 1944.

"Coach Walsh Is Permanent Resident Here." *Cleveland Plain Dealer*, December 17, 1945.

"Coach Walsh Says Champion Rams Confirmed His Season-Long Views." *New York Times*, December 17, 1945.

Cobbledick, Gordon. "Baseball Will Be Wise If It Continues Its Policy of Asking for No Favors." *Cleveland Plain Dealer*, November 16, 1943.

_____. "Clark and Conley Believe Strong College Squad Could Hold Its Own with Bears." *Cleveland Plain Dealer*, November 21, 1943.

_____. "Clark Rates Rams Better than 1939 Club, Cites Injuries as One Reason for Slump." *Cleveland Plain Dealer*, October 31, 1940.

_____. "Cleveland Boys, Mutryn and Lavelle, Lead Xavier to Upset of Eastern Eleven." *Cleveland Plain Dealer*, December 1, 1941.

_____. "'College Spirit' Blooms in Pro Camp; Rams Point for Grudge Battle with Lions." *Cleveland Plain Dealer*, November 14, 1939.

_____. "Dave Jones Stays as Browns' Chief." *Cleveland Plain Dealer*, January 6, 1961.

_____. "Diplomatic Denial or Bald-Faced Lie … Cases in Point … Not Limited to Sports." *Cleveland Plain Dealer*, February 9, 1946.

_____. "Donelli Gives Large Share of Credit for Rams' Success to Benton and Matheson." *Cleveland Plain Dealer*, October 18, 1944.

_____. "Hall and Goodnight Are Good, but Dutch Clark Desires Wing Back Who Can Carry Mail." *Cleveland Plain Dealer*, September 20, 1941.

_____. "Hirsch Leads All-Stars to 16–0 Victory Over Rams." *Cleveland Plain Dealer*, August 24, 1946.

_____. "Indians to Play Night Ball." *Cleveland Plain Dealer*, September 11, 1937.

_____. "Plain Dealing." *Cleveland Plain Dealer*, September 1, 1937.

_____. "Plain Dealing." *Cleveland Plain Dealer*, September 22, 1937.

_____. "Plain Dealing." *Cleveland Plain Dealer*, January 18, 1938.

_____. "Plain Dealing." *Cleveland Plain Dealer*, February 17, 1938.

_____. "Professional Football Is Over the Hump Here as Rams Make Good in Big Way." *Cleveland Plain Dealer*, November 27, 1939.

_____. "Rams' General Manager Cites Reasons for Not Fearing Threat of Pro Football Competition in Cleveland." *Cleveland Plain Dealer,* November 10, 1944.

———. "'Somebody Loves Me,' Could Be Theme Song of Rams After Booing They Received at Stadium." *Cleveland Plain Dealer,* November 5, 1941.

———. "Two Major Grid Games Draw 130,000 Fans, but Big Four Teams and Rams Are Ignored." *Cleveland Plain Dealer,* November 17, 1942.

———. "Walsh's Remarkable Organizational Job Assures City of Powerful Postwar Ram Team." *Cleveland Plain Dealer,* November 5, 1944.

Coenen, Craig R. *From Sandlots to the Super Bowl.* Knoxville: University of Tennessee Press, 2005.

Condon, David. "In the Wake of the News." *Chicago Tribune,* August 2, 1966.

Costello, Al. "Redskins Lose Title Battle to Rams, 15–14." *Washington Post,* December 17, 1945.

"Cowboy Drake Earns His Football Spurs." *Cleveland Plain Dealer,* December 26, 1940, 12.

Crowe, Jerry. "Thorny Start: USC–Penn State Matchup Rekindles Heated Memories of the 1923 Rose Bowl." *Los Angeles Times,* September 12, 1990.

Daley, Arthur. "Cleveland Coach Out to Upset Owen of Giants, His Ex-Mentor." *New York Times,* November 11, 1938.

———. "Pick of Country's College Gridiron Stars Drafted by National League Clubs." *New York Times,* December 12, 1937.

———. "Pro Football Musings." *New York Times,* January 15, 1946.

———. "Revisit to the Hall." *New York Times,* December 30, 1964.

Daly, Dan. *The National Forgotten League.* Lincoln: University of Nebraska Press, 2012.

———. "Sammy Baugh, 1943: The Greatest Season?" The MMQB. Accessed December 21, 2014. http://mmqb.si.com/2013/11/14/sammy-baugh-1943/

"Dan Reeves Dies; Owner of Rams." *New York Times,* April 16, 1971.

"Dan Reeves Moves West." *Coffin Corner* 20:1 (1998), Professional Football Researchers Association.

"Dan Reeves Proved Indians Were Gone." *Spartanburg* (South Carolina) *Herald-Journal,* April 18, 1971.

"Daniel Reeves Approves Merger." *New York Times,* August 19, 1941.

"Dante Magnani." *New York Times,* December 24, 1985. Accessed December 18, 2015. http://www.nytimes.com/1985/12/24/sports/dante-magnani.html.

Database Football. "1940 Notre Dame Fighting Irish." Accessed June 13, 2015. http://www.databasefootball.com/college/teams/teamyear.htm?TeamID=75&Season=1940.

"Day in a Coach's Life—Here's How Dutch Clark Polishes Up His Rams for Season Opener." *Cleveland Plain Dealer,* August 17, 1941.

DC3Airways.com. "American Airlines Timetable: September 24, 1939." Accessed February 11, 2016. http://www.dc3airways.com/flights/routes/american_airlines.htm.

"Debacle Angers Rams' President." *Cleveland Plain Dealer,* September 27, 1938.

Demographia. "U.S. Population by State from 1900." Accessed December 11, 2014. http://www.demographia.com/db-state1900.htm.

Dietrich, John. "Barons Hear That Title Triumph Climaxes League's Greatest Year." *Cleveland Plain Dealer,* April 12, 1941.

———. "Boston Irish Spank Rams Before 7,000." *Cleveland Plain Dealer,* October 19, 1936.

———. "Cardinals Score on 4 Plays, Win." *Cleveland Plain Dealer,* September 18, 1938.

———. "Chicago's Husky Bears Rip Rams." *Cleveland Plain Dealer,* October 11, 1937.

———. "Clark Greets 40 Rams Wednesday." *Cleveland Plain Dealer,* August 11, 1940.

———. "Cleveland Pros Stop Baugh; Gain First-Half Lead." *Cleveland Plain Dealer,* November 22, 1937.

———. "Corby Davis Says Rams Rate with Best in Pro League." *Cleveland Plain Dealer,* October 11, 1938.

———. "Detroit Outclasses Rams to Win Pro Grid Opener, 28–0." *Cleveland Plain Dealer,* September 11, 1937.

———. "Eagles Drop Rams into First-Place Tie, 28–14." *Cleveland Plain Dealer,* October 29, 1945.

———. "40 Rams Report for First Grid Workout of Year." *Cleveland Plain Dealer,* August 3, 1937.

———. "Greenwood, Ram Back, Eyes Berth with Browns." *Cleveland Plain Dealer,* February 6, 1946.

———. "How Good Are the Rams? You Can Look for a 'Pennant' If They Beat Eagles Decisively Sunday." *Cleveland Plain Dealer,* September 18, 1945.

———. "Huge Bear Line Men Oppose Rams Today." *Cleveland Plain Dealer,* October 10, 1937.

———. "Hutson Snares 2 Scoring Passes as Green Bay Blasts Rams, 42–7." *Cleveland Plain Dealer,* November 13, 1944.

———. "Hutson Snares Three Touchdown Passes to Whip Rams, 28–7." *Cleveland Plain Dealer,* October 31, 1938.

———. "Jacobs' 2 Touchdown Passes Win for Rams, 14–0." *Cleveland Plain Dealer,* September 28, 1942.

Bibliography

_____. "Laterals Fly as Rams Beat Syracuse, 26-0." *Cleveland Plain Dealer*, October 12, 1936.

_____. "Layden Praises Rams Before 800 at Fete." *Cleveland Plain Dealer*, December 13, 1945.

_____. "Lions Ruin Drake Day, Jolt Rams, 14-0." *Cleveland Plain Dealer*, November 3, 1941.

_____. "Magnani Dashes 93 Yards on Opening Kickoff, Rams Win, 17-14." *Cleveland Plain Dealer*, September 8, 1941.

_____. "Michigan Line Is Big Ohio Problem." *Cleveland Plain Dealer*, November 21, 1944.

_____. "National Football League's Public Be Damned Policy Kept Rams from Building Large Following." *Cleveland Plain Dealer*, February 10, 1946.

_____. "Need Triumph in Bid for 3d Place." *Cleveland Plain Dealer*, November 1, 1940.

_____. "Newman and Pincura Meet on Pro Field." *Cleveland Plain Dealer*, November 3, 1936.

_____. "1945 Could Be Rough Year for National League 'Big Four.'" *Football Fanfare*, Cleveland Rams vs. Chicago Cardinals, September 30, 1945.

_____. "'Observer' Idea Is a Little Late for Rams." *Cleveland Plain Dealer*, November 3, 1944.

_____. "Old 'Statue of Liberty' Gives Rams Tie, 7-7." *Cleveland Plain Dealer*, November 2, 1936.

_____. "Only Social Error; Rams Didn't Know Arizona Star Is a Junior." *Cleveland Plain Dealer*, March 28, 1938.

_____. "Packers Crush Rams, 35 to 10." *Cleveland Plain Dealer*, October 18, 1937.

_____. "Pro Grid War Looms Here, but Ideal Solution Would Give City One Home Game a Week." *Cleveland Plain Dealer*, March 30, 1945.

_____. "Ram Coach Welds Rookies into Outstanding Team." *Cleveland Plain Dealer*, December 9, 1945.

_____. "Rams Are in Dire Need of New Men." *Cleveland Plain Dealer*, November 30, 1941.

_____. "Rams Bag Beefy Rookies for 1938." *Cleveland Plain Dealer*, March 20, 1938.

_____. "Rams Bid for Backs in Draft Meeting Today." *Cleveland Plain Dealer*, December 9, 1939.

_____. "Rams Bowl Over Steelers, 21 to 0." *Cleveland Plain Dealer*, September 3, 1945.

_____. "Rams Build for Future, Sign 18 Star Gridders." *Cleveland Plain Dealer*, January 7, 1945.

_____. "Rams' Coach Favors Single Wing-Back." *Cleveland Plain Dealer*, July 21, 1937.

_____. "Rams Discounting 'Injury' to Baugh." *Cleveland Plain Dealer*, December 15, 1945.

_____. "Rams' Flat Pass Boomerangs, Cardinals Triumph, 7-0." *Cleveland Plain Dealer*, November 24, 1941.

_____. "Rams Forced to Run Gantlet in Pro Grid League." *Cleveland Plain Dealer*, November 2, 1944.

_____. "Rams' Freshmen Look Promising." *Cleveland Plain Dealer*, August 17, 1938.

_____. "Rams Get Battle from Cardinals, but Snare League Opener." *Cleveland Plain Dealer*, October 1, 1945.

_____. "Rams Gun for First Pro Grid Crown Today." *Cleveland Plain Dealer*, December 16, 1945.

_____. "Rams Halt Bears' Closing Rush for 2d Straight Upset, 14-7." *Cleveland Plain Dealer*, October 10, 1938.

_____. "Rams Hand Bears First Whitewashing in 59 League Games, 17-0." *Cleveland Plain Dealer*, October 8, 1945.

_____. "Rams Jolt Yanks, 20-7; Eagles Fall, Redskins Clinch Eastern Title Tie." *Cleveland Plain Dealer*, December 3, 1945.

_____. "Rams' Matheson Wins Berth on Associated Press All-Pro Eleven." *Cleveland Plain Dealer*, December 8, 1942.

_____. "Rams Plan Game with Collegians." *Cleveland Plain Dealer*, November 18, 1936.

_____. "Rams Plan Surprise for Lions in Opener." *Cleveland Plain Dealer*, September 5, 1937.

_____. "Rams Primed for Opening Kick-Off." *Cleveland Plain Dealer*, September 5, 1937.

_____. "Rams Reach Turning Point of Campaign as They Face Lions." *Cleveland Plain Dealer*, November 1, 1940.

_____. "Rams 'Satisfied' with Coach, Begin 1938 Rebuilding." *Cleveland Plain Dealer*, November 4, 1937.

_____. "Rams Search for Shifty Halfback." *Cleveland Plain Dealer*, August 3, 1941.

_____. "Rams Seek to Tame Lions at Stadium Friday Night." *Cleveland Plain Dealer*, September 5, 1937.

_____. "Rams Smash Bears, 19-7, to Send Pro Grid Title Hopes Soaring." *Cleveland Plain Dealer*, October 9, 1944.

_____. "Rams Steam into First 1938 Drill." *Cleveland Plain Dealer*, August 16, 1938.

_____. "Rams' Two Touchdowns in Last Quarter Rip Detroit, 21-17." *Cleveland Plain Dealer*, October 3, 1938.

_____. "Rams Win in Last Minute, Share Top." *Cleveland Plain Dealer*, November 9, 1936.

_____. "Rams Win World Pro Grid Crown, 15 to 14." *Cleveland Plain Dealer*, December 17, 1945.

_____. "Rams Withdraw from Pro Football League for Duration." *Cleveland Plain Dealer*, April 7, 1943.

———. "Reeves Becomes Sole Owner of Rams." *Cleveland Plain Dealer*, December 9, 1943, 20.

———. "Rival Fans Cheer for Rams as 'Miracle Team' Makes Comeback Stick; Lewis Praises 2 Ends." Cleveland Plain Dealer, October 25, 1938.

———. "Score on Fumble Beats Rams." *Cleveland Plain Dealer*, October 4, 1937.

———. "Smith Alternates with Hall, Janiak at Fullback." *Cleveland Plain Dealer*, November 6, 1942.

———. "10,677 See Barons Whip Pittsburgh in Hockey Thriller, 2–1." *Cleveland Plain Dealer*, February 10, 1938.

———. "35,000 Expected to See Rams Open Season; Lions Favored." *Cleveland Plain Dealer*, September 10, 1937.

———. "20,000 See Rams Face Green Bay Today in Opener." *Cleveland Plain Dealer*, September 11, 1938.

———. "Washington Redskins Install Special Grandstand Each Season; Rams May Adopt Same Set-Up." *Cleveland Plain Dealer*, November 13, 1945, 15.

———. "Waterfield Stars as Rams Bag First Victory Over Redskins, 21–0." *Cleveland Plain Dealer*, September 8, 1945.

Dietrich, Phil. "Over 6,000 Latecomers Miss Magnani's Touchdown Gallop." *Akron Beacon Journal*, September 8, 1941.

Dinner Program. "Testimonial Dinner Honoring the Cleveland Rams." Cleveland, Ohio, December 12, 1945. Jim Gillette's personal copy, privately held by Walker Gillette, Franklin, Virginia.

Donaldson, Ralph J. "Fleming Power to Fight for Life." *Cleveland Plain Dealer*, June 6, 1930.

"Donelli, Ex-Duquesne Mentor, Is Named Coach of Cleveland Rams." *Cleveland Plain Dealer*, July 4, 1944.

"Donelli Released by Navy." *New York Times*, December 16, 1945.

Doyle, James E. "Rams Will Have Powerful Postwar Team If War Doesn't Last Too Long." *Cleveland Plain Dealer*, May 6, 1944.

———. "The Sport Trail." *Cleveland Plain Dealer*, November 30, 1936.

———. "The Sport Trail." *Cleveland Plain Dealer*, August 14, 1944.

———. "The Sport Trail." *Cleveland Plain Dealer*, December 7, 1945.

———. "The Sport Trail." *Cleveland Plain Dealer*, December 14, 1945.

———. "The Sport Trail." *Cleveland Plain Dealer*, December 17, 1945.

———. "The Sport Trail." *Cleveland Plain Dealer*, January 1, 1946.

———. "The Sport Trail." *Cleveland Plain Dealer*, February 6, 1946.

———. "The Sport Trail." *Cleveland Plain Dealer*, August 30, 1946.

"Drake of Rams Is Picked on All-Pro Second Team." *Cleveland Plain Dealer*, December 14, 1937.

"Drake Will Accept Rams' New Offer." *Cleveland Plain Dealer*, July 17, 1938.

"Drake's Nose Broken." *Cleveland Plain Dealer*, November 23, 1937.

"Drake's 36 Points Lead Pro Scorers." *Cleveland Plain Dealer*, October 18, 1939.

"Dudley's 97-Yard Run Helps All-Stars Beat Redskins, 17–14." *Pittsburgh Post-Gazette*, December 28, 1942.

Dvorak, Bill. "Newspaper Strike Affected All Here." *Cleveland Press*, February 6, 1946.

Dvorchak, Robert. "1940s Put Steelers to Tests That Nearly Break Them." *Pittsburgh Post-Gazette*, September 16, 2007.

Dyer, Braven. "The Sports Parade." *Los Angeles Times*, May 19, 1946.

"The Eagles Are Screaming." *New York Times*, October 17, 1937.

eBay. "1940 Press Photo Jerry Dowd, Chuck Cherundolo & John Drake of Cleveland Rams." Accessed March 14, 2015. http://www.ebay.com/itm/1940-Press-Photo-Jerry-Dowd-Chuck-Cherundolo-John-Drake-of-Cleveland-Rams-/390961469059?pt=LH_DefaultDomain_0&hash=item5b07 1e9683.

"Elmer Layden Insists He Quit but Others Say He Was Ousted." *Pittsburgh Press*, January 13, 1946.

Encyclopædia Britannica. "Munich Agreement." Accessed February 3, 2015. http://www.britannica.com/EBchecked/topic/397522/Munich-Agreement.

Encyclopedia of Cleveland History. "Burton, Harold Hitz." Accessed March 14, 2015. http://ech.case.edu/cgi/article.pl?id=BHH

———. "Cleveland Barons." Accessed February 1, 2015. http://ech.case.edu/cgi/article.pl?id=CB3.

———. "Cleveland Municipal Stadium." Accessed September 20, 2015. http://ech.case.edu/cgi/article.pl?id=CMS5.

———. "Cleveland News." Accessed November 15, 2014. http://ech.cwru.edu/ech-cgi/article.pl?id=CN1.

———. "Cleveland Panthers." Accessed January 3, 2016. http://ech.case.edu/cgi/article.pl?id=CP1.

———. "Cleveland Rams." Accessed December 19, 2015. http://ech.case.edu/cgi/article.pl?id=CR3.

———. "Great Lakes Exposition." Accessed March 13, 2015. http://ech.cwru.edu/ech-cgi/article.pl?id=GLE

———. "Lewis, Franklin Allan Whitey." Ac-

cessed September 1, 2015. http://ech.case.edu/cgi/article.pl?id=LFAW
_____. "Nela Park." Accessed February 3, 2015. http://ech.case.edu/cgi/article.pl?id=NP1.
_____. "Print Journalism." Accessed October 19, 2015. http://ech.cwru.edu/ech-cgi/article.pl?id=PJ
_____. "Sutphin, Albert C. (Al)." Accessed January 16, 2016. https://ech.case.edu/cgi/article.pl?id=SAC4.
Encyclopedia of New York City. "Tammany Hall." Accessed April, 8, 2015. http://www.virtualny.cuny.edu/EncyNYC/tammany_hall.html.
ESPN. "NFL Attendance—2014." Accessed November 29, 2015. http://espn.go.com/nfl/attendance/_/year/2014.
_____. "Other Football Leagues of the Past." Accessed January 2, 2015. http://sports.espn.go.com/extra/afl/news/story?id=3764806.
"Evans Quits Pro Rams." *New York Times*, January 1, 1942.
"Ex-Brown Chet Adams Wins Top Lottery Prize." *Cleveland Plain Dealer*, October 31, 1975.
"Ex-Indian Boss Ellis Ryan Dies." *Cleveland Plain Dealer*, August 12, 1966.
"Ex-Rams Star Drake Is Dead." *Cleveland Plain Dealer*, March 29, 1972.
"Eye on Packers, Rams Start Job." *Cleveland Plain Dealer*, August 6, 1939.
Fan Base. "1941 UCLA Bruins Football Schedule." Accessed July 18, 2015. http://www.fanbase.com/ucla-bruins-football-1941/schedule.
Farmer, Sam. "Rams, Chargers, Raiders and Relocation Are Focus of NFL's Town Hall Meetings." *Los Angeles Times*, October 28, 2015.
Farrar, Harry. "Small Talk of Big Guy." *Denver Post*, July 15, 1961.
Feder, Sid. "Pro Football Rams Moved to Los Angeles." *Oregon Statesman*, January 13, 1946.
Federal Judicial Center. "Biographical Directory of Federal Judges: Freed, Emerich B." Accessed January 4, 2016. http://www.fjc.gov/servlet/nGetInfo?jid=793.
"Feller Proud to Serve in 'Time of Need.'" *New York Times*, December 16, 2010.
"Feller Shivers as Pitcher Waterfield Exhibits Control." Painesville (Ohio) *Telegraph*, December 17, 1946.
Fergusson, Tom. "Tiny Dippery, Rams' Trainer, Says Pro Champions Had as Much Spirit as Any College Team—Singles Out Gillette and Waterfield." *Norfolk Virginian-Pilot*, December 29, 1945.
Fernas, Rob. "Complete Package." *Los Angeles Times*, December 25, 1999. Accessed October 25, 2015. http://articles.latimes.com/1999/mar/17/sports/sp-18189.
"Final Whistle Brings a Near-Riot as Pirates Beat Cardinals, 17–13." *New York Times*, October 21, 1935.
Find a Grave. "Horace Greely Lipscomb." Accessed February 3, 2015. http://www.findagrave.com/cgi-bin/fg.cgi?page=gr&GRid=107139032.
_____. "Staton 'Jack' Waterfield." Accessed December 11, 2015. http://www.findagrave.com/cgi-bin/fg.cgi?page=gr&GRid=25713848.
_____. "Thomas Ellis Lipscomb." Accessed February 3, 2015. http://www.findagrave.com/cgi-bin/fg.cgi?page=gr&GRid=107139162.
"Football Attendance Drops 25 Per Cent." *Cleveland Press*, October 19, 1942.
Football Fanfare and Program. "Cleveland Rams vs. Washington Redskins, Cleveland Stadium." September 7, 1945.
Football Geography. "NFL Draft Locations." Accessed December 11, 2014. http://www.footballgeography.com/nfl-draft-sites/
"Football Stars to Appear at Palace." *Cleveland Plain Dealer*, October 16, 1936.
Forbes. "The Business of Football: The List." Accessed November 29, 2015. http://www.forbes.com/nfl-valuations/list/#tab:overall.
Ford, Mark L. "From Hollywood, It's the Los Angeles Rams!" *Coffin Corner* (37:4), July/August 2015, Professional Football Researchers Association.
_____. "The Hollywood Rams, Part Ii: The Sequel." *Coffin Corner* (38:1), January/February 2016, Professional Football Researchers Association.
Forgotten Four: The Integration of Pro Football. Documentary. Directed by Johnson McKelvy. 2014. New York: Epix, Ross Greenburg Productions. Television movie.
"Former Irish Captain Claimed." *Canton Repository*, January 14, 1985.
Foster, Chris. "UCLA's First Win Over USC Was a Battle, but Don't Dare Call It a War." *Los Angeles Times*, November 13, 2012. Accessed October 25, 2015. http://articles.latimes.com/2012/nov/13/sports/la-sp-1113-ucla-1942-usc-20121113.
"Founder Leaves Safeway Stores." *Cleveland Plain Dealer*, June 7, 1941.
"Four Brilliant Rookies Playing with Cleveland Rams This Year." *Prescott* (Arizona) *Evening Courier*, August 31, 1939.
Fowler, Clay. "Rams Fans Revel in Team's Return to Los Angeles Area." *Los Angeles Daily News*. Accessed March 6, 2016. http://www.dailynews.com/sports/20160115/rams-fans-revel-in-teams-return-to-los-angeles-area.
Fraley, Oscar. "Waterfield Makes Cleveland

Rams Tough Club to Beat." *Daily Times* (Beaver, Pennsylvania). November 6, 1945.

"Fred Levy Dies; Film Pioneer, 77." *New York Times*, March 26, 1955.

Friend, Tom. "A Farewell to Tinsel Town." *Los Angeles Times*, December 22, 1994.

"Fullback to Guard." *Cleveland Press*, July 12, 1939.

Furillo, Bud. "A Vote for Incumbent President." *Los Angeles Herald-Examiner*, November 1, 1965.

"Game Postponed." *Chicago Tribune*, October 12, 1938.

Game Program, World Championship Playoff: National Football League, Cleveland Rams vs. Washington Redskins, December 16, 1945.

"Gaylon Smith, Ex-Ram, Browns Fullback, Dies." *Cleveland Plain Dealer*, March 11, 1958.

"Georgia Attack in Last Quarter Beats U.C.L.A. Before 93,000 in Rose Bowl." *New York Times*, January 2, 1943.

Gibbons, Frank. "1946 Promises to Be Bouncing Baby for Cleveland Sports Fans." *Cleveland Press*, January 1, 1946.

Gietschier, Steve. "Go West, Young Rams." *Sporting News*, January 23, 1995.

Gill, Bob. "The Bulldogs: L.A. Hits the Big Time." *Coffin Corner* 5 (1984), Professional Football Researchers Association.

_____. "The St. Louis Gunners." *Fourth PFRA Annual* (1983), Professional Football Researchers Association.

Gillette, Marguerite, and Walker Gillette. Interview by James C. Sulecki. Personal interview. Franklin, Virginia, October 11, 2014.

Godley, Bob. "Dutch Gets Press Agent." *Cleveland Press*, September 9, 1937.

Goldstein, Herman. "Charles F. (Chile) Walsh." World Championship Playoff: National Football League Game Program, Cleveland Rams vs. Washington Redskins, December 16, 1945.

_____. "Gillette's Sharp Running." *Cleveland News*, December 17, 1945.

_____. "Pat on Back Pays Off with Colella." *Cleveland News*, October 9, 1947.

_____. "Pioneer in T." *Cleveland News*, September 1, 1945.

_____. "The 'T' Man Comes to Town." *Cleveland News*, May 2, 1945.

Goldstein, Richard. "Creighton Miller, 79, Lawyer and Notre Dame Halfback." *New York Times*, May 29, 2002.

_____. "Harry Newman, 90, Who Led Giants to Title Game as Rookie." *New York Times*, May 2, 2000.

_____. "Red Hickey, Who Introduced Shotgun to the N.F.L., Dies at 89." *New York Times*, April 3, 2006.

"Gomer Jones Barred for Helping Pro Game." *Milwaukee Journal*, August 24, 1937.

"Gomer Jones, Oklahoma Ex-Football Coach, Dies." *New York Times*, March 22, 1971.

Grant, Alison. "Airport Flew into History When It Opened in 1925." *Cleveland Plain Dealer*, July 5, 2015.

_____. "Thompson Hine Law Firm Takes Pride in Its Long Cleveland History." *Cleveland Plain Dealer*, November 19, 2011.

Grasso, John. *Historical Dictionary of Football*. Lanham, MD: Scarecrow Press, 2013.

Grayson, Harry. "Cleveland Boss Simply Gets His Interference in Front of Play." *NEA Service*, October 11, 1938.

Greater Buffalo Sports Hall of Fame. "Tommy Colella: Professional Football Player." Accessed December 11, 2015. http://buffalosportshallfame.com/member/tom-colella/.

"Green Bay Beats Rams, 26–17, on Herber's Passes to Hutson." *Cleveland Plain Dealer*, September 12, 1938.

"Green Bay Routs Cleveland by 35–7, Monnett's Passes Bringing 3 Touchdowns." *New York Times*, October 25, 1937.

"Green Bay Routs Cleveland, 35–10." *New York Times*, October 18, 1937.

Greenhouse, Linda. "Byron R. White, Longtime Justice and a Football Legend, Dies at 84." *New York Times*, April 16, 2002.

"Greenwood of Illinois Signs Ram Contract." *Cleveland Plain Dealer*, December 22, 1945.

Gridiron Uniform Database. "St. Louis Rams." Accessed March 14, 2015. http://www.gridiron-uniforms.com/rams.html.

Gries, Bob. *Five Generations: 175 Years of Love for Cleveland*. Shaker Heights, OH: Bob Gries, 2014. Accessed August 1, 2015. http://issuu.com/thebraungroup/docs/gries-5generations/1.

Gries, Robert D. Interview by James C. Sulecki. Personal interview. Shaker Heights, Ohio, August 1, 2015.

Griffin, Julian. "Poll Shows News Items Missed Most." *Cleveland Press*, February 6, 1946.

Grzegorek, Vince. "Ghosts of Football Past." *Cleveland Scene*, July 29, 2009.

"Halas Is Slated to Enter Navy." *Cleveland Plain Dealer*, October 22, 1942.

"Hall and Smith Are Not Signed by Rams." *Cleveland Plain Dealer*, June 4, 1939.

"'Halley' Harding, Noted Sportswriter, Dies at 56." *Jet*, April 20, 1967.

Ham, Bus. "Redskins Take Eastern Crown." Norwalk (Connecticut) *Hour*, December 10, 1945.

"Hanken, Pro Giants, Will Start at End." *New York Times*, October 20, 1937.

Heaton, Charles. "Scarry's Nose Broken 9 Times, but Reserve Coach Is Nostalgic About Pro-(Boscis) Football." *Cleveland Plain Dealer*, February 2, 1948.

Bibliography

Henkel, Frank M. *Cleveland Browns History.* Charleston, SC: Arcadia Publishing, 2005.

"Here Is the Story of Rams' Rise to Championship." *Football Fanfare and Program,* "Cleveland Rams vs. Boston Yanks, League Park, Cleveland, Ohio." December 2, 1945.

"He's a Touchdown Artist, Too." *Milwaukee Journal,* October 27, 1934.

Hession, Joseph. "Gil Bouley: 1945–1950." *Coffin Corner* 9:3 (1987), Professional Football Researchers Association.

Hinrichs, A.F. "Average Hourly Earnings in Manufacturing, 1933 to 1936." *Monthly Labor Review* 44 (April 1937): 838–858.

History.com. "Battle of Britain." Accessed March 14, 2015. http://www.history.com/topics/world-war-ii/battle-of-britain.

———. "1940: Franklin Roosevelt Approves Military Draft." Accessed March 14, 2015. http://www.history.com/this-day-in-history/franklin-roosevelt-approves-military-draft.

———. "1939: Germans Invade Poland." Accessed March 14, 2015. http://www.history.com/this-day-in-history/germans-invade-poland.

———. "V-J Day." Accessed August 13, 1945, http://www.history.com/topics/world-war-ii/v-j-day.

Horrigan, Joe. *Forgotten Four: The Integration of Pro Football,* documentary, directed by Johnson McKelvy, 2014, New York: Epix, Ross Greenburg Productions. Television show.

———. Interview by James C. Sulecki. Personal interview. Canton, Ohio, May 7, 2015.

———. "National Football League Franchise Transaction." *Coffin Corner* 4 (1982), Professional Football Researchers Association.

"Hudlin Strives for 11th Today." *Cleveland Plain Dealer,* July 23, 1937.

"Hugo Bezdek as a Player and Farmer." *Pittsburgh Post-Gazette,* June 11, 1942.

"Hugo Bezdek, Grid Coach, Ex-Buc Manager, Dies." *Pittsburgh Post-Gazette,* September 20, 1952.

"Hugo Bezdek Has Made Good." *Spokesman-Review* (Spokane, Washington), August 18, 1918.

"Hugo Bezdek Is Signed as Rams' Coach." *Cleveland Press,* May 25, 1937.

"Hugo Bezdek, 68, Football Coach." *New York Times,* September 20, 1952.

"Hugo Bezdek to Stick." *Lewiston* (Maine) *Daily Sun,* December 5, 1922.

Hunter, Bob. "In Hayden Building, NFL Had Its Infancy." *Columbus Dispatch.* Accessed January 10, 2016. http://www.dispatch.com/content/stories/sports/2010/12/21/in-hayden-building-nfl-had-its-infancy.html.

Huth, John F. "Rams Dazzle 30,690 Even as They Lose, 7–6." *Cleveland Plain Dealer,* November 27, 1939.

"In the Navy." *Cleveland Plain Dealer,* August 18, 1942.

"Inspired Rams Smash New York Giants, 13–0." *Cleveland Plain Dealer,* November 11, 1940.

Jacobs, Paul. "Marshman's 1936 Pro Grid Vision Comes True." *Cleveland News,* November 4, 1947.

"James Reeves, Led Food Chain." *New York Times,* October 12, 1957.

"Jane Russell Dumps the QB." *New York Post,* February 4, 1967.

Jewish Telegraphic Agency. "E.B. Freed Inducted as U.S. Attorney at Cleveland." August 18, 1933. Accessed January 4, 2016. http://www.jta.org/1933/08/18/archive/e-b-freed-inducted-as-u-s-attorney-at-cleveland.

"Jim Benton Dies at 84; Set Longtime Pass-Receiving Record." *New York Times,* April 3, 2001.

"Jim Benton Is 4-F—He'll Play for Rams." *Cleveland Plain Dealer,* February 4, 1944.

Jones, Day. "The Beginning of the National Firm." Accessed January 4, 2016. http://www.jonesday.com/principlesandvalues/firmhistory/beginningofthenationalfirm/

Jones, Harry. "Groza's Field Goal Is Signal for Celebration." *Cleveland Plain Dealer,* December 25, 1950.

Jordan, Jimmy. "Rams Threaten Packers' Hopes." *Tuscaloosa* (Alabama) *News,* October 16, 1944.

"Joseph G. Fogg." *Cleveland Plain Dealer,* December 3, 1946.

"Judge Upholds Chet Adams' Right to Stay with Browns." *Cleveland Plain Dealer,* August 30, 1946.

"Kabealo and Zontini Sign with Rams." *Cleveland Plain Dealer,* July 30, 1944.

Kable, Forrest. "All League Selections." *Pro Football Illustrated,* 1946 Edition.

Kaplan, Emily. "The NFL Wants L.A., but Is It a Requited Love?" The MMQB, July 23, 2015. Accessed October 27, 2015. http://mmqb.si.com/mmqb/2015/07/21/nfl-los-angeles-st-louis-rams-stan-kroenke.

Katzowitz, Josh. *Sid Gillman: Father of the Passing Game.* Covington, KY: Clerisy Press, 2012.

Kieran, John. "The Eagles Are Screaming." *New York Times,* October 17, 1937.

———. "Red Hot from Green Bay." *New York Times,* November 21, 1937.

———. "Rushing the Football Season." *New York Times,* September 7, 1937.

Kimes, Mina. "Dear NFL, Women Matter…." *ESPN the Magazine.* Accessed January 2, 2016. http://espn.go.com/espnw/news-com

mentary/article/11262500/espnw-why-ray-rice-light-punishment-bad-business-nfl.

King, Joe. "QB Houdini's Back ... as Coach." *New York World Telegram and Sun,* October 21, 1961.

Kirksey, George. "Record 1,176,476 Watch National Pro Grid Games." *Cleveland Plain Dealer,* December 19, 1937.

Knight, Jonathan. *Opening Day: Cleveland, the Indians, and a New Beginning.* Kent, OH: Kent State University Press, 2004.

"Know Your New Rams: Steve Pritko." *Cleveland Press,* September 24, 1944.

Kroll, John. "When Art Modell Fired Paul Brown: How the Plain Dealer Reported It." Cleveland.com. Accessed March 5, 2016. http://www.cleveland.com/browns/index.ssf/2012/09/when_art_modell_fired_paul_bro.html.

Krsolovic, Ken, and Brian Fritz. *League Park: Historic Home of Cleveland Baseball, 1891–1946.* Jefferson, NC: McFarland, 2012.

Kuenzel, William. "The Perfect Football Face." *LIFE,* December 28, 1936.

L.A. Rams Football Club: 1946 Guide for Press and Radio. Los Angeles: 1946.

Lanyon, James H. "Reeves Sues Browns to Keep Adams on Los Angeles Roster." *Cleveland Plain Dealer,* July 20, 1946.

Lauderdale, Vance. "Gaylon the Great." *Memphis Flyer,* November 4, 2008. Accessed January 4, 2016. http://www.memphisflyer.com/AskVanceBlog/archives/2008/11/04/gaylon-the-great.

Lawrence, Charles W. "Fans Just Can't Quit Baiting Umps." *Cleveland Plain Dealer,* October 12, 1936.

"Layden Confident Pro Grid League Can Open Season." *Cleveland Plain Dealer,* April 6, 1943.

"Layden Will Speak Here in Support of Rams." *Cleveland Plain Dealer,* April 10, 1941.

"League for Curry and J. Reynolds." *Cleveland Plain Dealer,* October 25, 1932.

"League Park: Cleveland's Original Ballpark." Cleveland Memory Project. Accessed August 15, 2015, http://www.clevelandmemory.org/league/

Lebovitz, Hal. "Ask Hal." *Cleveland Plain Dealer,* April 16, 1976.

———. "Ask Hal." *Cleveland Plain Dealer,* December 12, 1976.

———. "Hal Asks: Remember the Cleveland Rams?" *Cleveland Plain Dealer,* January 20, 1980.

———. "Old Pro Shuts Typewriter; Sports Scene Will Miss Him." *Cleveland Plain Dealer,* February 2, 1964.

———. "Remember the Cleveland Rams?" *Coffin Corner* 7 (1985), Professional Football Researchers Association.

"Left-Handed Passer Joins Rams' Squad." *Cleveland Plain Dealer,* August 29, 1944.

Levy, Alan H. "Jim Crows of a Feather: A Comparison of the Segregation and Desegregation Eras in Professional Baseball and Football." In *The Cooperstown Symposium on Baseball and American Culture, 2002,* edited by William M. Simons, series editor Alvin L. Hall, 154–166. Jefferson, NC: McFarland, 2002.

Levy, Bill. *Return to Glory: The Story of the Cleveland Browns.* Cleveland: World Publishing, 1965.

Lewis, Franklin. "AAC Surrender Promotes Browns to Big League." *Cleveland Press,* December 10, 1949.

———. "Bits and Bites of Sports Chosen and Chewed." *Cleveland Press,* December 17, 1945.

———. "A Few Tales of Adam Walsh, Coach of Year." *Cleveland Press,* December 19, 1945.

———. "Football Loses Real Star as Drake Retires." *Cleveland Press,* July 15, 1942.

———. "Gehrke Flies High as Airplane Artist, on Ground as Ram." *Cleveland Press,* November 1, 1945.

———. "Levy, Ex-Partner in Rams' Deal, Urged Removal." *Cleveland Press,* February 7, 1946.

———. "Our Hero Emerges from Vacuum of Sports Events." *Cleveland Press,* February 6, 1946.

———. "Rams' Waterfield Intends to Become Football Coach." *Cleveland Press,* August 30, 1945.

Lewis, Michael. "Aldo 'Buff' Donelli: The Man Who Ignited the Usa-Mexico Rivalry in 1934." *Guardian,* April 13, 2015. Accessed June 15, 2015. http://www.theguardian.com/football/2015/apr/13/how-aldo-buff-donelli-drew-first-blood-in-usas-rivalry-with-mexico.

Library of Congress. "Moving Image Section— Motion Picture, Broadcasting and Recorded Sound Division." Accessed November 29, 2015. http://memory.loc.gov/ammem/awhhtml/awmi10/television.html.

Lipscomb, Thomas E. "Era of Pro Grid Bum Over, Says Lipscomb." *Cleveland Plain Dealer,* August 18, 1940.

"Lipscomb, Ex-Head of Rams, Dies." *Cleveland Plain Dealer,* February 5, 1960.

"Lipscomb Is Named President of Rams." *Cleveland Plain Dealer,* April 6, 1938.

Livestrong. "Timeline: History of Football Pads." Accessed November 17, 2014. http://www.livestrong.com/article/363203-timeline-history-of-football-pads/

"Los Angeles Rams' Owner Dan Reeves Dies of Cancer." *The Palm Beach Post,* April 16, 1971.

Bibliography

Lost Lettermen. "Ohio State Buckeyes—1932 Database." Accessed November 17, 2014. http://www.lostlettermen.com/football/ohio-state/players/year/1932.
Loveland, Roelif. "Ram Looks Sheepish in Debut to 25,000." *Cleveland Plain Dealer*, September 11, 1937.
"Luck to Them Both." *Cleveland Press*, December 17, 1938.
Lustig, Dennis. "Whatever Happened To... Cliff Battles?" *Cleveland Plain Dealer*, January 14, 1973.
Lytle, James. "Leonard K. Firestone, Past Board of Trustees President, Dies." USC News. Accessed March 19, 2016. https://news.usc.edu/12356/Leonard-K-Firestone-Past-Board-of-Trustees-President-Dies/
MacCambridge, Michael. *America's Game: The Epic Story of How Pro Football Captured a Nation.* New York: Anchor, 2004.
"Managerial Maxims of Hugo Bezdek." *Pittsburgh Press*, July 25, 1918.
"Marlins Notes: Yelich Branches Off Family Football Tree." Sun-Sentinel.com. Accessed December 6, 2015. http://articles.sun-sentinel.com/2014-03-04/sports/fl-marlins-0305-20140304_1_christian-yelich-reeves-pioneer-award-fred-gehrke.
Marshman, Homer H. Homer H. Marshman to Solon Holt, Cleveland, Ohio, February 18, 1937.
"Mary Carroon Married to Daniel Reeves as Notables Among 800 Guests Look On." *New York Times*, October 25, 1935.
Mathis, Wes. "Sensational Comeback in Final 12 Minutes Wins for West Shrine." *San Jose News*, January 2, 1945.
"Mattos Can Shine Under Any System." *Cleveland Plain Dealer*, October 14, 1936.
"Max Padlow." Xenia (Ohio) *Daily Gazette*, August 19, 1971.
Maxymuk, John. *NFL Head Coaches: A Biographical Dictionary, 1920–2011.* Jefferson, NC: McFarland, 2012.
McCann, Dick. "Dick McCann Says": Washington (DC) *Times Herald*, December 17, 1945.
McGowen, Roscoe. "Cleveland Rams Transfer Eleven to Los Angeles." *New York Times*, January 13, 1946.
McKenna, Eddie. "Gillette Joins Cleveland; Cards Seek New Players." Kenosha (Wisconsin) *Evening News*, October 16, 1940.
McLemore, Henry. "Hugo Bezdek Recommends Drastic Changes in Rules." *Pittsburgh Press*, December 29, 1930.
Mendermach, Mark. "Rembrandt of the Rams." *Sports Illustrated*, September 5, 1994. Accessed November 29, 2015. http://www.si.com/vault/1994/09/05/131946/rembrandt-of-the-rams-fred-gehrke-got-out-his-brushes-and-changed-helmets-forever.
"Miami Alumni Will Attend Luncheon Today." *Cleveland Plain Dealer*, December 15, 1945.
Miami Redhawks. "Cradle of Coaches." Accessed December 26, 2014. http://www.muredhawks.com/ViewArticle.dbml?ATCLID=205437824.
Miller, Carol Poh, and Robert A. Wheeler. "Cleveland: The Making and Remaking of an American City, 1796–1993." in *Cleveland: A Metropolitan Reader*, edited by W. Dennis Keating, Norman Krumholz, and David Perry, 31–48. Kent, OH: Kent State University Press, 1995.
"Mini-Bio: Riley Matheson." *Coffin Corner* 16:2 (1994), Professional Football Researchers Association.
Missoulian. "Fun Facts About Anaconda, Montana." Accessed December 6, 2015. http://missoulian.com/news/state-and-regional/fun-facts-about-anaconda-montana/article_f6e1f944-d308-11e3-b51d-0019bb2963f4.html.
MM|QB. "A Ticket from Christmas Eve 1994: The Day the NFL Died in L.A." Accessed November 29, 2015. http://mmqb.si.com/2014/06/04/nfl-history-in-95-objects-last-day-of-football-in-los-angeles.
Muir, Brian. "Remembering Dutch." Detroit Lions–Baltimore Colts game program, August 26, 1978.
Murray, Jim. "It's 4th and One for Washington." (Fredericksburg, Virginia) *Free Lance-Star*, September 29, 1970.
_____. "Rams Should Pack in Thoughts of Move." *Los Angeles Times*, December 20, 1994.
"Nails Ram Back for Loss on Jaunt with No Drivers License." *Cleveland Plain Dealer*, November 7, 1936.
National Baseball Hall of Fame. "Billy Evans." Accessed April 11, 2015. http://baseballhall.org/hof/evans-billy.
National Football Foundation. "Hugo Bezdek." Accessed December 11, 2014. http://www.footballfoundation.org/Programs/CollegeFootballHallofFame/SearchDetail.aspx?id=20088.
National Football League. "Bernie Masterson." Accessed July 18, 2015. http://www.nfl.com/player/berniemasterson/2520308/profile.
_____. "History: 1931–1940." Accessed March 14, 2015. http://www.nfl.com/history/chronology/1931-1940.
_____. "Los Angeles Rams." *1946 Record and Rules Manual.*
_____. "NFC Championship Game Results." Accessed December 14, 2015. http://www.nfl.com/superbowl/results/championships.
_____. "NFL 1920 Regular Season Standings." Accessed November 15, 2014, http://www.nfl.com/standings?category=league&season=1920-reg.

_____. "Record & Fact Book: Team Records, Passing." Accessed April 22, 2015. http://www.nfl.com/history/randf/records/team/passing.

National Football League—**arranged chronologically**
_____. "1937 Regular Season Standings." Accessed January 3, 2016. http://www.nfl.com/standings?category=conf&season=1937-REG.
_____. "1938 Regular Season Standings." Accessed January 3, 2016. http://www.nfl.com/standings?category=conf&season=1938-REG.
_____. "1939 Regular Season Statistics." Accessed March 14, 2015. http://www.nfl.com/stats/player?seasonId=1939&seasonType=REG&Submit=Go.
_____. "1940 Regular Season Standings." Accessed January 3, 2016. http://www.nfl.com/standings?category=conf&season=1940-REG.
_____. "1941 Regular Season Standings." Accessed January 3, 2016. http://www.nfl.com/standings?category=conf&season=1941-REG.
_____. "1942 Regular Season Standings." Accessed January 3, 2016. http://www.nfl.com/standings?category=conf&season=1942-REG.
_____. "1944 Regular Season Standings." Accessed January 3, 2016. http://www.nfl.com/standings?category=conf&season=1944-REG.
_____. "1945 Regular Season Standings." Accessed January 3, 2016. http://www.nfl.com/standings?category=conf&season=1945-REG.

National Football League Operations. "Impact of Television: Key Moments of the NFL on Tv 1950–1978." Accessed November 29, 2015. http://operations.nfl.com/the-game/impact-of-television/
National Geographic Creative Photography. "Picture Id: 302609" (Riley Matheson). Accessed December 5, 2015. http://www.natgeocreative.com/photography/302609.
National Museum of American History. "Trade Catalogs from A.W. Hecker Co." Accessed November 27, 2015. http://americanhistory.si.edu/collections/search/object/SILNMAHTL_20379.
NCAA. "First Televised Football Game Featured Fordham, Waynesburg in 1939." Accessed February 14, 2016. http://www.ncaa.com/news/football/article/2014-09-28/first-televised-football-game-featured-fordham-waynesburg-1939.
Neill, Frank. "Exclusive Use of Coliseum Given Rams." *Deseret* (Utah) *News*, January 30, 1946.
"Nevers Is Reported as Rams' New Coach." *Cleveland Plain Dealer*, March 4, 1937.
"New Idea for Football Rules Is Advanced by Hugo Bezdek." *New York Times*, April 2, 1922.
"New Men Dot Rams' Roster." *Milwaukee Journal*, August 10, 1944.
"New Pro Grid Franchise Up." *Associated Press*, February 4, 1937.
"New Ram Coach Stresses Offense." *Football Fanfare*. Cleveland Rams vs. New York Giants, September 14, 1945.
"New Student View on Football Noted." *New York Times*, December 29, 1931.
Newborn, Isi. "Aldo (Buff) Donelli: Meet the Man Who Was Shamed into a Football Career, Whose Job Is to Rebuild Rams into a Pro Grid Power." *Cleveland Press*, August 21, 1944.
_____. "Benton Ends Retirement to Play for Rams Again." *Cleveland Press*, September 21, 1944.
_____. "Donelli to Receive 'One of Biggest Contracts in Football'—Walsh." *Cleveland Press*, November 22, 1944.
_____. "Gillette of the Rams—A Story of Irony and Grit." *Cleveland Press*, October 25, 1944.
"N.F.L. Puts O.K. on Sale of Rams to Reeves." *Chicago Daily Tribune*, February 8, 1963.
1945 NFL Championship. 1945. Mount Laurel, NJ: NFL Productions, 2014. DVD.
"90 Report for Adams Football." *Cleveland Plain Dealer*, September 2, 1938.
"Not His Brainchild, Says Hugo Bezdek." *Reading* (Pennsylvania) *Eagle*, October 19, 1935.
Oates, Bob. *The Los Angeles Rams*. Culver City, CA: Murray & Gee, 1955.
_____. "The New Hall of Famer." *Los Angeles Herald-Examiner*, February 7, 1967.
"Odds Shorten on Cleveland Rams." *Ellensburg* (Washington) *Daily Record*, December 14, 1945.
"Office Space." *Beaver County* (Pennsylvania) *Times*, September 5, 2004.
"Ohio Incorporations." *Cleveland Plain Dealer*, December 29, 1936.
Olderman, Murray. "Where the Elite Meet to Eat." *Tuscaloosa* (Alabama) *News*, March 8, 1972.
Oldest Living Pro Football Players. "Stephen 'Steve' Pritko." Accessed December 6, 2015. http://www.oldestlivingprofootball.com/stephenstevepritko.htm.
_____. "Top 3—Oldest Living Cleveland Rams." Accessed December 6, 2015. http://www.oldestlivingprofootball.com/oldestlivingclerams.htm.
Ole Miss Football. "Ole Miss Football Greats

Parker Hall and Bud Slay Pass Away." Accessed March 14, 2015. http://www.olemissports.com/sports/m-footbl/spec-rel/021105aac.html.
Oliver, Myrna. "Fred Gehrke, 83; Ram Player, Artist." *Los Angeles Times*, February 14, 2002.
Oller, Rob. "Shaw's Life Was Stuff of Hollywood." *Columbus Dispatch*. Accessed December 27, 2015. http://www.dispatch.com/content/stories/sports/2011/04/14/shaws-life-was-stuff-of-hollywood.html.
"On a Scale of One to 10?" *Cleveland Plain Dealer*, November 27, 1977.
"100,000 from War Held on West Coast." *New York Times*, December 19, 1945.
"One Star-a-Year Plan Works Well for Rams." *Cleveland Plain Dealer*, August 27, 1940.
"Opinions Divide on Football Criticism." *New York Times*, January 20, 1922.
Oriard, Michael. *King Football: Sport and Spectacle in the Golden Age of Radio and Newsreels, Movies & Magazines, the Weekly & the Daily Press*. Chapel Hill: University of North Carolina Press, 2001.
Orth, Samuel Peter. *A History of Cleveland, Ohio: Biographical*. Chicago: The S.J. Clarke Publishing Co., 1910.
"Oscar Fraley, 79, 'Untouchables' Author." *New York Times*, January 9, 1994.
Otis, Sam. "Brief News and Views on Sports." *Cleveland Plain Dealer*, October 30, 1941.
———. "Brief News and Views on Sports." *Cleveland Plain Dealer*, December 31, 1941.
———. "Brief News and Views on Sports." *Cleveland Plain Dealer*, April 8, 1943.
———. "Brief News and Views on Sports." *Cleveland Plain Dealer*, April 25, 1944.
———. "Brief News and Views on Sports." *Cleveland Plain Dealer*, November 12, 1944.
———. "Brief News and Views on Sports." *Cleveland Plain Dealer*, November 26, 1944.
———. "It's New to Most of You." *Cleveland Plain Dealer*, October 5, 1938.
———. "It's New to Most of You." *Cleveland Plain Dealer*, October 7, 1938.
"Packers Always Have Tight Squeeze Here." *Cleveland Plain Dealer*, November 4, 1942.
Packers News. "Chronicles of 1936, 1939 Seasons Through Former Press-Gazette Sports Editor's Eyes." Accessed March 14, 2015. http://archive.packersnews.com/article/20110128/PKR01/110128119/Chronicles-1936-1939-seasons-through-former-Press-Gazette-sports-editor-s-eyes.
"Packers Sign Jim Gillette." *Milwaukee Sentinel*, July 6, 1948.
"Padlow Is Reinstated by National." *Cleveland Plain Dealer*, September 28, 1938.
Page, Joseph S. *Pro Football Championships Before the Super Bowl: A Year-By-Year History, 1926–1965*. Jefferson, NC: McFarland, 2011.
Paine, Neil. "Revisiting the Greatest Show on Turf." FiveThirtyEight Sports. Accessed November 29, 2015. http://fivethirtyeight.com/features/revisiting-the-greatest-show-on-turf/
"'Pappy' Lewis Dead at 51." *The Miami News*, June 14, 1962.
PBS. "Kristallnacht: The November 1938 Pogroms." Accessed February 15, 2015. http://www.ushmm.org/information/exhibitions/online-features/special-focus/kristallnacht.
PBS Nova. "Discovering U-Boat 166." Accessed June 12, 2015. http://www.pbs.org/wgbh/nova/military/discovering-u-166.html.
Pegler, Westbrook. "Nobody's Business." *Chicago Tribune*, December 11, 1932.
Penn State Athletics. "All-Time Game-By-Game." Accessed December 17, 2014. http://grfx.cstv.com/photos/schools/psu/sports/m-footbl/auto_pdf/201-14/misc_non_event/12-YBY-SeriesResults.pdf.
"Penn State Ousts Bezdek from Post." *New York Times*, October 4, 1932.
Penner, Mike. "History of Pro Football in Los Angeles." *Los Angeles Times*, March 17, 1999. Accessed October 25, 2015, http://articles.latimes.com/1999/mar/17/sports/sp-18189.
"The Perfect Football Face…." *LIFE* magazine, December 28, 1936.
Perry, David C. "Cleveland: Journey to Maturity." In *Cleveland: A Metropolitan Reader*, edited by W. Dennis Keating, Norman Krumholz, and David Perry, 11–26. Kent, OH: Kent State University Press, 1995.
Peters, George. "Reeves and Levy Do Not Plan to Shift Grid Team." *Cleveland Plain Dealer*, June 12, 1941.
Piascik, Andy. *The Best Show in Football: The 1946–1955 Cleveland Browns*. Lanham, MD: Taylor Trade Publishing, 2007.
"'Play It Hard,' Is New Ram's Formula." *Cleveland Plain Dealer*, June 14, 1938.
Playback.fm. "1936 Top 60 Songs." Accessed January 8, 2016. http://playback.fm/charts/top-100-songs/1936/
Popelka, Greg. "Five Things Paul Brown Was Not—Reliving Yesteryear." Accessed February 21, 2016. http://www.waitingfornextyear.com/2014/11/five-things-paul-brown-reliving-yesteryear/
Popular Mechanics. "10 Steps in the High-Tech Evolution of Pro Football Helmets." Accessed November 17, 2014. http://www.popularmechanics.com/outdoors/sports/football/4281378.
Prell, Edward. "Adam Walsh Signs as Coach of Cleveland Rams." *Chicago Tribune*, March 15, 1945.

———. "Aug. 23 Homecoming for Ex-Bears Trafton, Snyder." *Chicago Tribune*, July 15, 1946.
———. "Cleveland Game Opens All-America Race Tonight." *Chicago Daily Tribune*, September 6, 1946.
———. "Rams Beat Redskins, 15–14, for Pro Title." *Chicago Daily Tribune*, December 17, 1945.
———. "Rams Champs at Gate in '52." *Chicago Daily Tribune*, December 17, 1952.
———. "Rams Offer Luke Johnsos $20,000 a Year." *Chicago Tribune*, March 6, 1945.
———. "Rams Shift Franchise to Los Angeles." *Chicago Sunday Tribune*, January 13, 1946.
———. "Walsh Tells Why Pro League Can't Keep Rams Fenced In." *Chicago Tribune*, November 20, 1945.
———. "Waterfield Is Man of Hour in Cleveland." *Chicago Daily Tribune*, December 18, 1946.
"The Presses Roll Again—." *Cleveland Press*, February 6, 1946.
Preston, Howard. "Snuggies, Gloves Help Rams Win Title." *Cleveland News*, December 17, 1945.

Pro Football Archives—**arranged chronologically**
———. "1935 Detroit Lions (NFL)." Accessed January 2, 2015. http://www.profootballarchives.com/1935nfldet.html.
———. "1936 Boston Shamrocks (AFL)." Accessed November 17, 2014. http://www.profootballarchives.com/1936aflbos.html.
———. "1936 Cleveland Rams (AFL)." Accessed November 17, 2014. http://www.profootballarchives.com/1936aflcle.html.
———. "1936 Detroit Lions (NFL)." Accessed January 2, 2015. http://www.profootballarchives.com/1936nfldet.html.
———. "1936 New York Giants (NFL)." Accessed February 3, 2015. http://www.profootballarchives.com/1936nflnyg.html.
———. "1936 New York Yankees (AFL)." Accessed November 17, 2014. http://www.profootballarchives.com/1936aflnewy.html.
———. "1937 Cleveland Rams (NFL)." Accessed January 2, 2015. http://www.profootballarchives.com/1937nflcle.html.
———. "1937 Green Bay Packers (NFL)." Accessed January 2, 2015. http://www.profootballarchives.com/1937nflgb.html.
———. "1938 Cleveland Rams (NFL)." Accessed February 1, 2015. http://www.profootballarchives.com/1938nflcle.html.
———. "1938 New York Giants (NFL)." Accessed September 20, 2015. http://www.profootballarchives.com/1938nflnyg.html.
———. "1938 NFL Leaders and Leaderboards." Accessed January 16, 2015. http://www.pro-football-reference.com/years/1938/leaders.htm.
———. "1939 Chicago Bears (NFL)." Accessed February 14, 2015. http://www.profootballarchives.com/1939nflchib.html.
———. "1939 Cleveland Rams (NFL)." Accessed March 14, 2015. http://www.profootballarchives.com/1939nflcle.html.
———. "1940 Cleveland Rams (NFL)." Accessed March 14, 2015. http://www.profootballarchives.com/1940nflcle.html.
———. "1940 Green Bay Packers (NFL)." Accessed March 14, 2015. http://www.profootballarchives.com/1940nflgb.html.
———. "1940 NFL Leaders and Leaderboards." Accessed January 16, 2015. http://www.pro-football-reference.com/years/1940/leaders.htm.
———. "1941 Cleveland Rams." Accessed April 11, 2015. http://www.profootballarchives.com/1941nflcle.html.
———. "1941 Season: National Football League." Accessed April 11, 2015, http://www.profootballarchives.com/1941.html.
———. "1944 Detroit Lions (NFL)." Accessed June 13, 2015. http://www.profootballarchives.com/1944nfldet.html.
———. "1944 New York Giants (NFL)." Accessed June 13, 2015. http://www.profootballarchives.com/1944nflnyg.html.
———. "1944 Philadelphia Eagles (NFL)." Accessed June 13, 2015. http://www.profootballarchives.com/1944nflphi.html.
———. "1944 Washington Redskins (NFL)." Accessed June 13, 2015. http://www.profootballarchives.com/1944nflwas.html.
———. "1945 Cleveland Rams (NFL)." Accessed December 11, 2015. http://www.profootballarchives.com/1945nflcle.html.
———. "1945 Hollywood Bears (PCFL)." Accessed October 25, 2015. http://www.profootballarchives.com/1945pcflhol.html.
———. "1946 Cleveland Browns (AAFC)." Accessed November 29, 2015. http://www.profootballarchives.com/1946aafccle.html.
———. "1946 Green Bay Packers." Accessed June 13, 2015. http://www.profootballarchives.com/1946nflgb.html.
———. "1946 Los Angeles Rams (NFL)." Accessed November 29, 2015. http://www.profootballarchives.com/1946nfllarm.html.
———. "1946 Philadelphia Eagles (NFL)." Accessed June 13, 2015. http://www.profootballarchives.com/1946nflphi.html.
———. "1947 Green Bay Packers (NFL)." Accessed June 13, 2015. http://www.profootballarchives.com/1947nflgb.html.
———. "1947 Philadelphia Eagles (NFL)." Accessed June 13, 2015. http://www.profootballarchives.com/1947nflphi.html.
———. "1948 Los Angeles Rams (NFL)." Ac-

Bibliography

cessed November 29, 2015. http://www.profootballarchives.com/1948nfllarm.html.
_____. "1948 Philadelphia Eagles (NFL)." Accessed June 13, 2015. http://www.profootballarchives.com/1948nflphi.html.
_____. "1949 Los Angeles Rams (NFL)." Accessed November 29, 2015. http://www.profootballarchives.com/1949nfllarm.html.
_____. "1949 Philadelphia Eagles (NFL)." Accessed June 13, 2015. http://www.profootballarchives.com/1949nflphi.html.
_____. "1950 Cleveland Browns (NFL)." Accessed November 29, 2015. http://www.profootballarchives.com/1950nflcle.html.
_____. "1950 Philadelphia Eagles (NFL)." Accessed June 13, 2015. http://www.profootballarchives.com/1950nflphi.html.
_____. "1955 Los Angeles Rams (NFL)." Accessed November 29, 2015. http://www.profootballarchives.com/1955nfllarm.html.
_____. "1957 Los Angeles Rams (NFL)." Accessed November 29, 2015. http://www.profootballarchives.com/1957nfllarm.html.
_____. "1970 San Diego Chargers (NFL)." Accessed September 21, 2015. http://www.profootballarchives.com/1970nflsd.html.
_____. "1994 Los Angeles Rams (NFL)." Accessed November 29, 2015. http://www.profootballarchives.com/1994nfllarm.html.

Pro Football Archives. "Olie Cordill." Accessed April 11, 2015. http://www.profootballarchives.com/cord00400.html.
_____. "Riley Matheson." Accessed December 5, 2015. http://www.profootballarchives.com/math00850.html.
_____. "Vic Spadaccini." Accessed April 11, 2015. http://www.profootballarchives.com/spad00400.html.

"Pro Football Championship Game 1945." YouTube video, 1:35, posted by "History Comes to Life." August 2, 2011, https://www.youtube.com/watch?v=XxdlIwh0XfU

Pro Football Hall of Fame. "Hall of Famers: Bob Waterfield." Accessed July 18, 2015. http://www.profootballhof.com/hof/member.aspx?PlayerId=226.
_____. "Hall of Famers: Dan Reeves." Accessed October 25, 2015. http://www.profootballhof.com/hof/member.aspx?PLAYER_ID=178.
_____. "History: 1937 Draft." Accessed December 11, 2014. http://www.profootballhof.com/history/general/draft/1937.aspx.
_____. "NFL Champions 1920–2014. Accessed December 18, 2015. Http://Www.Profootballhof.Com/Football-History/NFL-Champions-1920-2014/
_____. "The 1941 NFL Draft Picks." Accessed December 18, 2015. http://www.profootballhof.com/timeline/1940/the-1941-nfl-draft/

_____. "St. Louis Rams: Team Facts." Accessed March 8, 2016. http://www.profootballhof.com/teams/st.-louis-rams/team-facts.

"Pro Football Loop Meets June 19–20." *Cleveland Plain Dealer*, May 30, 1943.

Pro Football Reference. "Adam Walsh." Accessed August 9, 2015. http://www.pro-football-reference.com/coaches/WalsAd0.htm.
_____. "Akron Indians Franchise Encyclopedia." Accessed October 19, 2015. http://www.pro-football-reference.com/teams/akr/
_____. "Al Donelli." Accessed June 12, 2015. http://www.pro-football-reference.com/players/D/DoneAl20.htm.
_____. "Arizona Cardinals Franchise Encyclopedia." Accessed December 18, 2015. http://www.pro-football-reference.com/teams/crd/
_____. "Bill Conkright." Accessed August 13, 2015. http://www.pro-football-reference.com/players/C/ConkBi20.htm.
_____. "Bob Snyder." Accessed December 12, 2015. http://www.pro-football-reference.com/players/S/SnydBo20.htm.
_____. "Branko Smilanich." Accessed February 1, 2015. http://www.pro-football-reference.com/players/S/SmilBr20.htm.
_____. "Buzz Wetzel." Accessed February 3, 2015. http://www.pro-football-reference.com/players/W/WetzBu20.htm.
_____. "Canton Bulldogs Franchise Encyclopedia." Accessed October 19, 2015. http://www.pro-football-reference.com/teams/cbd/
_____. "Chet Adams." Accessed December 27, 2015. http://www.pro-football-reference.com/players/A/AdamCh20.htm.
_____. "Chicago Bears Franchise Encyclopedia." Accessed October 19, 2015. http://www.pro-football-reference.com/teams/chi/
_____. "Cleveland Browns Training Camp Locations." Accessed August 13, 2015, http://www.pro-football-reference.com/teams/cle/training-camps.htm.
_____. "Coaches, Records, and Coaching Totals." Accessed November 29, 2015. http://www.pro-football-reference.com/coaches/
_____. "Dante Magnani." Accessed March 14, 2015. http://www.pro-football-reference.com/players/M/MagnDa20.htm.
_____. "Don Greenwood." Accessed August 11, 2015. http://www.pro-football-reference.com/players/G/GreeDo24.htm.
_____. "Don Hutson." Accessed June 13, 2015. http://www.pro-football-reference.com/players/H/HutsDo00.htm.
_____. "Elbie Schultz." Accessed August 11, 2015. http://www.pro-football-reference.com/players/S/SchuEl20.htm.
_____. "Elroy Hirsch." Accessed August 9, 2015.

http://www.pro-football-reference.com/players/H/HirsEl00.htm.
____. "Floyd Konetsky." Accessed August 11, 2015. http://www.pro-football-reference.com/players/K/KoneFl20.htm.
____. "Frankford Yellow Jackets Franchise Encyclopedia." Accessed October 19, 2015. http://www.pro-football-reference.com/teams/fyj/
____. "Fred Gehrke." Accessed March 14, 2015. http://www.pro-football-reference.com/players/G/GehrFr20.htm.
____. "Gaylon Smith." Accessed December 6, 2015. http://www.pro-football-reference.com/players/S/SmitGa21.htm.
____. "Gil Bouley." Accessed June 12, 2015. http://www.pro-football-reference.com/players/B/BoulGi20.htm.
____. "Jack Jacobs." Accessed June 12, 2015. http://www.pro-football-reference.com/players/J/JacoJa20.htm.
____. "Jim Benton." Accessed June 12, 2015. http://www.pro-football-reference.com/players/B/BentJi00.htm.
____. "Jim Gillette." Accessed March 14, 2015. http://www.pro-football-reference.com/players/G/GillJi20.htm.
____. "Joe F. Carr Trophy (MVP) Winners." Accessed March 8, 2016. http://www.Pro-Football-Reference.Com/Players/Award_Jfct.Htm.
____. "Mike Lazetich." Accessed August 9, 2015. http://www.pro-football-reference.com/players/L/LazeMi20.htm.
____. "Mike Scarry." Accessed December 12, 2015. http://www.pro-football-reference.com/players/S/ScarMi20.htm.

Pro Football Reference—**arranged chronologically**
____. "1920 APFAtandings, Teams & Offensive Statistics." Accessed January 3, 2016. http://www.pro-football-reference.com/years/1920_APFA/
____. "1937 Cleveland Rams." Accessed December 12, 2015. http://www.pro-football-reference.com/teams/ram/1937.htm.
____. "1937 NFL Opposition & Defensive Statistics." Accessed January 2, 2015. http://www.pro-football-reference.com/years/1937/opp/htm.
____. "1937 NFL Standings, Team & Offensive Statistics." Accessed January 2, 2015. http://www.pro-football-reference.com/years/1937/
____. "1938 Cleveland Rams." Accessed February 6, 2016. http://www.pro-football-reference.com/teams/ram/1938.htm.
____. "1938 Leaders and Leaderboards." Accessed February 15, 2015. http://www.pro-football-reference.com/years/1938/leaders.htm.
____. "1938 NFL Draft." Accessed February 1, 2015. http://www.pro-football-reference.com/years/1938/draft.htm.
____. "1939 Cleveland Rams." Accessed December 6, 2015. http://www.pro-football-reference.com/teams/ram/1939.htm.
____. "1939 NFL Leaders and Leaderboards." Accessed December 6, 2015. http://www.pro-football-reference.com/years/1939/leaders.htm.
____. "1939 NFL Standings, Team & Offensive Statistics." Accessed March 14, 2015. http://www.pro-football-reference.com/years/1939/#rushing_and_receiving.
____. "1940 NFL Leaders and Leaderboards." Accessed March 14, 2015. http://www.pro-football-reference.com/years/1940/leaders.htm.
____. "1940 NFL Pro Bowlers." Accessed April 30, 2015. http://www.pro-football-reference.com/years/1940/probowl.htm.
____. "1941 NFL Leaders and Leaderboards." Accessed April 15, 2015. http://www.pro-football-reference.com/years/1941/leaders.htm.
____. "1942 Cleveland Rams." Accessed June 12, 2015. http://www.pro-football-reference.com/teams/ram/1942.htm.
____. "1944 Cleveland Rams." Accessed June 12, 2015. http://www.pro-football-reference.com/teams/ram/1944.htm.
____. "1944 NFL All-Pros." Accessed June 13, 2015. http://www.pro-football-reference.com/years/1944/allpro.htm.
____. "1944 NFL Draft." Accessed June 12, 2015. http://www.pro-football-reference.com/years/1944/draft.htm.
____. "1944 NFL Leaders and Leaderboards." Accessed June 12, 2015. http://www.pro-football-reference.com/years/1944/leaders.htm.
____. "1945 Cleveland Rams." Accessed March 8, 2016. http://www.pro-football-reference.com/teams/ram/1945.htm.
____. "1945 NFL Leaders and Leaderboards." Accessed August 15, 1945. http://www.pro-football-reference.com/years/1945/leaders.htm.
____. "1946 Cleveland Browns." Accessed August 11, 2015. http://www.pro-football-reference.com/teams/cle/1946.htm.
____. "1947 Cleveland Browns." Accessed August 11, 2015. http://www.pro-football-reference.com/teams/cle/1947.htm.
____. "1951 Los Angeles Rams." Accessed August 9, 2015. http://www.pro-football-reference.com/teams/ram/1951.htm.

Pro Football Reference. "NFL Single Game Receiving Touchdowns Leaders." Accessed December 27, 2015. http://www.pro-football-reference.com/leaders/rec_td_single_game.htm.
____. "NFL Single Game Receiving Yards Leaders." Accessed August 15, 2015. http://

www.pro-football-reference.com/leaders/rec_yds_single_game.htm.
———. "Parker Hall." Accessed December 6, 2015. http://www.pro-football-reference.com/players/H/HallPa20.htm.
———. "Philadelphia Eagles Franchise Encyclopedia." Accessed December 18, 2015. http://www.pro-football-reference.com/teams/phi/
———. "Pittsburgh Steelers Franchise Encyclopedia." Accessed December 18, 2015. http://www.pro-football-reference.com/teams/phi/
———. "Providence Steam Roller Franchise Encyclopedia." Accessed October 19, 2015. http://www.pro-football-reference.com/teams/prv/
———. "Riley Matheson." Accessed April 28, 2015, http://www.pro-football-reference.com/players/M/MathRi20.htm.
———. "St. Louis Rams Franchise Encyclopedia." Accessed July 18, 2015. http://www.pro-football-reference.com/teams/ram/
———. "Sid Gillman." Accessed December 6, 2015. http://www.pro-football-reference.com/coaches/GillSi0.htm.
———. "Steve Pritko." Accessed June 12, 2015. http://www.pro-football-reference.com/players/P/PritSt20.htm.
———. "Tom Colella." Accessed December 11, 2015. http://www.pro-football-reference.com/players/C/ColeTo20.htm.
———. "Tom Fears." Accessed August 9, 2015. http://www.pro-football-reference.com/players/F/FearTo00.htm.
———. "Walker Gillette." Accessed June 12, 2015. http://www.pro-football-reference.com/players/G/GillWa00.htm.
———. "Walter West." Accessed June 12, 2015. http://www.pro-football-reference.com/players/W/WestWa20.htm.
———. "Woody Strode." Accessed March 17, 2016. http://www.pro-football-reference.com/players/S/StroWo20.htm.

Pro Football Researchers Association— **arranged chronologically**
———. "1937 National Football League." Accessed January 15, 2015. http://profootballresearchers.com/members-only/Linescores/1937Linescore.pdf.
———. "1938 National Football League." Accessed February 3, 2015. http://profootballresearchers.com/members-only/Linescores/1938Linescore.pdf.
———. "1939 National Football League." Accessed March 14, 2015. http://profootballresearchers.com/members-only/Linescores/1939Linescore.pdf.
———. "1941 National Football League." Accessed March 13, 2016. http://profootballresearchers.com/members-only/Linescores/1941Linescore.pdf.
———. "1942 National Football League." Accessed June 12, 2015. http://profootballresearchers.com/members-only/Linescores/1942Linescore.pdf.
———. "1944 National Football League." Accessed June 13, 2015. http://profootballresearchers.com/members-only/Linescores/1944Linescore.pdf.
———. "1945 National Football League." Accessed June 12, 2015. http://profootballresearchers.com/members-only/Linescores/1945Linescore.pdf.
———. "1951 National Football League." Accessed November 29, 2015. http://profootballresearchers.com/members-only/Linescores/1951Linescore.pdf.
———. "1955 National Football League." Accessed November 29, 2015. http://profootballresearchers.com/members-only/Linescores/1955Linescore.pdf.
———. "1957 National Football League." Accessed March 6, 2016. http://profootballresearchers.com/members-only/Linescores/1957Linescore.pdf.

"Pro Football Rules Are Changed to Curb Out-Of-Bounds Kickers." *New York Times*, April 11, 1938.
Pro Football Writers of America. "Dick McCann Award." Accessed September 23, 2015. http://www.profootballwriters.org/off-field-awards/pfwa-dick-mccann-award/
"Pros Swing Fists." *Lawrence* (Kansas) *Journal-World*, October 21, 1935.
Quirk, James P., and Rodney D. Fort. *Pay Dirt: The Business of Professional Team Sports*. Princeton: Princeton University Press, 1992.
"Ram Officials Shift Gridiron to Bring Game Closer to Spectators." *Cleveland Plain Dealer*, July 20, 1941.
"Ram Owners Buy Grid Farm Team." *Cleveland Plain Dealer*, August 20, 1941.
"Ram Prexy Passes Cigars." *Cleveland Plain Dealer*, August 31, 1941.
"Ram Reserve List Impressive." *Football Fanfare*, Cleveland Rams vs. Chicago Bears, October 7, 1945.
Ram Rumblings: Published by the Cleveland Rams Football Club 1:1 (September 1941).
"Rams Again Upset Chicago Bears, 23–21." *Cleveland Plain Dealer*, October 24, 1938.
"Rams Balk, Game's Off." *Pittsburgh Press*, November 16, 1936.
"Rams Beat White and Pirates, 13–7." *Cleveland Plain Dealer*, December 5, 1938.
"Rams Bid for Sid Luckman in Pro Football Draft Today." *Cleveland Plain Dealer*, December 9, 1938.
"Rams Break Pro Record, Draw 86,080." *Cleveland Press*, October 31, 1949.

"Rams Charge on Packers Again." *Cleveland Plain Dealer*, October 24, 1937.

"Rams Clinch Crown Beating Lions, 28–21." *New York Times*, November 23, 1945.

"Rams Close $656,000 Deal for Television." *Cleveland Plain Dealer*, August 18, 1950.

"Rams Connect 11 of 17 Passes for Smashing 17–0 Upset of Dodgers." *Cleveland Plain Dealer*, November 2, 1942.

"Rams Cut Prices for Home Games." *Cleveland Plain Dealer*, November 6, 1936.

"Rams Draft 3 All-Americans." *Cleveland Plain Dealer*, December 12, 1937.

"Rams Drop Moan as Squad Is Cut." *Cleveland Plain Dealer*, September 29, 1939.

"Rams Face 1,652 Pounds of Bear Line Here Today." *Cleveland Plain Dealer*, October 9, 1938.

"Rams' First String Backfield Is Now Signed for Next Fall." *Cleveland Plain Dealer*, December 27, 1945.

"Rams' Game Off; Demand Pitt Ouster." *Cleveland Plain Dealer*, November 16, 1936.

"Rams Get 40–21 Ride at Boston." *Cleveland Plain Dealer*, November 25, 1946.

"Rams Have 26 Players Signed for '41 Season." *Cleveland Plain Dealer*, July 2, 1941.

"Rams Held to Scoreless Tie." *Cleveland Plain Dealer*, October 29, 1936.

"Rams Land 3 All-Americans—Hall, Roth and Smith—In Draft." *Cleveland Plain Dealer*, December 10, 1938.

"Rams Launch Grid Practice Tomorrow." *Cleveland Plain Dealer*, August 1, 1937.

"Rams Lure Davis into Camp with Attractive Offer." *Cleveland Plain Dealer*, June 9, 1938.

"Rams' Magnani Has Chance to Lead Ground Gainers in National League." *Cleveland Plain Dealer*, September 17, 1942.

"Rams May Be Big Factor in Pro Grid Loop." *Sunday Morning Star* (Wilmington, DE), June 25, 1939.

"Rams Move 3 Games to League Park Field." *Cleveland Plain Dealer*, August 13, 1944.

"Rams Need Strengthening at End and Tackle Posts." *Cleveland Plain Dealer*, August 27, 1944.

"Rams Obtain Court Order to Probe Deal of Browns for Adams." *Cleveland News*, August 12, 1946.

"Rams Out to Do It for Clark Today." *Cleveland Plain Dealer*, November 19, 1939.

"Rams Owners to Seek Title and Big Crowds." *Cleveland Plain Dealer*, June 18, 1941.

"Rams Pick New Training Camp." *Cleveland Plain Dealer*, July 8, 1945.

"Rams Please Coach in First Scrimmage." *Cleveland Plain Dealer*, August 18, 1940.

"Rams' President Joins Air Corps." *Cleveland Plain Dealer*, September 21, 1942.

"Rams Return to City Next Sunday as Enemy." *Cleveland Plain Dealer*, December 18, 1950.

"Rams Score Twice in Last Period to Upset Green Bay, 27–24." *Cleveland Plain Dealer*, October 2, 1939.

"Rams Seek Court Aid in Player Grab." *Brooklyn Daily Eagle*, July 24, 1946.

"Rams' Shift Is Surprise." *Zanesville* (Ohio) *Signal*, January 13, 1946.

"Rams Sign Snyder to New Contract." *Cleveland Plain Dealer*, July 30, 1938.

"Rams Sign Walsh to Handle Line." *Cleveland Plain Dealer*, December 8, 1941.

"Rams Slated for Five Home Games." *Cleveland Plain Dealer*, February 18, 1938.

"Rams Strive for Decisive Victory." *Cleveland Plain Dealer*, November 5, 1939.

"Rams' Success Predicted." *Cleveland Plain Dealer*, August 16, 1939.

"Rams Suffer 2nd Straight Setback." *Cleveland Plain Dealer*, September 21, 1939.

"Rams to Exhibit Colorful Attack." *Cleveland Plain Dealer*, October 8, 1936.

"Rams to Open Training with 13 Veterans." *Associated Press*, August 11, 1944.

"Rams to Remain Here, Walsh Says." *Cleveland Plain Dealer*, March 13, 1945.

"Rams to Test New Offense in Camp at Hiram." *Cleveland Plain Dealer*, August 9, 1942.

"Rams Vanquish Lions by 20–17 in Late Rally for Third in Row." *New York Times*, October 15, 1944.

"Rams Vote to Resume Play in 1944." *Associated Press*, September 21, 1943.

"Rams Will Be Back." *Cleveland Plain Dealer*, September 22, 1943.

"Rams Will Play Only Four of 13 Games at Home." *Cleveland Plain Dealer*, April 24, 1944.

Rathbone, Basil. *In and Out of Character*. Garden City, NJ: Doubleday, 1962.

"Ready, Rams!" *Cleveland News*, September 3, 1941.

Real Clear Sports. "Top 10 Most Despised Owners: 7. Georgia Frontiere (Rams)." Accessed November 29, 2015. http://www.realclearsports.com/lists/top_10_despised_owners/georgia_frontiere_rams.htm.

"Record Ground-Gainer Slated for Rams' Job." *Cleveland Plain Dealer*, December 8, 1938.

Reed, Tom. "How Moving a Franchise from Cleveland to L.A. Benefited the Browns and Fostered Social Change." Cleveland.com. Accessed December 18, 2015. http://www.cleveland.com/browns/index.ssf/2014/02/cleveland_rams_browns_move_to_los_angeles.html.

Reedy, William T. "Penn State Football Coach Address Penn Wheelmen." *Reading* (Pennsylvania) *Eagle*, January 24, 1926.

Reeves, Dan. Interview by James C. Sulecki. Personal interview. Santa Ynez, California, January 29, 2016.
Reeves, Daniel F. Daniel F. Reeves to Richard P. McCann, Beverly Hills, California, April 23, 1962.
Reeves Ranch Vineyard. "Our Story." Accessed December 6, 2015. http://www.reevesranch vineyard.com/ourstory.php.
"Resignation of Hugo Bezdek." *Pittsburgh Press*, January 22, 1930.
Richardson, William D. "Giants Overcome by Rams, 21 to 17." *New York Times*, November 5, 1945.
———. "Rams Top Redskins for Title." *New York Times*, December 17, 1945.
"Rodak Likely to Sign with Rams." *Cleveland Plain Dealer*, March 17, 1939.
"Rooney Tells How Big Deal Was Arranged." *Pittsburgh Post-Gazette*, December 10, 1940.
Ross, Charles K. *Outside the Lines: African Americans and the Integration of the National Football League*. New York: New York University Press, 1999.
Russell, Jane. *My Path & My Detours: An Autobiography*. New York: Franklin Watts, 1985.
———. Telegram to Bob Waterfield, September 26, 1942.
Samford, H.L. "Ram Game Sets Receipts Record." *Cleveland Plain Dealer*, October 6, 1941.
"Sammy Baugh Suffering from an Old Rib Injury." *Milwaukee Journal*, December 13, 1945.
Sauerbrei, Harold. "Browns Win World Title, 30–28." *Cleveland Plain Dealer*, December 25, 1950.
SB Nation Land-Grant Holy Land. "Gold Pants: An Ohio State Football Tradition." Accessed November 15, 2014. http://www.landgrantholyland.com/2013/6/3/4381740/gold-pants-an-ohio-state-football-tradition.
SB Nation. "Leather-Bound Lions: Dutch Clark." Accessed February 1, 2015. http://www.prideofdetroit.com/2010/6/3/1498784/leather-bound-lions-dutch-clark.
Scanlon, Tom. "Historical Football Career Comes to End for Mo Scarry." *Pittsburgh Post-Gazette*, January 30, 1986.
Schlemmer, Jim. "Rams and Eagles Display Championship Possibilities." *Football Fanfare*, Cleveland Rams vs. Philadelphia Eagles, September 23, 1945.
Schmidt, Raymond. "All-America Football Conference." In *Sports in America: From Colonial Times to the Twenty-First Century*, edited by Steven A. Reiss, 86–87. London: Routledge, 2011.
Scholl, Bill. "Lazetich—Charger with Song in His Heart, Football in Blood." *Cleveland Press*, November 1, 1974.
———. "Scarry Tales of Browns' Glory Days." *Cleveland Press*, November 16, 1979.
"Schultz Traded to Rams." *New York Times*, August 1, 1945.
Sell, Jack. "Donelli Must Start Over Again After War." *Pittsburgh Post-Gazette*, March 22, 1945.
"7 Former Ohio State Stars on Team Here." *Cleveland Plain Dealer*, September 26, 1936.
Shatto, Carl. "Hugo Bezdek Is Signed as Rams' Coach." *Cleveland Press*, May 25, 1937.
"Shaw Books Two Night Grid Games." *Cleveland Plain Dealer*, January 8, 1938.
Sheehan, Joseph M. "Rams Reveal Balance and Depth in Outstanding Backfield Squad." *New York Times*, November 1, 1945.
Sher, Jack. "The Bob Waterfield Story." *SPORT*, November 1951.
Sherman Oaks Patch. "Property Where Jane Russell Lived Is Up for Sale." Accessed July 18, 2015. http://patch.com/california/shermanoaks/the-property-where-jane-russell-lived-is-up-for-sale.
"Sid Gillman, 91, Innovator of Passing Strategy in Football." *New York Times*, January 4, 2003.
Sillcox, Scott. "The Evolution of Colors." Los Angeles Rams video, 1:50. February 11, 2013. http://www.therams.com/videos/videos/Evolution-of-the-Rams-Colors/164595b6-f383-4af0-a9d1-141d1fba0c18.
Silverman, Alvin. "All That Glitters Is Not Told." In *Cleveland in Full Face*, edited by Ed Bang, Gordon Cobbledick, Winsor French, Franklin Lewis, and Alvin Silverman. Cleveland: Gruber Hollenden Foundation, 1955.
———. "Sees 'Way Clear' on Stadium Snow." *Cleveland Plain Dealer*, December 15, 1945.
———. "60,135 See Browns in Debut Here." *Cleveland Plain Dealer*, September 7, 1946.
———. "Snowdrifts Hold Line Against City on Stadium Gridiron." *Cleveland Plain Dealer*, December 13, 1945.
———. "Stadium Snow on Way Out; Straw Is Next." *Cleveland Plain Dealer*, December 14, 1945.
———. "Time Out." *Cleveland Plain Dealer*, December 25, 1945.
Skinner, Chads O. "C. of C. Cheers Grid Heroes; Rams and Lions Vie for Burton Trophy." *Cleveland Plain Dealer*, November 18, 1939.
———. "Grid 'Eskimos' Survive Zero Hour at Game." *Cleveland Plain Dealer*, December 17, 1945.
———. "Wife of Rams' Owner Jinxes Team If She Sits with Him." *Cleveland Plain Dealer*, December 8, 1945.
Slater, Tom. Tom Slater, Mutual Broadcasting System, to Bob Waterfield, New York, New York, January 18, 1945.

"Slip Madigan and Keeshin Visitors." *Cleveland Plain Dealer*, December 14, 1945.

"Slonacker to Talk About Smilanich." *Prescott (Arizona) Evening Courier*, March 31, 1938.

"Smith Back in Town; Picks Cleveland Rams." *The Milwaukee Journal*, December 13, 1945.

Sneaker Report. "The Surprising and Unexpected Evolution of the Football Cleats." Accessed December 21, 2014. http://sneakerreport.com/news/the-surprising-and-unexpected-evolution-of-the-football-cleat/7/

"Snow Here for a Week, Traffic Badly Snarled." *Cleveland Press*, December 11, 1945.

"Snow Will Not Prevent Rams' Game." *Cleveland Plain Dealer*, November 26, 1936.

Society for American Baseball Research. "Billy Evans." Accessed April 11, 2015. http://sabr.org/bioproj/person/540a0fa3.

———. "Jack Graney, the First Player-Broadcaster." Accessed November 17, 2014. http://research.sabr.org/journals/jack-graney.

Song Lyrics. "Bing Crosby—San Fernando Valley Lyrics." Accessed July 18, 2015. http://www.songlyrics.com/bing-crosby/san-fernando-valley-lyrics/

Spartano, Phil. "Cleveland Rams Will Win Pro Title, Gillette Says on Visit to Utica." *Observer-Dispatch* (Utica, NY), December 6, 1945.

"Sport: Okinawa's All-Americans." *TIME*, September 24, 1945. Accessed January 4, 2016. http://content.time.com/time/magazine/article/0,9171,886603,00.html.

"Sports Bigwigs Fry on Writers' Griddle." *Cleveland Plain Dealer*, February 9, 1939.

Sports-Central.org. "NFL Dynasties and Hall of Famers." Accessed December 6, 2015. http://www.sports-central.org/sports/2012/07/10/nfl_dynasties_and_hall_of_famers.php.

Sports on Earth. "The Battle of Ohio." Accessed March 14, 2015. http://www.sportsonearth.com/article/64052854/

Sports Reference/College Football— **arranged chronologically**

———. "1939 Stanford Cardinal Schedule and Results." Accessed July 18. 2015, http://www.sports-reference.com/cfb/schools/stanford/1939-schedule.html.

———. "1940 Stanford Cardinal Schedule and Results." Accessed July 18, 2015. http://www.sports-reference.com/cfb/schools/stanford/1940-schedule.html.

———. "1941 Pacific Coast Conference Year Summary." Accessed July 18, 2015. http://www.sports-reference.com/cfb/conferences/pcc/1941.html.

———. "1941 Stanford Cardinal Schedule and Results." Accessed July 18, 2015. http://www.sports-reference.com/cfb/schools/stanford/1941-schedule.html.

———. "1942 UCLA Bruins Schedule and Results." Accessed July 18, 2015. http://www.sports-reference.com/cfb/schools/ucla/1942-schedule.html.

———. "1943 UCLA Bruins Schedule and Results." Accessed July 18, 2015. http://www.sports-reference.com/cfb/schools/ucla/1943-schedule.html.

———. "1944 UCLA Bruins Schedule and Results." Accessed July 18, 2015. http://www.sports-reference.com/cfb/schools/ucla/1944-schedule.html.

"Stadium Game Will Supplant All-Star Event." *Cleveland Plain Dealer*, April 2, 1942.

"Stadium Snow Licked, 50,000 to Hail Rams." *Cleveland Plain Dealer*, December 16, 1945.

"Star Washington Back Will Quit Job at Columbia." *Cleveland Plain Dealer*, December 7, 1938.

"Statement of Federal & State Tax Collected During November for Football Game at League Park." The Cleveland Baseball Club, November 1945. Document privately held by Donald Gries, Shaker Heights, Ohio.

Steelers.com. "Eagles-Steelers Share a Long History." Accessed April 8, 2015. http://www.steelers.com/news/article-1/Eagles-Steelers-share-a-long-history/2c8b7482-7d9c-42de-885d-57e5baca0460.

Stewart, Dixon. "Football Kills 32 in Most Disastrous Year." *Cleveland Press*, December 4, 1931.

Stewart, Larry. "Longtime Tv and Radio Sportscaster in L.A. Also Appeared in a String of Films." *Los Angeles Times*, December 27, 2007.

Storck, Carl L., ed. *Official Guide of the National Football League: 1939*. New York: American Sports Publishing Co., 1939.

———. *Official Guide of the National Football League: 1940*. New York: American Sports Publishing Co., 1940.

Strickler, George. "Bezdek, Once Maroon Star, Directs Rams." *Chicago Tribune*, October 29, 1937.

———. "Cardinals Beat Rams, 31–17; Set Pair of Records." *Chicago Tribune*, November 28, 1938.

———. "Cardinals End Season Today Against Rams." *Chicago Tribune*, November 27, 1938.

———. George Strickler telegram to Bob Waterfield, January 2, 1946.

———. "Rams See Only Packers in Way of Championship." *Chicago Tribune*, October 25, 1938.

"Strike Ended by Pressmen at 3 Dailies." *Cleveland Plain Dealer*, February 6, 1946.

Strode, Woody. *Goal Dust: The Warm and Candid Memoirs of a Pioneer Black Athlete and Actor*. Lanham, MD: Madison Books, 1990.

Strother, Shelby. "Postwar Classic." In *NFL Top*

Bibliography

40: *The Greatest Pro Football Games of All Time*, 32–35. New York: Viking, 1988.

Sulecki, Jerry. Interview by James C. Sulecki. Personal interview. June 14, 2014.

Supreme Court Historical Society. "William R. Day." Accessed January 4, 2016. http://supremecourthistory.org/timeline_day.html.

Surdam, David George. *Run to Glory and Profits: The Economic Rise of the NFL During the 1950s*. Lincoln: University of Nebraska Press, 2013.

"Sutphin Says He's Interested in Buying Rams." *Cleveland Plain Dealer*, January 15, 1938.

"T. E. Lipscomb Leaves $256,000 to Vanderbilt." *Cleveland Plain Dealer*, March 30, 1960.

"Tampering Says Walsh." *Chicago Daily Tribune*, July 24, 1946.

Tandler, Rich. "1945 NFL Championship Game: Cleveland Municipal Stadium." in *The Redskins from A to Z: The Games*, 34. Midlothian, VA: Walking Encyclopedia Publications, 2002.

"31 Ram Fans Hurt at League Park as Temporary Stands Fall." *Cleveland Plain Dealer*, November 12, 1945.

Thomas, Robert McG., Jr. "Buff Donelli, College Football Coach, Dies at 87." *New York Times*, August 11, 1994.

"3 Cleveland Rams Enter Armed Services." *Cleveland Plain Dealer*, February 28, 1942.

"Three Long Runs Help Lions Vanquish the Rams, 27 to 7." *New York Times*, November 8, 1937.

"Thumbnail Sketches of Cleveland Rams." Official Program, Eagles vs. Rams, October 28, 1945.

Thurman, Jim. "10 L.A. Sports Venues That Are No More." *L.A. Weekly*, December 23, 2013.

"Toledo Coach Resigns Post." *St. Petersburg* (Florida) *Times*, November 3, 1951.

"Toledo Names Dunn to Succeed Greenwood." *Cleveland Plain Dealer*, November 2, 1951.

Toman, James A. *Cleveland Stadium: Sixty Years of Memories*. Cleveland, OH: Emerson Press, 1991.

"Tony Butkovich Dies on Okinawa." *Milwaukee Sentinel*, May 4, 1945.

"Tribe Attendance Drop Is Largest." *Cleveland Plain Dealer*, October 3, 1942.

Trickey, Erick. "Eliot Ness and J. Edgar Hoover." *Smithsonian*, September 2014.

"20 Backers of New Rams Team Named." *Cleveland Plain Dealer*, February 4, 1937.

"29 Oct 1944 Cleveland Rams at Chicago Bears." YouTube video, 5:27, posted by "Kanal Von B14ckd34th." February 3, 2010, https://www.youtube.com/watch?v=kbJs9LLgFyA

"23 Games Launch School Football." *Cleveland Plain Dealer*, September 12, 1938.

"Two Seek Pro League Berths." *Milwaukee Journal*, February 9, 1936.

"UCLA vs. Washington State College, 1941." YouTube video, 25:21, posted by "Wazzulibrary." April 10, 2014, https://www.youtube.com/watch?v=8xWCHOLzUaQ

"U.C.L.A. Wins, 14–7; Selected to Play in the Rose Bowl." *New York Times*, December 13, 1942.

Underwood, Paul S. "Rams Upset Pro League Predictions." *St. Petersburg* (Florida) *Times*, October 14, 1944.

United States Bureau of the Census. "Population of the 100 Largest Urban Places: 1930." Accessed December 11, 2014. https://www.census.gov/population/www/documentation/twps0027/tab16.txt.

_____. "Population of the 100 Largest Urban Places: 1940." Accessed October 24, 2015. https://www.census.gov/population/www/documentation/twps0027/tab17.txt.

United States Holocaust Memorial Museum. "Liberation of Nazi Camps." Accessed August 9, 2015. http://www.ushmm.org/wlc/en/article.php?ModuleId=10005131.

U.S. Soccer. "90-Year Anniversary Articles: Aldo 'Buff' Donelli." Accessed June 12. 2015. http://www.ussoccer.com/stories/2014/03/17/12/40/90-year-anniversary-articles-aldo-buff-donelli.

University of Arkansas. "Hugo Bezdek and the Razorbacks." Accessed December 14, 2014. http://www.uark.edu/rd_vcad/urel/info/campus_map/446.php.

University of Chicago. "Jay Berwanger, First Winner of the Heisman Trophy, 1914–2002." Accessed December 11, 2014. http://www-news.uchicago.edu/releases/02/020627.berwanger.shtml.

University of Connecticut. "Voices from the Second World War: Timeline of Selected Events 1931–1945. Accessed June 12, 2015. Http://Sp.Uconn.Edu/~wwwcoh/Timeline.Htm

Van Natta, Don, Jr., and Seth Wickersham. "The Wow Factor." ESPN, February 29, 2016. Accessed March 8, 2016. http://espn.go.com/espn/feature/story/_/id/14752649/the-real-story-nfl-owners-battle-bring-football-back-los-angeles.

"Varied Ram Attack Subdues Bears, 17–0." *New York Times*, October 8, 1945.

Vischansky, Peter. "A Football Man—Coach Bob Snyder." *Coffin Corner* 22:1 (2000), Professional Football Researchers Association.

_____. "The Life and Times of Fred Gehrke." *Coffin Corner* 22:3 (2000), Professional Football Researchers Association.

Wallace, William N. "Dan Reeves Dies; Owner of Rams." *New York Times*, April 16, 1971.

_____. "Sid Gillman, 91, Innovator of Passing Strategy in Football." *New York Times*, January 4, 2003.
_____. "Sid Luckman, Star for the Bears, Dies at 81." *New York Times*, July 6, 1998.
Walsh, Charles F. Charles F. Walsh to Mrs. S. E. Waterfield, Cleveland, Ohio, September 13, 1945.
"Walsh, GM of Rams' '45 Title Club, Dies." *Cleveland Plain Dealer*, September 7, 1971.
Walsh, Leonard P. Leonard P. Walsh, president of the Touchdown Club, Washington, D.C., telegram to Bob Waterfield, December 20, 1945.
"Walsh, Ram Aid, Is Orator, Too." *Cleveland Plain Dealer*, October 3, 1942.
Ward, Arch. "In the Wake of the News." *Chicago Tribune*, December 23, 1953.
_____. "Remember Him?" *Chicago Tribune*, January 11, 1937.
_____. "Talking It Over." *Chicago Tribune*, January 5, 1937.
_____. "U.C.L.A. Says Man to Watch in Rose Bowl Is Our Waterfield." *Chicago Tribune*, December 31, 1942.
Ward, Gene. "Rams Zoom to Pro Peak Through Cutie and QB" *New York Daily News*, November 11, 1945.
"Washington Halts Cleveland by 16–7." *New York Times*, November 22, 1937.
Water and Power Associates. "Early Views of the San Fernando Valley." Accessed August 26, 2015, http://waterandpower.org/museum/Early_Views_of_the_San_Fernando_Valley_Page_1.html.
Waterfield, Bob. Scrapbook. Ca. 1930s. Privately held by Buck Waterfield, Santa Maria, California.
Waterfield, Buck. Interviews by James C. Sulecki. Personal interview by phone, September 27, 2014; and in Santa Maria, California, January 30, 2016.
Waterfield, Frances. Bob Waterfield Scrapbook. Ca. 1940s. Privately held by Buck Waterfield, Santa Maria, California.
"Waterfield Pitches Three Touchdown Passes to Humble Bears, 24 to 14." *Cleveland Plain Dealer*, December 18, 1950.
"Waterfield Signs to Coach Rams." *Cleveland Plain Dealer*, January 13, 1960.
"We Want the Rams." *Cleveland Plain Dealer*, April 9, 1941.
"The Weather Over the Nation and Abroad." *New York Times*, November 30, 1936.
Weber, Tracy. "The Rams: Bound for St. Louis." *Los Angeles Times*, January 16, 1995.
"Welcomes Rams' Move." *New York Times*, January 14, 1946.
West Virginia Mountaineers. "Art 'Pappy' Lewis." Accessed April 11, 2015, http://www.wvusports.com/hallOfFame.cfm?func=viewProfile&hofID=122.
"Wetzel Gets New Job." *Cleveland Plain Dealer*, February 23, 1939.
"Wetzel Out as Ram Boss." *Cleveland Press*, September 14, 1938.
"Wetzel Resigns as Ram Official." *Cleveland Plain Dealer*, September 15, 1938.
What Was Here. "Hotel St. Regis." Accessed July 18, 2015. http://www.whatwasthere.com/browse.aspx#!/ll/41.503601,-81.630917/id/68080/info/details/zoom/14/
"Where Are They Now?: Johnny Drake." *Cleveland Press*, February 9, 1954.
"Where Are They Now?: Parker Hall." *Cleveland Press*, January 10, 1955.
"WHK to Take Pro Football Opener Sunday." *Cleveland Plain Dealer*, October 9, 1936.
"Why This or That Cleveland Ram 'Ain't in the Army.'" *Detroit News*, week of September 21, 1942.
Wiebusch, John. "NFL Championship: A Look Back: A Long Winter's Day: The Improbable Saga of the 1945 NFL Championship Game." *Los Angeles Times*. Accessed September 23, 1945. http://articles.latimes.com/1986-01-10/sports/sp-956_1_press-box.
Williamson, Ben. "His Players Wanted Bezdek Kept; Rams' Owners Need Tough Manager for Selves." *Cleveland Press*, September 29, 1938.
_____. "Pardon This Heat, but Drake Is Back on Range; and Here's How Indians Still Can Win It." *Cleveland Press*, August 16, 1938.
Willis, Chris. *Dutch Clark: The Life of an NFL Legend and the Birth of the Detroit Lions*. Lanham, MD: Scarecrow, 2012.
_____. *Joe F. Carr: The Man Who Built the National Football League*. Lanham, MD: Scarecrow, 2010.
Wisconsin Historical Society. "Green Bay Stadium Field Before NFL Championship Game." Accessed February 26, 2016. http://www.wisconsinhistory.org/Content.aspx?dsNav=N:4294963828-4294955414&dsNavOnly=N:1135&dsRecordDetails=R:IM6661.
Wogenrich, Mark. "The Wonder Team During Their Undefeated 1937 Season, Northmapton's Koncrete Kids Were Virtually Unstoppable—Scoring 58 Points a Game While Allowing Only 25." *Morning Call* (Allentown, Pennsylvania), January 28, 2000.
Wolff, Alexander. "The NFL's Jackie Robinson." *Sports Illustrated*, October 12, 2009. Accessed October 25, 2015, http://www.si.com/vault/2009/10/12/105865272/the-nfls-jackie-robinson.
"Yankees Downed by Cleveland, 27–0." *New York Times*, October 26, 1936.

"Yellow Cab Asks Cleveland Test of Radio Dispatching." *Cleveland Plain Dealer,* September 1, 1944.

Yelsky, Milton. "Rams Will Pick Colorado's Whizzer White in Pro Football Draft." *Cleveland Plain Dealer,* December 8, 1937.

Yonkers, Bob. "Benton Battling Flu, Is Doubtful Starter Sunday; 800 Fans Fete Rams." *Cleveland Press,* December 13, 1945.

_____. "Browns Aim to Make Fans Forget Departed Rams." *Cleveland Press,* February 6, 1946.

_____. "Browns Willing to Play Rams in 1946." *Cleveland Press,* December 30, 1945.

_____. "Champ Rams Get $1469 Each, Vanquished Redskins $902." *Cleveland Press,* December 17, 1945.

_____. "Cleveland Loses Rams' Franchise to Los Angeles." *Cleveland Press,* January 14, 1946 (page proof).

_____. "Coach Snyder Latest Ram to Pass Up Rival League." *Cleveland Press,* December 29, 1945.

_____. "Colella Sparks Winning Three-Touchdown Rally." *Cleveland Press,* October 5, 1945. Inscribed copy privately held by Walker Gillette, Franklin, Virginia.

_____. "Outwitting Quarterback Gains Matheson Stardom." *Cleveland Press,* November 30, 1945.

_____. "Pritko, Steady End, Has Definite Place in Rams' League Opening Game Sunday." *Cleveland Press,* September 2, 1945.

_____. "Rams May Play Redskins, Eagles Here Next." *Cleveland Press,* December 27, 1945.

_____. "Rams Ruin Packers' Passing, Coast on Early Lead." *Cleveland Press,* November 12, 1945.

_____. "Reeves Denies Rams Will Move to Los Angeles." *Cleveland Press,* January 11, 1946 (page proof).

_____. "Star Lineman May Jump to New League in '46." *Cleveland Press,* December 18, 1945.

_____. "Waterfield Leads Rams to Title, Signs Three-Year Contract." *Cleveland Press,* December 17, 1945.

Yost, Mark. *Tailgating, Sacks, and Salary Caps: How the NFL Became the Most Successful Sports League in History.* Chicago: Kaplan, 2006.

Young, A.S. (Doc). "Dedicated Writers and Editors Paved Way for Integration of Major Sports." *Ebony,* October 1970.

Zillow. "16014 Hartland St, Van Nuys, Ca 91406." Accessed July 18, 2015. http://www.zillow.com/homedetails/16014-Hartland-St-Van-Nuys-CA-91406/19962937_zpid/

Zirin, Alex. "Rams Are in League to Stay, Walsh Says." *Cleveland Plain Dealer,* May 5, 1944.

_____. "Rams Expected to Remain Here." *Cleveland Plain Dealer,* April 19, 1941.

_____. "Waterfield Signs 3-Year Contract with Rams for Reported $60,000." *Cleveland Plain Dealer,* December 17, 1945.

Index

Numbers in ***bold italics*** refer to pages with photographs.

ABC radio network 165
ABC television ***205***–206
Adams, Chet 13, 74, 79, 106, 112–113, 115, 184, 217; controversy over signing with the Cleveland Browns 196–199, 217, 222
Admiral Corp. 207
Admittance to the National Football League 42–43, 53, 162, 221
African American sports writers' opposition to Rams playing in the Los Angeles Coliseum 188–191; *see also* Los Angeles Memorial Coliseum
African Americans in early pro football 32–33, 190
Aguirre, Joe 169–172
Akins, Frank 168
Akron, Ohio 10, 17, 74, 112, 117, 129
Akron Beacon Journal 102
Akron Pros (American Professional Football Association) ***18***, 190
Akron Rubber Bowl 101–***102***, ***108***, 151
Aldrich, Ki 170–171
All-America Football Conference 10, 112, 128, 142–145, 155, 175–176, 178, 180–182, 188, ***191***, 193–194, 201–203, 217–219, 221, 223; founding 124–125, 143
Allentown Bears 69
Alphonse, Jules 69, 71
Ambassador Hotel (Los Angeles) 138
Ameche, Don 90, 179
American Airlines 84
American Football Association 100–101; *see also* Jersey City Giants
American Football Coaches Association 49
American Football League 19, 21–23, 26, 29, 33, 35–41, 52–53, 55–56, 58, 60, 62, 73, 81, 90–91, 103, 124, 143, 201, 207, 219–221; Rams' canceled championship game 37; Rams' debut 26–30, 82; Rams' departure from 38–39; Rams' first touchdown 30, 219; Rams' first victory 30
American Hockey League 62, 91
American League (baseball) 26, 124
American Professional Football Association ***18***; *see also* National Football League

Anaheim, California 1, 213
Anaheim Stadium 212
Arkansas A&M 217
Associated Press 21, 37, 113, 115
Athens, Ohio 22
attendance: link to winning percentage ***59***; Rams in Cleveland 9, 34, 57–***59***, 62, 85, 104, 158, 166, 178, 200, 206; Rams in Los Angeles/southern California ***191***, 200–201, 205, 207–208, 210–213
Autry, Gene 210

Bagarus, Steve 170
Baldwin, Burr 137
Baldwin-Wallace College 66
Baltimore, Maryland 2, 7, 12, 84, 115, 220
Baltimore Colts (All-America Football Conference) 203
Baltimore Colts (National Football League) 212, 220, 222
Bang, Ed 186
Banta, Jack 199–200
Barrett, Emmett ***108***
Battles, Cliff 73, 95
Baugh, Sammy 3, 40, 61, 83, 85, 118, 127, 160, 168, 185, 220; safety in 1945 NFL championship game 169–170
Baugh/Marshall Rule 169
Baylor University 111
Bear Mountain, New York 153
Begarus, Steve 170
Belichick, Bill 64
Belichick, Stephen 64
Bell, Bert 41, 49, 89–90, 114
Benton, Jim 7–***8***, 61, 67, 70, 72–74, 76, 79, 82–83, 85–86, 88, 102, 109, 112–113, 115, 124, 126–127, 129, 146–148, 151–152, 156, 158, 164, 168, 170–***174***, 176, 199, 208, 213, 217, 220, 222; championship season with the Chicago Bears 116, 121, 217; performance in 1945 NFL championship game 173; 303 yards receiving in one game 12, 156, 158, 217
Berea, Ohio 78
Berwanger, Jay 45
Bezdek, Hugo 45–***47***, 48–51, 54–58, 60–61,

268

66–69, 73–75, 81, 89, 103, 114, 120, 147, 194, 203, 217, 221; firing by the Rams 69–71; hiring as Rams coach 49; Pennsylvania State University 47–49
Bidwill, Charles 39, 90, 180
Blozis, Al 109
Boone, Jack 112
Bornstein, Larry 209
Bossard, Emil 165
Boston, Massachusetts 7, 22, 34, 36, 89, 92, 117, 145, 179; Rams' near-move to 91, 97–98, 179, 185
Boston Braves/Redskins (National Football League) 10, 21, 33, 40, 95; *see also* Washington Redskins
Boston College 119, 146
Boston Shamrocks (American Football League) 22, 26–27, 30, 33–36, 40, 58, 62; canceled American Football League championship game 37
Boston University 218
Boston Yanks (National Football League) 115, 117, 125, *150*, 157–158, 199, 219, 222
Bouley, Gil *8*, 119, 146–147, 150–151, 176, 182, 199, 205, 208
Bowdoin College 105, 144–145, 147, 203, 223
Bowling Green State University (Ohio) *148*–149, 173, 198, 219
Braves Field (Boston, Massachusetts) 35
Briggs Stadium (Detroit, Michigan) 156, *191*
Brooklyn Dodgers (All-America Football Conference) 194
Brooklyn Dodgers/Tigers (National Football League) 10, 17, 20, 40, 41, 56, *59*, 61, 96, 112, 115, 121, *150*, 175
Brooklyn/Los Angeles Dodgers (Major League Baseball) 13, 194
Brooklyn/Rochester Tigers (American Football League) 35
Brown, Paul 25, 101–*102*, 123, 143, 160, 173, 181, 183, 194, 196–198, 200
Bruch, Edward P. *63*–64, 90–91, 97–98
Brumbaugh, Carl 50, 52, 57, 71
Buffalo, New York 21, 41, 84, 90, 112, 218
Buffalo All-Americans (American Professional Football Association) *18*
Buffalo Bills (All-America Football Conference) 217
Burton, Harold H. 29, 54, 82; Trophy 82–83
Buruma, Ian 142
Butkovich, Tony 119

Caddell, Ernie 56
Calgary Stampeders (Canadian Football League) 221
California, Rams' first game in 73
California Eagle 188
Camden, New Jersey 96
Canadian Football League 221
Canisius College 123, 218
Canton, Ohio 10, 15, 17, 19, 145, 180

Canton Bulldogs (American Professional Football Association/National Football League) *18*, 19, 168, 182
"Card-Pitts" (merged Chicago Cardinals/Pittsburgh Steelers team) 118, 125, *126*, 128, 146
Carnegie Tech 125
Carr, Joe F. 17, 19–20, 33, 38–43, 53, 58, 64, 85; Trophy for league most valuable player 78, 83, 111, 113, 128, 174, 208, 224
Carroon (Reeves), Mary *94*, 95, 153–154, 191–192; *see also* Reeves, Daniel F.
Case School of Applied Science 64
Central Armory 164
Chagrin Valley Hunt Club 22
Champaign, Illinois 130
Cherundolo, Chuck 60, 79, 113
Chicago, Illinois 20, 23, 42, 46, 53, 114, 124–125, 127, 145, 155, 180, 199
Chicago Bears (National Football League) 7, 15–16, 19, 21, 27, 39–40, 50, 52, 57–58, *59*, 60, 62, 71–73, 76–77, 82, 85–86, 90, 97, 101, 103–104, 109–110, 112–116, 126–127, 134, 136, 143, 149–*150*, 151–152, 156–157, 160, 162, 179, 188, 193, 201, 205, 218, 221, 223
Chicago Cardinals Quarterback Club 155
Chicago Hornets (All-America Football Conference) 201
Chicago Rockets (All-America Football Conference) 145, 182
Chicago/St. Louis/Arizona Cardinals (National Football League) 13, 17, *18*, 29, 40, 49, 53, 56–57, *59*, 62, 65, 68, 73, 85, 90, 103, 105, 110, 112, 118, 125, *126*, 149–*150*, 151, 155, 180, 220, 222
Chicago Tigers (American Professional Football Association) *18*
Chicago Tribune 4, 49, 57, 69, 124, 143–144, 201
Chillicothe, Ohio 21
Cincinnati, Ohio 7, 20, 91, 96, 115, 173; contingency plan to move Rams to 181, 187
Cincinnati Bengals (American Football League/independent) 53, 221
Cincinnati Reds (Major League Baseball) 91
Cincinnati Reds (National Football League) 40, 91, 110
City Stadium (Green Bay, Wisconsin) 57, *191*
Clark, Earl "Dutch" 13, 55, 58, 61, 70–72, 76–*79*, 81–82, 85–86, 88, 101, 103–104, 106–*107*, 109–110, 113, 119, 125, 129, 145, 152, 160, 194–195, 203, 218–219, 221, 223; hiring as Rams coach 75, iconic image 74–75, 100, 102; resignation from Rams 114
Clarke's, P.J. (New York City) 96, 193
Cleveland, Ohio 1–25, 30–31, 36, 38–39, 42, 49–50, 53–55, 64, 66, 68, 74, 76, 83–85, 88, 90, 92, 94, 96, 98–100, 104–106, 115, 117–118, 121, 123–125, 127–129, 140, 142, 144–146, 149–150, 153–154, 156–158, 162–164, 166, 171, 173, 176–188, 190–*192*, 193–210, 212–215, 217, 220, 223; business community 22–23, 214,

221; description of, 1930s 31–32; efforts to keep the Rams 91–92, 104, 128; first pro football playoff game 166; "sleeping giant" for pro football 158, 201; sports 6, 19
Cleveland Advertising Club 91
Cleveland Arena 41
Cleveland Athletic Club 81
Cleveland Barons (American Hockey League) 62, 91
Cleveland Browns (All-America Football Conference/National Football League) 2, 3, 10–*11*, 12–14, 23–25, 34, 41, 64, 68, 74, 78, 85, 98, 115, 117, 123, 125, 128, 142–143, 145–146, 148, 151, 157–158, 160, 162, 166, 169, 175–177, 179, 181–184, 187, *191*, 193–194, 196–198, 200–203, *205*, 213–214, 217–223; admittance to the National Football League 201–203; attendance 200–201; debut in All-America Football Conference 200–201; role in the Rams leaving Cleveland 10, 125, 179, 182, 202; versus Rams in 1950 NFL championship game 203, 205–207; versus Rams in 1951 NFL championship game 207–208; versus Rams in 1955 NFL championship game 208
Cleveland Buckeyes (Negro League baseball) 184
Cleveland Bulldogs (National Football League) 6, 9, 19–20, 101, 183–184
Cleveland Cavaliers (National Basketball Association) 41
Cleveland Chamber of Commerce 91–92, 184
Cleveland Convention and Visitors Bureau 91
Cleveland Indians (Major League Baseball) 15, 24–26, 28, 50, 68, 114, 157
Cleveland Indians (National Football League) 6, 19–20, 43, 182–183
Cleveland Municipal Stadium 4, 16, 20, 43, 50, 54–55, 63, 65, 70, 82–83, 85, 96, 98, 103–105, 112–113, 125, 144, 150, 153–154, 157, 160, *164*–166, 168, 170–*174*, 175–176, 179, 185–186, *191*, 195, 200, 202, 205–207; description 2, 6, *11*, 76–77, 162; inadequacy for football 77, 100, 126; straw insulation for the 1945 NFL championship game 162–163
Cleveland News 23, 69, 101, 124, 151, 177, 186, 202
Cleveland Panthers (American Football League) 19–20, 143
Cleveland Plain Dealer 3, 4, 12, 15, 20, 23–26, 28, 31, 33, 37, 52, 54–55, 62, 69, 72, 82–84, 91, 97, 99–101, 104, 111, 113, 115, 117, 119, 126, 128, 130, 143–144, 158, 166, 176–177, 182–183, 185–187, 197, 199–200, 203
Cleveland Press 5, 9, 50, 64, 69, 75, 96, 103, 105, 121–123, 139, 152, 166, 177, 183, 186–187, 201, 210
Cleveland Skeletons (semi-pro football) 20–21
Cleveland South High School 29–30
Cleveland Spiders (Major League Baseball) 140
Cleveland State University 5

Cleveland Tigers (American Professional Football Association) 6, 18, 20, 183
Cleveland Touchdown Club 110
Clowser, Jack 9, 186
Cobb, Ty 28
Cobbledick, Gordon 4, 15, 62, 84–85, 104, 113, 115, 119, 183, 185
Coenen, Craig R. 5, 181
Colella, Tommy 13, *122*–123, 126–128, 146–147, 151–152, 197, 201, 218
College All-Stars 52, 199
College Football Hall of Fame 217, 223
Collins, Bud 79
Collins, Ted 115
Colorado College 77
Colorado Springs, Colorado 83, 113, 129
Columbia University 123, 218
Columbus, Ohio 16–18, 21, 39, 42, 103
Columbus Bullies 81
Columbus Panhandles (American Professional Football Association) *18*, 39
Come-to-Cleveland Committee 91
Comiskey Park (Chicago, Illinois) 57, 73, 128, 155, *191*
Commodore Hotel (New York City) 179, 213
Compton Junior College (Compton, California) 196
Conkright, Bill "Red" 13, 77, 85, 104, 115, 121, *122*–123, 197–198, 218
Cooper, Bill *31*, 52–53, 60
Corcoran, Jerry 20
Cordill, Olie 85–86, 103
Cornell University 49
Cotton Bowl (Dallas, Texas) 180
County Stadium (Green Bay, Wisconsin) 152
Crosby, Bing 32, 74, 131
Crosley, Powel, Jr. 91

Daley, Arthur J. 69, 188
Dallas, Texas 180
Davis, Al 218
Davis, Bob 71
Davis, Corbett "Corby" 61, 65, 67–68, 71, 73–74, 76, 85, 103, 108, 112
Davis, Glenn 206
Day, Luther 198–199
Dayton, Ohio 10, 111
Dayton Triangles (American Professional Football Association) *18*
Debut, Rams' American Football League 26–30; National Football League 54–56, 82, 100, 164
Decatur Staleys (American Professional Football Association) *18*
DeGroot, Dudley 168
Delauer, Bob 173, 200
Dempsey, Jack 157
Denison College 33
Denver Broncos (National Football League) 135, 219
Des Moines, Iowa 110

Detroit, Michigan 20, 54, 111, 127, 149, 158
Detroit Heralds (American Professional Football Association) 18
Detroit Lions (National Football League 12, 22, 40, 54–56, 58, *59*, 61–62, 65, 70–71, 73–77, 79, 82–83, 85–86, 89, 103, 111, 113–115, 119, 121, 123, 126, 128–129, 137, 143, 147, 149, *150*, 153–154, 156, 158, 218–219, 221
Detroit News 74
Detroit Stadium, University of Detroit 77
Deutsch, Sam 20
Dietrich, John 3, 31, 33, 35, 52, 54–57, 72, 84–85, 101, 115, 126–128, 144, 147, 149, 154–156, 158, 176, 183, 185–186; collapse of temporary bleachers at League Park as "decisive blunder" 154; "public be damned" accusation 185; recommendation to hire Paul Brown 143; role in naming Rams 25
dinner, testimonial for 1945 Rams 11, 158, 160, 163, 198; program *159*
Dippery, Leroy (Tiny) 127, 152, 156
Donelli, Aldo "Buff" 123, 127–130, 143, 145–146, 160, 195, 203, 218; coached college and NFL teams simultaneously 120; induction into the Navy 129; soccer career 120–121, 218
Donelli, Allen 120
Downes, Bill 171
"Downtown Coaches" (Rams' founding investors) 10, 63–64, 66–71, 72, 74, 81–82, 84–85, 89–92, 98, 101, 126, 194, 202, 214
Doyle, James E. 12, 37, 176, 182, 186, 199
Doylestown, Pennsylvania 49, 70
Drake, Johnny 41, 43, 56, 58, 60–62, 65, 67, 70, 73, 76, 79, 82, 85–86, 88, 103, 111, 113, 139, 195, 218; first Rams player to score an NFL touchdown 56, 218
dress code, Rams' 52, 82
Duke University 41
Dumont Television Network 207
Duquesne University 120–121, 123
Dye, Les 170–171
Dyer, Braven 186

Earhart, Amelia 32
Eason, Roger 208
East Cleveland, Ohio 56, 76
Eastern Division (National Football League) 97, 156, 157
Ebbets Field (Brooklyn, New York) 17, 56, 112
Eisenhower, Dwight D. 157, 174
Eisner, Mannie 68, *107*
Elmira, New York 131
Elway, John 13, 135
English Football League 120
entertainment industry, Rams' involvement with 13, 195, 205
equipment, football: cost to equip a team (1941) 101; mandatory helmets 115; 1940s *108*; 1930s 27
Euclid Beach Park 108
Evans, Billy 99–100, 109

Fawcett, Jake 121, *122*
Fears, Tom 9, 145–146, 207
Feller, Bob 6, 28, 86, 99, 114, 160
Fenway Park (Boston, Massachusetts) 29, *191*, 199
Field, Harry Nuuanu 17
Filchock, Frank 12, 168, 170–172
financial losses, Rams': in Cleveland (1936) 34, 37–38; in Cleveland (1937) 59; in Cleveland (1937–1939) 84; in Cleveland (1941) 104; in Cleveland (1941–1944) 117; in Cleveland (1941–1945) 193; in Cleveland (1945) 9, 160, 178; in Los Angeles (late 1940s) 193, 201, 210
Firestone, Leonard *80*, 81, 210
First NFL home victory, Rams' 70–71, 77
First NFL points at home, Rams' 57
First NFL regular-season game in the West, Rams' 83
First NFL touchdown, Rams' 56, 223
First NFL victory, Rams' 56
Fogg, Joseph G. 64
Football Digest 209
Forbes Field (Pittsburgh, Pennsylvania) 16, 36, *126*, *191*
Ford, Gerald 16, 35
Fordham University 25, 123
Fort Benning, Georgia 138, *139–140*
"Four Horsemen" 92, 125, 144, 223; *see also* University of Notre Dame
Fraley, Oscar 154
Freed, Emerich B. (U.S. federal judge) 198–199, 202
Friedman, Benny 20, 101, 139
From Sandlots to the Super Bowl 5, 181
Frontiere, Georgia 212–213

Gable, Clark 209
Gabriel, Roman 209
Gardner, Ava 137–138
Gehrig, Lou 28
Gehrke, Fred 7–*8*, 13, 86–88, 123, 146–149, 154, 156, 158, *159*, 170–171, 175–176, 197, 199, 208, 218–219; Daniel F. Reeves Pioneer Award 12, 219; design of Rams' helmets 13, 87, 204–206, 219, 223
General Electric/NELA Park (East Cleveland, Ohio) 65
Georgetown University 10, 74, 95
Georgia Tech 49
Gibbs, Ronald 168
Gibson, Joe 115, 121
Gillette, Jim 7, *8*, *87*–88, 123, 127–128, 141, 146–*148*, 151, 157–158, *159*, 160, 169–*174*, 175–176, 184, 199, 219; service in World War II *87*, 109; statistics in 1945 NFL championship game 173
Gillette, Marguerite 5, 88, 109, 123, 141, 157, 160, 175, 184
Gillette, Walker 3, 5, *87*, 109, 162, 219
Gillman, Sid 13, 21, 27, 30, 33, 35, 38, 53, 160,

207–209, 219, 221; Rams franchise's first touchdown (American Football League) 30, 219
Gilmore Stadium (Los Angeles, California) 73, 187
Glenville (Cleveland neighborhood) 53, 139
Goddard, Ed 67
Goldstein, Herman 151, 186
Graham, Otto 119, 143, 199, 206, 208, 222
Graney, Jack 28
Grange, Red 16, 19, 52, 188
"Greatest Show on Turf" 212
Green Bay, Wisconsin 19, 22, 127, 152
Green Bay Packers (National Football League) 7, 17, 27, 30, 40, 50, 53, 57, **59**, 60–61, 67, 73, 77, 81–83, 86, 88, 97, 103, 111–115, 127–128, 149, **150**, 152, 154–156, 158, 160, 193, 201, 217–220, 222, 224
Greenwood, Don 7, **8**, 13, 130, 146–147, 152, 154, 158, 165, 171, 176, 197, 199, 201, 219
Gries, Robert D. (Bob) 3, 5, 24, 34, 220
Gries, Robert H. 13, 24, **34**, 41, 64, 97–98, 125, 145, 220
Griffith Stadium (Washington, D.C.) 69, 127, 157, **191**
Groza, Lou 200, 206
Grygo, Al 127
Guardian Building 43
Guy, Dick 36

Hadden, John A. 23
Halas, George 15–18, 39, 42, 72, 112, 179, 181
Hall, Parker "Bullet" 74, 76, 78–79, 82–83, 85–87, 102, 112–113, 139, 195, 220; first National Football League passer to complete more than 100 passes in a season 83; Joe F. Carr Trophy (league most valuable player) 78, 83, 86, 111, 220
Hamilton, Ray 71, 208
Hammond Pros (American Professional Football Association) **18**
Hanley, Dick 49
Hanna, Daniel (Dan) Rhodes, Jr. 23, 27, 38, 43, 99, 124
Hanna, Daniel Rhodes, Sr. 23
Hanna, Marcus A. 23
Harding, Halley 188, 190
Harding, Roger 171
Hardy, Jim 200
Harlem Globetrotters 190
Harmon, Tom 101
Hartland Street 131, **133**; *see also* Van Nuys, California
Harvard University 22, 144
Hastings, Nebraska 108
Hay, Ralph 18
Hayden, John A. 64
Heisman Trophy 45, 137
Henderson, Elmer (Gloomy Gus) 47
Hickey, Howard "Red" 13, 106, 111, 147, 172, 205–206, 208, 220

Hiemstra, Ed **108**
Hightower, Ben 112, 115
Hill, Herman 188, 190–191
Hinkle, Clarke 57–58
Hiram College 124
Hirsch, Elroy "Crazylegs" 9, 145–146, 199, 207
Hoffman, Bob 200
Hollenden Hotel 18
Holliday, Billie 32
Hollywood, California 105, 110, 131, 134, 144, 148, 153, 223
Hollywood Bears (Pacific Coast Football League) 190
Hope, Bob 103, 210
Horrell, Edwin "Babe" 134–135
Horrigan, Joe 5, 12, 20, 62, 92, 142, 180, 183, 187, 194, 204
Hotel Alexandria (Los Angeles) 196
Hotel Carter 160
Hotel Cleveland 100, 175
Hotel St. Regis 140, 153
Houston, Texas 42
Houston Oilers (National Football League) 219
Hoyt, Elton, II 81
Hutson, Don 16, 57, 61, 67, 74, 77, 81, 83, 86, 113, 128–129, 152, 155, 156, 158, 217, 220

Incorporation as a business, Rams' 41
Indiana University 52, 61
Indianapolis, Indiana 212
inequity in regular-season game scheduling for Rams 118, 124, 129, 149, **150**, 176, 185, 201
Inglewood, California **214**
Irsay, Robert 211–212
Irvine, California 3

Jackson, "Shoeless" Joe 28
Jackson, Ohio 22
Jacobs, "Indian" Jack 111–112, 147
Jersey City Giants (American Football Association) 100
Jessup, Roger 191
Johnson, Robert 32
Johnsos, Luke 143
Jones, Deacon 209
Jones, Edgar "Special Delivery" 200
Jones, Gomer 21, 29, 53, 90, 220
Jones, Day, Cockley & Reavis (Cleveland law firm) 198

Kabealo, Mike **122**
Karrs, John **122**
Kebble, Joe 56
Keeshin, John 182
Kelley, Bob 55
Kenosha Cardinals (semi-pro football) 88
Kezar Stadium (San Francisco, California) 138
Kieran, John 57–58
Kinard, Frank 62

Index

King, Joe 154
Kirtland Country Club (Kirtland, Ohio) 22, 82, 89
KNBH-TV (Los Angeles) 207
Koch, George *159*, 160
Konetsky, Floyd *122*, 147, 156, 169
Kovatch, Johnny 71
Kroenke, E. Stanley 1, 2, 213
Kuenzel, William 74–75

L.A. Rams Football Club: 1946 Guide for Press and Radio 12, 196
Lahr, Warren 206
Lake Erie College (Painesville, Ohio) 51, 54
Lambeau, Earl "Curly" 57
Landreth, Orian 64
LaSalle Hotel (Chicago, Illinois) 72
Lavelli, Dante 206
Layden, Elmer 92, 101–*102*, 117–118, 120, 144, 160, 175
Lazetich, Bill 108, 146, 221
Lazetich, Milan "Mike" 7–*8*, 146–147, 170, 176, 199, 205–206, 208, 220
Lazetich, Pete 146, 221
League Park 10, 16, 26, 28, 33, 35, 37, 46, 54–58, 65, 71–73, 76, 126, 128–129, 144, 150–151, 153–154, 157–158, 176, 179, 185, 187, *191*, 195, 212; collapse of temporary bleachers 154–155, 186; Daniel F. Reeves' proposed expansion 173; description *28*–29; Rams' last game 157
Leahy, Frank 143, 146
Lebovitz, Hal 4, 184
legal action to force move of Cleveland players to Los Angeles 196–199, 217, 222–223
Levy, Fred, Jr. 99–101, 106, 111–113, 115–116, 210; purchase of Rams with Daniel Reeves 97–98, 222; role in Rams' move to Los Angeles 96–97, 181, 187
Lewis, Art "Pappy" 65–67, 69–73, 75–76, 78–*79*, 81, 88, 103, 105, 110, 114, 120, 126, 194, 203, 221
Lewis, Franklin 4, 96, 103, 105, 139, 166, 183, 185–187, 201, 210
LIFE magazine 74, 153
Liles, Sonny 173
Lipscomb, Thomas E. 41, 64–66, 68–69, 74–75, 78, 79, 81–82, 97–99, 160, 198–199
Little Rock, Arkansas 124
Littlefield, Carl "Moon Eyes" 72
Livingston, Ted 79, 85–86
Logos, early Rams logo 43–*44*
Lombardi, Vince 25
Lorain, Ohio 30, 123, 172
Los Angeles, California 1–5, 7, 9–10, 14, 18, 21, 25, 41–42, 48, 73, 84, 90, 95, 97–98, 101, 116, 125, 131, 134, 138, 143, 145, 154, 164, 175, 177–181, 183–184, 186–188, 190–*192*, 193–204, 207–*214*, 215, 219–220, 222–223; distance from rest of National Football League 9, 84, 178–182, 188, 195, 198

Los Angeles Angels 210
Los Angeles Buccaneers (National Football League) 41
Los Angeles Bulldogs (American Football League) 58
Los Angeles Bulldogs (Pacific Coast Football League, independent) 73, 124
Los Angeles Coliseum Commission 188, *189*, 191
Los Angeles Dons (All-America Football Conference) 179, 181, 201, 205
Los Angeles Forum *214*
Los Angeles Memorial Coliseum 2, 9, 12, 95, 135, 137, 179, *189*–190, *191*, 192, 199–200, 205, 207–208, 211–212, *214*, 223; exclusion of pro football 188; Rams' negotiation to secure use 188–191, 223
Los Angeles Raiders (National Football League) 212
Los Angeles Sentinel 188
Los Angeles Times 4, 135, 186, 209, 212–213
Los Angeles Tribune 188
Louis, Joe 32
Louisiana State University 46
Louisville, Kentucky 96
Luckman, Sid 77, 116, 127, 134, 152, 223
Luna Park 20

Magnani, Dante 14, 85, 102, 112–113, 115–116, 208
Major League Baseball 45–46, 50, 84, 97, 114, 124, 194, 217
Mara, Timothy 20, 39, 179, 181
Mara, Wellington 112
March Field Fliers (military football team) 111
Marienthal, Mike 137
Marshall, George Preston 42, 91, 95, 97, 168–169, 179, 181
Marshman, Homer H. 21–25, 27–28, 34–38, 40–43, 45, 49–50, 52–53, 57–62, 64–65, 67–69, *80*, 99–100, 120, 145, 202, 221; cofounder of the Rams 24–25, 221; minority owner of the Cleveland Browns 98, 221; sale of Rams to Daniel F. Reeves 98–99, 221; *see also* Wetzel, Damon "Buzz"
Martin, Dean 192
Massillon, Ohio 17
Masterson, Bernie 134–135
Matheson, Riley "Rattlesnake" 7–*8*, 78–79, 81, 88, 103, 112–115, 121, *122*, 126–127, 129, 146–148, 157–158, 169, 171, 175, 199, 208, 218, 221
Mattos, Harry "Horse" 30–*31*, 35, 52–53, 56, 60, 135
May, Jack 73
May Company department store 24, 34, 36, 220
McAuley, Ed 186
McBride, Arthur B. "Mickey" 23, 25, 85, 98, 124–125, 143, 145, 176, 179, 196, 198, 201, 220; offer to buy Rams from Daniel F. Reeves 85, 115, 125, 202

McCann, Dick 166, 175, 180
McCooey, John H. 95
McDonald, Don 153
McIntosh, Gregory 64
Memphis, Tennessee 220
Memphis *Commercial Appeal* 78
Miami, Florida 84, 112, 175, 180
Miami Dolphins (National Football League) 222
Miami Seahawks (All-America Football Conference) 200
Miami University (Ohio) 160
Middleport, Ohio 65
Miller, Charles "Ookie" 52
Miller, Creighton 125
Miller, Don 125
"Millionaire's Row" 33, 64
Millner, Wayne 169–170
Milwaukee, Wisconsin 96, 193
Modell, Art 1, 2, 12, 24, 34, 64, 125, 183, 220–221
monetary value of Rams franchise 98, 101, 211, 213–214, 222
Montreal, Quebec 194
Motley, Marion 194
move to L.A.: Cleveland Browns' role 202–203; Cleveland Rams 3, 9–11, 13, 41, 178–179, 181–187, 192–193, 195, 200, 200–203, 208, *214*, 222–223; NFL owners' initial opposition to 178–180; reaction in Cleveland 181–187, 203
Mucha, Rudy 90, 103, 111, 147
Muhlenberg College 49
Muncie Flyers (American Professional Football Association) *18*
Murphy, Raymond "Fido" 134
Murray, Jim 135, 193, 212
Muscle Beach 133; *see also* Santa Monica, California

Nagurski, Bronko 16, 39, 52, 57, 61, 108–109
naming as Rams 25
Nashville, Tennessee 64
National Agricultural College 70, 218
National Basketball Association 41
National Football League 1, 6–14, 15, 17–18, 26, 29–30, 32–33, 38–45, 47, 50–51, 53–56, 58, 60–62, 64, 67–68, 70, 73–77, 81, 83–87, 89–92, 95, 97–100, 103–106, 110, 112–114, 117, 119, 125, 128–130, 139, 142–145, 147, 149, 154, 156, 158, 160, 162, 169, 172–176, 179, 181–183, 185–186, 188, 193–194, 199, 201, 203, 210–215, 217–223; ban of African Americans 32–33, 188, 190–191, 196; championship games 2, 4, 6–7, *11*, 16, 35, 37, 40, 68, *87*, 90, 109, 113, 116, 123, 127, *133*, 136, 145, 156–157, 160, *174*, 177, 182, 187, 196–197, 199, 203, *205*–208; dominance by the "big four" teams 7, 13, 50, 59, 60; early instability 19–20; first fully designed helmets 204; first NFL game in New Orleans 73; first team to exceed 1 million in season attendance 210; first televised game 84; founding franchises *18*; inequity in regular-season game scheduling *150*; insularity of early owners 21, 23, 124, 180; league records set in 1945 championship game 175; 1945 championship game 162–*165*, 166–*167*, 168–176; 1-million-plus attendance for the first time 84; owners' opposition to the Rams' move to Los Angeles 178–180; program, 1945 NFL championship game *167*; Rams' admittance 42–43; Rams' debut 54–56, 82, 100, 164; Rams' first touchdown 56; Rams' first victory 56; reintegration by African American players 13, *189*, 191, 193–194; stadium capacities (1945-1946) *191*; westward movement 12, 194; World War II impact on rosters 108–112, *126*
National League (baseball) 46, 124
Negro League (baseball) 184
Nemeth, Steve *159*
Ness, Eliot 32
Nevers, Ernie 49
New Orleans, Louisiana 73
New York Bulldogs (National Football League) 222; *see also* Boston Yanks
New York City 9–10, 18–20, 40–41, 54, 73, 94, 96, 123, 145, 158, 177, 179, 188, 191–193, 211, 213, 220, 222
New York Daily News 154
New York Giants (National Football League) 7, 10, 20, 27, 35, 40, 50, *59*, 60, 73, 84, 86, 97, 104, *108*, 112, 115, 122, 129, *150*–151, 153–154, 156–157, 160, 179, 185, 203, 222
New York/San Francisco Giants (Major League Baseball) 13, 194
New York Times 4, 11, 14, 17, 57–58, 69, 97, 103, 172, 182, 188
New York World Telegram and Sun 154
New York Yankees (All-America Football Conference) 181, 201
New York Yankees (American Football League) 26–27, 33–35, 37
New York Yankees (Major League Baseball) 175
New York Yanks (National Football League) 217
Newman, Harry 35
Newspaper Enterprise Service 72
newspaper strike in Cleveland 4, 12, 177–178, 181, 183, 185; effect on fans' reaction to Rams' move 182–184
newspapers, influence of 4, 183–184
Norfolk Virginian-Pilot 152
Northwestern University 49

Oakland, California 212
Oakland Raiders (American Football League) 218
Oates, Bob 18
O'Brien, Davey 86
Ohio College All-Stars 76

Index

The Ohio State University 14–16, 21, 25, 27, 29–30, 33, 60, 102, 143, 184, 200, 214, 219–222
Ohio University 22, 65, 74, 147
O'Keefe, Declan 35
Olsen, Merlin 209
107th Cavalry Armory (Shaker Heights, Ohio) 164
O'Neill, Bill 52, 56
O'Neill, Steve 24
Oregon State University 136–137
O'Shea, Michael 134
Otis, Sam 100, 104, 115, 128, 187
Owens, Jesse 32

Pacific Coast Football League 124, 190
Padlow, Max 21, 35, 53–54, 221
Paige, Satchel 190
Painesville, Ohio 51
Palm Beach, Florida 21, 96, 221
Parker, Clarence "Ace" 41
Parkersburg, West Virginia 66
Pasadena, California 137
Pasqua, Joe 115
Pauley, Ed 210
Pegler, Westbrook 49
Pennsylvania State University 47–49, 54, 60, 66
Philadelphia, Pennsylvania 18, 90, 118, 153, 158, 180
Philadelphia Athletics 50
Philadelphia Eagles (National Football League) 10, 17, 21, 40–41, 49, 53, 56–57, *59*, 61, 83, 85, 89–90, 95, 111–112, 114, 117, 119–120, 129, 146, *150*–151, 153, 180, 199, 201, 205
Philadelphia Phillies (Major League Baseball) 48
Photo Developing Co. 96
Pincura, Stan 30, 52–53, 57, 60, 70–71, 73, 184; Rams franchise's first touchdown pass (American Football League) 30
Pittsburgh, Pennsylvania 16, 36, 90, 120, 126, 143
Pittsburgh Americans (American Football League) 26–27, 34, 36, 52, 147
Pittsburgh Courier 188
Pittsburgh Pirates (Major League Baseball) 46–47, 52
Pittsburgh Pirates/Steelers (National Football League) 10, 16–17, 40–41, *59*, 61, 73, 89, 91, 95, 97–98, 101–*102*, 103, 114, 117, 120–121, 129, 146, 149–*150*, 184, 202; near-merger with Rams 117–118, *126*, 184
Pittsburgh Post-Gazette 89
Plessy v. Ferguson 188
Plunkett, Warren *108*, 110–111
Pollard, Frederick Douglass "Fritz" 18, 190
Polo Grounds (New York City) 10, 86, 153, 162, *191*
Portsmouth, Ohio 22, 77
Portsmouth Spartans (National Football League) 20, 22, 75, 77, 114, 218; *see also* Detroit Lions
Prell, Edward 201
press pin, Rams—1945 championship game *165*
Pritko, Steve *8*, 115, *122*–123, 126–127, 146, *148*, 151–152, 156, 158, 170, 175–176, 199, 208, 222
pro football: attainment of college degrees among players 45; increasing popularity 33, 39, 59, 84, 98, 104, 109, 187–188, 201–202, 211, 214; low pay for players 43, 110, 123, 139; negative early reputation of players 19, 21
Pro Football Archives 5
Pro Football Hall of Fame 5, 12, 13, 15, 20, 30, 40, 53, 63, 77, 92, 95, 119, 142, 160, 180, 193, 204, 218–219, 222–223; Daniel F. Reeves Pioneer Award 12, 219
Pro Football Illustrated 158
Pro Football Reference 5
Professional Football Researchers Association 5
Providence, Rhode Island 20
Providence Steam Roller 20
Pueblo, Colorado 74
Purdue University 41, 52–53, 119
Pyle, C.C. ("Cash and Carry") 19

Ram Rumblings (team newsletter) 99–101
Rams' 80-Piece All-American Band 82
Rathbone, Basil 192
Reeves, Dan, Jr. 3, 5, 92, 95, 116, 180–181, 210–*211*, 222
Reeves, Daniel (brother) 94
Reeves, Daniel F. 2, 8, 9–13, 20, 41, 74, *80*, 92, *93*–*94*, 97, 99–*102*, 104, 106–*107*, 109–110, 112–117, 125–126, 128–129, 135, 139, 143–145, 151, 153–156, 160, 164, 172–173, 176–183, 185–188, 191–*192*, 194, 196–199, 201–204, 207–210, *211*, 213–214, 217, 219, 222–223; denial the Rams would leave Cleveland 178, 183–185; description 95–96; failed attempts to buy the Philadelphia Eagles and the Pittsburgh Steelers 10, 95; Los Angeles lifestyle 192–193; Pioneer Award 12, 219; purchase of Rams franchise *93*, 97–98, 220–221; sale of Rams franchise by family 211
Reeves, Daniel, Inc. *93*, 94–95
Reeves, Edward 95, 179
Reeves, James A. 92, 94, 211
Reeves Ranch Vineyard *211*
Reisz, Albie 123, 127, 146, 151, 172, 197, 206
Rice, Jerry 222
Rice University 85
Richards, George A. 74, 79
Rickey, Branch 22, 194
Riffle, Chuck *122*
Roach, Leonard 190
Robb, Harry 168
Robinson, Abie 188, 190
Robinson, Jackie 13, 136, 194

Index

Rochester, New York 26
Rochester Jeffersons (American Professional Football Association) *18*
Rock Island Independents (American Professional Football League) *18*
Rockne, Knute 110, 223
Rome, New York 144
Rooney, Art 16, 39, 41, 61, 73, 89–90, 97–98, 114, 118, 120, 202
Rooney, Mickey 137–138
Rose Bowl 46–48, 97, 136–139, 144
Rosenbloom, Carroll 212
Rosequist, Ted 52
Roseville, Ohio 15
Rozelle, Pete 210
rumors the Rams might leave Cleveland 7, 9, 85, 115, 143–145, 177–178, 182, 184, 187, 202, 223
Run to Glory and Profits 201
Russ-Field Productions 209
Russell, Jane 2, *8*, 132–*133*, 135–140, 151, 153–154, 160, 174, 179, 208; in Georgia 138–*139*; marriage to Bob Waterfield 119, 138, 209, 223; notoriety from Howard Hughes movie *The Outlaw* 138
Ruth, Babe 28–29, 77
Ruthstrom, Ralph 157
Ryan, Ellis W. 24, 64

Sadosky, Len 30
Safeway Stores *93*, 95
St. Louis, Missouri 1–3, 14, 96, 125, 180, 212–213
St. Louis Gunners 40, 91, 110
St. Louis University 10
St. Mary's College 85, 120
sale of Rams to Daniel F. Reeves 97–99, 101, 221
San Diego Chargers (American Football League/National Football League) 146, 162, 219, 221
San Fernando Valley, California 131, 208
San Francisco, California 10, 84, 138, 180, 194
San Francisco 49ers (All-America Football Conference) 112, 178–179, 181, 201, 203, 220, 221
San Francisco 49ers (National Football League) 220–211, 219
Santa Barbara, California *211*
Santa Clara University 136, 144
Santa Monica, California 133
Scarry, Mike "Mo" 7–*8*, 13, *122*–123, 146, 158, 166, 168, 176, 197, 199, 218, 222; first-ever televised football game 123, 222
scheduling, unbalanced game *150*; see also National Football League
Schmidt, Francis 16, 27
Schramm, Tex 210
Schultz, Eberle "Elbie" *8*, 146–147, 169, 176, 199, 208
Seattle Bombers (American Football League) 218

Sebastian, Mike *31*, 35
Second Air Force Bombers (Pacific Coast Service Football League) 103
Seley, Hal 210
Seymour, Bob 171
Shaker Heights, Ohio 164
Shaughnessy, Clark 136, 145, 204
Shaw, Bob 222
Shaw Stadium 65, *66*, 68, 70–71, 74, 76–77, 195
Sher, Jack 208
Sherby, Dan 145, 182
Sherman Oaks, California *133*, 208
Shibe Park (Philadelphia, Pennsylvania) 129, 153, *191*
Shula, Don 222
Sillcox, Scott 67
Sinkwich, Frankie 123, 126–128, 137
Skinner, Chads O. 82, 166
Smilanich, Bronko 63–64, 90
Smith, Alfred E. 94
Smith, Gaylon 13, 74, 78–79, 103, 106, *108*, 111–112, 197–199, 201, 222–223
Snelling, Ken 137
Snyder, Bob *8*, 13, 52, 56, 60, 65, 67, 70, 72–73, 77, 79, 116, 148–149, 151, 156, 176, 193, 199, 204, 223; first Ram to throw an NFL touchdown pass 56, 223; role in creation of Rams' designed helmets 204, 223
Soldier Field (Chicago, Illinois) 199
South Bend, Indiana 143
Southwestern University 74
Southworth, Billy 47
Spadaccini, Vic 83, 86, 102–103, 111
SPORT magazine 208
Sporting News 7, 8
Stagg, Amos Alonzo 46
Staley, A.E., Manufacturing Co. 17
Standard Oil Company 140
Stanford University 136
State College, Pennsylvania 50
State Fair Park (Milwaukee) *191*
Staten Island, New York 20
Statler Hotel (Detroit, Michigan) 156
"Steagles" (merged Pittsburgh Steelers/Philadelphia Eagles team) 114, 118, 146
Stengel, Casey 47
Street and Smith's Football Year Book 142
Strickler, George 9, 57, 69
Strode, Woody 111, 190, 193–194, 200
Stuart, Roy 115
Stydahar, Joe 206
Sulecki, Chester 171
Sulecki, Jerry 5, 169
Super Bowl 124, 184, 208–209, 212
Surdam, David George 201
suspension of Rams operations (1943): dispersal draft 115, 122, 222; World War II 114–116, 120, 180, 202, 217, 222; *see also* World War II

Sutphin, Albert C. "Al" 41, 62, 64, 91
Sweeney, Bill 27
Swifty, Jr. (mascot) 164
Swifty the Ram (mascot) 51, 56
Syracuse, New York 114
Syracuse/Rochester Braves 26–28, 30, 33, 55

T-formation offense 90, 103, 110–111, 121, 130, 134–137, 142, 145–148, 173, 218, 220
Tana, Dan 193
Telenews Theater 95
televised NFL games, Rams' early role in 205–207
Texas Christian University 137
Texas School of Mines 78
Thompson, Alexis 89–90, 112
Thompson, Hine & Flory (Cleveland law firm) 64, 198
Thompson Products 147
Thorpe, Jim 19
Thurlow, Paul 22–24, 35–38, 43
Times-Herald (Washington, D.C.) 166
Toledo, Ohio 42
Topping, Dan 10, 96, 112, 175, 181
Trafton, George *8*, 147, 199
Trippi, Charley 137
Trosky, Hal 99
Tulane Stadium (New Orleans, Louisiana) 73
Tunney, Gene 68
Turley, Doug 169
Tyler, Ed 137–138

uniforms, Rams' 13, 27, 55, 67, 81, 86, 87, 102, 149, 168, 204–*205*, 206–207, 219, 223
Union Club 38, 43, 64, 69, 89
Union Commerce Building 25, 100, 106–*107*
Union Station (Cleveland) 157
United Press (International) 58, 63, 154
United States District Court 196, 198
United States Employment Service 164
Universal Stadium (Portsmouth, Ohio) 77
University of Alabama 16
University of Arizona 63, 90
University of Arkansas 46, 61
University of California–Berkeley 136–137
University of California–Davis 49
University of California–Los Angeles 119, 130, *133*–138, *139*, 148, 190, 192–194, 200
University of Chicago 46
University of Detroit 77, 218
University of Georgia 137–138
University of Illinois 46, 130
University of Michigan 16, 35, 146, 220
University of Mississippi 74, 78
University of Montana 220
University of Notre Dame 92, 110, 124–125, 143–144, 223
University of Oklahoma 53, 111, 220
University of Oregon 46
University of Oxford 61
University of Pennsylvania 27

University of Southern California 9, 48, 95, 134, 137, 188, 191, 200
University of Toledo 219
University of Utah 86
University of Virginia 87, 123
University of West Virginia 221
University of Wisconsin 49

Van Brocklin, Norm 207–208, 224
Van Buren, Steve 119, 151
Vanderbilt University 64
Van Nuys, California 131, *132*–*133*, 134, 150, 173, 208
Veeck, Bill 24
Villanova University 122

Wagner, Honus 46
Waite Hill, Ohio 22, 24–25, 37
Wallack, Nate 148, 153–154, 157
Walsh, Adam *8*, 145–146, *148*–149, 154, 156, 162, 168, 170, 173–*174*, 179, 187, 199, 223; hiring as Rams' head coach 144; NFL coach of the year (1945) 173, 223; resignation as Rams' head coach 203; style of coaching 147–148
Walsh, Charles "Chile" *8*–9, 40, 105, *107*, 109–112, 114–122, 128–129, 139, 156, 160, 175, 178–179, 185–188, 190–191, 194, 198–199, 202–203, *214*, 223; assurances the Rams would remain in Cleveland 143–144, 148, 150–155, 178, 184; influence on Rams' move to Los Angeles 187, 204, 223; negotiation to move the Rams to the L.A. Coliseum 188–191, 223; resignation as Rams' general manager 203; success in drafting and recruiting players 8–9, 13, 109–110, 114, 139, 145–146, 203–204; vision for pro football 13, 110
War Memorial Stadium (Buffalo, New York) 149
Ward, Arch 124, 137, 143
Warner, Kurt 213
Warner Brothers 148
Washington, Kenny 134, 136, 190–191, 193–194, 199–200
Washington and Lee College 103
Washington, D.C. 40, 69, 91, 97, 127, 166, 179
Washington Post 168
Washington Redskins (National Football League) 7, 10, 42, 50, 53, 58–*59*, 60, 62, 69, 73–74, 84, 86, 90–91, 97, 104, 111–113, 115–116, 121, 127, 129, 149–*150*, 156–157, 160, 164, 166–*174*, 178–179, 185, 200, 205–206, 212, 218, 222; *see also* Boston Redskins
Washington State College 135
Waterfield, Bob 2, 6, 7, *8*, 12–13, 77, 86, 119, 130–*132*, *133*–140, 145–*148*, 149–156, 158, 160, 164, 168–*174*, 176, 179, 182, 193, 196–197, 199–200, 204–208, 213, 223; apartment in Cleveland with Jane Russell 140, 153; first/only pure quarterback to take his team to an NFL title as a rookie 173, 223; military

service 138, *139–140*; NFL's most valuable player (1945) 174, 208, 224; Rams head coach 209; Rams salary 139, 160; 303 yards passing to Jim Benton 156
Waterfield, Buck 3, 5, 132–136, 208–209
Waterfield, Frances 131–*132*, *133*–134, 138, 150
Waterfield, Staton "Jack" 131–*132*, 209
Waynesburg College 123
weather for Rams' games in Cleveland 6–7, *11*, 37, 156, 160, 162–*163*, 164–165, 168, 175, 177–178, 195, 205–206
West, Pat 147, 153, *159*, 168, 170–172, 175, 200, 208
West, Walter *122*–123
West Virginia Wesleyan College 95
Western Division (National Football League) 16, 40, 58, 73, 81, 97, 111, 114, 127–128, 153, 155–156; Rams as champions 156–158, *159*, 199
Western Reserve University 16
Wetzel, Damon "Buzz" 14–17, 21–30, *31*, 33–34, 36, 40–43, 49–52, 55, 60–62, 65, 67, 70–71, 73, 86, 89, 98, 114, 120, 194, 200, 207, 219, 221, 224; co-founder of the Rams 24–25, 221, 224; firing by Rams 67–68; *see also* Marshman, Homer H.
Wetzel, Henry "Buzz" 15, 24
WGAR radio, Cleveland 55
White, Byron "Whizzer" 61, 86

Williamson, Ben 64, 67, 69–70
Willis, Bill 194
Willis, Chris 114
Wilson, Jack 111
Wilson, Johnny 1, 104, 112
Winslow, Kellen 222
Wismer, Harry 165
Wojciechowicz, Alex 62
World War I 46
World War II 7, 8, 60, 68, 81, 87–88, 101, 105, 117–119, 121, 129, 138, 142, 190, 214, 217; end 109, 149; impact on NFL rosters 106–*107*, 108–112, *126*; impact on sports attendance 114; Rams' suspension of operations 14, 114–116, 120, 217, 222
Wrigley Field (Chicago, Illinois) 72–73, 113, 115, 127, 152, *191*
Wrigley Field (Los Angeles, California) 187

Yale University 61, 64, 144
Yankee Stadium (New York City) 175, 181
Yonkers, Bob 177–178, 184–185
Young, Cy 28, 46

Zanesville, Ohio 24
Zanesville Greys (minor league baseball) 17
Zirin, Alex 117
Zoll, Dick 52

www.ingramcontent.com/pod-product-compliance
Ingram Content Group UK Ltd.
Pitfield, Milton Keynes, MK11 3LW, UK
UKHW041929140426
5217IPUK00014B/386